Sustainable Marketing Planning

This book provides practical insights, tools and frameworks to help readers produce tactically and strategically appropriate marketing plans.

Showing how to embed sustainability in these plans, students will be shown how to implement changes while being encouraged to reflect on why they are needed. The text reflects on contemporary themes that impact on sustainable marketing planning, including consumer behaviour, entrepreneurialism, internal marketing, services, international marketing, event management and digital marketing. The second edition has been fully updated with a greater focus on the issues surrounding sustainability, including the environmental challenges facing businesses, sustainable accreditation and integrating the UN SDGs. It provides background on the value discourses that underpin sustainability, incorporates new examples and case studies from broader regions around the world and introduces TBL-based loyalty. Full of tools and frameworks to improve comprehension, including chapter-by-chapter learning outcomes, summaries, exercises, applied activities and mini case studies, it bridges the gap between theory and practice effectively and accessibly.

Presenting contemporary themes and challenges at the cutting edge of business research and practice, this book provides core reading for advanced undergraduate and postgraduate students of sustainable marketing, marketing planning and marketing strategy, as well as professionals seeking to improve the competitive advantage of their organisations.

Online resources for the use of instructors include PowerPoint lecture slides and a multiple choice questions section.

Neil Richardson is an experienced marketing/business practitioner with substantial private sector experience, working for (and with) world-class companies and as a director of a social enterprise and other SMEs. Since 2005, Neil has taught Leeds Business School undergraduate, postgraduate and professional students. He now focuses on driving sustainability into the curriculum, is the lead academic in (sustainable marketing) research funding bids and supervises several doctoral tutees.

Sustainable Marketing Planning

Second Edition

Neil Richardson

Routledge
Taylor & Francis Group
LONDON AND NEW YORK

Second edition published 2024
by Routledge
4 Park Square, Milton Park, Abingdon, Oxon OX14 4RN

and by Routledge
605 Third Avenue, New York, NY 10158

Routledge is an imprint of the Taylor & Francis Group, an informa business

First edition published by Routledge 2020

British Library Cataloguing-in-Publication Data
A catalogue record for this book is available from the British Library

Library of Congress Cataloging-in-Publication Data
Names: Richardson, Neil Andre Asselbroug, author.
Title: Sustainable marketing planning / Neil Richardson.
Description: Second Edition. | New York, NY : Routledge, 2024. |
Revised edition of the author's Sustainable marketing planning, 2020. |
Includes bibliographical references and index.
Identifiers: LCCN 2023050238 (print) | LCCN 2023050239 (ebook) |
ISBN 9781032561738 (hardback) | ISBN 9781032561721 (paperback) |
ISBN 9781003434214 (ebook)
Subjects: LCSH: Green marketing. |
Consumption (Economics)–Environmental aspects. |
Social responsibility of business.
Classification: LCC HF5413 .R53 2024 (print) |
LCC HF5413 (ebook) | DDC 658.8/02–dc23/eng/20231030
LC record available at https://lccn.loc.gov/2023050238
LC ebook record available at https://lccn.loc.gov/2023050239

ISBN: 9781032561738 (hbk)
ISBN: 9781032561721 (pbk)
ISBN: 9781003434214 (ebk)

DOI: 10.4324/9781003434214

Typeset in Sabon
by Newgen Publishing UK

Access the Support Material: www.routledge.com/9781032561721

Contents

List of Figures x
List of Tables xii

Introduction 1

1 Sustainability and Sustainable Development (SD) 3
1.1 Sustainability – An Historical Perspective 3
1.2 Corporate Social Responsibility (CSR) 5
1.3 Stakeholder Theory 7
Strong Versus Weak Stakeholder Theory 9
Friedman Versus Freeman 11
1.4 Sustainable Development (SD) 13
Wicked Problems 13
Defining Sustainability 14
The Business Case for Adopting Sustainability 15
Corporate Social Irresponsibility 17
United Nations Sustainable Development Goals (SDGs) 19
B Corporation Accreditation 22
The 5 Planets Theory 24
Three Rs 24
1.5 Systems and SD 25
Economic Systems 25
Circular Economies 26
Organisational Systems 29

2 Critical Thinking and Marketing 36
2.1 Marketing – A Definition 37
The Role and Nature of Markets 38
2.2 Sustainable Marketing (SM) and Its Predecesors 41
Social Marketing 41
Societal Marketing 43
Green Marketing 43
Sustainable Marketing (SM) 45
2.3 Critical Marketing 47
Myths Perpetuated by (or About) Marketers 48

2.4 *Value(s) 51*
Corporate Values 52
The Value Proposition (VP) 54
Consumer Values 54
Co-Creation of value 55

3 Sustainable Buyer Behaviour 59
3.1 *Consumer Buyer Behaviour 59*
Needs, Wants and Norms 60
The BAU Consumer (B2C) Decision-Making Process (DMP) 61
Individual Internal Influences 64
The Decision-Making Unit (DMU) 66
3.2 *Organisational Buyer Behaviour 67*
The B2B Market 67
Influences on Business Buyers 68
3.3 *TBL-Based Consumer Buyer Behaviour 69*
The Elusive Sustainable Consumer 70
A TBL-Based B2C DMP 73
TBL Support for 'Information Search' and 'Information Evaluation' DMP Stages 75
Limitations 76

4 The Marketing Mix 79
4.1 *Communications (a.k.a. 'Marcomms' a.k.a. 'Comms') 80*
Noise 81
Word of Mouth (WoM) 83
Push, Pull and Profile Strategies 83
The 'Comms' Mix 84
Digital Platforms 87
The Use of Communications Agencies 89
4.2 *Convenience (a.k.a. Place a.k.a. Distribution) 90*
Marketing Channels 90
The Use of Intermediaries 91
Brick and/or Click 91
Market Coverage 92
4.3 *Customer Benefits (a.k.a. Product) 93*
Consumer-Purchasing Scenarios 93
Anatomy of a Product 95
Classification of Goods 96
The Product Portfolio 97
Product Life Cycle (PLC) 99
The Product Adoption Curve (a.k.a. the Diffusion Curve) 103
New Product Development (NPD) 104
Boston Control Group (BCG) Matrix 108
Directional Policy Matrices 110
4.4 *Cost to Customers (a.k.a. Price a.k.a. Value-for-Money) 112*
Pricing Perspectives 113

Pricing Techniques 115
Vouchers and Cashback 117
4.5 *Services 117*
'Services Marketing' Versus 'Marketing Services' 118
Customer Involvement 119
Characteristics of Services 120
The Extended Marketing Mix for Services 120
People 121
Process 121
Presence (a.k.a. Physical Evidence) 122
Service Quality 123
4.6 *Using the Mix to Coordinate Sustainability Adoption 123*
Choice Editing 126
Integrated Marketing Communications (IMC) and Sustainability 127
Sustainable Distribution 130

5 Sustainable Marketing (SM) Planning 137
Planning Frameworks 138
5.1 *Goal Setting – Mission (or Purpose) Statements, Corporate Objectives and Scenario Planning 141*
Mission and Purpose Statements 141
Corporate Objectives 142
Scenario Planning 144
5.2 *Strategic Decisions: STP and Strategy Formulation 145*
Marketing Audits 147
Internal Environment Analysis 148
Micro-Environment Analysis 151
Core Competence 155
Value Systems 159
Communities and Networks 159
Macro (External) Environmental Analysis 163
Economics 164
Politics 165
Socio-Cultural 166
Technology 167
Legal 168
Environment 170
Ethical 171
Issues with the Environmental Tools and Frameworks 171
The SWOT Summary 172
Generating SM Objectives 173
TOWS Analysis 174
5.3 *Strategy Formulation and Tactical Implementation 175*
Segmentation 175
Ethical Targeting 180
Sustainable Positioning 181
Strategy Formulation 186

Schumpeter's Creative Destruction 187
Mintzberg's Deflected and Realised Strategies 188
5.4 *Implementation – Monitoring, Evaluation and Control* 192
Control and Measuring Value 193
Key Performance Indicators (KPIs) 193
540° Feedback 194
Hard and Soft Controls 194
Budget 195
SM Benchmarking 196
Environment Social and Governance (ESG) Benchmarking 196
5.5 *Barriers to Adopting SM Planning* 199
Planning in a Crisis 199
Responsibility for Ownership 200
Shareholder Dominance – Monitoring Management 200
Multiple Stakeholder Interests 201
Short-Termism 201
Overcoming Barriers to Adoption 202

6 Internal Marketing (IM) 207
RUTH M. GOSNAY

6.1 *Organisational Orientations* 208
Market Orientation (MO) – A Definition 211
Benefits of Adopting an MO 211
Marketing's Role in Supporting the MO 212
6.2 *IM and Its Associated Orientation (IMO)* 213
Dimensions of IMO 214
6.3 *IM and the Marketing Mix* 216
Internal Supplier–Customer Relationships (ISCRs) 216
People 217
Communication 218
Internal and External Communication 218
Tacit (or Implicit) Communication 219
The Internal Brand Champion and Becoming a Brand Ambassador 220
Practical Steps Towards Implementing IM 220
6.4 *IM'S Influence on Strategic Decision-Making* 221
IM and Segmentation 221
6.5 *IM Benefits and Criticisms* 222
The Future of IM 224

7 Relationship Marketing and Loyalty 229
7.1 *Defining Relationship Marketing (RM)* 230
The Marketing Information System (MkIS) and Customer Relationship Management (CRM) 232
7.2 *The BAU Building Blocks of RM* 234
Identity 234
Segmentation and RM 234

7.3 *Loyalty 237*
A TBL-Appropriate Loyalty Ladder 237
Loyalty Versus Satisfaction 239
Measuring and Monitoring Online Loyalty 240
Negative Aspects of Loyalty 241
Loyalty and IM 241
7.4 *Benefits of RM 242*

8 Themes 247
8.1 *Sustainable Entrepreneurship (SE) 247*
Value, Norms, Motivations and SE 248
SE and Communities 250
Ownership and SE 250
Growth 250
Environmental Resilience 251
8.2 *Sustainable Branding 252*
Brand Personalities 253
Brand Equity 253
Brand Positioning 254
Brand Communities 256
Reputation 257
8.3 *Global Sustainable Marketing 258*
Key Factors in Global Marketing 259
Trans-National Corporations (TNCs) 260
Foreign Direct Investment (FDI) 260
Vulnerable States 261
Global Marketing and the 'Macro' Environment 262
Investment, SD and 'Environmental, Social and Governance' (ESG) 263
Socio-Cultural Factors 264
Gender Balance 265
Technology Factors 265
Global Marketing and the Marketing Mix 265
Sustainable Distribution 266
8.4 *SMEs and Micro-Enterprises 268*
SMEs and Sustainability 269
Tools and Frameworks 270
8.5 *Charities, Not-for-Profit and Third Sector 271*

Index 276

Figures

1.1	Carroll's CSR pyramid	6
1.2	Stakeholder connectedness	8
1.3	BAU stakeholder typology	10
1.4	Stakeholder bargaining strength	11
1.5	The CSI v CSR dichotomous model and potential outcomes	18
1.6	Circular economy – Flow of goods and consumer decisions	27
2.1	Schools of thought	47
2.2	Chronology of changes in 'value'	55
3.1	The BAU Decision-Making Process (DMP) for consumers	62
3.2	Maslow's Hierarchy of Needs	64
3.3	Herzberg's dual factor theory of motivation	65
3.4	The Decision-Making Unit (DMU)	67
3.5	Business (B2B) DMP applied to a TV manufacturer	68
3.6	Sustainable stakeholder typology (SST)	73
3.7	The TBL-based DMP for consumers	75
4.1	Linear model of communications	80
4.2	One and two-step communications	82
4.3	Expanded communications mix	87
4.4	Brick versus click distribution	92
4.5	Anatomy of a product	95
4.6	The generic product life cycle (PLC)	99
4.7	Differing PLC scenarios	101
4.8	Product adoption or diffusion curve	103
4.9	New product risk continuum	105
4.10	New Product Development (NPD) Process	106
4.11	Boston Control Group (BCG) Product Matrix	108
4.12	Directional Policy Matrix (DPM)	110
4.13	SERVQUAL – A gaps model of service	124
4.14	Using IMC to co-ordinate sustainability adoption	128
5.1	The POST model	143
5.2	Relationship between corporate and functional objectives	143
5.3	Gap analysis	145
5.4	Marketing environments influencing value creation	146
5.5	Porter's value system	159
5.6	Flowchart for information requests under GDPR	169
5.7	SWOT summary for a restaurant chain opening a vegan outlet in Leeds	174

5.8 Two widely used BAU segmentation frameworks 177
5.9 Possible sustainability behaviours of consumer versus citizen 'segments' attending festivals 179
5.10 Sustainability Perception Continuum influenced by heuristics 184
5.11 TBL positioning grid 185
5.12 Mintzberg's realised versus intended strategies 188
5.13 Two ways to portray Porter's Generic Strategy 189
5.14 Porter's Generic Strategy applied to retailers 190
5.15 A TBL-based sustainable strategy 192
5.16 Sustainable Marketing (SM) Benchmarking Framework 197
5.17 Polar diagram plotting sustainability results against targets 198
6.1 Kotler's service profit chain 208
6.2 The dimensions of internal market orientation (IMO) 215
6.3 Boundary spanning employees (BSEs) at the internal–external markets interface 218
6.4 Internal marketing (IM) segmentation 222
6.5 Benefits of IM expressed as organisational performance indicators 223
7.1 Customer value pyramid 231
7.2 Marketing Information System (MkIS) 232
7.3 Sustainable Marketing (SM) loyalty ladder 239
7.4 Customer satisfaction versus loyalty matrix 240
8.1 Kapferer's brand identity prism applied to a vegan coffee shop 255
8.2 The small firm value chain analysis (VCA) 271

Tables

1.1 Strong versus weak stakeholder theory 9
1.2 Elkington's 7 revolutions to a sustainable future 16
1.3 Ethics and legality matrix 17
1.4 UN Sustainable Development Goals (SDGs) 21
1.5 Antecedents of the circular economy 26
2.1 Marketing definitions 37
2.2 The role and nature of markets 39
2.3 A chronology of different approaches to consumption and consumer value 51
3.1 Contrasting consumer barriers and facilitating factors 70
3.2 How aspects of consumption relate to sustainably motivated consumers 72
4.1 Key 'Comms' mix tools with considerations 85
4.2 Purchasing scenarios (a.k.a. problem-solving situations or buy-classes) 94
4.3 B2C and B2B product classifications 96
4.4 Product line mix and depth applied to Procter & Gamble 98
4.5 DPM criteria – industry attractiveness vs business strength 111
4.6 Weightings for DPM criteria 111
4.7 The three perspectives of pricing 112
4.8 Balancing factors germane to pricing 114
4.9 Pricing techniques 115
4.10 Benefits sought in service encounters 118
4.11 Contrasting the nature of services being directed at people or possessions 119
4.12 Characteristics of services 121
4.13 Where the extended services mix and SERVQUAL overlap 125
4.14 Adoption vs adaptation of mix components to target sustainable segments 129
5.1 Militaristic origins of strategic language 139
5.2 BAU planning process models and frameworks 140
5.3 REACH NEW heights planning framework 140
5.4 Operational versus strategic gaps 146
5.5 BAU 'Internal' frameworks 149
5.6 BAU 'Micro' frameworks 152
5.7 Original offerings and related substitutes 153
5.8 Balanced scorecard showing typical strategic objectives, measures and information sources 154
5.9 Internal and Micro summary for Biffy – A fictional dog grooming products importer 156
5.10 Core competencies – client versus agencies 157

5.11 Mendelow grid featuring sources of Power 163
5.12 PEST and other macro frameworks 164
5.13 GDPR fines 170
5.14 Generic SWOT summary 173
5.15 TOWS analysis with detailed objectives for vegan restaurant 176
5.16 Mapping the Mix against marketing objectives from the TOWS analysis 177
5.17 APPROVES – a sustainable segmentation framework 178
5.18 Segments for meat-eating versus plant-based eating 179
5.19 Contrasting differing positioning factors and approaches 181
5.20 Positioning strategies contrasting price and quality 182
5.21 Hart's Environmental Sustainability Portfolio 183
5.22 Sustainable Marketing Matrix 184
5.23 Three 'Grand' generic strategies 186
5.24 Ansoff's strategy matrix 190
5.25 Key mobile metrics 194
6.1 Attributes of pre-sustainability organisational orientations 209
7.1 Contrasting traditional and social media loyalty ladders with TBL-based sustainable segments 238
8.1 Contrasting BAU brand personality frameworks with a sustainable alternative 254
8.2 Kapferer's positioning model applied to three sustainable scenarios 256
8.3 Push and pull factors for global marketing 258
8.4 Dynamic versus static Foreign Direct Investment (FDI) 262
8.5 PLATFORM macroenvironmental analysis framework 263
8.6 Incoterms for all modes of transport 267
8.7 Attributes in relation to company size 269

Introduction

First, may I thank you for buying this book. Having bought it, you're now one of my customers, which means a lot to me. As you progress through the chapters, you'll recognise the theme of marketers creating value for customers. My sincere hope is that you will take value from this book during your studies and later in your professional career.

Marketing draws on many of the great discourses, namely philosophy, sociology, economics and psychology. Indeed, many marketers see it as a form of applied psychology, shaping how managers make decisions and implement changes (based on these decisions). Hence, this text will be a practical resource to those studying marketing decision-making and implementation. It supports undergraduate, postgraduate and professional students. The fundamental principles provide a thorough underpinning for strategy, planning and metrics-related modules. Furthermore, the text features teaching tools to improve comprehension, e.g. each chapter has learning outcomes, key findings, applied activities and practical examples. It critiques the theory and brings the real world into the classroom.

Throughout my career I've worked for (and with) organisations ranging from charities to SMEs to genuinely world-class companies. I've witnessed management decision-making that has at times been inspired but often ill-informed. Marketing managers face two parallel challenges: first how to adapt to changes (of fragmenting markets, hyper-competition, over-supply or globalisation); and second, how to grow a business whilst practicing recognisably sustainable practices. Companies must align their values with their customers who increasingly seek products and services that create customer value whilst being People and Planet friendly.

Organisational drivers rarely change (e.g. attracting/retaining customers, developing customer relationships and growing satisfaction), however the sustainability challenges are introducing previously unseen complexities into everyday business. Marketing is changing almost daily, e.g. media ethics (think Leveson), emergent consumer concerns (Banking, Fairtrade etc.) and ever-evolving business needs. Using Sustainable Marketing (SM) techniques to create value ultimately leads to improved customer satisfaction, better professional relationships and increased effectiveness. This text is unique in that it extensively covers marketing planning AND addresses key sustainability challenges simultaneously.

All business students must be interested in the issues of corporate failure, recovery and turnaround techniques. No doubt there are many factors that contribute to failure and

DOI: 10.4324/9781003434214-1

each scenario is unique. I'll discuss these factors throughout the text, however I have no doubt that

"the largest threat to a company's future is likely to be ineffective marketing"

... poor marketing, nothing more nothing less. Many (ill-informed) people think marketing is superficial, ephemeral or at worst deceptive. So, I'll consider its role for critical marketers, the persistent marketing myths and why scepticism exists.

Sustainability is increasingly disrupting business practices. Sustainability reporting started in the late 1990s. Since then, Environmental, Social and Governance (ESG) has been widely adopted globally. Whilst this may have been incremental, increasingly research suggests ESG supports those who think sustainability is Schumpeterian. Initially ESG reports were little more than an afterthought or even greenwashing. Nowadays, however, they are increasingly seen as essential and are undoubtedly given more emphasis with each passing year. This has been accelerating since the introduction of the United Nations' Sustainable Development Goals (SDGs) in 2015. Adopting Sustainable Development (SD) approaches has benefited both consumers and companies. Social media can make it easier for marketers to collaborate with communities and achieve reputational endorsement. Alternatively, it can be the source of many societal and 'green' problems for companies. Think of the child-labour scandals that arise and the reputational damage they inflict. Potential buyers will seek to take value from certain brands above others in the same product category. To achieve this, companies strive to build brand awareness and equity. However, such brands are increasingly being viewed through the prism of sustainability. The two issues are now inextricably linked.

Many marketing texts focus on larger, manufacturing organisations. They promote theories or tools that don't apply (meaningfully) to many enterprises today. Hence, this text is for students interested in all organisations, virtual, large or small, new or old, profit-making, ecological or charitable. Planning is absent from many current sustainable texts hence this one provides a bottom-up approach with the latest thoughts on tactical and strategic Sustainable Marketing (SM). It reflects on the role of sustainability in the contexts of contemporary themes including (amongst others) entrepreneurialism, international marketing, small firms and charities (amongst others).

Finally, employers increasingly want graduates to be better marketing practitioners rather than simply 'academics'. Most texts fail to address this; hence this book bridges this gap by adopting a 'Pracademic' approach. Students will be given insights into 'How' to implement whilst being encouraged to reflect on 'Why'.

> "There's a saying that 'Climate doom is the new climate denial'. Essentially, with climate denial we don't take action because we don't think it's a problem, but with climate doom we don't take action because we think it's a problem we can't solve".
>
> (Marcy Franck, author of *The Climate Optimist* newsletter)

Climate optimism "isn't about denying what we can see with our own eyes, or ignoring our grief for what we've lost. It's understanding that we know how to prevent things from getting worse and that we're making progress" (*ibid*). Indeed, the key aim of this book is to make a small contribution to making progress.

Best Wishes
Neil Richardson

1 Sustainability and Sustainable Development (SD)

Abstract

This chapter first considers the antecedents of sustainability. Corporate Social Responsibility (CSR) pre-dates the sustainability discourse and is still a key component of sustainability. Stakeholder theory is used to identify Business-As-Usual (BAU) segments. Friedman's questionable position on the role of business in society is discussed. The United Nations Sustainable Development Goals (SDGs) are identified. As are indices for overtly sustainable organisations including the most rigorous accreditation, i.e. that awarded by the B Corporation (BCorp). Finally, it considers the role of systems and their influence on adopting sustainable practices.

Learning Outcomes

At the end of this chapter students will be able to

- discuss the historical influences on sustainability
- examine the role of Corporate Social Responsibility (CSR)
- assess Stakeholder theory's influence on the sustainability discourse
- evaluate the application of the UN Sustainable Development Goals (SDGs)
- discuss the contribution made by B Corporations
- explain how systems influence adopting sustainable practices.

1.1 Sustainability – An Historical Perspective

Whilst other texts pre-date Adam Smith (e.g. Sun Tzu's Art of War), his *Wealth of Nations* (Smith, 1776) is regarded by many as the first modern 'business' book. Whilst undoubtedly important, it is not a blueprint for business. Organisations were not high on his agenda as he devoted only two paragraphs to corporations. He insisted that the only organisations with a real future would be in canal building and banking (*ibid*). Donaldson (2008, p 173) describes Adam Smith as a

> "young moral philosopher (who) suggested that we throw out the assumption of the zero sum game (i.e. assuming that there was a fixed amount of wealth) and begin to talk about how wealth is created, especially through labour and voluntary exchange".

DOI: 10.4324/9781003434214-2

However, his discussion of the (economic only) value of slaves is repugnant to all right-minded people in the twenty-first century. Adam Smith may well have been a 'moral' philosopher of his time, however societal values and attitudes to slavery have rightly changed. This supports those who argue that value is always temporal (Heinonen *et al*, 2010). Sustainability is a value-laden concept and 'value' is a common thread throughout this book.

Smith's idea of the pursuit of growth could be argued to be the genesis of the 'Dominant Social Paradigm' (DSP) ultimately leading to the neo-liberal agenda (Jackson, 2005) and globalisation based on the assumption that the march of progress is not only inevitable but is also an ideal to be striven towards (Jones *et al*, 2009).

Economists expressed alarm during the Industrial Revolution over the lack of social wealth (Tilley & Young, 2009). In the seventeenth century, Hobbes noted the pervasive anxiety of a society characterised by unlimited materialist value perspectives. Victor Hugo suggested that the two main problems faced by nineteenth- century society were the production of wealth and its distribution (Jackson, 2005). Gerald Alonzo Smith's (1996) review of the historic perspective of the purpose of wealth, suggested many nineteenth-century economists questioned the proposition that economic growth was an end rather than a means. He cited John Ruskin as stating: 'Something was wrong with an economy that produced so much quantity with so little quality, yet brutalised so many people in doing it.' GA Smith also cited Sismondi (1834), a Swiss economist who specialised in French and Italian history, who opined 'The too much of everything is the evil of the day' which resonates with the oversupply and fragmentation of today's society.

The nineteenth-century economist Thomas Malthus was concerned with the production of food and suggested that supply would be outstripped by population growth, developing the idea that nature is not a never-ending resource. Marx (and many others) decried the 'fetishism of commodities' that characterised capitalism. On the cusp of the twentieth century, American economist and sociologist Thorsten Veblen coined the phrase 'conspicuous consumption' which still resonates today. His critique of unfettered capitalism is captured in his text *The Theory of the Leisure Class* (see Veblen, 1898).

From the time of Adam Smith through to the present day, organisations have been allowed (or even encouraged) to develop in line with capitalist, neo-liberal traditions. Herein, Business-As-Usual (BAU) is used to represent the traditional business approach where shareholders and profits dominate. Developments since the adoption of the neo-liberal agenda (such as globalisation and deregulation) mean "some corporations have gradually come to replace the most powerful institution in the traditional concept of citizenship, namely government" (Garriga & Mele, 2004, p 57). With Facebook, Amazon, Alphabet Inc, and Microsoft (amongst others) this is arguably more relevant today than ever before. It is, however, too simplistic to say that globalisation has generated only negative impacts. It can be argued that material well-being has increased dramatically for many people (Rosling, 2010).

Clear divides were evident in the mid-twentieth century. Bowen, regarded by many as the 'father' of CSR, produced his seminal text (Bowen, 1953) entitled *Social Responsibilities of the Businessman*, which brought the issue to the wider community. Davis (1960) attacked the assumption of the classical economic theory of perfect competition that restricts the involvement of the firm in society to the creation of wealth. Davis warned whoever does not use social power responsibly will lose it. Agle *et al* (1999) refer to this as Davis's 'iron law'. If ethics has any meaning whatsoever and is meaningful it will be because "we need to justify our lives to ourselves and to others, as Sartre and other thinkers have shown us ... (and if) ... business is on one side and ethics is on the other, then we'll have a gap that may come to be known as 'corporate social responsibility'".

(Freeman, 2008, p 164)

1.2 Corporate Social Responsibility (CSR)

The CSR discourse predates that of sustainability. For some, CSR is the prime value that should be sought in businesses. Alternatively, the inestimable Rev Professor Simon Robinson (a renowned expert on applied ethics) insisted 'responsibility' is the value sought with both CSR and sustainability representing value-types (see Richardson & Cassop Thompson, 2023) that combined to create the value. For the purposes of this book, CSR and responsibility are keys components (i.e. value-types) of the over-arching sustainability meta-narrative.

CSR is complex as it draws on economics, politics, social integration and ethics (Garriga & Mele, 2004). For those interested in CSR, the Garriga & Mele paper provides an excellent underpinning. CSR is an eclectic field with loose boundaries, multiple memberships, different training/perspectives, broad rather than focused, multidisciplinary and interdisciplinary (Carroll, 1994). Larger companies often address ethical and societal concerns by adopting CSR policies, which may benefit both the company and their stakeholders. Richardson (2015) raised concerns regarding levels of awareness of the term CSR amongst micro-enterprises and Small-to-Medium-size employers (SMEs), finding few recognised the term but many had adopted recognisably ethical practices (*ibid*).

Professors Archie Carroll (see Carroll, 1979;1991) and Donna Wood (see Wood, 1991) are widely cited as having played key CSR roles. When Carroll developed the original four-part construct of CSR (1979) and pyramidal depiction (1991), it was clearly done with American-type capitalistic societies in mind (Carroll, 2016). Carroll defined the different levels at which organisations respond to social responsibilities (Figure 1.1).

The idea (as with most pyramid conceptualisations – see Maslow) is that organisations should progress upwards until they reach the 'Discretionary' level. Jones *et al* (2009) cite a number of issues with Carroll's Pyramid namely:

- the levels are not mutually exclusive
- as a staged hierarchy, movement results from (not necessarily appropriate) fixed criteria
- the dynamism of the social, economic and business world is only partially captured
- as a theoretical abstract it lacks the complex realities of the world it seeks to explain.

Like all 'staged' frameworks, organisations may struggle to know when they move from one stage to another. Arguably, it gets harder to move up the pyramid, the higher an organisation progresses. Also, these positions are dynamic, hence it is possible to fall down the pyramid if good practices lapse. Baden (2016) argued for the Economic and Ethical stages to exchange places allowing for businesses to operate and be trusted

"with the production and allocation of scarce natural resources and inherently valuable human resources, it needs to first and foremost accept its ethical responsibility to do no harm and conform to society' s ethical norms and expectations. Secondly business needs to be compliant with legal responsibilities, and only once it has accepted these responsibilities is it free to make a profit and pursue its economic objectives".

(*ibid*, p 11)

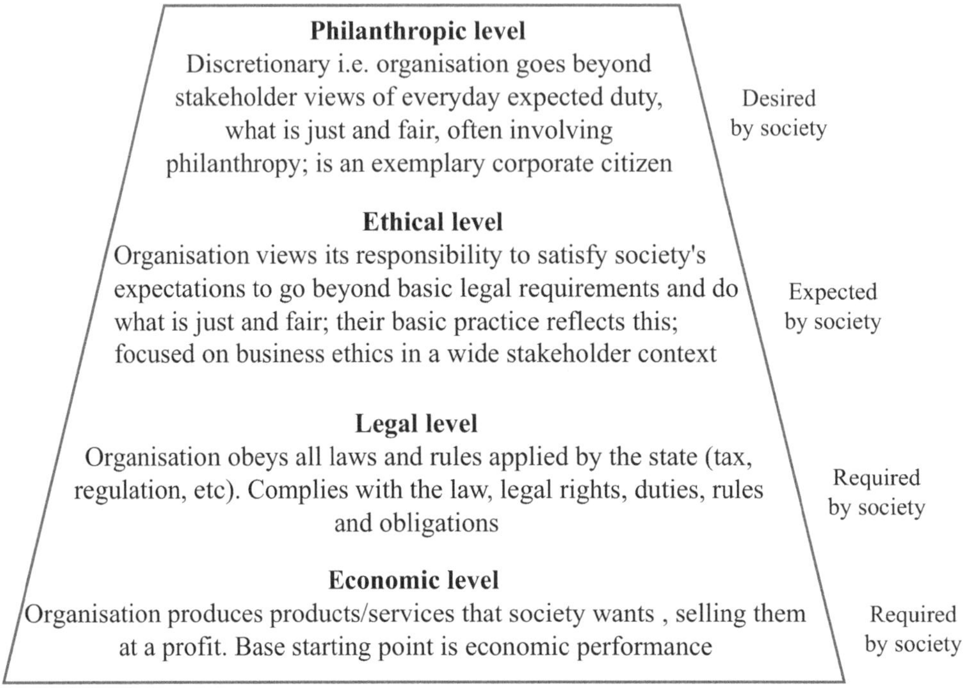

Figure 1.1 Carroll's CSR pyramid.

Source: Adapted from Caroll (1991).

Carroll accepted that other researchers would continue to explore the applicability of the Pyramid to different global, situational, and organisational contexts. This is how theory and practice develop (Carroll, 2016). It remains a useful framework as it improves understanding of how companies position themselves 'ethically'.

Many studies have found positive correlations between improved profitability and adopting CSR measures including progressive employee relations, product innovation/safety, environmental stewardship, community relations (Richardson & Cassop Thompson, 2023) or positive Word-of-Mouth (WoM). Where companies seek (unfair) competitive advantage by abusing the reporting of their CSR practices, the reactions are often swift and hostile. Social media sites often form the platforms for well-organised pressure groups to coordinate their communications efforts in order to influence corporate behaviour. Marketers must monitor such sites and respond clearly, articulating their company's position via a 'marcomms' campaign (see Section 4.1) highlighting positives from sustainability audits as well as identifying how changes will be implemented.

Customers may be the forgotten stakeholders (Belz & Peattie, 2012) as organisations may be inconsistent, i.e. their CSR commitment may change with time. Patterns exist in the adoption of CSR across differing organisations. Highly motivated companies may adopt idealistic stances or even one of enlightened self-interest whereas stakeholders on whom they rely may only adopt CSR practices when coerced (Haberberg *et al*, 2010). This poses risks for companies who must trust their supply networks (see Chapter 4), e.g. Nike's poor PR due to allegations of child labour generated negative publicity that spread rapidly via social media.

CSR cannot be assumed to be central to organisational culture and beliefs as it may simply be an 'add on' feature to a business operation, an afterthought (Jones *et al*, 2009) or deemed voluntary in nature (Barkemeyer, 2009). Gordon (2002) referred to the flagrant violation of societal standards in the corporate scandals of recent years. Sadly, in 2023 this comment still resonates (e.g. Libor rate fixing and the Volkswagen 'defeat device' debacle). It questions whether society and stakeholders can trust organisations.

1.3 Stakeholder Theory

> "The 21st Century is one of 'Managing for Stakeholders.' The task of executives is to create as much value as possible for stakeholders without resorting to trade-offs. Great companies endure because they manage to get stakeholder interests aligned in the same direction".
>
> (R Edward Freeman)

Stakeholder theory is not widely used by strategic management scholars to explain competitive advantage (Harrison *et al*, 2017). Organisations who attend to the needs of a broad group of stakeholders may enjoy a competitive advantage. The key is to better understand the primary stakeholders' utility functions, increasing the likelihood of recognising value-creating opportunities (*ibid*). There has been a shift from shareholder interests reigning supreme, to different stakeholders competing to influence the business agenda. Hence, shareholder interests are simply one of many. Businesses must meet increasing public expectations, addressing legal obligations around environmental and sustainability issues (Jones *et al*, 2009). The need to make profit can align (or conflict) with a company's stated ethical aims and objectives.

Sustainability should be viewed in terms of commitment within the wider context of stakeholder relationships. To improve relationship management (see Chapter 7) requires an understanding of stakeholders who may have interpersonal or person-to-firm perspectives. Competing stakeholders with differing needs, rights and obligations must be managed to minimise conflict. Whether stakeholders can be managed is a moot point. Reasons for involving stakeholders include:

- needing to understand the cultural system's complexity
- ensuring management systems identify potential conflicts
- resolving areas of conflict and counterbalancing existing patterns of interaction

(Mendes *et al*, 2009)

Freeman's award-winning book (Freeman, 1984) provided a language and framework for examining how companies relate to stakeholders. It established legitimacy for parties, other than shareholders, whose interests shape managerial actions (Margolis & Walsh, 2003). He defined stakeholders as groups or individuals who can affect (or be affected by) the achievement of the organisation's objectives (Freeman, 1984). This can be beneficial or harmful and was developed to include those whose rights may be violated, who should be respected by the business or claim ownership in organisational activities (Mendes *et al*, 2009).

Figure 1.2 is useful as it maps the stakeholders in terms of their connectedness to the organisation. Those directly employed have the highest degree of connection (and control by management) as they usually have contractual obligations. It develops the notion of employees to include internal customers (ICs) and Boundary Spanning Employees (BSEs) (see Figure 6.3). Shareholders have no contractual obligations *per se* as they can always sell their shares. They do, however, have legal recourse should managers act negligently. Large institutional investors have greater power and access whereas small shareholders have little real power. There are, of course, exceptions, one being the role of co-operatives. Both the Mondragon Cooperative Group (established 1984) in Spain and the UK's John Lewis (established 1864) use a co-operative business model where their staff own shares in the business and benefit from regular profit shares. So, for John Lewis and Mondragon, the employee shareholders would be at the centre of Figure 1.2.

Agle *et al* (1999, p 521) refer to "a stakeholder class system in which shareholders, employees, and customers were privileged, and government and communities were less so". 'Primary' stakeholders are those without whom the company cannot survive, whereas 'Secondary' stakeholders represent those who influence or affect (or are influenced or affected by) the company but are not essential for survival. Hence, a power-based ranking system can be established ranging from only having (low-power) interest to having an affect (medium power) to assuming (high power) ownership (see Mendelow grid in Table 5.1). Acknowledging this (power and interest) has, to a degree, encouraged businesses to re-evaluate their activities. Indeed, Freeman himself argued that

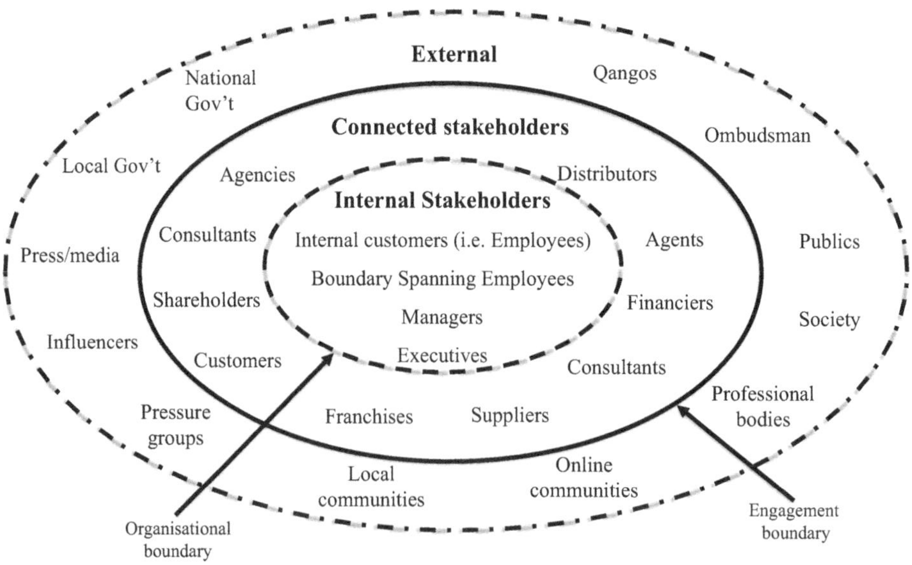

Figure 1.2 Stakeholder connectedness.

Source: Adapted from Richardson (2020).

"maximizing profits is more like creating value for stakeholders than others might read in Capitalism and Freedom (Friedman, 1962). Does that mean that I believe that 'maximizing profits' is the goal or purpose of the corporation? Absolutely not ... it is an outcome of a well-managed company, and that stakeholder theory is an idea about what it means to be well-managed ... (and) ... is not about markets and how they work ... It's not a theory of the firm. Rather it is a very simple idea about how people create value for each other".

(Freeman, 2008, pp 164–166)

Freeman insists better stakeholder theory focuses us on the ways that "companies and entrepreneurs are out there creating value, making our lives better, and changing the world" (*ibid*). The notion of personal and organisational 'value' (and the value types that combine to create that 'value' – see Richardson & Cassop Thompson, 2023) is central to marketers.

Strong Versus Weak Stakeholder Theory

Strong stakeholder theory suggests all stakeholders, irrespective of power and/or interest, are dealt with equally. Table 1.1 summarises the key issues regarding strong versus weak stakeholder theory.

In Table 1.1 the classical interpretation of 'strong versus weak' stakeholder theory has been juxtaposed with a range of tactics proposed by Float (2023). Float misuses the term 'strategies' (see Chapter 5 for an explanation of the difference between strategies,

Table 1.1 Strong versus weak stakeholder theory

View	*Attribute*	*Comment*	*Float's Stakeholder management 'tactics'*
Strong	Each stakeholder has a legitimate claim on management attention Management must balance stakeholder demands	Managers who account to everyone, account to no-one; With no criteria for performance, managers cannot be evaluated meaningfully; Managers decide on the balance between stakeholders; It confuses a stakeholder's interest in a firm with a person's citizenship of a state	1. Identify stakeholders 2. Conduct purposeful stakeholder analysis 3. Focus on engaging stakeholders 4. Establish clear goals and expectations 5. Develop strong stakeholder relations 6. Communicate effectively 7. Consult regularly 8. Involve stakeholders in decision making
Weak	Satisfying stakeholders is a good thing because it enables the firm to satisfy its primary purpose – long-term owner wealth growth	People have interests but this does not give them rights; Stakeholder attributes are variable rather than steady states; Stakeholder priorities can change for any group or stakeholder-manager relationship	9. Designate an owner for project stakeholder management 10. Address concerns quickly 11. Adapt as needed

Sources: Adapted from Jensen (2008); Agle *et al* (1999); Float (2023).

objectives and tactics) however their suggestions are sensible. A critique of strong stakeholder theory is it assumes

> "managers would do the right thing so as to benefit society as a whole. That position is naive ... (as they) ... would have no way to know how to best benefit society ... furthermore there would be widespread disagreement on how and what to do".
>
> (Jensen, 2008, p 168)

Marketers must be aware of the degree of urgency, interest and/or power stakeholders possess. Figure 1.3 clearly illustrates a range of stakeholders with differing combinations of attributes (i.e. power, legitimacy and urgency) resulting in different saliences (Mitchell *et al*, 1997).

'Power' alludes to the degree to which managers prioritise competing stakeholder claims. Such 'salience' is often attributed to shareholders, customers, government and communities. Institutional shareholders can be dominant stakeholders and therefore salient to a degree, however it is heightened shareholder urgency that concerns senior management. The idea of the 'non-stakeholder' is replaced in marketing by a 'public', which represents a stakeholder with interest in the organisation but no direct involvement or connection. Naturally today's 'public' could easily become tomorrow's engaged stakeholder. Stakeholders will have differing attributes due to combinations of power, legitimacy and also urgency (Figure 1.3). Questions that must be considered are

- Which publics are important and is the degree of importance changing?
- How strong are company-stakeholder relationships?
- What is the impact of corporate actions on these publics and vice versa?

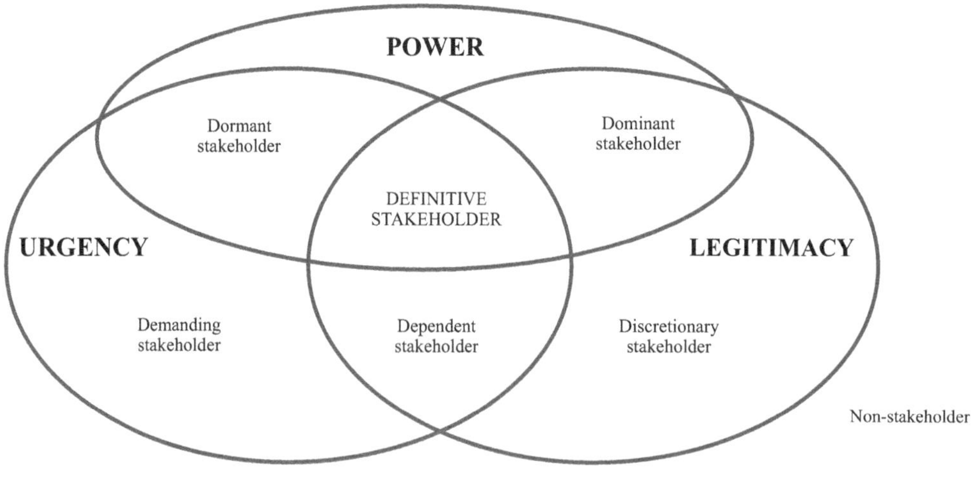

Figure 1.3 BAU stakeholder typology.

Source: Adapted from Mitchell *et al* (1997, p 874).

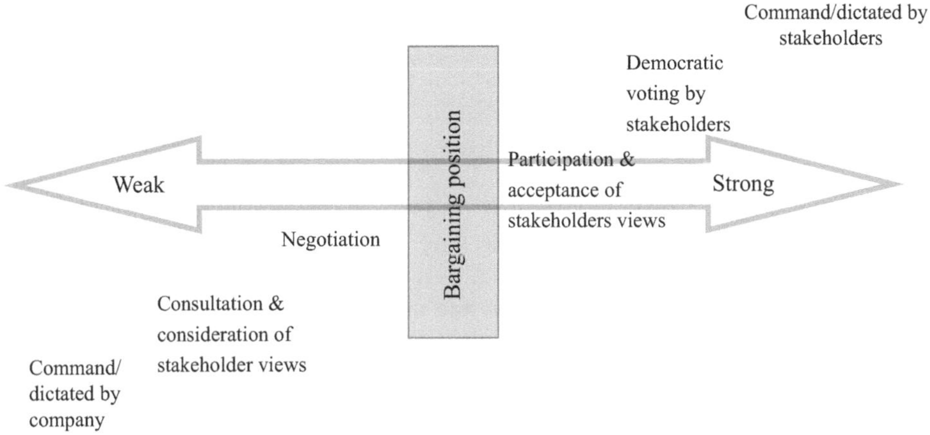

Figure 1.4 Stakeholder bargaining strength.

Source: Author.

- How do the interests of the relevant publics differ?
- Which groups pose a threat and which an opportunity?

This raises the challenging issue of bargaining power and communication (Figure 1.4). As Figure 1.4 illustrates, stakeholder bargaining represents a continuum ranging from companies with inclusive cultures to authoritarian organisations. The use of a continuum is appropriate as organisational decisions are rarely as 'clear cut' as many business models and/or frameworks suggest. Progressive marketers recognise that consumers are more discerning and have more choice than ever before. The ill-treatment of stakeholders can create reputational damage. Marketers must be transparent in their communications and should consult with networks of suppliers and stakeholder communities.

Friedman Versus Freeman

For centuries "family run businesses with social value such as Cadbury, Lever and Rowntree had shown that businesses could be run in ways that were profitable and that benefited others, particularly employees and the local community" (Emery, 2012, p 11). These enterprises complemented the traditional 'bottom line' with other values. Indeed, they thrived whilst refuting the BAU approach in favour of mutual benefit.

In 1970 Friedman challenged firms that contemplated making investments in social objectives and public interests other than economic ones. His article is widely cited often by libertarians who insist enterprises should have no objectives other than those with an economic focus, i.e. the bottom line. He insisted property rights, the invisible hand of the market and the government are entrusted to solve society's problems whereas corporate managers should play no direct role in ensuring the social welfare of society (Friedman, 1970). For Friedman, the only responsibility of business towards society is the maximisation of profits to the shareholders. Often paraphrased as "the business of business is business", this is arguably one of the most cited quotes in organisational management theory literature. It should not, however, be taken at face value as Friedman qualified this by stressing the business should work within the legal framework and the ethical custom of the country (*ibid*).

Friedman was not alone in voicing this view. Jensen (2008) argued 200 years' worth of work in economics and finance indicate that social welfare is maximised when all firms in an economy maximise total firm value. Jensen conceded that companies must attend to multiple constituencies in order to succeed but that, ultimately, they should be guided by wealth creation only (Margolis & Walsh, 2003) and that long-term market value is the one objective that best advances social welfare. Those supporting this view believe that if shareholder wealth is maximised, social welfare is maximised as well (*ibid*). In 2023, with wealth inequality increasing across the globe, such notions of trickle-down economics are increasingly challenged. However, as "long as society wants high investment returns, job security and higher wages, and lower prices, CEOs are bound to respect these norms" (Agle *et al*, 1999, p 522).

It can be argued that Friedman was merely reflecting a view from society as he did not "deny the existence of social problems; he simply claimed that it is the state's role to address them" (Margolis & Walsh, 2003, p 272). In other words, money should not be taken as 'rent' from the shareholders. It is worth noting that Jensen (2008, p 167) suggests there is nothing special

> "about stockholders in the firm ... (and) ... maximizing the value of a firm's equity will not produce maximum value of the firm as a whole. And it will certainly not produce maximum value for society".

Regarding the conflict between taking account of relevant stakeholders and attending to long-run interests, Jensen (2008, p 170) argues:

> "When I look at the maladaptive behavior in corporations (and goodness knows there's lots of it), what shocks me is how much of it is purposeless. ... the behavior doesn't accomplish what the people who are taking those actions nominally want to accomplish, which let us assume is power and wealth".

These arguments illustrate the fundamental problem with Friedman's position, in that business is a part of (and not apart from) society. Whilst in no way belittling the role of organisations in modern society, it is important that they are not demonised. 'Business' has rights as well as obligations, with competing needs to address. These rights, obligations and needs change over time and between contexts (Jones *et al*, 2009).

Another flaw in Friedman and his supporters' arguments, is the role of (and anticipated reaction from) society and stakeholders therein. Clearly, they expect stakeholders (and society) to be passive, which has long been understood not to be the case. Ranganathan (1998) listed 47 initiatives where investors have 'pressured' firms to be more responsive to social problems. Margolis & Walsh (2003, pp 289–290) cited street protests against the World Trade Organization (WTO), the International Monetary Fund (IMF) and the World Bank. In 2023, Extinction Rebellion and Just Stop Oil are raising similar issues, i.e. the need for sustainable practices. Wood (2008, p 160) insisted "we know too much about the institutional role of business in society to be persuaded by arguments about the glories of unfettered free markets with actors solely in pursuit of maximizing their economic self-interest". Clarkson (1988) argued it had been demonstrated that the pursuit of this single measure was self-defeating. Hence stakeholder theory is relevant even if it runs contrary to maximising shareholder returns.

> **Example:** Since England privatised its water supplies in 1989, not a single reservoir has been built (despite population growth). Less was invested in 2018 than in 1990. Water bills rose by 40% in real terms (according to the National Audit Office) and the water companies were (according to John McDonnell MP) losing enough water for 20 million people daily. Since the 1990s, investment from the privatised English water companies has gone down 15%, whilst amassing a debt mountain of over £60 billion (underwritten by taxpayers). Meanwhile, shareholders have received £72 billion – £2 billion a year on average (WeOwnIt, 2023). The English water companies are more than 70% owned by shareholders abroad (*ibid*), face increasingly bad PR including being deemed by many to be privatised monopolies. In 2023, support for renationalising water was at 83%, higher than for any other privatised utility.

Ultimately, most economic models focused on BAU rather than a societal (or even customer) centric position. However, studies have consistently found that with or without a stakeholder focus, corporate performance is very much the same. This suggests stakeholder-focused management does no harm to shareholder interests while also benefiting a larger constituency (Agle *et al*, 1999).

1.4 Sustainable Development (SD)

Scholars have long been criticised for paying too little attention to the relationship between the firm and society, focusing too much on internal organisational processes, to the neglect of any analysis of the societal effects of the firm (Walsh *et al*, 2003). This is remiss as ethics, social responsibility and sustainability in business have moved from marginal to mainstream and it can no longer be argued that the business of business is purely business (Emery, 2012).

Wicked Problems

In 1973, Horst Rittel and Melvin Webber coined the term 'wicked problem', drawing attention to the challenges of addressing planning and social policy problems (Rittel & Webber, 1973). Wicked problems are multifaceted and highly complex societal problems, such as poverty, obesity and environmental degradation (Kennedy & Parsons, 2012). Hastings & Domegan (2023) argue the wicked problems now faced, demand more than nudges and off-the-shelf solutions. They need everyone to take responsibility and engage in finding intelligent solutions. Wicked problems include impersonal interactions that require institutional guidance and (normative) frameworks. These, in turn, present vehicles for solving social problems. What, how, and how much is exchanged is decided by society and perpetuated through institutions (Kennedy, 2015).

There are those who describe sustainability as a 'megatrend' (Prothero & McDonagh, 2015) as it is larger in magnitude, longer in duration and deeper in its effects than normal trends, fads or fashion (Mittelstaedt *et al*, 2014). If it is a megatrend, the issues raised by businesses adopting and implementing sustainability are relevant. Sustainability-related solutions should be government led, however Tadajewski & Hamilton (2014) argue political action is not as effective as it should be. Consumers increasingly consider problems to be beyond the capacity of government alone. This must be seen in the context of unforeseen global phenomena e.g. the 2007 credit crunch and COVID-19. Post-credit crunch, 'austerity' programmes were introduced by some national governments (often at the behest of central banks) based on cutting social (i.e. care) budgets to 'save money'. Ironically there is increasing evidence, in 2023, that these austerity measures substantively reduced the capacity for societies to respond to the pandemic.

Defining Sustainability

Defining sustainability has proven to be challenging with many terms (i.e. 'ethical', 'organic', 'eco', 'green' or 'fair trade') being used interchangeably (Barkemeyer *et al*, 2009) when clearly they are not (Richardson, 2015, 2020, 2022). Some consumers find the terms confusing with new terms regularly being added to the sustainability lexicon such as upcycling (Bonera *et al*, 2020) and slow-fashion (Legere & Kang, 2020). It is not surprising that many terms are used to represent new concepts such as sustainability. Even well-established terms such as the 'environment', are used in myriad ways in differing texts and in some cases by the same author.

Consumers often connect with broader environmental issues (see Section 3.3). Their environmental interaction is important, often emotional and often influences their purchasing decisions. In companies, terms such CSR and sustainability are vague enough to gloss over varieties in definition, stakeholder interest and involvement whilst at the same time being powerful enough to draw the commitment of many different actors, including consumers, other companies and (inter)national organisations (Skov & Meier, 2011).

The widely cited 1987 Brundtland Commission's defined sustainability as development that meets the needs of the present without compromising the ability of future generations to meet their own needs (WCED, 1987). In 1994 the issue was brought to wider audiences when Elkington coined the phrase 'Triple-Bottom-Line' (TBL) in the Harvard Business Review (Elkington, 2018). In TBL, the traditional BAU economic focus is complemented by the addition of new foci, namely societal and ecological responsibility. Since TBL was coined, the sustainable business development concept has grown, often being referred to as 'People-Planet-Profit'. This may still be new to many practitioners (and academics) however elements therein have been practiced for centuries.

Example: The UK Co-operative (hereafter Co-op) retail movement can trace its principles and practices back to the Rochdale Pioneers of 1844 (ICA, 2023). Amongst their guiding principles were education, training, information and concern for the community through sustainable development (Davies & Burt, 2007). Often, they have been leaders in actions including product labelling, health education, fair trade and changing local workers' attitudes towards taking responsibility for their own welfare. Indeed, the Co-op not only channelled funds but existed "to serve the community in which it traded" (*ibid*, p 159). Co-operatives have cultural, industrial and historical origins which Hess (2004) considered important and they create 'societal' embeddedness. Two further forms of embeddedness attributed to co-operatives are 'network' (the composition and structure of the network relationships) and 'territorial' (the relationships in 'place' with local firms, consumers and regulations). Whilst other retailers or banks may not want to share all the Co-op's altruistic aims, their longevity, differentiation and customer retention (partially attributed to their form of 'societally embedded' retailing) suggests further consideration is prudent. Mainstream retailers have followed the Co-op's lead by espousing their green credentials (Jones *et al*, 2007).

The Business Case for Adopting Sustainability

It has been argued that Friedman's 'Libertarian' position leads to acting in a non-sustainable way. Pursuing short-term profits over all other considerations contributed to the 2008 economic meltdown. Companies must position (or reposition) themselves within their markets to make effective decisions. Two questions all marketers must answer:

1 How does the company create value in terms of sustainability?
2 How do customers seek sustainable value from the company?

If there is a mismatch in perceptions (i.e. a perceptual gap) then the organisation must implement changes, or be subject to a disadvantage which the competition could exploit. Creating sustainable value may be subject to time constraints or impossible given certain resource allocations. While some can implement sustainable practices immediately, others need time to accrue the resources to initiate change (Pacheco *et al*, 2010) or face disadvantage by pursuing 'costly' sustainable actions that may not be borne by BAU competitors (*ibid*).

Many companies have flagged their ecological credentials. However, simply insisting they are 'green' is no longer sufficient. Such claims are often challenged and those who engage in 'green-washing' (i.e. seeking to gain from false or exaggerated environmental claims) have suffered both reputational and collateral damage to their brand. Marketers must respond to the narrative AND demonstrate they operate in increasingly sustainable ways.

Elkington (2004) argued that the BAU approach was changing as a result of seven 'revolutions' (Table 1.2) which were changing businesses' behaviours and leading to a more sustainable future.

Clearly, the 'revolutions' do not stand apart, rather they can energise or alternatively constrain each other. Nor are they chronologically linear or constant across different cultures. The complex nature of the revolutions is exacerbated by the need for all functions in companies to engage. In practice it is not always clear where Sustainability 'ownership' resides, i.e. should it be hosted by marketing (representing the customer), HR (representing the staff), production (reducing 'green' impacts), Quality Control (ethical supply policies), purchasing (if greening the supply chain) or all of the above? This is partly due to differing approaches regarding what should be sustained, where and when. A way to address ownership issues is to arrange for cross-functional, inter-departmental teams to contribute to (and coordinate) sustainability-related matters.

Some organisations recognise sustainability's importance with elements in their mission statements (see Section 5.1). Increasingly Purpose Statements are used where organisations clearly state their differing objectives and related stakeholders. This helps

Table 1.2 Elkington's 7 revolutions to a sustainable future

Revolution	*Paradigm*		*Comment*
	Old	*New*	
Markets	Compliance	Competition	Increased competition in more demanding, volatile markets making businesses more susceptible to the effects of economic crises
Values	Hard	Soft	Worldwide shift in human / societal values making businesses susceptible to values-based crises when society finds them wanting
Transparency	Closed	Open	Increased transparency from more open access to information, stakeholder authority scrutiny and reporting systems
Life-cycle technology	Product	Function	Prioritising products' point of sale diminishes; focus shifts to whole supply network from raw materials to manufacture, transport, storage, disposal or recycling post-consumption
Partnerships	Subversion	Symbiosis	Partnerships will become more varied as pressure groups enter relationships with business organisations once regarded as enemies
Time	Wider	Longer	Sustainability issues lengthen time considerations making planning for sustainable business a matter of years, decades even generations
Corporate governance	Exclusive	Inclusive	Evolving governance to include representing ALL relevant stakeholders, keeping the board focused on the sustainable agenda.

Source: Adapted from Elkington (2004).

when sustainability responsibility is spread across stakeholders, e.g. the company, the consumer, the community, the regulator or the government. Consumers and others 'downstream' can develop different types of involvement with activities, objects, ideas or even social issues. Higher involvement results from stakeholders being committed to a cause or alternatively being affected such as the local community.

Some sustainable ventures do not seek to grow their enterprises (see Section 8.1), being content to remain in their niche. Hockerts & Wüstenhagen (2010) argue those who are active in a high-end social niche, but with no intention to broaden their impact on a wider market, are 'social bricoleurs' who worry about abandoning their ideals. This is harsh as new entrants will simply see the opportunity and strive to grow their company whilst the sustainable first mover continues or declines.

Marketers are put under pressure to be global and local, centralised and decentralised, large and small, planned yet flexible, and to serve differing markets, with standardised and customised products, at premium and penetration prices, through restricted and extensive distribution networks, and supported by national yet targeted promotional campaigns (Brown, 1995). With these demands it is no surprise that companies fail.

Table 1.3 Ethics and legality matrix

		Legality		
		High	*Low*	*Zero*
Ethicality	High	A	B	C
	Low	D	E	F
	Zero	G	H	I

Source: Author.

The cause is often due to their inappropriate marketing. The term 'inappropriate' covers not only poorly implemented marketing but also that which is neither legal nor ethical. It can be argued that anything that is sold is marketed. Hence those involved in, say, prostitution or ticket touting could be argued to be marketers. The counter to this argument is to be ethical in everything. If there are doubts about the ethical or environmental impact of a company's actions (Table 1.3), they should think carefully before proceeding.

Table 1.3 covers the full spectrum of marketing activities. Thankfully, it is harder than ever before to keep illegal and/or unethical practices secret. Most marketers are ethical and comply with the law. Table 1.3 is useful as it can be used to test customer perceptions of companies. A company who self-rates as being in position 'A', but research suggests its customers see it as Position 'E', can address the perceptual gap. They can reposition from E to A in one step or two (E-B-A or E-D-A).

A basic premise of this book is that in acting sustainably, marketers will be more likely to build trust. Too often marketing has focused on what needs to be done '*to*' customers whereas modern, progressive marketers should be asking themselves (and their colleagues) what they can do *for* their customers. This mindset will improve relationships with consumers and other stakeholders.

Corporate Social Irresponsibility

Corporate Social Irresponsibility (CSI) is arguably better suited to describing the workings of the BAU business models whereas CSR is more applicable to the workings of the stakeholder business model. CSI extends Carroll's work on definitional constructs by re-examining some of the theoretical frameworks that underpin, inform and guide CSR (Figure 1.5).

Jones *et al* (2009) describe their model as a conduit of corporate governance that enables action and assists planning. It facilitates a potentially better managed, more productive, socially responsible and profitable business (*ibid*). It can be inferred (from Figure 1.5) that some organisations may be positioned towards CSR on some issues whilst closer to CSI on others. Companies with clear, coherent CSR strategies should gravitate towards one end. The CSI–CSR continuum provides a useful tool for organisational positioning and benchmarking. It does, however, suffer the drawback of not informing managers how they should implement changes. It is worth noting that the continuum includes ecological concerns within the 'social' concept of CSR which some may deem incongruous. Although CSR predates the sustainability SM movement (Emery, 2012), despite including ecological matters, it fails to provide a complete answer to the issues raised by the sustainability agenda (*ibid*).

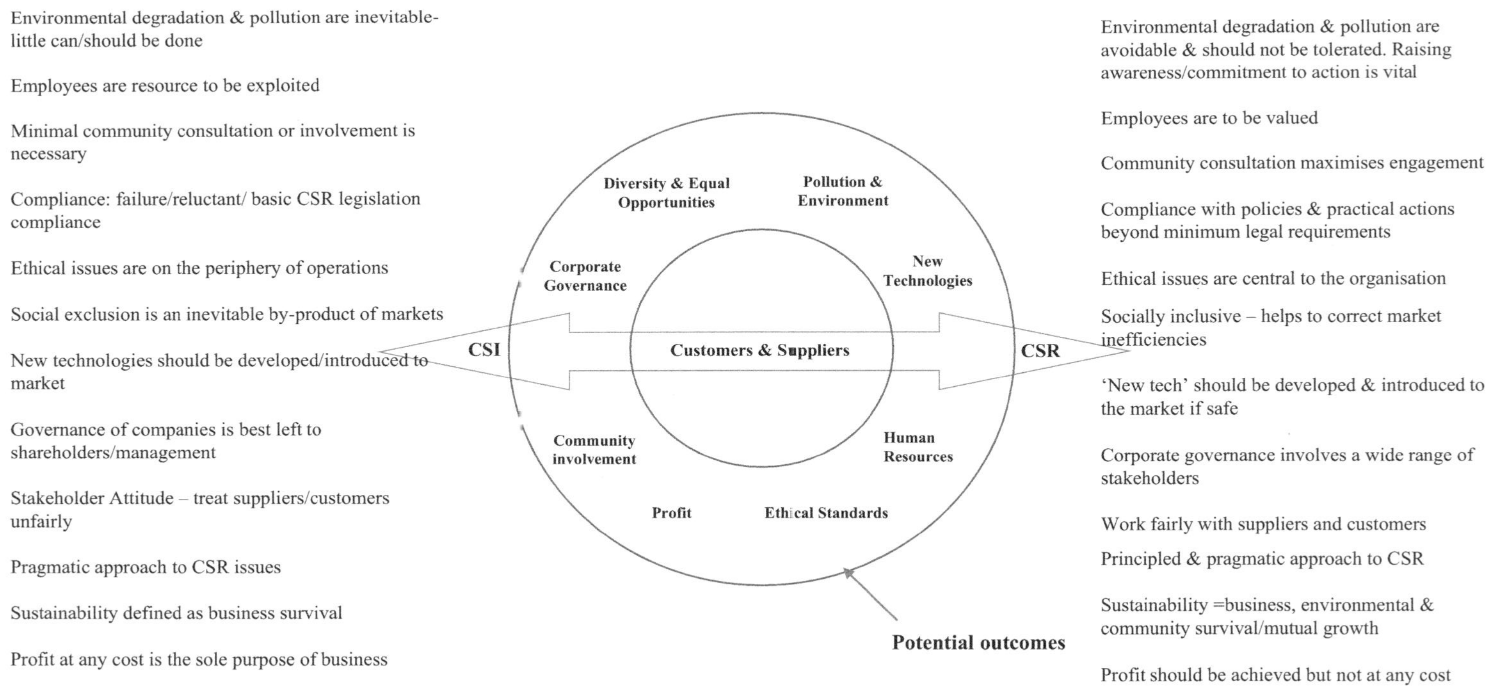

Figure 1.5 The CSI v CSR dichotomous model and potential outcomes.

Source: Adapted from Jones *et al* (2009, pp 301–304).

The Public Relations (PR) industry has, at times, been associated with CSI by producing propaganda, often during times of conflict or unrest. PR has been used by dictators when the messages communicated were based on a twisted form of idealism rather than reality. Criticism is often aimed at businesses and organisations who do not 'practice what they preach' or spin the story to include a heavily biased opinion in favour of the message sender (see Section 4.1). PR practitioners (often referred to as 'spin doctors') representing political parties, are frequently criticised for their part in manipulating (or being economical with) the truth. Sometimes their role has been more insidious as was demonstrated in the Bell Pottinger debacle in South Africa in 2018.

In the UK there are laws to protect against libel and slander. Increasingly cases are being brought for online comments. The law applies whether online or in hard copy. Cases of libel action being brought against PR practitioners are rare but high-profile practitioners have found themselves facing high court rulings for promoting stories that were falsified. Similarly, newspapers are treated with the same legal action for reporting stories, often promoted by PR practitioners, that are defamatory and may cause huge anxiety for those misrepresented.

United Nations Sustainable Development Goals (SDGs)

Whilst we (arguably) may not be able to see the impact of climate change today, it unarguably presents us a future few neither truly comprehend nor want; a future that experts predict will not be compatible with human life on our planet (Figueres & Rivett-Carnac, 2020). Without significant changes to the way we live our lives, this future may become a reality within most of our lifetimes (UNIPCC, 2018). World leaders have recognised the problem for over 50 years and have spent the last 25 debating the solutions (Alstine *et al*, 2013). Societies faced with a radical imperative to achieve a socially, economically and ecologically sustainable basis (within a historically short time) must reappraise most aspects of organisations therein.

The 1991 Rio Earth Summit produced Agenda 21; the official document signed by all attending nations (Bell, 2016). The word 'education' appears in every Agenda 21 chapter with a particular focus in Chapter 36 entitled 'Promoting Education, Public Awareness, and Training' (UN, 2021). Many paths to sustainability are mentioned in the Agenda 21's 40 chapters (UNESCO, 2023). Education is one of these paths, however on its own it cannot achieve a more sustainable future; that said, without education and learning for sustainable development (SD), that goal (i.e. sustainability) will not be reached (*ibid*).

In 2000, the United Nations launched the UN Global Compact as a call to companies everywhere to align their operations and strategies with ten universally accepted principles in the areas of human rights, labour, environment and anti-corruption (UN, 2017). The UN Global Compact is built on the fundamental belief that business plays a critical role in improving our world – and it starts by doing business responsibly (*ibid*).

The United Nations Decade of Education for Sustainable Development (2005–2014) sought to mobilise the educational resources of the world to help create a more sustainable future. In 2009, the UNECE Steering Committee on Education for Sustainable Development (ESD) offered a range of core feasible competencies to facilitate (ESD's) integration into educational programmes at all levels (UNECE, 2011). Furthermore, they provided guidelines for the development of these competencies among educators (*ibid*).

Example: The EAUC organises an annual UK & Ireland Green Gown Awards (see www.greengownawards.org) delivered in association with UK Research and Innovation (UKRI). EAUC invites applicants from across the Higher and Further Education sectors to apply across a diverse array of categories, where institutional and individual sustainability work can be showcased. Since 2006, Campus Responsables have run 'Les trophées des campus responsables', a French-speaking edition of the Green Gown Awards, open to all (French-speaking) universities across the world. In 2010 the Awards were introduced to Australasia, delivered by ACTS (see www.acts.asn.au/) open to all tertiary education institutions in Australia and New Zealand. Finally, the International Green Gown Awards (see www.greengownawards.org/international-green-gown-awards) are supported by the UN Environment Programme and are open to any university or college across the world. In 2023, there were 92 finalists representing 25 countries. This represented a 64% increase in the number of finalists in 2022. Universities across the globe should engage with the Green Gown awards.

By 2017, the UN Global Compact was the largest corporate sustainability initiative in the world, with more than 9,500 companies and 3,000 non-business signatories in over 160 countries, with activities supported by 76 Local Networks (UN, 2017). To accelerate progress, in 2015, the 193 participating countries in the UN agreed to an ambitious 2030 Agenda for Sustainable Development (*ibid*). This new global action plan sought to promote sustainability worldwide (by 2030), leaving no one behind, calling for action to end poverty and fight climate change. The new Agenda augmented the former 8 Millennium Development Goals (MDGs) to become 17 Sustainable Development Goals (SDGs) covering social, economic and environmental topics (Table 1.4)

The 'Short titles' (Table 1.4) are used extensively by the UN for example in their use of graphical representations. The SDGs provide a framework for a better, more sustainable future for all (UN, 2023) and enable a focus on the global issues of poverty, health and education, through which enormous advances have been monitored (Dean *et al*, 2018). Progress has been made – in the last 30 years, the world has: reduced extreme poverty by half; increased the number of school children in primary school in Sub-Saharan Africa; reduced maternal mortality by 45%; and experienced success in the fight against AIDS, Malaria and TB (*ibid*). Clearly, the need to create the SDGs is, in itself, a criticism of the efficacy of the neo-liberal agenda.

Example: In the UK, students (SOS, 2023) and academics in 'The Alliance for Sustainability Leadership in Education' (EAUC, 2023) come together annually to organise a month of 'Teach-ins'. It is an international campaign, calling on trainers, lifelong and workplace learning facilitators and formal and informal educators across all disciplines and levels globally, to adopt the UN SDGs in their teaching, training, and learning through case studies, debate, discussion, group work, team tasks, or simulations relating to topics included within the SDGs. The 2022 campaign saw over 770 educators reach nearly 140,000 students in discussions around the SDGs and their relevance to their subject. According to SOS-UK research, 84% of students would like to see SD actively incorporated and promoted through their learning, and the Teach In is a great springboard for meaningful engagement in this area. The Teach In aims to:

- Raise awareness of the importance of SD
- Catalyse curriculum reform and test new ideas
- Embed sustainability and social responsibility across all learning
- Link teaching, learning, and assessment to local and global concerns
- Prepare students with the knowledge, skills, and attributes to tackle the world's greatest challenges.

Table 1.4 UN Sustainable Development Goals (SDGs)

SDG	*Short titles*	*Explanation*
1	No Poverty	End poverty in all its forms everywhere
2	Zero Hunger	End hunger, achieve food security & improved nutrition; promote sustainable agriculture
3	Good Health and Well-Being	Ensure healthy lives & promote well-being for all at all ages
4	Quality Education	Ensure inclusive & equitable quality education; promote life-long learning opportunities for all.
5	Gender Equality	Achieve gender equality; empower all women and girls
6	Clean Water and Sanitation	Ensure availability & sustainable management of water/sanitation for all
7	Affordable and Clean Energy	Ensure access to affordable, reliable, sustainable, modern energy for all
8	Decent Work and Economic Growth	Promote sustained, inclusive & sustainable economic growth; full, productive employment; decent work for all
9	Industry, Innovation and Infrastructure	Build resilient infrastructure; promote inclusive, sustainable industrialisation; foster innovation
10	Reduced Inequalities	Reduce inequality within and among countries
11	Sustainable Cities and Communities	Make cities & human settlements inclusive, safe, resilient & sustainable
12	Responsible Consumption and Production	Ensure sustainable consumption and production patterns
13	Climate Action	Take urgent action to combat climate change and its impacts
14	Life Below Water	Conserve and sustainably use the oceans, seas and marine resources for SD
15	Life on Land	Protect, restore & promote sustainable use of terrestrial ecosystems; sustainably manage forests; combat desertification; halt & reverse land degradation & biodiversity loss
16	Peace Justice and Strong Institutions	Promote peaceful & inclusive societies for SD; provide access to justice for all; build effective, accountable, inclusive institutions at all levels
17	Partnerships for the Goals	Strengthen the means of implementation; revitalise the global partnership for SD

Source: Adapted from UN (2017).

The UN SDGs (Table 1.4) are a global call to action to eradicate poverty, safeguard the environment, and guarantee that everyone lives in peace and prosperity. The SDGs do not stand apart; rather they are interdependent and can energise each other. SD is predicated on Elkington's Triple Bottom Line (TBL) and supports the UN SDGs. Walker (2021) provides an excellent analysis of the issues germane to micro-plastics when viewed through the lens of the SDGs. He cites the 169 targets, used to monitor the 17 SDGs which generate 247 unique indicators. He argues

> "despite pervasive global pollution from (micro)plastics, there is only one indicator (14.1.1b) under Goal 14, specifically related to reducing impacts from (micro)plastics ... (and) ... reliable reporting and monitoring of 247 SDG indicators present unique challenges for governments and organizations".
>
> (*ibid*, p 1)

B Corporation Accreditation

> "I see a bright ray of hope coming from the high-energy world of B Corporations".
>
> (Elkington, 2018)

Companies who self-identify as sustainable may be found on indices that measure their performance regarding strong Environmental, Social and Governance (ESG) practices. Transparent management and clearly defined ESG criteria make indices, e.g. FTSE4Good, suitable tools to be used by a variety of participants when creating or assessing sustainable investment products. Other Indices include the Dow Jones Sustainability Index (DJSI, 2023) and the Better Business Bureau (BBB, 2023). The most rigorous accreditation is found amongst organisations who attain B Corporation certification (Kim & Schifeling, 2022; Ferioli *et al*, 2022).

By 2023, 7,227 companies, with over 646,000 workers in 93 countries across 161 industries (BCorp, 2023a) have been successful in applying for 'B Corporation' (hereafter BCorp) status. Interestingly, most applications are rejected as applicants must undertake a rigorous process (BCorp, 2023b) featuring a 200-plus question 'assessment test' based on their size, sector and market. Applicants must disclose past public complaints, fines or sanctions and provide full disclosure of their corporate practices (Marks, 2021). The certification requires the provision of legal protection for directors when considering the interests of all stakeholders (not just shareholders). It requires companies to create additional rights for shareholders to hold directors accountable.

Example: Chloé, a French luxury fashion house founded in 1952, was the first such organisation to attain BCorp Certification and pioneer sustainability within the luxury world; their A/W21 collection (featuring recycled wool and cashmere knits, puffer jackets made using surplus textiles and reworked vintage handbags) led to a year-on year CO_2 reduction of 400%. They stated by

> "becoming BCorp certified, we reinforce our ongoing commitment to taking accountability for our impact on people and the planet. Rather than a final goal, this certification marks a new stage in our transformation towards a purpose-driven model, reinventing how we do business".
>
> (Bellini, 2021)

Customers buying sustainable luxury fashion items may have less experience of purchasing such items. By nature, these products tend to involve a longer customer commitment and expectations, i.e. Chloé customers may want their trainers to last several years. Luxury fashion retailers need to recognise that prospective customers (or prospects) may spend longer moving through the 'Information Search' and 'Information Evaluation' steps (see Chapter 3). Chloé supports (amongst others) UN SDGs 3, 8, 9 and 12 (see Table 1.4).

Companies are motivated to seek BCorp accreditation because "a new generation of workers and customers are pushing today's business leaders to consider things beyond just profits. And many smart leaders are responding to the call" (Marks, 2021). The number of companies in the indices (including the 7,227 BCorp companies) is still relatively small, however it supports the notion that companies are increasingly adopting sustainable practices and, to an extent, provides a rationale for this book. It is not easy; Sean Russell, founded Danish BCorp accredited beauty company Skandinavisk in 2012. He observes

> "it become obvious to me that if we are to represent a better version of the world, then we must live it as well. That we needed to lead by example. What followed was the arduous task of becoming a Certified B Corporation, to reach a threshold that represents such better practice. But what the certification process taught me was even more powerful: that of the tremendous difference between how good you think you are and how good you truly act. The gap was uncomfortable, to say the least, and, ever since, I've been determined to reduce it".
>
> (Russell, 2022)

These BCorps are leading the way towards a more sustainable and regenerative planet by putting their impact on the air, climate, water, land and biodiversity first in their business practices. These companies excel in environmental performance by offering products or services designed to solve an environmental issue or through their facilities, materials, emissions, and resource and energy use, as well as transportation/ distribution channels and the environmental impact of their supply chain (Alpro, 2023).

Example: In 2022, Belgium-headquartered Alpro was recognised as 'Best For The World' in the BCorps Environment category.

> "For two years in a row, we have been recognized as Best for the World 2022 in the environmental category since our last re-certification in 2021. We gained almost 20 points in the environment category of the B Impact Assessment thanks to the hard work we put in. We are not the best IN the world but we do our best FOR the world. So, this recognition is so much more than just a badge of honor, it gives us more motivation to keep increasing our efforts. We are always looking at other inspirational BCorps who have amazing practices related to the environment in place but also at the same time thrive in other areas".
>
> Juliane Greff, Sustainability Expert
> Plant-Based Europe at Alpro (Alpro, 2023)

The 5 Planets Theory

To a degree the Malthusian idea of a never-ending population explosion has been countered and those interested should seek out the works of Hans Rosling. Rosling (2010) predicts the planet's population plateauing at 9–10 billion by 2050 (assuming average family sizes continue to reduce in developing countries). The earth's population is still growing, but it will level out. The issue is how will we all live together? In 2019 scientists produced a diet that could feed a global population of 10 billion whilst using current levels of technology. This would entail wholesale changes to eating patterns with much less red meat being consumed. Still, it is useful to see positive solutions being offered. A simple means of illustrating how problems of increasing consumption (resulting from population growth) continue to this day is the 5 Planets Theory. This is used to benchmark countries' consumption. If all countries consumed resources in the same way as the USA, four planets would be needed. For the UK it is 2.7 planets whereas for India it is only 0.4 planets. Two points. First the UK figure has reduced from three planets. So, post-industrial societies can change their impact for the better. Second, if all countries had India's impact, the Earth's population would be able to co-exist with current levels of resources. Realistically this will not happen as the current economic systems are not 'geared up' to make the necessary changes.

Three Rs

Manufacturers and retailers should encourage and support consumers to:

- reuse what they can
- recycle what cannot be reused
- repair what is broken
- re-manufacture what cannot be repaired (Stahel, 2016).

From this, the oft-cited 'Three Rs' has arisen. This mnemonic seems simple but has far-reaching implications for buyer behaviour. Those strongly committed to sustainable causes (i.e. green, charitable or ethical), will be more critical and (willing to) undertake further research prior to purchase (see Figure 3.7). The most popular version is "Reduce, Reuse, Recycle". It is worth noting that alternatives exist, e.g.

- Rescue, Restore, Reuse
- Refuse, Reduce, Reuse, Repurpose, Recycle
- Repair, Remake, Refuse, Remember, Respect, Restore.

Example: One of the leaders of the repairable, upgradeable revolution is Dutch startup Fairphone and its eponymous smartphone, which is now in its fourth generation (Guardian, 2023). The Fairphone 4 is an Android-based device with all the usual features, including water resistance, packed into a slightly chunky design that hides fully modular parts. Consumers can change the battery (without tools), while everything else needs a small screwdriver. Fairphone offers a five-year warranty and aims to provide updates for up to seven years. That said, it is not the fastest, the camera is a lower 'spec' than its competitors and, at £499, it is more expensive, spec-for-spec, than its rivals. There are cheaper alternatives, such as a handful of Nokia phones costing about £120 and upwards, with user-replaceable parts. However, they are not as easy to fix as the Fairphone and Nokia only provides up to three years of updates from release (*ibid*).

Many activists believe that modern business practices advocate 'selling more' whilst 'Sustainability' is about consuming less. Marketers may need to adapt to address stakeholders' concerns. Sustainability is not simply about damage limitation, rather it is an opportunity to promote good practices. BAU cannot continue and the good news is that companies and even countries are changing their behaviour. For example, in 2014, copper use in China featured 80% recycled metal. This was driven by increasing copper prices; however it illustrates how changes can be made, e.g. use of fuel, recycling, waste.

1.5 Systems and SD

> "One of the great deficiencies of our education is that few of us are taught systems theory. Yet everything of material importance to us – the human brain, the human body, human society, ecosystems, the atmosphere, the oceans, the financial system, the food system – is a complex system. The behaviour of these systems, because so few of us study them, repeatedly takes us by surprise".
>
> (Monbiot, 2023)

Dr Hannah Ritchie is lead researcher at Our World in Data. She suggests the answer to almost every climate dilemma is 'We need both' i.e.

> "we need renewables and nuclear energy (even if that means just keeping our existing nuclear plants online). We need to tackle fossil fuels and our food system; fossil fuels are the biggest emitter, but emissions from food alone would take us well past a temperature rise of 1.5C and close to 2C. Not everyone can commute without a car, so we need electric vehicles and cycle-friendly cities and public transport networks. We can't decarbonise without technological change, but we need to rethink our economic, political and social systems to make sure they flourish".
>
> (Richie, 2023)

Economic Systems

> "TBL's stated goal from the outset was *system change* – pushing toward the transformation of capitalism. It was never supposed to be just an accounting system. It was originally intended as a genetic code, a triple helix of change for tomorrow's capitalism, with a focus was on breakthrough change, disruption, asymmetric growth (with unsustainable sectors actively side-lined), and the scaling of next-generation market solutions".
>
> (Elkington, 2018)

There are three kinds of industrial economy: linear, circular and performance. A linear economy uses natural resources, e.g. raw materials, to manufacture products that hopefully create customer value. The linear 'take, make, dispose' economic model relies on large quantities of cheap, easily accessible materials and energy (Macarthur, 2015). When the decision-making process is completed, ownership and responsibility transfer to the consumer. At the end of the product's useful life, the consumer decides if the product should be disposed, reused, recycled, repurposed or remanufactured. This assumes that they are aware of their choices or, indeed, are motivated to do so. Within a linear economy, consumers are assumed to be continuously seeking the next best thing in what is often a saturated, fragmented, over-supplied market where goods are disposable. Linear economies involve overcoming scarcity whilst wasting resources.

Example: Apropos the linear plastics economy, Walker (2021) insists a dramatic shift is needed to achieve SDG 9 (Table 1.4). He insists innovation is required to move from reliance on unsustainable fossil fuel-based plastics to sustainable bio-based plastic alternatives to help contribute to a circular economy. Although bio-based plastics may offer a sustainable alternative, they account for <2% of plastics, because of low-cost of fossil-based plastics, intense requirement for land use, and undeveloped recycling options. Therefore, cradle-to-grave life cycle assessment of bio-based alternatives is urgently required (*ibid*).

Circular Economies

The concept of the circular economy has been around since the early 1970s. It has evolved from a number of key antecedents (Table 1.5).

Moving to a 'circular economy' would change economic logic because it replaces production with sufficiency (Stahel, 2016). It seeks to avoid sending goods to landfill or for incineration. Rather, it advocates turning goods at the end of their serviceable life into resources for others, closing loops in industrial ecosystems and minimising waste. It is restorative and regenerative by design, keeping products, components or materials at their highest utility and value at all times (Macarthur, 2015).

Table 1.5 Antecedents of the circular economy

Key Authors	*Topic*
Lifset & Graedel (2001)	Industrial Ecology
McDonough & Braungart (2003)	Cradle to Cradle Design
Benyus (2003)	Biomimicry
Stahel (2006)	The Performance Economy
Hawken, Lovins & Lovins (2008)	Natural Capitalism
Pauli (2010)	Blue Economy

Source: Adapted from Macarthur (2015).

Example: The Vestiaire Collective is a BCorp accredited Parisian resale platform with a vast offering (i.e. Chanel bags, Dior jackets or Alexander McQueen scarves). They were the world's first pre-owned fashion site to become BCorp Certified, with particular recognition of achievements in the 'Workers' and 'Governance' areas. It has over 500 employees across France, Germany, America, Hong Kong and Singapore; 60% of its staff are women, covering 48 nationalities (Bellini, 2021). In 2020, it appointed a chief sustainability and inclusion officer and launched five employee diversity and inclusion task forces, including Ethnic diversity, LGBTQIA+, Women's empowerment, Disability and Equal opportunity (*ibid*). Clearly, Vestiaire provides a service that addresses both ethical and environmental concerns. By facilitating the sale of pre-owned fashion, the company reduces the need for new clothes (and raw materials) whilst preventing clothes at the end of their initial life cycle being sent to landfill. Vesitaire supports UN SDGs 5, 8, 9, and 12 (amongst others).

Vestiaire's activities can be deemed as 'Reuse' and/or 'Recycle'. Many of those driving towards a circular economy provide such services. This could be extended to include 'Repair' and/or 'Repurpose' functions. The remanufacturing, repair or repurposing of products creates skilled jobs and is better for the environment (Figure 1.6).

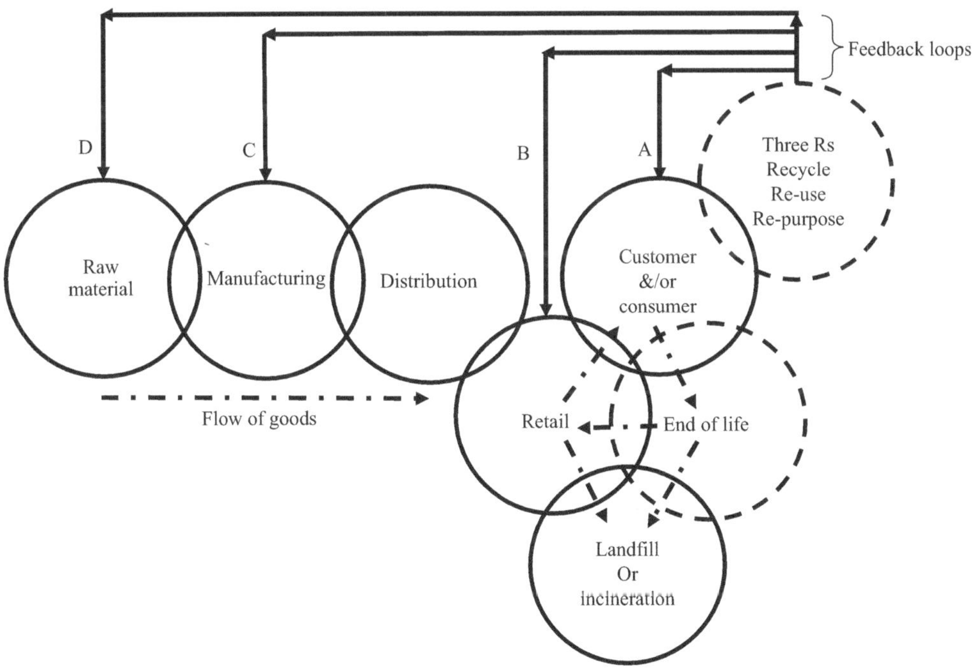

Figure 1.6 Circular economy – Flow of goods and consumer decisions.

Source: Author.

Figure 1.6 illustrates the typical flow of goods from raw material via retailers to customers. The feedback loops are suggested to improve the likelihood of achieving a circular economy. At the end of the product's life the consumer decides whether any of the Three Rs are viable or sadly the item has reached its end of life (Position A). Can the consumer return the item to the retailer for disposal (as happens with white goods items such as fridges)? Does the retailer support (and inform) the customer at this touchpoint? Issues that impede the Three Rs need to feed back and (as suggested) this can involve feedback through the supply network even to the selection of raw materials. Furthermore, retailers must address the issue of 'terminal stock', i.e. items that are taking up valuable floor space but are no longer deemed saleable. Do these simply go to landfill or can alternatives be found?

Example: The United Repair Centre (URC), in Amsterdam employs refugees, who are tailors, to help extend the lifespan of clothing by repairing garments for brands and their customers. Founded in 2022, URC's work is a small part of Amsterdam's effort to become a circular economy (BBC, 2023). "Circularity is the hottest topic in the fashion industry right now ... Every brand is looking at how they can be sustainable. Repairs will be part of the future of circularity for brands ... There needs to be a systematic solution if change is to happen ... It's not going to happen through the consumer" says Thami Schweichler, CEO of URC. Currently working with five brands including Patagonia, Scotch & Soda and Decathlon, garments needing repairs are sent to URC, with a typical turnround of a week. Currently repairing 400 repairs each week, or roughly 20,000 a year, the target is to reach 200,000 repairs per year by 2026 (*ibid*).

Each feedback loop and interaction between stages creates opportunities for new jobs to be created and, therefore, systems are needed at each step. Consumers will need access to collection points to return products to the manufacturers. Communications will have to be tailored to ensure consumers are aware of the processes involved (see Figure 3.7). Initially incentives may need to be offered, however, in time, new behaviours will become the norm and sustainable practices will proliferate. A study of seven European nations found that a shift to a circular economy would reduce each nation's greenhouse-gas emissions by up to 70% and grow its workforce by about 4% (Stahel, 2016). Circular-economy business models either

- promote reuse and extended Product Life Cycles through repair, remanufacture, upgrades and retrofits; or
- repurpose pre-owned items into new offerings featuring recycled materials.

The reprocessing of goods and materials saves energy while reducing resource consumption and waste. A milk bottle that is used 20-30 times has a lower carbon footprint than that of a single-use plastic bottle. Dairies report common recycling figures of 40–50 re-uses per bottle. Cleaning a glass bottle and using it again is faster and cheaper than recycling the glass or making a new bottle from minerals. In a circular economy, the objective is to maximise value at each point in a product's life.

A performance economy features renting, leasing and sharing goods rather than selling them. The supplier retains ownership of the product and is responsible for its upkeep. Taxis are facing competition from car clubs in major cities and the users are not faced with issues such as depreciation, maintenance or servicing. The performance economy features replacing buying products with service-based solutions and is inherently inclined towards reducing waste. Alvis and Avison (2021) argue against BAU as it assumes little progress on the circular economy. They insist under BAU

- recycling rates will remain at low levels
- there will be little or no growth in remanufacturing, repair or rental services
- there will be minimal growth related to recycling and repair.

Organisational Systems

When discussing audits with practitioners it is rarely long before the political nature of companies is discussed. Companies are made up of different systems that interact with each other and their respective environments. Some managers protect their departments jealously, possibly lacking a vision of the bigger picture. These departments or functions (e.g. HR, Accounts, Logistics or Marketing) often have their own systems, which do not necessarily interact harmoniously. This may result from companies being too 'inward' focused or having 'systems' that do not create value for the customer. Such companies are often process or systems driven when they should be customer driven.

Mintzberg argues that organisational success will be dictated by the 'overlaps' between systems, e.g. how well does the HRM system recruit, motivate and reward marketing staff? Are recruits customer-centric? How well do the systems interact with the environment in which business activity takes place? Systems have natural and man-made boundaries e.g. departmental structures. Organisations have within them systems that are

- technical
- informational and
- social.

These systems can be closed systems, open systems or hybrid (semi-open). Open systems connect and interact freely with the organisation's environments. Hence, they are influenced by the company's environments (see Figure 5.4). These influences can energise the organisation or alternatively they can act as constraints. Open systems, i.e. wikis, tend to be stable but continuously changing due to the user-generated nature of the content. There are issues regarding the reliability of the data contained therein as contributors may not be experts or may have vested interests.

Closed systems are isolated from the company's environments, i.e. the system is independent with no influence exerted either way. For example, production may use a Distributed Process Control (DPC) system. In practice, few systems are entirely closed. Many are semi-open meaning some stakeholders in the business environments can access the systems' information or even input data. Hence there is a degree of influence depending on the stakeholders and the nature of the system. Universities have Virtual Learning

Environments (VLEs) where the students have password access. Often the university staff can upload lectures whereas the students can file assessments online to modules. Semi-open systems connect and interact with their environments with user access dictated by passwords.

Senior management often access a Management Information System (MIS) where others input data. Different sectors use differing systems, e.g. for retailers service tills (EPOS) and Radio Frequency ID tags (RFID) are visible elements of process systems. Whereas booking systems for festivals, hotels or concert venues represent 'back-office' elements. Interestingly, there are very few contemporary discussions in the marketing literature about information systems despite the inexorable rise of Big Data.

Effective decision-making is almost always underpinned by relevant data and analysis. The focus on data has increased in recent years, facilitated by the innovations presented by the digital marketing environment. There is an increasing number of categories including product data, mobile data, campaign data, website data, funnel data, engagement data and customer data amongst others. Big Data is defined as high-volume, high-velocity and high-variety assets that demand cost-effective, innovative forms of information processing for enhanced insight and decision-making (Richardson *et al*, 2015). The key points to take from this are Big Data

- uses increasingly large data sets recorded and stored using technology.
- is generated at speed and requires timely responses to exploit the opportunities it presents
- is complex coming from many different sources and in various formats.

Big Data presents the following challenges to marketers:

- identifying which data is relevant, which data actually matters
- being able to analyse, form insights and react quickly
- bringing together the 'quant' and 'qual' data from different platforms in a cohesive, coherent format.

The task of taking various data sets (from a variety of data sources, with varying degrees of relevance, accuracy and validity) and giving it structure through matching, cleansing and linkage is daunting. Marketers increasingly use visualisation software to shape the huge volumes of data into meaningful results. These visual representations can highlight patterns and trends that can support decision-making. Undoubtedly operational aspects and systems are important but not at the expense of customer focus. In building and operating such systems the mnemonic RATIFI is useful:

- Raw data must be processed to provide useful and useable information
- Agreement must be reached as to what information is needed and to whom it may be communicated
- The information system must drive strategy and planning
- Information dissemination must be effective
- Feedback loops must be incorporated so the implementation of the marketing plan informs the data (and quality) of the information system
- Information gathering must be a continuing process not a one-off.

Key Findings

1. Corporate Social Responsibility (CSR) pre-dates the sustainability discourse and is still a key component of sustainability. There are still definitional issues relating to sustainability.
2. Stakeholders increasingly influence the achievement of organisational objectives.
3. All companies need to be aware of their ethical positioning in order to make appropriate strategic and operational decisions.
4. The United Nations Sustainable Development Goals (SDGs) should be adopted in teaching, learning and practices.
5. Indices provide benchmarking opportunities for overtly sustainable organisations including the most rigorous accreditation, i.e. B Corporation.
6. Systems can influence adopting sustainable practice. They must inform decision-making, knowledge management and support internal implications, e.g. training needs.

Activities

1. For more insights into stakeholder theory, see Freeman's site (https://redwardfreeman.com/).
2. Review BCorp-accredited organisations and reflect on whether insights can translate to other companies adopting sustainability.
3. Reflect on the Co-operative's world-class CSR platform (it is transparent and independently audited).
4. For insights into the role of systems read George Monbiot's 'The Hunger Gap' (see Monbiot, 2023).
5. For more information on the B Corps Best for the World™ awards see https://bcorporation.eu/best-for-the-world/.
6. The Climate Optimist has many interesting articles. See www.hsph.harvard.edu/c-change/climateoptimist/

References

Agle, B.R., Mitchell, R.K., & Sonnenfeld, J.A. (1999) Who matters to CEOs? An investigation of stakeholder attributes and salience corporate performance and CEO values. *Academy of Management Journal*, 42(5), pp. 507–525. DOI:10.5465/256973

Alpro (2023) *Alpro: Promoting Healthier Eating and Sustainable Living*. https://bcorporation.eu/case_study/alpro-promoting-healthier-eating-and-sustainable-living/ (accessed 29-08-23).

Alstine, J.V., Afionis, S. & Doran, P. (2013) The UN conference on sustainable development (Rio +20): A sign of the times or 'ecology as spectacle?' *Environmental Politics*, 22(2), pp. 333–338. DOI:10.1080/09644016.2013.765162)

Alvis, S. & Avison, Z. (2021) *Levelling up through Circular Economy Jobs* Green Alliance policy insight paper August 2021. www.green-alliance.org.uk (accessed 20-10-22).

Baden, D. (2016) A reconstruction of Carroll's pyramid of corporate social responsibility for the 21st century. *International Journal of Corporate Social Responsibility*, 1(8), pp. 1–15. DOI:10.1186/s40991-016-0008-2

Barkemeyer, R. (2009) Beyond compliance — below expectations? CSR in the context of international development. *Business Ethics: A European Review*, 18(3) 273–289.

BBC (2023) *Can Amsterdam Make the Circular Economy Work?* www.bbc.co.uk/news/business-65696083 (accessed 20-09-2023).

B Corp. (2023a) *Make Business a Force for Good*. Website. www.bcorporation.net/en-us/ (accessed 08-08-23).

B Corp. (2023b) *Certification Requirements*. Website. https://bcorporation.net/certification/meet-the-requirements (accessed 14-04-23).

Bell, D. (2016) Twenty-first century education: Transformative education for sustainability and responsible citizenship. *Journal of Teacher Education for Sustainability*, 18(1), pp. 48–56, DOI:10.1515/jtes-2016-0004

Bellini, L. (2021) *The Glossary's B Corp Fashion Guide: The Ethical Fashion Brands to Know-From Luxury Fashion Houses to Innovative Footwear Brands, these are the Trailblazing Names Doing Their Bit for the Planet*. 21 October 2021

Belz, F-M. & Peattie, K. (2012) *Sustainability Marketing — A Global Perspective*, 2nd Edition. Chichester: Wiley & Sons.

Bonera, M., Codini, A. P., & Miniero, G. (2020) The great Millennials' trouble: Leading or confused green generation? An Italian insight. *Italian Journal of Marketing*, pp. 289–308. DOI:10.1007/s43039-020-00015-4

Bowen, H.R. (1953) *Social Responsibilities of the Businessman*. Federal Council of the Churches of Christ in America.

Brown, S. (1995) *Postmodern Marketing*, London: Routledge.

Carroll, A.B. (1979) A three-dimensional conceptual model of corporate performance. *Academy of Management Review*, 4(4), pp. 497–505. DOI:10.2307/257850

Carroll, A.B. (1991) The pyramid of corporate social responsibility: Toward the moral management of organisational stakeholders. *Business Horizons*, July–Aug, pp. 39–48. DOI:10.1016/0007-6813(91)90005-G

Carroll, A. B. (1994). Social issues in management research: Experts' views, analysis, and commentary. *Business & Society*, 33(1), pp. 5–29. DOI:10.1177/000765039403300102

Carroll, A.B. (2016) Carroll's pyramid of CSR: Taking another look. *International Journal of Corporate Social Responsibility*, 1(3). DOI:10.1186/s40991-016-0004-6

Clarkson, M.B.E. (1988) 'Corporate social performance in Canada 1976–86' in *Research in Corporate Social Performance and Policy*, L.E. Preston (Ed.), vol 10, pp. 241–265. Greenwich: JAI Press.

Davies, K. & Burt, S (2007) Consumer co-operatives and retail internationalisation: problems and prospects. *International Journal of Retail & Distribution Management*, 35(2), pp. 156–77.

Davis, K. (1960) Can business afford to ignore corporate social responsibilities? *California Management Review*, 2(3), Spring, pp. 70–76. DOI:10.2307/41166246

Dean, B.A., Gibbons, B. & Perkiss, S. (2018) An experiential learning activity for integrating the United Nations sustainable development goals into business education. *Social Business*, 8(4), pp. 387–409. DOI:10.1362/204440818X15445231830058

DJSI (2023) *DJSI Index Family*. www.spglobal.com/esg/performance/indices/djsi-index-family (accessed 10-09-23).

Donaldson, T. (2008) 'Two stories'. Article from Academy of Management 2007 Symposium in B.R. Agle, T. Donaldson, R.E. Freeman, M.C. Jensen, R.K. Mitchell, & D.J. Wood, (2008) Dialogue: Toward Superior Stakeholder Theory. *Business Ethics Quarterly*, 18(2), pp. 153–190. DOI:10.5840/beq200818214

EAUC (2023) *The Alliance for Sustainability Leadership in Education*. Website. www.eauc.org.uk/ (accessed 26-04-23).

Elkington, J. (2004) 'Enter the triple bottom line' in A. Henriques & J. Richardson, (Eds), (2004) *The Triple Bottom Line: Does it all add up?* London: Earthscan.

Elkington, J. (2018) *25 Years Ago I Coined the Phrase "Triple Bottom Line." Here's Why It's Time to Rethink It*. https://hbr.org/2018/06/25-years-ago-i-coined-the-phrase-triple-bottom-line-heres-why-im-giving-up-on-it (accessed 02-09-23).

Emery, B. (2012) *Sustainable Marketing*. Harlow: Pearson Education.

Ferioli, M., Gazzola, P., Grechi, D. & Vătămănescu, E-M. (2022) Sustainable behaviour of B Corps fashion companies during Covid-19: A quantitative economic analysis. *Journal of Cleaner Production*, 374, November, DOI:10.1016/j.jclepro.2022.134010

Figueres, C. & Rivett-Carnac, T. (2020) *The Future We Choose: Surviving the Climate Crisis*. London: Manilla Press.

Float (2023) *11 Strategies for Effective Stakeholder Management*. www.float.com/resources/stakeholder-management/ (accessed 08-08-23).

Freeman, R.E. (1984). *Strategic Management: A Stakeholder Approach*. Boston: Pitman.

Freeman, R.E. (2008). Ending the so-called 'Friedman-Freeman' debate. *Business Ethics Quarterly*, 18(2), pp. 153–190.

Friedman, M. (1962) *Capitalism and Freedom*. University of Chicago Press

Friedman, M. (1970) The social responsibility of business is to increase its profits. *New York Times Magazine*, 13 September 1970.

Garriga, E. & Mele, D. (2004) Corporate social responsibility theories: Mapping the territory *Journal of Business Ethics*, 53, pp. 51–71. DOI:10.1023/B:BUSI.0000039399.90587.34

Gordon, J.N. (2002) What Enron means for the management and control of the modern business corporation: Some initial reflections. *University of Chicago Law Review*, 69, pp. 1233–1250.

Guardian (2023) *Say Hello to Longlife Tech That Can Challenge Our Throwaway Culture*. www.theguardian.com/money/2023/jul/30/say-hello-to-longlife-tech-that-can-challenge-our-throwaway-culture?CMP=Share_AndroidApp_Other (accessed 18-09-23).

Haberberg, A., Gander, J., Rieple, A., Martin-Castilla, J-I. & Helm, C. (2010) Institutionalizing idealism: The adoption of CSR practices *Journal of Global Responsibility*, 1(2), pp. 366–381. DOI:10.1108/20412561011079443

Harrison, J.S., Bosse, D. & Phillips, R.A. (2017) Stakeholder theory and competitive advantage. *Academy of Management Proceedings*, 1, DOI:10.5465/ambpp.2007.26530469

Hastings, G. & Domegan, C. (2023) 'Delivering global change-How social marketing can make a difference' in *Social Marketing – Principles and Practice for Delivering Global Change* 4th Edition, G. Hastings, & C. Domegan, (Eds), Abingdon: Routledge. DOI:10.4324/9781003200086.

Heinonen, K. Strandvik, T. Mickelsson, K.J. Edvardsson, B. Sundström, E. Andersson, P. (2010) A customer-dominant logic of service. *Journal of Service Management*, 21(4), pp. 531–548.

Hess, M. (2004) Spatial' relationships? Towards a reconceptualization of embeddedness. *Progress in Human Geography*, 28(2), pp. 165–186. DOI:10.1191/0309132504ph479oa

Hockerts, K. & Wüstenhagen, R. (2010). Greening goliaths versus emerging Davids — Theorizing about the role of incumbents and new entrants in sustainable entrepreneurship. *Journal of Business Venturing*, 25(5), pp. 481–492.

ICA (2023) *The Rochdale Pioneers*. International Cooperative Alliance website. www.ica.coop/en/rochdale-pioneers (accessed 02-09-23).

Jackson, T. (2005) *Motivating Sustainable Consumption – A Review of Evidence on Consumer Behaviour and Behavioural Change*; A report to the Sustainable Development Research Network January 2005. Funded by the Economic and Social Research Council's Sustainable Technologies Programme (STP).

Jensen (2008) 'Non-rational behavior, value conflicts, stakeholder theory, and firm behavior article from academy of management 2007 symposium' in B.R. Agle, T. Donaldson, R.E. Freeman, M.C. Jensen, R.K. Mitchell, & D.J. Wood, (2008) Dialogue: Toward Superior Stakeholder Theory. *Business Ethics Quarterly*, 18(2), pp. 153–190.

Jones, B.T., Bowd, R. & Tench, R. (2009) Corporate irresponsibility and corporate social responsibility: Competing realities. *Social Responsibility Journal*, 5(3), pp. 300–310. DOI:10.1108/17471110910977249

Jones, P., Comfort. D. & Hillier, D. (2007) What's in store? Retail marketing and corporate social responsibility. *Marketing Intelligence & Planning*, 25(1), pp. 17–30.

Kennedy, A-M. (2015), Macro-social marketing. *Journal of Macromarketing*, 36(3), pp. 1–12.

Kennedy, A-M. & Parsons, A. (2012), Macro-social marketing and social engineering: A systems approach. *Journal of Social Marketing*, 2(1), pp. 37–51.

Kim, S. & Schifeling, T. (2022) Good corp, bad corp, and the rise of B corps: How market Incumbents' diverse responses reinvigorate challengers. *Administrative Science Quarterly*, 67(3), pp. 674–720. DOI:10.1177/00018392221091734

Legere, A. & Kang, J. (2020). The role of self-concept in shaping sustainable consumption: A model of slow fashion. *Journal of Cleaner Production*, 258(120699), pp. 1–12. DOI:10.1016/j.jclep ro.2020.120699

Macarthur, E. (2015) *Towards a Circular Economy: Business Rationale for an Accelerated Transition*. Published by the Ellen MacArthur Foundation. November 2015.

Margolis, J.D. & Walsh, J.P. (2003) Misery loves companies: Rethinking social initiatives by business. *Administrative Science Quarterly*, 48, pp. 268–305. DOI:10.2307/3556659

Marks, G. (2021) *Good Business Isn't Just Making Money — It's also Doing Good. There's a Way to Show It*. www.theguardian.com/business/2021/apr/14/us-small-business-certified-b-corporation?CMP=Share_AndroidApp_Other (accessed 14-04-21).

Mendes, J., Guerreiro, M. & Valle, P. (2009) Sustainable planning for community venues. Chapter 15 in *Event management and Sustainability*. R. Razaq, & J. Musgrave, (Eds), Oxon: CABI.

Mitchell, R.K., Agle, B.R. & Wood D.J. (1997) Toward a theory of stakeholder identification and salience- defining the principle of who and what really counts. *Academy of Management Review*, 22(4), pp. 853–866. DOI:10.2307/259247

Mittelstaedt, J.D., Shultz, C.J., Kilbourne, W.E. & Peterson, M. (2014) Sustainability as megatrend: Two schools of macromarketing thought. *Journal of Macromarketing*, 34(3), pp. 253–264. DOI:10.1177/0276146713520551

Monbiot, G. (2023) The Hunger Gap. Written Submission to the Environmental Audit Committee's *Inquiry on Environmental Change and Food Security*, 3 March 2023. www.monbiot.com/2023/03/09/the-hunger-gap/ (accessed 08-08-23).

Pacheco, D.F., Dean, T.J. & Payne, D.S. (2010) Escaping the green prison: Entrepreneurship and the creation of opportunities for sustainable development. *Journal of Business Venturing*, 25(5), pp. 464–480. DOI:10.1016/j.jbusvent.2009.07.006

Prothero, A. & McDonagh, P. (2015) Introduction to the special issue: Sustainability as megatrend II. *Journal of Macromarketing*, 35(1), pp. 7–10. DOI:10.1177/0276146714556818

Ranganathan, J. (1998) *Sustainability Rulers: Measuring Corporate Environmental and Social Performance*, World Resources Institute. www,wri,org/meb/sei/state,html

Richardson, N. (2015) *The Adoption of Sustainable Marketing Practices within the UK Music Festivals Sector*. PhD thesis. University of Leeds. https://etheses.whiterose.ac.uk/13578/ (accessed 06-07-23).

Richardson, N. (2020) *Sustainable Marketing Planning*. Abingdon: Routledge.

Richardson, N. (2022) How new sustainability typologies will reshape traditional approaches to loyalty. *Italian Journal of Marketing*. Special issue: S.I. Sustainable Marketing and Performance Management, DOI10.1007/s43039-022-00047-y

Richardson, N. & Cassop Thompson, M. (2023) How improved understanding of what constitutes 'value' may lead to better underpinning of Corporate Social Responsibility (CSR). *Journal of Global Responsibility*, pp. 2041–2568, DOI:10.1108/JGR-10-2022-0115

Richardson, N., James, J. & Kelley, N. (2015) *Customer-Centric Marketing- Supporting Sustainability in the Digital Age*. London: Kogan Page.

Richie, H. (2023) *The Big Idea: Why Climate Tribalism Only Helps the Deniers*. www.theguardian.com/books/2023/jul/10/the-big-idea-why-climate-tribalism-only-helps-the-deniers?CMP=Share_AndroidApp_Other (accessed 19-09-2023).

Rittel, H.W. & Webber, M.M. (1973). Dilemmas in a general theory of planning. *Policy Sciences*, 4(2), pp. 155–169.

Rosling, H. (2010) *Hans Rosling: Global Population Growth, Box by Box*. TED talks. Published 9 Jl 2010. www.youtube.com/watch?v=fTznEIZRkLg (accessed 09-07-23).

Russell, S. (2022) *If You Want to Go Far, Go Together- Beauty B Corps Join Forces to Raise the Bar*. https://bthechange.com/if-you-want-to-go-far-go-together-988b78378963 (accessed 28-08-23).

Skov, L. & Meier, J. (2011) Configuring sustainability at fashion week. Chapter 11 in *Negotiating Values in the Creative Industries-Fairs, Festivals and Competitive Events*, B. Moeran & J. Strandgaard Pedersen, (Eds), (2011), Cambridge: Cambridge University Press.

Smith, A. (1776) *The Wealth of Nations*. London: Stramen.

Smith, G.A. (1996) 'The purpose of wealth: A historical perspective' in *Valuing the Earth: Economics, Ecology, Ethics*, H.E. Daly & K.N. Townsend, (Eds), London: MIT Press, pp. 183–209.

SOS (2023) *Students Organising for Sustainability UK*. Website. www.sos-uk.org/ (accessed 26-04-23).

Stahel, W. (2016) The circular economy. *Nature*, 531, pp. 435–438. DOI:10.1038/531435a

Tadajewski, M. & Hamilton, K. (2014) Waste, art, and social change: Transformative consumer research outside of the academy? *Journal of Macromarketing*, 34(1), pp. 80–86. DOI:10.1177/0276146713509631

Tilley, F. & Young, C.W. (2009) Sustainability entrepreneurs — Could they be the true wealth generators of the future? *Greener Management International*, 55, pp. 70–92, Greenleaf Publishing. DOI:10.9774/GLEAF.3062.2006.au.00008

UN (2017) *2017 United Nations Global Compact Progress Report- Business Solutions to Sustainable Development*. https://unglobalcompact.org/library/5431 (accessed 10-08-23).

UN (2021) *Agenda 21. Chapter 36. Promoting Education, Public Awareness and Training. UN Documents Cooperation Circles. Gathering a Body of Global Agreements*. www.un-documents.net/a21-36.htm (accessed 10-06-21).

UNECE (2011) *Learning for the Future: Competences in Education for Sustainable Development*. United Nations Economic Commission for Europe, Steering Committee on Education for Sustainable Development, (ECE/CEP/AC.13/2011/6)

UNESCO (2023) *UN Decade of ESD*. Online article https://en.unesco.org/themes/education-sustainable-development/what-is-esd/un-decade-of-esd (accessed 24-04-23).

UNIPCC (2018) *An IPCC Special Report on The Impacts of Global Warming of 1.5 °C*', UN Intergovernmental Panel on Climate Change. www.ipcc.ch/sr15/ (accessed 23-04-23).

Veblen, T. (1898). *The Theory of the Leisure Class*. New York: Macmillan.

Walker, T.R., 2021. (Micro) plastics and the UN sustainable development goals. *Current Opinion in Green and Sustainable Chemistry*, 30(100497), pp. 1–9. DOI:10.1016/j.cogsc.2021.100497

Walsh J.P., Weber, K. & Margolis J.D. (2003) Social issues and management: Our lost cause found. *Journal of Management*, 29(6), pp. 859–881. DOI:10.1016/S0149-2063_03_00082-5

WCED (1987) *Our Common Future*. World Commission on Environment and Development. Oxford: Oxford University Press.

WeOwnIt (2023) *Let's Take Back Our Water*. Online article. https://weownit.org.uk/public-ownership/water (accessed 02-09-23).

Wood, D.J. (1991) Corporate social performance revisited. *The Academy of Management Review*, 16(4), pp. 691–718. DOI:10.2307/258977

Wood, D.J. (2008) Corporate Responsibility and Stakeholder Theory: Challenging the Neoclassical Paradigm. Academy of Management 2007 Symposium in B.R. Agle, T. Donaldson, R.E. Freeman, M.C. Jensen, R.K. Mitchell, & D.J. Wood, (2008) Dialogue: Toward Superior Stakeholder Theory. *Business Ethics Quarterly*, 18(2), pp. 153–190.

2 Critical Thinking and Marketing

Abstract

Marketing, as a theoretical domain, has only been meaningfully considered since the early twentieth century. Whilst it is a relatively new social science, the debates about markets, consumer behaviour and consumerism are ancient. Hence this chapter first critiques widely used definitions of marketing. Then the antecedents that led to Sustainable Marketing (SM), namely green, social and societal marketing, are considered. Furthermore, SM cannot ignore the criticisms aimed at marketing, hence critical marketing is discussed as are the nature of markets and persistent myths associated with marketing. Finally, this chapter considers the role of value (and value-types) and their influence on adopting sustainable practices.

Learning Outcomes

At the end of this chapter students will be able to

- discuss the historical influences on Sustainable Marketing (SM)
- examine widely used definitions of marketing
- assess the long-standing myths attached to marketing
- evaluate the role of the Critical Marketing school
- understand how value and its constituent parts inform the sustainability narrative.

> "You can please some of the people all of the time, you can please all of the people some of the time, but you can't please all of the people all of the time".
>
> –John Lydgate

This may be a cliché, but it has some truth in it and partially illustrates the challenges facing Sustainable Marketing (SM). For example, marketers must be able to answer the crucial question 'Why would clients buy your products or services rather than those of a competitor?' One answer is that when buying goods, consumers increasingly buy from companies who are motivated by more than Business-As-Usual (BAU). Another answer is that consumption is social and when 'buying' consumers take on the attitudes, beliefs, opinions or values of others. These are increasingly shaped by information shared digitally, often by people 'outside' the companies. Hence, those companies unaware of

DOI: 10.4324/9781003434214-3

changes in society risk alienating customers. This is the case with sustainability which, despite historically being missing from many marketing texts, is increasingly important to key stakeholders.

2.1 Marketing – A Definition

Singularly the most important stakeholders for marketers are 'customers'. The work organisations undertake (not just the marketing department) should be designed and implemented to delight customers. This should be reflected in any definition (Table 2.1).

The CIM definition is cited widely and is useful for understanding the key facets of marketing. That said there are issues. Firstly, marketing is seen as a management process. Undoubtedly, marketing can only be fully embedded into an organisation if it has 'buy-in' from senior management. However, all employees influence customers (and/or prospects), including those not involved in sales and marketing i.e. accounts, logistics or 'tech support'. However, customers do not distinguish between the differing roles if they are dissatisfied. They see the company holistically. Hence marketing is everybody's responsibility as everyone plays a part in creating the 'customer experience'.

As the CIM definition suggests, marketing is an ongoing process. It is neither linear nor a 'one-off'. As customers change, businesses must adapt appropriately. Marketers must 'anticipate' customers' future wants, needs and values; organisations must focus on the future. It can take years to develop new products (or services), hence marketers must be aware of changing customer perceptions.

The AMA definition complements the CIM equivalent by introducing value and the role of society. The BAU view is that customers buy products and services from organisations in exchange for money. This simple exchange view is somewhat outdated. In reality, organisations cannot 'give' customers value (a mistake repeated in many marketing texts). Some argue that the exchange brings the organisation and the customer together where a co-creation of value takes place. Others argue that customers provide money so they can seek value from companies (see Richardson & Cassop Thompson, 2019). Marketers must focus on creating circumstances where customers can seek, co-create or simply take value. Awareness of co-creation and value-seeking reduces the risk for organisations as they promote a customer-centric approach. Since value-seeking and taking involve bringing (at least) two parties together, relationships form; marketers must capitalise upon that initial relationship by finding out as much as they can about the customer and their needs.

Table 2.1 Marketing definitions

Marketing Body	*Definition*
Chartered Institute of Marketing (CIM)	'… the management process responsible for identifying, anticipating and satisfying customer requirements profitably'.
American Marketing Association (AMA)	'the activity, set of institutions, and processes for creating, communicating, delivering, and exchanging offerings that have value for customers, clients, partners, and society at large'.

Sources: Adapted from CIM (2023); AMA (2023).

The Role and Nature of Markets

Marx famously said that the only constant is change. Customer needs constantly change and technology is enabling quicker, easier decision-making. Consider the impact on the markets of cost-comparison websites (i.e. Gocompare.com and moneysupermarket.com) which not only compete with each other but also with organisations who 'represent' the customer such as Which? For many organisations, the marketplace is a difficult, dynamic and highly competitive arena. When the market or environment changes, marketers must adapt, otherwise they risk being left behind. Those that do not adapt may incur customer dissatisfaction and suffer attrition, i.e. lose their customers to the competition. If the customer has a positive experience, they are more likely to tell their family and friends (see Word of Mouth in Chapter 4); if they have a bad experience, the likelihood is they will tell even more people.

Example: The needs of the core customers of retail giant Toys "R" Us were changing and new competition entered the High Street. Changes occurred in the wider external environment, for example young children were increasingly being given smartphones and tablets as presents. These were available extensively online and from a much wider range of suppliers. Business rates had increased, while the UK Government introduced new taxes such as the Apprenticeship Levy. Toys "R" Us, like many retailers, were paying high rent values to landlords. Furthermore, their cash flow was inherently seasonal. Consequently, they were vulnerable, despite a sustained period of success.

Individuals can become complacent when not challenged. Is it surprising that organisations run by humans can react similarly? Companies who survived similar market-changing scenarios to Toys "R" Us went through a process of recovery, making changes, including to their management culture. They increasingly focused on identifying, anticipating and delighting customers. Many addressed social issues relating to supply chains and later adopted sustainable policies. That said, most organisations have limited financial, staff or equipment resources. Therefore, they must seek to satisfy their customers efficiently (with as little waste as possible) and profitably. However, now more than ever, business activities should be undertaken in an environmentally friendly and socially responsible manner.

There are many ways to create, grow or maintain market share, depending on the type of market, resources available (both hard and soft), leadership skills, entrepreneurialism and serendipity (sheer luck). Economists suggest three types of markets exist (Table 2.2).

Forecasting and projecting sales (amongst other things) is challenging particularly when entering nascent, new or turbulent markets. Many organisations are overzealous with their future plans offering 'wish lists' rather than something based on sound research. Targets must be achievable. This is particularly problematic if investment is secured against planned targets. Incipient markets pose problems for companies who want to provide solutions based on customer dialogue. Customer dialogue is usually needed for successful launches. Two exceptions (where the drivers were internal rather than external from the market) are the Sony Walkman in the late 1970s and the iPhone

Table 2.2 The role and nature of markets

Market type	*Traditional role*	*Customer-centric implications*
Existing markets	Customers are satisfied with existing products or services. Competition is largely based on price and promotional spend. Innovation/additional benefits seem to be absent	Customers or consumers benefit from progressively lower prices for given categories of products or services. This in turn requires companies to pay close attention to costs and marketing 'spend' to maintain profitability suggesting a cost leadership approach often found in production orientation.
Latent markets	Needs are defined but not yet met, e.g. much-improved battery technology to support the introduction of genuinely non-polluting vehicles or cures for Alzheimer's disease or Type 2 diabetes	Investment needed in technology, new diagnostic tools and therapies. These require the application of 'high tech' which lends itself to production and product orientations.
Incipient markets	Customers do not yet recognise their need or problems that need solving however the appearance of a new solution triggers their recognition	Research with customers will not show support for genuinely innovative products and services

Source: Adapted from Richardson *et al* (2015, pp 28–29).

in 2007. Both were radical examples of technological competence being matched with a vision and understanding of the application of that specific technology.

Some markets have many similar products with little differentiation. Markets can be niche or alternatively widely spread amongst many small competitors. Niche markets can offer real potential for growth and developing new brands. Blue Ray DVD recording units were high value specialty purchases whereas DVD players were low cost almost routine purchases sought largely by laggards (and subsequently dropped by retailers as consumers increasingly used streaming services). Markets can be growing, static or declining. They can be monopolistic, duopolistic, oligopolistic or competitive. A company can be a market leader, challenger or follower. Young markets may be subject to rapid growth that will plateau at an (as yet) unknown level.

Fragmentation of markets is a challenge for marketers. There may be hundreds of, say, domestic appliances, however a retailer may only want to stock the 20 best sellers. As electrical appliances are now rated according to their power consumption, consumers are increasingly aware that their electricity bills can be reduced substantially over the lifetime of the product. Hence, retailers will increasingly stock A-rated appliances. Some market shifts are driven by technology, e.g. retailers made a conscious decision to stop stocking old-fashioned CRT televisions and adopted flat screen variants. These are easier to transport, to display and, as a by-product, use less electricity.

Developing a more sustainable economy will require costs associated with sustainability being factored into markets and their prices. This can happen through voluntary action, or additional taxation (such as a carbon tax on fossil fuels). Pricing can be used to 'demarket' harmful products such as cigarettes or scarce or finite products like fossil fuels. Developing more sustainable markets may require switching emphasis away from the purchase price of products towards the lifetime cost of ownership and usage, thus encouraging the design, purchase and consumption of products with greater energy efficiency and/or longevity (*ibid*).

Globalisation is a key influence on markets. The E7 countries (Brazil, Russia, India, China, Mexico, Indonesia and Turkey) are forecast to grow at a faster rate than the G7, who they will eventually outgrow by 2030. In 2023, India became the world's fifth-largest economy. The E7 will rely on each other more than other nations. In 2023, Russia continued to be a major supplier of oil and gas to India and China despite the Ukraine conflict. Markets will continue to open in the E7, which brings opportunities for Western companies. Companies may want to avoid becoming over-reliant on the growing E7 economies as this can lead to complacency.

Example: In 2018 Jaguar Land Rover (JLR) announced 4,500 redundancies among their UK workforce. Brexit had some role as it had lowered the value of sterling, diesel engines had suffered reputational damage from the VW emission cheat debacle and some local authorities were actively considering introducing pollution charges in cities akin to the Congestion Charge in London. But above everything else, the Chinese economy slowed down and their burgeoning middle-classes bought JLR products in smaller numbers. By 2023 the Chinese economy had regained momentum and JLR figures improved correspondingly with an order book of 200,000 units reflecting strong client demand, particularly for Range Rover, Range Rover Sport and the Defender. These premium products represent 76% of the JLR order book.

It is possible that the Country of Origin (CoO) effect may have influenced the initial downfall, as Chinese consumers may have preferred to buy products made locally. The competitive landscape is dynamic and presents challenges. Companies have to balance cutting losses (in market share or profitability) against staying in the market long enough to ride out recessional difficulties.

Chinese investors have acquired hundreds of European companies over the last decade. Many of these were German or British companies including those in the automotive sector, e.g. Rover (UK); MG (UK); and Volvo (Sweden). This saw cars previously manufactured in Europe now being made in China.

Example: To-date, Chinese manufacturers have played a minor role apropos automotive European market share. However, their brands, i.e. MG, made significant progress in 2022. Among all car groups, they gained the most market share, with registrations jumping from 66,100 units in 2021 to 152,400 units in 2022. Combined, Chinese brands outsold established manufacturers including Mazda and Suzuki. Many of the sales corresponded to vehicles designed and manufactured by Chinese-owned brand MG, whose volume increased by 116% to almost 114,000 units, outselling Jeep and Honda. DR Automobiles, an Italian company that sells rebadged vehicles manufactured by Chinese brand Chery in Spain and Italy, outsold Smart and Subaru with an increase in registrations of 197% to almost 25,000 units. MG and DR vehicles accounted for 91% of the volume registered by all Chinese brands.

(Motortrader, 2023)

Clearly the forces stimulating the development and growth of E7 markets has seen indigenous companies reciprocate, i.e. seek to become established in developed countries. The nature, or orientation, of the companies will largely shape their approach to selling domestically and internationally. A sector where China will take an even bigger market share globally, is Zero-Emission Vehicles (ZEVs). The G7 countries (with the exception of Japan) have been tardy in developing ZEV products, particularly as California Air Resources Board (CARB) first adopted the ZEV requirement in 1990 as part of the Low-Emission Vehicle regulation (LEV).

Example: Six decades before Teslas began populating the automotive landscape, Nissan was pioneering early electric vehicle technology. Facing scarce oil reserves in post-war Japan, Nissan developed the Tama in 1947, a small battery-powered urban taxi. Years later, the Hypermini (2000) and Pivo (2005) offered whimsical takes on electrified urban mobility. But Nissan's ground-breaking move came in 2010 when it launched the Nissan Leaf, the first 'mass-produced' electric vehicle in history.

(Motortrend, 2023)

2.2 Sustainable Marketing (SM) and Its Predecesors

Marketing is a social science. Hence, matters are rarely 'clear cut'. Answers to questions are often conditional and shaped by the context. In some ways, context is everything as answers taken out of context may be damaging. Hence to improve conceptualisation (i.e. better understanding) of SM it is sensible to reflect on its antecedents, namely 'Social', 'Societal' and 'Green' marketing.

Social Marketing

Kotler and Levy proposed the extension of marketing technologies into non-business arenas. In their seminal article (Kotler & Levy, 1969) they advocated Social Marketing as an approach for social ideas and causes, which can be applied to places (cities, regions, nations) or people. Kotler later defined it as

> "the design, implementation, and control of programs seeking to increase the acceptability of a social idea, cause or practice among a target group"
>
> (Kotler & Armstrong, 2006, p 239)

This suggests a range of approaches and different solutions to differing problems, which is not ideal from a sustainability perspective where global solutions are needed. Furthermore, it can be inferred (from the definition) that what matters is the supply-side selling of products and services through programmes. Social Marketing is often used to influence consumer behavioural change however many people do not have the information or the processing capability in certain situations to make logical choices (Kennedy, 2015). When auxiliary products (e.g. educational programs) support change, then people must be told how to obtain them and what actions constitute a purchase (*ibid*, p 5). Hence Kotler's 'inward-out' orientation may contribute to cognitive dissonance lacking, as it does, specifics with respect to social responsibility, ethics, community or environmental sustainability.

A further definitional challenge is that Social Marketing can be undertaken by commercial, non-profit, and government organisations (Kotler & Lee, 2005) not all of whom will necessarily be *au fait* with 'commercial marketing'. The International Social Marketing Association (ISMA) develop this by suggesting it

> "seeks to develop and integrate marketing concepts with other approaches to influence behaviours that benefit individuals and communities for the greater social good. Social Marketing practice is guided by ethical principles. It seeks to integrate research, best practice, theory, audience and partnership insight, to inform the delivery of competition sensitive and segmented social change programmes that are effective, efficient, equitable and sustainable".

This refinement provides a better balance between the supply and demand side. It supports the notion that actors in a marketing system can be individuals, groups, businesses, or networks (Kennedy, 2015) and offers clear overlap with sustainable consumption (see Jackson, 2005). Dibb *et al* (2006) discussed 'social responsibility and marketing ethics' which chimes with the ethical element of the ISMA definition. Ultimately marketers cannot force customers (and other stakeholders) to be happy, satisfied or green. All they can hope to achieve is to create the circumstances where value-seeking customers and influencers can 'take value' from the company (Vargo & Lusch, 2004).

Furthermore, national governments are increasingly 'washing their hands' and devolving social causes to the private and 'third' sectors (see Section 8.5). Third sector enterprises practice Social Marketing (see Chapter 2), which is "inherently political, especially when undertaken by public sector organizations" (Kennedy, 2015, p 5). Belz and Peattie (2009) insist many social problems remain stubbornly intractable. Local governments, along with communities, institutions, and individuals may need to be part of long-term plans to create such society-wide change (Kennedy & Parsons, 2014). Questions should be raised about whose values are being implemented and hope that in democratically elected and governed societies, democratic values are the ones implemented (*ibid*). However, it is difficult to challenge this logic in times of reduced 'purse' as national and local governments may not share the same values. Kennedy (2015) alludes to the use of Social Marketing by those who shape the social context, seeking societal rather than individual-level change. The implementation of such policies will be more effective if both societal and individual level change is sought. Social Marketing has traditionally focused on socio-cultural change when more emphasis is needed on sustainable value creation. Whilst Social Marketing was a key stepping stone, it has not addressed growing ecological concerns in the way sustainability does.

Societal Marketing

In 1972 Kotler introduced the 'Societal Marketing' concept, later defined as:

> "a principle of enlightened marketing that holds that a company should make good marketing decisions by considering consumers' wants, the company's requirements, consumers' long run interests and society's long run interests".
>
> (Kotler & Armstrong, 2006, p 642)

Societal Marketing questions the implicit assumptions of marketing and more broadly the Dominant Social Paradigm (Belz & Peattie, 2009). It extends Kotler's previous model to include society and consumer dimensions, however, it lacks specifics regarding ethics or environmental sustainability. The term 'enlightened' is vague. That said, Societal Marketing proposed a broader relationship between consumers, businesses and society as a whole, promoting long-term consumer and/or public welfare without sacrificing the standard organisational goal of profitability (Emery, 2012). It introduces the notion that long-term relationships and 'society's long-run interests' are broad enough to imply the inclusion of ecological concerns. Kotler and Lee (2005) addressed some of the issues with Societal Marketing when they sub-divided CSR into six distinct social initiatives: cause promotions, cause-related marketing, corporate social marketing, corporate philanthropy, community volunteering and socially responsible business practices. From a TBL perspective, the absence of 'Planet'-related measures is problematic.

Sadly, despite decades of academic debate on the efficacy of Societal Marketing, many problems remain stubbornly intractable (Belz & Peattie, 2009). Indeed, Societal Marketing does not take into account the multiple intricacies of the sustainable business environment (Emery, 2012). Brassington and Pettitt (2007) however link 'Societal' Marketing with ethical marketing as elements of CSR (see Section 1.2) which (they say) should inexorably lead to 'Sustainable' Marketing.

Green Marketing

Green Marketing came to prominence in the 1970s. The AMA hosted a 1975 workshop entitled "Ecological Marketing" which led to a similarly titled book (Henion & Kinnear, 1976). Nearly two decades later, seminal texts were written by Martin Charter (see Charter, 1992) and Ken Peattie (see Peattie, 1992) in the UK and Jacquelyn Ottman (see Ottman, 1993) in the USA. These authors have co-authored many key texts subsequently (e.g. Belz & Peattie, 2009) and undoubtedly laid down many fundamentals that influenced later commentators (see Jackson, 2005).

Green marketing, is defined as a holistic and responsible management process that identifies, anticipates, satisfies and fulfils stakeholder requirements, for a reasonable reward, that does not adversely affect human or natural environmental well-being (Charter, 1992). Peattie and Charter (1999, p 593) refined this by defining it as also being responsible for

> "identifying, anticipating and satisfying the needs of customers and society, in a profitable and sustainable way".

In the absence of adequate regulation, free markets can run out of control. Consumerism has been described as the 'shame of marketing' for the simple reason that if sellers were marketing oriented (see Section 6.2), the interests of buyers would be given equal attention (to those of sellers), thus avoiding conflicts of interest that bring many marketing practices into disrepute (Baker, 2009). Consider the matter of UK waste in 2020–21 as follows:

- The Waste from Households (WfH) recycling rate fell across the UK in 2021 except in Northern Ireland. The rates were England (44.1%), Northern Ireland (48.4%), Scotland (41.7%) and Wales (56.7%).
- biodegradable municipal waste (BMW) sent to landfill increased to 6.8 million tonnes in 2021 from 6.1 million tonnes in 2020.
- 63.2% of packaging waste in 2021 was recycled, similar to 2020 (63.1%).
- England generated circa 34 million tonnes of commercial and industrial (C&I) waste in 2020 and 2021respectively, 84% of the UK total.
- 222.2 million tonnes of total waste were generated in 2018, with England responsible for 84% (187.3 million tonnes) of the total.

(Adapted from UKGOV, 2023)

Clearly there is much room for improvement. Consumers alone cannot be responsible for the total amount of waste recycled. Responsibility also falls on manufacturers, government (local and national) and recycling organisations. Most of the plastic food containers that householders clean after use and put in the recycling bin cannot be recycled by local government authorities due to the use of (often poor quality) polymers.

> "Well over half of the household plastic packaging the government claims is recycled is sent abroad, most of it going to countries with very low recycling rates and a serious problem with plastic waste being dumped or burned illegally".
>
> (Greenpeace, 2021)

53% (593,000 tonnes) of the UK plastic packaging, declared as recycled, was processed in the UK, with 47% (519,000 tonnes) exported. Hence the packaging's CO_2 footprint is increased, amid concerns about the working conditions of those tasked with recycling, with child labour working in poor conditions being common. Turkey remained the main destination for UK exports in 2021, though less was sent than in 2020 (Recoup, 2022).

Example: Microwave meals are often supplied in black plastic, as it is deemed aesthetically appealing, conveying a sense of 'luxury' and suggesting a premium product. However, materials can only be recycled once they have been sorted. Some manual sorting takes place, however as recycling volumes increases, optical scanners are increasingly used. However, black cannot be easily scanned by recycling machines; changing the colour would significantly increase the recycling rate. Margarine and ice cream tubs often contain the polymer polypropylene, which is difficult to recycle. An alternative approach would be to make them from the same plastic as water bottles, which is easily recycled. Yoghurt pots are often made from a mixture of polypropylene and polystyrene. An alternative is to use polyethylene terephthalate, which is also used in plastic bottles and can be easily recycled (*ibid*).

Recoup (2022) expressed concern that auditing material market flows remains challenging. They suggest that precise information and transparency about the end destinations of exported materials should be high on the UK's agenda, as it shapes future strategy (*ibid*). The UK introduced its plastic packaging tax (PPT) in April 2022, which sought to encourage using recycled plastic instead of new plastic packaging. It applies to plastic packaging manufactured in (or imported into) the UK incorporating less than 30% recycled plastic (CIPS, 2023). The tax was charged at £200 per tonne, rising to £211 by 2023. Around 20,000 packaging producers and importers, manufacturing or importing 10 or more tonnes annually, must register for the tax. Small operators, importing or manufacturing less than 10 tonnes of plastic packaging annually are exempt. Only 3,426 businesses paid the tax between its inception (April 2022) and February 2023, i.e. 17% of the eligible firms. More than 254m tonnes of plastic packaging were declared by companies, with nearly two-thirds (61%) being registered as tax-exempt. HMRC collected £195m between April 2022 and January 2023, i.e. just under the initial estimate (£200m) for the entire year. However, the revenue is not ringfenced and spent on improving the UK's recycling infrastructure or expanding the country's capacity to recycle plastic. Instead, the money goes to the Treasury, representing a missed opportunity to increase investment in UK recycling (*ibid*).

The annual cost of dealing with UK household packaging is circa £1billion. In 2023, UK GDP was estimated at £2.52 trillion (over 3% of global GDP from 0.008% of the global population). So, £1 billion is a minuscule amount (i.e. 0.0004% of UK GDP). However, as always, someone will have to pick up the cost. Often it is the consumer as BAU companies seek to maintain profits and shareholder dividends. A better alternative may be to incentivise marketers to adopt easily recyclable materials and designs. This carrot and stick argument has been around as long as companies have existed.

Green Marketing, whilst influential, has struggled to gain a foothold amongst academics and practitioners. In 1997, *Harvard Business Review* published 'Beyond Greening' which brought the need for broadening the narrative to include sustainability to the wider business community. The public expects companies to be problem solvers. However, inertia, lack of clarity or fear of change are often cited as reasons for businesses to be conservative or risk averse. Companies need clear definitions and Sustainable Marketing (SM) tools or frameworks.

Sustainable Marketing (SM)

Theodore Levitt coined the term 'Marketing Myopia' in 1960 for organisations that 'short-sightedly' prioritised short-term goals over long-term growth and business needs over customer needs. Companies with Marketing Myopia often lack transparency and consultation, potentially suffering customer attrition and business failure. To be more successful, organisations must be externally focused, not just internally focused upon production techniques, products and processes. However, the current business environment is so turbulent, all marketers are, to a degree, blind to the future. Belz and Peattie (2009) developed Levitt's notion when they introduced the term 'Sustainability Marketing Myopia' which can lead to an exaggerated focus on the socio-ecological attributes of the product over the core consumer values, a distortion of the marketing process which may lead to the product failing or remaining confined in a small alternative niche (*ibid*).

Van Dam and Apledoorn (1996) coined the phrase 'Sustainable Marketing' (SM) in 1996 when discussing the inadequacy of green and/or ecological marketing. SM is the process of creating, communicating and delivering value to customers in such a way that both natural and human capital are preserved or enhanced throughout (Martin & Schouten, 2013). Richardson (2020, p 19) offered a refined definition, suggesting SM

> "is principled and predicated on the foci of the Triple Bottom Line. SM decisions should be ethically and ecologically sound and companies should divert profits into People and Planet foci to enable implementation. Sustainable business practices must be informed by continuous dialogues with all stakeholders. Ultimately this is the only way to resolve the tensions between customer (and stakeholder) demands, long-term interests, companies' requirements, society's long run interests and the need for environmental balance".

This definition should act as a springboard for companies. SM needs to be 'sold' on the basis of future gains using communications platforms for external stakeholders and internal marketing (IM) techniques (see Chapter 6) to overcome resistance to change. It should inform mission/vision/purpose statements, marketing objectives, strategies and tactics. SM may need adapted frameworks and tools. Certainly, marketers will have to adapt the information used to make decisions **and** the criteria used to measure performance, hence, sustainability audits may be required.

SM involves cascading information regarding best sustainable practices to producers, stakeholders and consumers alike. It advocates environmental stewardship, based on minimising the depletion of non-renewable resources while promoting environmental regeneration. SM is inherently long-term and an evolution of being market oriented (see Section 6.2). Marketers will have to sacrifice short-term profit by incorporating environmental and social costs into pricing decisions.

Some use the term 'sustainability' or 'sustainability-driven' marketing to reflect the values of marketers who associate with the process of sustainability as opposed to the process of sustaining anything (Tilley & Young, 2009). These terms have some merit, however, as the notion of driving values is problematic as, ultimately, marketers cannot force customers to (say) be happy, satisfied or green. All marketers can hope to achieve is to create circumstances where value-seeking customers can 'take value'. Even those who use Sustainability Marketing have also used Sustainable Marketing; indeed Kemper and Ballantine (2019, p 6) suggest

> "Several scholars see the merging of relationship, social, green and ethical marketing combining to create a new concept of 'Sustainable Marketing'".

From a semantic point of view, no-one is using the term Sustainability Development; the universally accepted term is Sustainable Development (see Chapter 1). So why use Sustainability Marketing, if a more widely used term (Richardson, 2022) with a better fit is available? Furthermore, Sustainability Marketing may be construed as the marketing of sustainability. The challenge this presents is that sustainability may not be prioritised and deemed yet another thing to address (*ibid*). Sustainable Marketing (SM) is all-encompassing, holistic and should be embedded into the orientation of the organisation. The term Sustainable Marketing is more coherent and now, more than ever, it encourages marketers to align their values with the increasingly ethical and/or green behaviour of consumers.

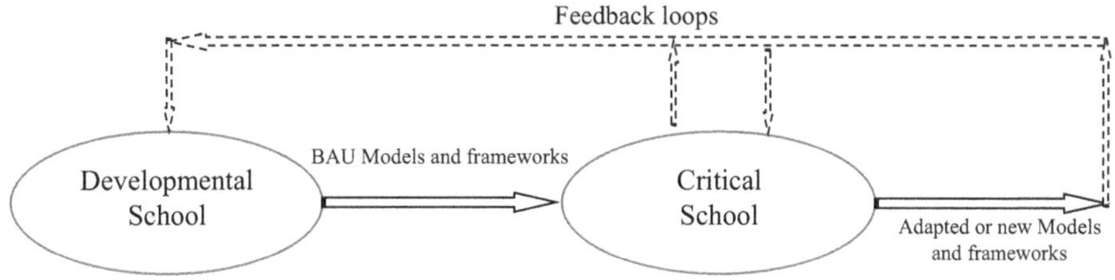

Figure 2.1 Schools of thought.

Source: Adapted from Mittelstaedt *et al* (2014).

2.3 Critical Marketing

Mittelstaedt *et al* (2014) identified two different schools of Marketing thought (Figure 2.1); the Developmental School sees markets and marketing systems as part of the solution to the problems of the human condition; the Critical School sees markets and marketing as part of the problem. What they 'have to say about sustainability rests on the acceptance or rejection of the context in which questions of sustainability have emerged' (*ibid*, p 253).

Critical Scholars are more suspicious of the social consequences of markets or marketing and have long played a key role in challenging BAU. Critical Marketers (Brownlie & Saren, 1992; Brown, 1995; Tadajewski & Brownlie, 2008 amongst others) provide useful reminders of why models (and frameworks) need adapting (or new versions adopted). Developmental Scholars (see McDonald, 2016) provide continuity and may be resistant to change. They often criticise Critical Scholars for not providing useful terms and tools. Indeed, van Dam & Apledoorn (1996), aligned with the Critical School (see their paper in Tadajewski & Brownlie, 2008), did not offer a clear definition, nor tools or frameworks to help practitioners. Many years later, Critical Marketers Gosnay and Richardson (2008) offered a TBL-based Sustainable Marketing Benchmarking Framework. This was subsequently updated (see Richardson, 2015, 2018, 2020). This book is positioned in the Critical School as it results from the Developmental School's failure to offer TBL-based alternative models and frameworks.

The duality of the 'Schools' (Mittelstaedt *et al*, 2014) can be found throughout marketing domains (Figure 2.1). Apropos loyalty, Critical Marketers identify 'unsustainable' aspects which (they argue) need to be discussed more frequently in academia. Many large service providers have customers who are not totally satisfied with their services. Often the consumer feels 'locked-in' (Jackson, 2005; Murray & Haubl, 2007; Harrison *et al*, 2012) or a possibly unhealthy sense of compulsion (Guido *et al*, 2020). The effort needed to switch suppliers tends to make customers stay with the existing provider. This is 'unsustainable' and results from inertia, risk aversion, apathy and 'working life conditions, which favour a work-and-spend lifestyle, the conditions of urban living or the effects of pervasive marketing' (Sanne, 2002, p 286).

An argument is whether profit should be exclusively used to improve Return on Investment (RoI), Return on Marketing Investment (RoMI) or alternatively invested into a Return on Objectives (RoO) designed to satisfy stakeholders other than shareholders.

RoI is the performance measure used to evaluate the economic efficiency of an investment whereas RoO gauges an investment's efficiency in achieving other corporate and/or functional objectives. Marketers are put under pressure to be global and local, centralised and decentralised, large and small, planned yet flexible, and to serve differing markets, with standardised and customised products, at premium and penetration prices, through restricted and extensive distribution networks and supported by national, yet targeted, promotional campaigns (Brown, 1995). With so many high-profile cases in recent years marketers should not be shocked to hear that there is much cynicism towards marketing.

Myths Perpetuated by (or About) Marketers

Marketing practitioners, unlike some business 'functions' (e.g. HR, Accounts, Production etc.), must challenge the orthodoxy. No marketer will be appointed if their pitch involves doing the same as the previous incumbent. Being a continuity candidate will not land the job. No marketing agency will win deals if they are offering the same as their predecessor. Marketers must be agents of change. However, in seeking such change they are often accused of

- Creating false wants and fostering materialism
- Producing too few social goods
- Creating cultural pollution and bombarding people with adverts
- Having too much political power
- Driving prices higher by adding to the cost of the product or service
- Deceiving consumers about pricing, promotion and packaging
- Lacking a customer focus concentrating on closing the deal
- Selling products that lack quality
- Designing goods with built-in obsolescence to accelerate replacement.

This list is not exhaustive and clearly marketers must reflect on why other stakeholders hold such views. These views have accumulated over a considerable period of time. As consumers become more discerning, marketers need to recognise and react to scepticism. Worryingly, some of the more cynical perceptions are often held by fellow professionals who should really know better. Partially, this may be due to the often-cited Marketing Myths, such as:

1 Marketing is just advertising

Marketing is not merely advertising and promotional work. People perceive it as such because promotional work (i.e. advertising, PR or sales promotions) is often a highly visible part of a marketing campaign. Increasingly other 'comms' tools and vehicles are being used progressively to engage in meaningful dialogue with consumers and stakeholders.

2 A satisfied customer is a loyal customer

Satisfied, loyal customers are more likely to provide good Word of Mouth (WoM), improved reputation and customer acquisition (i.e. more new customers). Managers often confuse satisfaction with loyalty (see Chapter 7). In some cases, loyalty is simply down to customer apathy as the perceived benefits of changing supplier does not outweigh the 'hassle' of moving. This is often the case with retail banking and utilities such as gas suppliers who arguably have an over-reliance on systems. This poses the question:

> "Has being good at systems e.g. Customer Relationship Management (CRM) replaced identifying customers thoughts, feelings and concerns?"

3 A strong brand is invincible

Strong brands are far from invincible. Microsoft is undoubtedly one of the world's strongest brands and yet it is under attack from all sides. On one front it is the advance of open-source software (e.g. Linux, Mozilla, Google's Chrome) and shareware. Another threat comes from technological changes such as cloud computing or the challenges presented by 5G mobiles. They recognise such threats and have the financial strength to diversify. The Xbox range cost billions of dollars to develop, however Microsoft saw it as a future hub for home communications. In 2014 they acquired Nokia's mobile phone division for around $8billion. Within a matter of months, they announced 18,000 jobs were to be cut many of which were in Scandinavia, much to the concern of those who built the Nokia brand.

4 A big-name brand can sustain a higher price

Critical marketers are often scathing about the most widely used tools i.e. the marketing mix (see Brownlie & Saren, 1992). Pricing is a contentious issue and presents many challenges for marketers (see Section 4.4). Dell has high levels of brand awareness and recognition; however, they offer a value-for-money (vfm) proposition. McDonalds is one of the world's most easily recognisable brands and yet their prices are by no means excessive. Ultimately, what matters is whether the customer sees value in the goods or services. Remember it is not about being the cheapest, as many iPhone owners think their phone is the best vfm available.

5 The customer is always right!

The customer is not always right but they are always the customer and are undoubtedly the most important 'stakeholders' for companies. Organisations must place them at the heart of all the decision making and planning (not just the marketing) decisions (see Chapter 6). Customer insights and engagement (which can only be achieved by entering into regular, honest dialogue) must drive business decisions. Every time marketers receive customer feedback, their organisation grows stronger.

Example: Microsoft launched Office versions for the iPad in 2014, four years after Apple effectively created a new tablet market. This was clearly a result of muddled thinking on Microsoft's part. It lacked customer-centricity. As soon as the iPad was launched, Microsoft should have launched Office. That said, Apple themselves have been equally obstinate (to the detriment of customers) as to this day older iPads cannot have their iOS updated beyond certain levels even if the item is fully functional. This prevents access to key sites such as LinkedIn. So, customers who bought an iPad would have a different level of support to those who bought a

MacBook on the same day for a similar price. This form of built-in obsolescence may explain why Apple lost their first-mover advantage in tablets.

6 Members of distribution channels do not influence marketing

Distribution channels are often key to organisational success. At best poor distribution can irritate customers. At worst, it can lead to organisational failure. Technology has made it easier for companies to distribute their goods and services. This is what Chris Andersen calls the 'long tail' where everything is available online somewhere. Marketers must not confuse being online with being popular or profitable. Thousands of apps on the Apple store have never been downloaded even though the 'distributor' is highly visible with brand recognition of the highest level.

7 Advertising always affects sales

It must be recognised that some advertising campaigns are poor. Good advertising has a long-term effect though most seek a short-term sales boost. Mobile advertising is gaining ground as it has the unique ability to be seen by the user. This and other technological changes are causing havoc in the advertising industry. Customers have evolved into multi-taskers who access differing social media sites using a range of platforms (online, mobile, tablet and/or TV) which creates challenges for those wishing to target them with marketing communications (see Section 4.1).

8 Marketing is only used by large organisations

Small companies are different in nature to larger ones (see Section 8.4). Despite this, traditional approaches to marketing are largely derived from experiences in larger companies. Organisational size and shape influence the ability to communicate with differing stakeholders. A 'market' orientation (see Table 6.1) is important for SMEs who do not have the low-cost base or substantial financial resources of large companies. However, SMEs can be flexible, adapting quickly to changing customer needs (making them feel valued) and market dynamics.

9 Business causes the problems rather than solving them

Some argue that business is part of the problem not the solution apropos sustainability which should be the concern of politicians and governments. This approach is incoherent as trade largely takes place between companies not governments. In 2022 the value of world merchandise trade rose 12% to US$ 25.3 trillion, while commercial services trade increased 15% to US$ 6.8 trillion (WTO, 2023). Hence 'Business' has enormous potential to promote sustainable trade patterns. 'Business', rather than government, has the knowledge and skills to trade sustainably as well as helping to shape global sustainability guidelines and practices. If the Co-operative can thrive for 160 years, so can other businesses.

2.4 Value(s)

Value is what is sought by customers and other stakeholders. Value-types combine to create the sought value (see Richardson & Cassop Thompson, 2019, 2023). If sustainability is the sought value, altruism may be a value type. Altruism may derive from an individual's life-orientation possibly relating to a particular life-cycle stage and personal or social circumstances (Spedale & Watson, 2014). This can unfold over a lifetime being shaped by personal history, present circumstances and a host of broad and/or specific cultural and discursive factors (*ibid*). Sustainability is a value-laden concept. Furthermore, globally politicians, elements of the media and those with vested interests are perpetually cynical about climate change and the need for social justice. It has been insightful watching many environmental pressure groups use recognisable guerrilla marketing tactics. Extinction Rebellion has a distinct logo and uses social media efficiently and effectively. Marketing is, however, a part of society, it is not apart from society. Hence it has a role to play in the journey towards living sustainably. The notion of equifinality applies i.e. there are many routes to a destination.

Whilst the notion of the sustainable consumer is relatively recent, the debates about consumption, value, consumer behaviour and consumerism are ancient (Table 3.1).

The list of commentators interested in Table 2.3 is not exhaustive. Christopher Falzon, for example, elaborated on value. Adam Smith recognised the idea of voluntary

Table 2.3 A chronology of different approaches to consumption and consumer value

Author	*Date*	*Topic*
Aristotle	353 BC	Pleonexia (the 'insatiable desire for more')
Nicolas Barbon	1690	Value in use
Adam Smith	1776	Value in exchange; value in use
Thomas Malthus	1798–1803	The Principle of Population: affects future improvement of society
David Ricardo	1821	Labour value theory
Karl Marx	1867	Value in exchange; value in use
Thorsten Veblen	1889	Conspicuous consumption
Pierre Bordieu	1979	Analysis of social distinction
Abraham Maslow	1943–1971	Humanistic psychology
J.K. Galbraith	1958	Socio-political critique of the affluent society
Jean Baudrillard	1968–72	Semiotic analysis
Mary Douglas	1970	Symbolic interpretive anthropology – how cultural symbols are used to improve understanding of particular societies
Edward O. Wilson	1975	Establishing sociobiology as a new scientific field
Fred Hirsch	1977	Positional goods – valued by how they are distributed among the population
Duane Elgin	1976–81	Voluntary simplicity – reducing, depending less on technology and spending less money
Richard Dawkins	1982	Evolutionary biology: the effects of genes stretch into the environment
Juliet Schor	1992	Downshifting and upscaling
Thomas Princen	2005	Sufficiency-moderating energy needs and materialism

Sources: Adapted from Jackson, 2005; Richardson and Cassop Thompson (2023).

exchanges, i.e. transactions between producers and consumers where both parties gained a benefit (Smith, 1776). Smith suggested abandoning the assumption of the zero-sum game (i.e. that there was a fixed amount of wealth) and talked about wealth creation, especially through labour and voluntary exchange.

Organisation and Management Theory scholars have long been criticised for paying too little attention to the relationships between firms and society. They have focused excessively on internal organisational processes and the adaptation of firms to their proximate environment, neglecting analysis of the firm's effects on society (Walsh et al, 2003). Many marketing texts draw from the experiences of large American companies, who were often behind the curve on key areas such as value, sustainability and customer-centricity. The company's relationship to 'the problem' also influences how it ought to respond to a societal ill. Three perspectives are:

- a problem created (or exacerbated) by the firm, imposes a stronger duty to act than one not of their making;
- the relevance of the firm's capabilities and resources to the societal ill, shape the strength of necessity to respond; and
- the response required varies with a company's proximity to the community in which the need arises (*ibid*)

G E Moore (as cited in Freeman, 2010, p 164) posed the 'open question argument'. Namely for any decision that a manager or organisational stakeholder makes, can the following questions be answered? If this decision is made ...

1 For whom is value is created and destroyed, who is harmed and/or benefits?
2 Whose rights were enabled or not?
3 What kind of person will I be if I make this decision this particular way?

Some businesses can and do fail through not answering these questions, which clearly link value with sustainability. Value types that may be addressed include the monetary outlay to buy a related product, but also include time, energy and social/psychological costs of obtaining or not obtaining a product or undertaking behaviour (Kennedy, 2015).

Value (whether sustainable or other) cannot be 'given' to consumers. Consumers can co-create or take value, but companies cannot simply give it. It is generally accepted that the larger the organisation, the more difficult it is to change direction. The size and structure of larger companies add layers of complexity when change is required. Inertia results from a combination of complacent executives, the abundance of procedures/processes inherent in large organisations and the dominant corporate values.

Corporate Values

Values exist in groups, organisations, subcultures, networks, communities and societies. Such social institutions are made up of beliefs, practices, codes, values, and behaviours (Kennedy, 2015). Clearly, 'values' vary between organisations and have the potential to create positive or negative outcomes. A critical factor is whether those leading large organisations can transform themselves, in everchanging markets (see Figure 5.4). Some companies have failed after a long period of success (think Wilko or Woolworths). This may result from internal inertia, being risk averse, subject to Marketing Myopia or incapable of satisfying value-seeking customers. Leaders must do two things well; they must make decisions and then implement changes (based on those decisions). Clearly there is no room for complacency in marketing. Hiding behind the 'status quo' or being unwilling to accept the need for continuous change will ultimately lead to failure. That said, it must be the right value-laden change. Change for its own sake is rarely a recipe for long-term success.

For a number of key sectors (banking, insurance, transport or energy) government regulations will continue to be key. Companies must recognise this and develop appropriate values. Where sectors misbehave, they are given the opportunity to self-regulate; however, increasingly governments are legislating (if companies do not regulate). Some deregulation is likely to be reversed e.g. there is increasing support for renationalising the railways in the UK.

Example: LNER was renationalised in 2018 to replace the repeated failed attempts of the private sector. In 2021 it was estimated that for every £1 spent running and investing in LNER's services, at least £2 is generated in Gross Value Added (GVA) impact and an additional £0.83 is generated in wider societal impacts, including environmental benefit. All profit goes to the UK government rather than international shareholders.

Many service providers in developed markets addressed the impacts of crises, e.g. the 2008 credit crunch and the COVID–19 pandemic. They must also manage changes introduced by GDPR (see Figure 5.6). Changes in technology (particularly digital technologies) have impacted substantially on companies. Blackberry had little option other than to change their business model. Blackberry no longer sees itself as a smartphone provider, rather they provide technological solutions to problems in the growing Internet of Things (IoT). Some companies cannot react in time to changes, whereas others may be able to buy themselves time to change.

Example: Music Shops. In 2018 HMV was in administration for the second time in six years. Such turbulence is the norm in the music industry. Graham Jones, in his excellent text 'The Last Shop Standing', cites over 2,000 record shops closing since the advent of the compact disc (Jones, 2014). Also, music sales have shrunk as established music companies struggle to adapt to the distribution of digital content online and a new generation of consumers do not appear to respect traditional Intellectual Property. DVD sales declined as streaming gathered momentum. Whether HMV can survive these changes in the long-term will be of interest to music fans. The remaining 250 independent music shops are showing signs of health having diversified (into selling 'gig' tickets and vinyl) they are now in a position to better serve customers. In 2023 HMV stores sell merchandise as well as vinyl decks.

Unless organisations and their leaders look beyond their companies, they risk reinforcing attractive but dangerous assumptions. In marketing terms, companies must recognise and engage effectively with the values of all stakeholder groups. Large organisations must be wary of the 'group think' phenomenon where employees accept organisational values and norms set by the executive. Managers often refuse to challenge leaders because they think they can benefit from silence (i.e. will career opportunities be available for those who 'rock the boat'). Alternatively, they fear sanctions if they do not agree with autocratic leaders. Weak leaders only seek inputs from those with 'Halos' and refuse to interact with those with 'Horns'. This may be acceptable in certain areas, however in marketing the orthodoxy must be challenged.

The Value Proposition (VP)

Much marketing research is based on models featuring the creation of 'value' by goods manufacturers. In these models (see Table 5.5), manufacturers 'give' value to customers through what is referred to as a 'value proposition' (VP), a term deemed increasingly contentious (Richardson *et al*, 2015). It implies that consumers should purchase particular products or services where they will be 'given' value to a greater extent than other competing offerings. However, VPs are rarely unique (think Baker's JND as against a USP) and they may not adequately capture the customers' values and priorities. VPs may even contribute to 'locked-in' customers (see Section 1.3), promoting in their place values and social constructs that reflect the priorities of the company (Blowfield, 2005). With SM, neither the methods, nor sought changes are value free. Marketers often try to encourage, or change, the norms and values of a target group (Kennedy, 2015). Despite this, Jensen (2008, p 171) protests

> "value issues go unaddressed. These important issues are not getting nearly enough attention from those of us in business and in economics, as well as in the rest of the social sciences".

That said, the fundamental flaws of the VP are that value only resides in the minds of those receiving it and whilst it can be co-created, it cannot be given, only taken.

Consumer Values

If seeking value-for-money (vfm) as a value, the value types may include the cost, but also include the time, energy and social/psychological costs of obtaining or not obtaining a product or undertaking behaviour (Kennedy, 2015). Meaning is a value-laden concept. Consumer preferences are not formed on the basis of the products themselves, but on the meaning they confer, the attributes they possess and the individual consumer's value-system (Jackson, 2005). Marketers should recognise that consumers have value in themselves, which is shaped by the social context. Furthermore, different value orientations co-exist in the same individual and may all influence behaviour (*ibid*). Consumers' values, which they may attach to sustainability criteria in decision-making (see Chapter 3), can be functional, emotional, cognitive, social or conditional. Hence, decision-making is far from simple.

The notion of value creation is central to current marketing thinking and Marketers should tailor their strategies towards a new approach, focusing on their relationship / interaction /co-operation with consumers. Vargo and Lusch (2004) reached a similar conclusion, recognising consumers as co-creators of value rather than 'targets'. The emergence of consumers as co-creators or seekers of value has stimulated much interest in marketing circles.

Co-Creation of Value

Key commentators such as Kotler and Porter have argued that companies should concentrate their resources into value-building investments and activities, as marketers

> "may raise sales in the short run but add less value than would actual improvements in the product's quality, features or convenience. Enlightened marketing calls for building long-run consumer loyalty and relationships, by continually improving the value that consumers receive … By creating value for customers, the company can capture value from consumers in return".
>
> (Kotler *et al*, 2009, pp 97–98)

Capturing value from consumers in return is a form of value co-creation. Clearly, key issues need to be addressed. First, not all stakeholders are equal, with customers being the primary stakeholder for marketers; second, value can only be meaningfully added in how customers perceive organisations, rather than, say, between departments, within databases, in the supply chain or elsewhere in the micro-environment; finally, value is not permanent, rather it can be created or destroyed.

Co-creation of value counters the idea of giving or proposing value by suggesting it is mutually created. The notion is not new, indeed Freeman (1984) suggests just as people have been watching the stars for a long time, they have also been creating value and

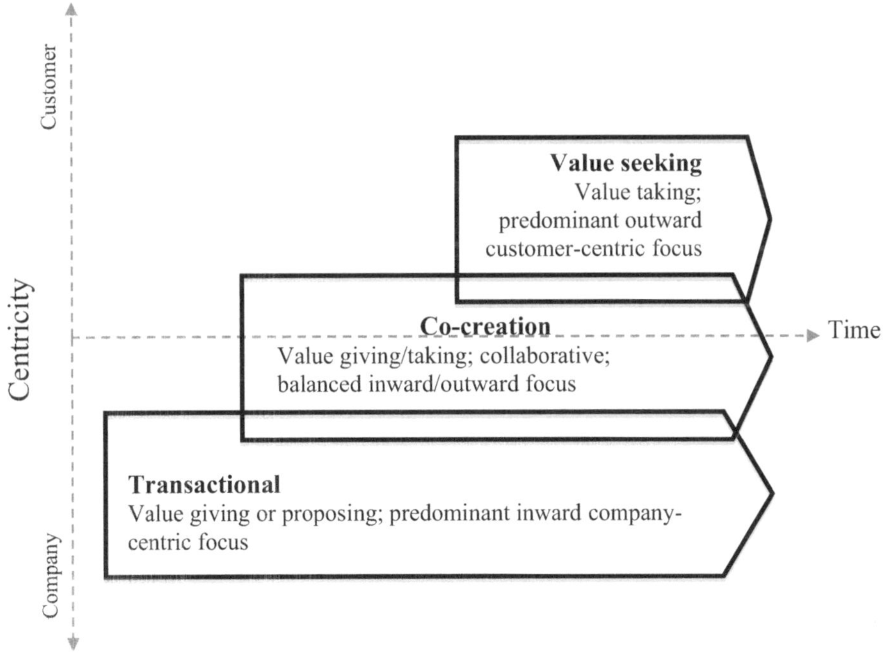

Figure 2.2 Chronology of changes in 'value'.

Source: Adapted from Richardson *et al* (2015, p 22).

trading with each other since long before there were corporations. This is a challenge for marketers as decisions may be linked and supported by common values. Alternatively, they may be unconnected and affected by the external (situational) environment (see Section 5.2). The notion of value propositions or proposed value simply being 'given' has been challenged by those who argue for the co-creation of value or enabling value-seeking (Figure 2.2).

Figure 2.2 shows the chronology of how value has evolved. Whilst transactional companies exist (think the low involvement nature of withdrawing money from an ATM) the move towards more services being offered (see Section 4.5) has led to companies increasingly seeing 'value' from the customer's perspective. Some want to co-create the value whereas others believe that the best they can do is to create the circumstances where customers will seek to take value from their company. Co-creation and enabling value-seeking are inherently more customer centric than the traditional notion of a value proposition.

Key Findings

1 The debates about markets, consumer behaviour and consumerism are ancient.
2 Sustainable Marketing (SM) has evolved from green, social and societal marketing.
3 Progressive managers remove barriers to adopting sustainability.
4 Two schools of thought exist, Developmental and Critical. Critical marketers see the flaws inherent in BAU marketing.
5 Myths exist relating to marketing and its negative perception.
6 Companies are increasingly seeing 'value' from the customer's perspective. Value only resides in the minds of those receiving it and whilst it can be co-created, it cannot be given, only taken.

Activities

1 The International Social Marketing Association (ISMA – see https://isocialmarketing.org/) has useful information and is worth a visit.
2 The Sustainable Marketing Knowledge Network (Smart: Know-Net) exists to bring together the worlds of marketing and sustainability www.cfsd.org.uk/smart-know-net/.
3 Useful insights that can inform sustainability adoption are Sustainable Value (www.sustainablevalue.com).
4 Purpose Disruptors have built a network of 4,000 advertising industry insiders. Look for insights on their website (www.purposedisruptors.org/about-us).

References

AMA. (2023) *Definition of Marketing*. www.ama.org/the-definition-of-marketing-what-is-marketing/ (accessed 04-08-23).

Baker, M. (2009) *Aided Recall and Marketing Mnemonics* Guest Lecture presented By Professor Michael Baker to Leeds Business School, November 2009.

Belz, F-M. & Peattie, K. (2009) *Sustainability Marketing — A Global Perspective*. Wiley & Sons: Chichester.

Blowfield, M. (2005) Corporate social responsibility: Reinventing the meaning of development? *International Affairs*, 81(3), pp. 515–524. DOI:10.1111/j.1468-2346.2005.00466.x

Brassington, F. & Pettitt, S. (2007) *Essentials of Marketing*. Pearson: Harlow.

Brown, S. (1995) *Postmodern Marketing*. London: Routledge.

Brownlie, D. & Saren, M. (1992) The four Ps of the marketing concept: Prescriptive, polemical, permanent and problematical. *European Journal of Marketing*, 26(4), pp. 34–47. DOI:10.1108/03090569210012408

Charter, M. (1992) *A Greener Marketing Approach to Business*. Sheffield: Greenfield Publishing.

CIM. (2023) *What is Marketing?* www.cim.co.uk/content-hub/quick-read/what-is-marketing/ (accessed 04-08-23).

CIPS. (2023) *Plastic Packaging Tax Deemed 'Not Fit for Purpose*. www.cips.org/supply-management/news/2023/april/plastic-packaging-tax-deemed-not-fit-for-purpose/ (accessed 09-08-23).

Emery, B. (2012) *Sustainable Marketing*. Harlow: Pearson Education.

Freeman, R.E. (1984). *Strategic Management: A Stakeholder Approach*. Pitman: Boston.

Gosnay, R.M. & Richardson, N. (2008) *Develop Your Marketing Skills*. London: Kogan Page.

Greenpeace. (2021) *What Really Happens to Your Plastic Recycling?* www.greenpeace.org.uk/news/plastic-recycling-export-incineration/#:~:text=Well%20over%20half%20of%20the,being%20dumped%20or%20burned%20illegally. (accessed 08-08-23).

Guido, G., Amatulli, C., Peluso, A.M., De Matteis, C., Piper, L. & Pino, G. (2020) Measuring internalized versus externalized luxury consumption motivations and consumers' segmentation. *Italian Journal of Marketing*, 1 pp. 25–47. DOI:10.1007/s43039-020-00002-9

Harrison, M.P., Beatty, S.E., Reynolds, K.E. & Noble, S.N. (2012) Why customers feel locked into relationships: Using Qualitative research to uncover the lock-in factors. *Journal of Marketing Theory and Practice*, 20(4), Fall, pp. 391–406. DOI:10.2753/MTP1069-6679200403

Henion, K.E. & Kinnear, T.C. (1976). *Ecological Marketing*. Chicago: American Marketing Association.

Jackson, T. (2005) *Motivating Sustainable Consumption- A Review of Evidence on Consumer Behaviour and Behavioural Change*; a report to the Sustainable Development Research Network January 2005. Funded by the Economic and Social Research Council's Sustainable Technologies Programme (STP).

Jensen (2008) *Non-Rational Behavior, Value Conflicts, Stakeholder Theory, And Firm Behavior. Academy of Management 2007 Symposium* in B.R. Agle, T. Donaldson, R.E. Freeman, M.C. Jensen, R.K. Mitchell, & D.J. Wood, (2008) Dialogue: Toward Superior Stakeholder Theory. *Business Ethics Quarterly*, 18(2), pp. 153–190.

Jensen, M.C., Mitchell, R.K., & Wood, D.J. (2008) Dialogue: Toward superior stakeholder theory. *Business Ethics Quarterly*,18(2), pp. 153–190.

Jones, G. (2014) *Last Shop Standing- What Ever Happened to Record Shops? 6th Edition*. London: Proper Music Publishing.

Kemper, J.A. & Ballantine, P.W. (2019). What do we mean by sustainability marketing? *Journal of Marketing Management*, February. DOI:10.1080/0267257X.2019.1573845

Kennedy, A-M. (2015) Macro-social marketing. *Journal of Macromarketing*, 35(3), pp. 1–12. DOI:10.1177/0276146715617509

Kennedy, A-M. & Parsons, A. (2014) Social engineering and social marketing: Why is one "good" and the other "bad"?", *Journal of Social Marketing*, 4(3), pp. 198–209. DOI:10.1108/JSOCM-01-2014-0006

Kotler P. & Armstrong G. (2006). *Principles of Marketing, 11th Edition*. Upper Saddle River, New Jersey: Prentice-Hall.

Kotler, P., & Lee, N. (2005). *Corporate Social Responsibility: Doing the Most Good for Company and Your Cause*. Chichester: John Wiley & Sons.

Kotler, P. & Levy, S.J. (1969) Broadening the concept of marketing. *Journal of Marketing*, 33(1), pp. 10–15. DOI:10.2307/1248740

Kotler, P., Wong, V., Saunders, J. & Armstrong, G. (2009) *Principles of Marketing, 5th European Edition*. Harlow: Prentice Hall.

Levitt, T. (1960). Marketing myopia. July/August 1960, Harvard Business Review.

Martin, D. & Schouten, J. (2013) *Sustainable Marketing*. Harlow: Pearson Education. ISBN-13: 9781292040899

McDonald, M. (2016) *Malcolm McDonald on Marketing Planning – Understanding Marketing Plans and Strategy,* 2nd Edition. London: Kogan Page.

Mittelstaedt, J.D., Shultz, C.J., Kilbourne, W.E. & Peterson, M. (2014) Sustainability as megatrend: Two schools of macromarketing thought. *Journal of Macromarketing*, 34(3) pp. 253–264. DOI:10.1177/0276146713520551

Motortrader. (2023) Chinese brands make 'significant progress' in sales across Europe. by J Kirwan. www.motortrader.com/motor-trader-news/automotive-news/chinese-brands-make-significant-progress-sales-across-europe-02-02-2023 (accessed 07-08-23).

Motortrend. (2023) Nissan leaf history: The EV that launched a movement- Nissan's trailblazing EV paved the way for the Japanese automaker's electrified future. www.motortrend.com/features/nissan-leaf-ev-history-pioneer-future/#:~:text=But%20the%20carmaker's%20groundbreaking%20move,produced%20electric%20vehicle%20in%20history (accessed 08-08-23).

Murray, K.B. & Häubl, G. (2007) Explaining cognitive lock-in: The role of skill-based habits of use in consumer choice. *Journal of Consumer Research*, 34(1), pp. 77–88. DOI:10.1086/513048

Ottman, J.A. (1993). *Green Marketing: Challenges & Opportunities for the New Marketing Age.* Chicago: NTC Business Books.

Peattie, K. (1992) *Green Marketing.* The M & E handbook series. London: Pitman.

Recoup. (2022) *UK Household Plastic Packaging Collection Survey 2022* www.recoup.org/ (accessed 08-08-23).

Richardson, N. (2018) Entrepreneurial insights into sustainable marketing: A case study of U.K. music festivals. Strategic Change. Special Edition: The Creation of Value through Sustainable Development. Part 1. pp. 559–570. DOI:10.1002/jsc.2239

Richardson, N. (2020) *Sustainable Marketing Planning.* Abingdon: Routledge.

Richardson, N. (2022) How new sustainability typologies will reshape traditional approaches to loyalty. *Italian Journal of Marketing. Special issue: S.I. Sustainable Marketing and Performance Management*, February. DOI:10.1007/s43039-022-00047-y

Richardson, N. & Cassop Thompson, M. (2019) A new positioning framework for organizational value: Juxtaposing organizational value positions with customer centricity. Strategic Change. Special edition: *Sustainable Business Models.* pp. 1–10. DOI:10.1002/jsc.2253

Richardson, N. & Cassop Thompson, M. (2023) How improved understanding of what constitutes 'value' may lead to better underpinning of corporate social responsibility (CSR). *Journal of Global Responsibility*, pp. 2041–2568. DOI:10.1108/JGR-10-2022-0115

Sanne, C. (2002) Willing consumers – or locked in? Policies for a sustainable consumption. *Ecological Economics*, 42, pp. 273–287. DOI:10.1016/S0921-8009(02)00086-1

Spedale, S. & Watson, T.J. (2014) The emergence of entrepreneurial action: At the crossroads between institutional logics and individual life-orientation. *International Small Business Journal*, 32(7), pp. 759–776. DOI:10.1177/0266242613480376

Tadajewski, M. & Brownlie, D. (2008) *Critical Marketing – Issues in Contemporary Marketing.* Chichester: Wiley.

Tilley, F & Young, C.W. (2009) Sustainability entrepreneurs – Could they be the true wealth generators of the future? *Greener Management International*, 55, pp. 70–92, Greenleaf Publishing. DOI:10.9774/GLEAF.3062.2006.au.00008

UKGOV. (2023) *Official Statistics. UK statistics on waste –Updated 28 June 2023* www.gov.uk/government/statistics/uk-waste-data/uk-statistics-on-waste (accessed 08-08-23).

van Dam, Y.K. & Apeldoorn, P.A.C. (1996) Sustainable marketing. *Journal of Macromarketing*, 16(2), pp. 45–56. DOI:10.1177/027614679601600204

Vargo, S.L. & Lusch, R.F. (2004) The four service marketing myths – remnants of a goods-based manufacturing model. *Journal of Service Research*, 6(4), pp. 324–335. DOI:10.1177/1094670503262946

WTO. (2023) Global trade outlook and statistics. World Trade Organisation www.wto.org/index.htm (accessed 09-08-23).

3 Sustainable Buyer Behaviour

Abstract

This chapter first reflects on the historical view of consumption. It provides underpinning for consumer decision making including a better understanding of needs, wants and norms. The limitations of the BAU B2C Decision Making Process (DMP) are considered. Individual influences are identified, particularly key models relating to motivation. A definition of the elusive sustainable consumer is offered. The role of the Decision-making Unit (DMU) is addressed in relation to sustainability. The notion of organisational behaviour is considered including how consumer barriers to adoption. TBL-based sustainable segments are identified. Finally, a TBL-appropriate B2C DMP is discussed.

Learning Outcomes

At the end of this chapter students will be able to

- discuss the historical influences on consumption
- examine the role of the B2C Decision-Making Process (DMP)
- appreciate key aspects of organisational buying behaviour
- evaluate a definition of sustainable consumers
- assess the role of the Decision-Making Unit (DMU) in B2B and B2C scenarios
- explain the benefits of adopting a TBL-based DMP for consumers.

3.1 Consumer Buyer Behaviour

Consumer Behaviour is one of the oldest and most studied marketing domains. In the 1960s John Howard and Jagdish Sheth posited the Theory of Buyer Behaviour (Howard & Sheth, 1969). Furthermore, a group of US academics laid the foundations for what is identified as consumer behaviour theory today. James Engel, David Kollat, Roger Blackwell and Paul Miniard (amongst others) studied how consumers generally move through a psychological process when purchasing products. They published dozens of articles culminating in the Consumer Decision Model (Engel *et al*, 1968; Blackwell *et al.*, 2001). Their collective works are seminal and of such importance that many refer to the EKB model (see Ashman *et al*, 2015), however the most widely used term is the 'Decision Making Process' (DMP). DMP is preferred as it relates to the model's functionality rather than its authors. Nearly 70 years later, this model still informs teaching and practice.

DOI: 10.4324/9781003434214-4

Kollat *et al* (1972) recognised that consumer behaviour is influenced by various phenomena interacting in complex ways. Sustainability is one such phenomenon. Poor sustainability practices can lead to reputational damage whereas good ones can enhance not only corporate reputations but also acceptance and perceptions of companies' activities (Gomez-Trujillo *et al*, 2020).

Marketers who identify the key influences affecting decision-making, will better understand customers' behaviour and be better placed to create value for them. To remain competitive, innovative and attractive to customers, marketers must constantly develop their products, services and even organisations. Occasionally brands have a USP (unique selling point), which enables them to be recognised in a crowded marketplace. These are few and far between. Many brands have what Professor Michael Baker calls a JND (just noticeable difference). Sometimes, a price advantage may itself attract attention. Companies with little or no differentiation or price advantage will struggle.

Needs, Wants and Norms

Needs and wants are the basic building blocks of buyer behaviour. A need refers to the gap between a consumer's actual state and their ideal or desired state. When the gap is sufficiently large, consumers are motivated to satisfy the need. Needs can be physical or psychological, e.g. hunger and thirst are physical whereas status is psychological. Wants are culturally and socially influenced. Needs may produce very different wants for different consumers. Needs theorists argue 'true' human needs are finite, few and universal (Maslow, 1954). Part of progressing towards a more sustainable economy will require a greater understanding of what constitutes a 'want' as compared to a 'need' as "humans have a complex set of wants and needs that can interact and even conflict" (Belz & Peattie, 2009, p 74).

Consumers do not buy products, rather they buy benefits. A product or service should provide the consumer with a benefit that satisfies a need or want. They

- can see products as solving multiple problems and thus providing multiple benefits
- are attracted to the products offering the largest blend of benefits.

The term 'norm' refers to a standard of conduct or rule of behaviour. Norms can be cultural, social or personal and reflect what is normally (or should be) done. They exist in social settings to the extent that an individual's behaviour may lead to the approval, disapproval or even sanctioned by others if not acting 'appropriately'. Sanctioning behaviour may be essential for the existence of a norm. Norms bring uniformity of behaviour, encouraging conformity. Margolis and Walsh (2003) argue 'normative' refers to the underlying justification that gives moral weight. Moral weight implies a degree of risk, e.g. when food and drink choices are based on cultural norms (Mitchell & Harris, 2005) of, say, health concerns or 'conscience' consumption.

Personal norms invoke feelings of strong moral obligation when engaging in prosocial behaviour and may determine further pro-social behaviours. What appears to interfere with personal norms in the success of pro-environmental behaviours is the existence of external social or institutional constraints (Jackson, 2005). Social norms reflect the behavioural expectations in light of the moral rules and guidelines of the 'tribe'. Jackson argues the existence of social norms can be a powerful force both in inhibiting and in encouraging pro-environmental behaviour. Social norms either provide behavioural examples that may be helpful in selecting appropriate behaviour or they relate to the social outcomes associated with the performance of a given behaviour (*ibid*).

Examples of 'sustainable' norms include codes of conduct, behaviour contracts, partnership agreements and third-party certification programmes (e.g. Forest Alliance, Fairtrade, Soil Association). Such evidence of sustainable norms is attractive to the ever-increasing numbers of consumers who are concerned about sustainability and buy food products that are identified as Fairtrade or other ethically produced goods (Co-op, 2021). Harnessing social norms is important for pro-sustainability behaviour (Belz & Peattie, 2009).

Some consumers are not willing actors in the consumption process, capable of exercising rational or irrational choice in the satisfaction of their own needs and desires. They find themselves 'locked into' unsustainable patterns of consumption, either by social norms or the constraints of institutional contexts (Jackson, 2005). It can be argued modern consumer society is locked into a 'social pathology' driven to consume by a mixture of greed, social norms and the persuasive power of unscrupulous producers (*ibid*). This implies consumers are passive which is clearly not always the case. It does, however, explain some antipathy towards marketing and underpins the argument for co-creation of value.

Clearly, it is useful to know how to support customers' decision-making when they are buying products or services and what influences these processes. Sustainable consumers are often willing to pay more for the blend of benefits. Sustainable marketers must communicate the benefits of the 'People, Planet and Profit' approach. Through understanding the value sought and behaviour, marketers can provide them with information and the resources to support their decision-making.

The BAU Consumer (B2C) Decision-Making Process (DMP)

The 'business-to-consumer' (B2C) market is where the consumer (end user) buys the offering for their own personal consumption, for the use of their family and/or friends and not for profit-making purposes. Whilst other forms exist (e.g. B2G, C2B and C2C), the two most widely considered by marketers are B2C and 'business-to-business' (B2B).

The DMP was first-and-foremost a BAU framework i.e. designed to increase contributions to the bottom line. It was designed as an economic framework for marketers, not consumers. This was the case with most tools and frameworks in the 1960s, 1970s and 1980s. A quick inspection of Porter's 5 Forces (see Table 5.6) reveals it lacks any reference to ecology. The original Macro situational-review framework PEST had to be augmented to include societal (People) and/or environmental (Planets) elements (see Table 5.12).

The BAU Consumer DMP contains a number of simple steps, however there are many things that exert influence.

Figure 3.1 is an aggregate of many variations of the DMP. Engel, Miniard and Blackwell did not refer to the Marketing Mix for example. Furthermore, they cited situational influences without specifying the most widely used framework PEST. It is worth noting that their early models included Disposal however "Marketing rarely considered the post-use behaviour of consumers beyond the opportunity for a repeat purchase" (Belz & Peattie, 2009, p 76). Often BAU DMP models (see Brassington & Pettit, 2006; Ashman *et al*, 2015; Dudovskiy, 2022) ignore the increasingly important aspect of disposal, i.e.

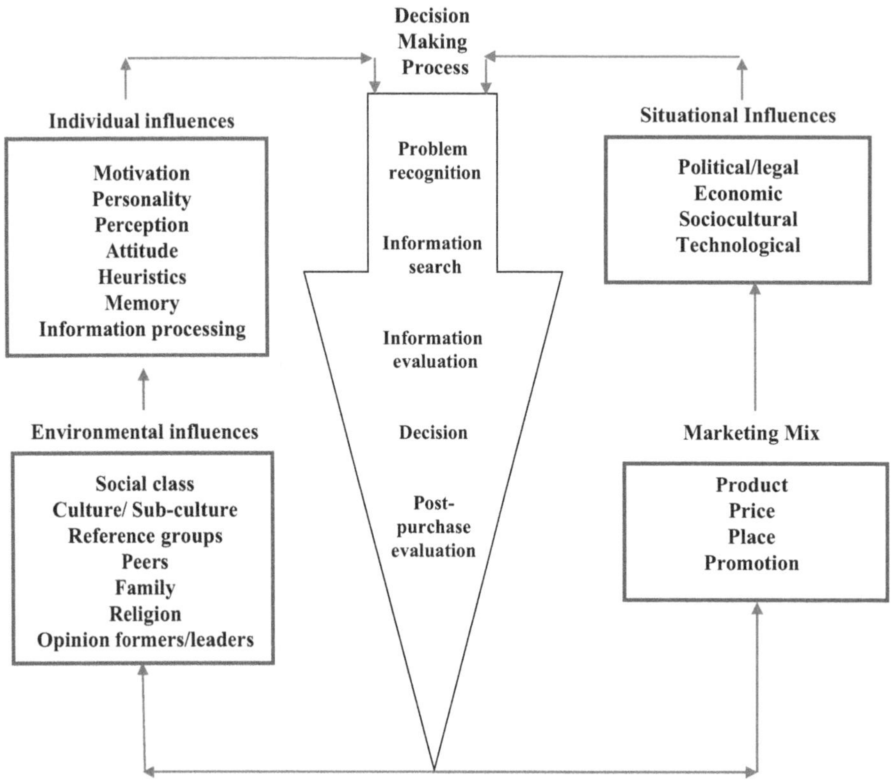

Figure 3.1 The BAU Decision-Making Process (DMP) for consumers.

Sources: Adapted from Brassington and Pettitt (2006); Dibb *et al* (2006).

the fate of goods after their useful life. This is remiss. Increasingly those designing goods are thinking of disposal. Historically cars were designed to last as long as possible for the amount spent. Today, cars are designed to last AND have 90% of their parts recyclable on disposal.

Figure 3.1 portrays key internal characteristics that influence the B2C DMP. These are not prioritised and may influence one another. In Figure 3.1 the arrows represent the flow of influences on the BAU DMP.

Within 'Problem Recognition' the word 'problem' seems to be problematic for many students. A problem is simply a need, want or desire that needs to be satisfied. Most consumers start the buying process when they realise they have a problem, e.g. their washing machine has broken, they want food or their car needs a service.

The 'Information Search' and 'Information Evaluation' stages (Figure 3.1) are those most impacted by communications (see Section 4.1) as the consumer searches for information on brands that will provide a solution. This search could involve a diverse range of sources including websites, magazines, newspapers, social media or even retail outlets. Different consumers will have differing degrees of complexity of decision-making owing to their use of information. Information seeking is present to some degree for all consumers. The challenge for marketers is to employ a variety of information sources as part of their Integrated Marketing Communications (IMC). Consumers spend little time searching for information and evaluating the alternatives when buying staple goods involving repeat purchases and low risk, i.e. for Fast Moving Consumer Goods (FMCG) such as a loaf of bread. Consumers trust their peers and 'independent' third parties, both of whom can generate word of mouth (WoM), arguably the most powerful and trusted form of communication. A range of means to evaluate alternatives exist such as the JD Power survey which uses consumer feedback for three-year-old cars and covers a range of issues such as reliability, economy and service quality.

Having considered the options, consumers make their 'purchasing decision'. For more sophisticated purchasing scenarios (see Table 4.2) say, buying a luxury handbag or piece of jewellery, consumers deal with complex choices by eliminating options. They select key aspects (i.e. price, location, line-up, facilities or 'green') or combine them to form heuristics. Using heuristics allows consumers to make important but complex decisions in an informed, intelligent way that reduces risk and effectively simplifies going through the DMP. The irony of 'pricing' being a simple shortcut will not be lost on marketers who will recognise that it represents one of the most complex issues in the domain. Consumers also deal in general perceptions rather than comparing every detail, so emotive issues such as ethics or green goods could easily shape decision-making (Mitchell & Harris, 2005). Understanding the role of heuristics may explain how criteria interact and support or create barriers when the consumer is forming priorities.

Some may question their own decision before, during and after the purchase. This 'cognitive dissonance' is more likely when the item bought has a higher level of risk (socially and financially). These doubts are natural and marketers should allay the customer's fears. It can be as easy as congratulating the customer on the wisdom of their choice. This is why most consumer durables are accompanied by literature supporting their choice, re-affirming the benefits or highlighting the security the guarantee brings.

Once consumers have worn their new item of clothing, they form opinions about the product during the 'Post-Purchase Decision Review'. If, say, the perception is that it is poorly made, they may avoid the brand in future. Their car may still be 'going strong' and remaining reliable several years later. This could lead to a repeat-purchase. Increasingly they create Consumer Generated Media (CGM) which includes comments, posts, brand complaints, reviews, testimonials, social media posts or simply sharing experiences within brand communities (see Section 5.4).

Example: Tripadvisor is now widely cited in the hotel sector. Customers leave a star rating and often much more insightful qualitative feedback, some of which can be hard hitting. Tripadvisor has, however, acknowledged the issue of fake reviews. It recognises that some unethical companies have made "huge businesses" out of fake reviews and that this may ultimately corrupt the whole platform. Worryingly, some businesses now create fake Tripadvisor reviews for hotels wanting to make unethical progress. The vast majority of reviews are genuine, but will this always be the case with the increasing use of 'bots' and AI?

Consumer knowledge can be a cause of high power with retail patrons being better informed than those involved in other services. Traditionally, marketing campaigns often simply listed features of the product. Before Web 2.0 this may have been enough to satisfy customers, but today's customers are seeking information on benefits. Consumers always move through the DMP, however, they prefer acquiring information at their own pace and answering their own questions (Jackson, 2005), depending upon the purchasing scenario (see Table 4.2) and items sought (see Table 4.3). Marketers should stop trying to sell what they think consumers want. Rather they must find out what information consumers need to make better decisions. Those who are too focused on trying to 'close the deal' may struggle.

Individual Internal Influences

The DMP contains several simple steps, however, many things exert influence (Figure 3.1). As the details of the BAU influences are well covered elsewhere (see Richardson, 2020, pp 48–53) this chapter focuses on motivation. Marketers need a clearer understanding of consumers' "motivations and the barriers they face to making sustainable choices" (Belz & Peattie, 2009, p 82). Those who are highly motivated may pay higher prices. People are motivated to know and understand what is going on, to learn, discover and explore (Jackson, 2005). They are motivated to participate and play a role in what is going on around them. However, they hate being disoriented, confused, feeling incompetent or helpless (*ibid*).

Often consumers can have multiple motivations. Two widely cited motivational models are Abraham Maslow's "Hierarchy of Needs" (Maslow, 1954) and Frederick Herzberg's 'dual factor' theory (Herzberg *et al*, 1959). It is inferred from Maslow's hierarchy (Figure 3.2) that consumers need to satisfy needs in a rising scale from physiological

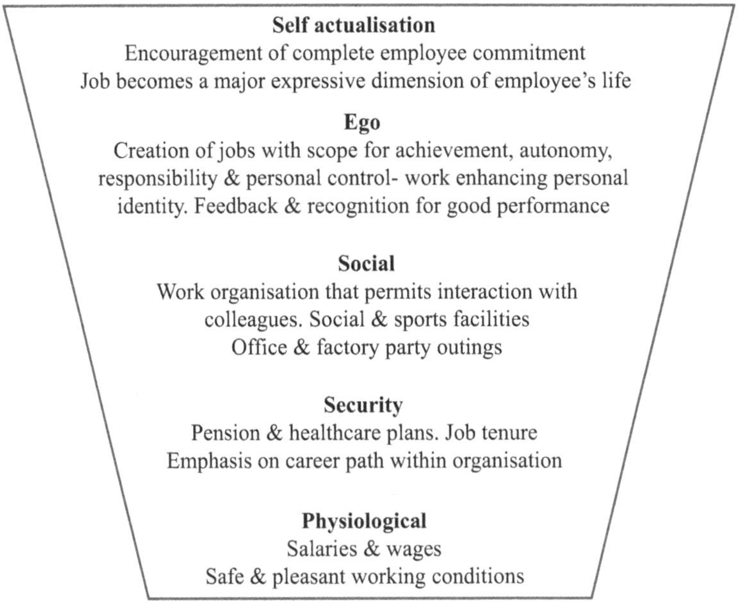

Figure 3.2 Maslow's Hierarchy of Needs.

Source: Adapted from Maslow (1954).

needs to safety, belonging, esteem and finally self-actualisation. It is a simplistic tool, however it serves a number of useful purposes for marketers. It reminds marketers that consumers may have a substantial concern that they wish to address first. If the marketer is trying to communicate other issues (deemed lesser by the consumer) these will effectively be 'noise' (see Figure 4.1) and will have little 'cut-though'. Hence, the lesson is to deal with the big issue first. Furthermore, it should be noted that the position within the hierarchy depends on the context. Someone who is established in a community may feel safe and have a sense of belonging. They may strive to improve their achievement and esteem. Should they move to a different community, they will adopt a new position lower down in the hierarchy and start to climb the stages again. Finally, self-actualisation is largely an abstract concept, particularly in western materialistic societies. Maslow himself said that only 1% of 1% would self-actualise. Apparently, there is always a new gadget to buy for western consumers. This may be changing, however, there is a long way to go.

Herzberg's Theory (Figure 3.3) suggests a distinction should be made between factors causing satisfaction (i.e. motivators) and those that could lead to dissatisfaction (i.e. hygiene factors). Hygiene factors cover those things that people take for granted (e.g. health and safety in the workplace, equitable treatment of suppliers or the sensible disposal of waste materials). People do get a sense of satisfaction from these factors; however it is short term. Motivators can have a longer-term impact and derive from achievement, recognition, responsibility and/or personal growth. The values associated with sustainability can be motivators or hygiene factors depending on the circumstances. Consumers assume councils will recycle the items placed in a green bin. This is taken for granted and is a hygiene factor. Those who support, say, protecting and replenishing threatened marine life will be motivated to support the establishment of Marine Conservation Zones.

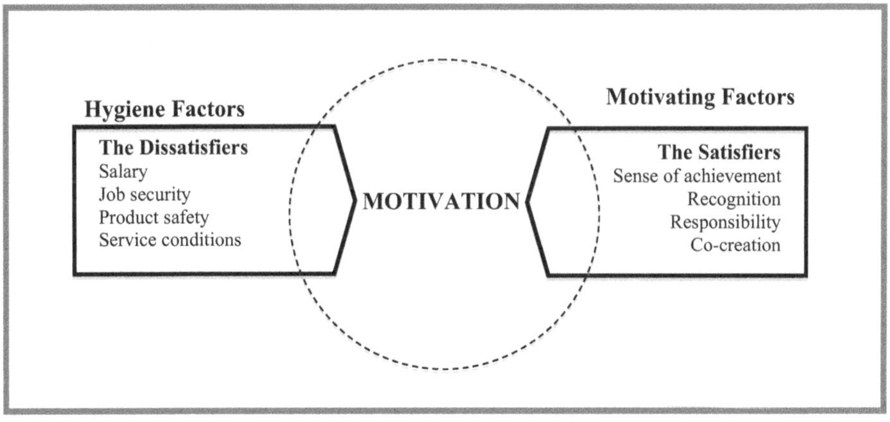

Figure 3.3 Herzberg's dual factor theory of motivation.

Source: Adapted from Herzberg *et al* (1959).

A key finding is that the removal of a dis-satisfier would not necessarily produce satisfaction. Marketers should avoid dis-satisfiers and actively promote major purchasing satisfiers.

The degree of involvement is another factor. Involvement is an unobservable state of motivation, arousal or interest; consumers can develop many different types of involvement with activities, objects, ideas or even social issues (Houston & Rothschild, 1978). Consumers can develop many different types of involvement with activities, objects, ideas or even social issues. Certainly, consumers experience involvement when objects or events 'connect' to important goals or centrally held values, e.g. being environmentally friendly (Mitchell & Harris, 2005). This 'connectedness' with the broader environment features intense emotional commitments which, in turn, increasingly influence their consumption. Research into consumer behaviour cites differing modes of involvement, namely:

- interest in a product or service
- pleasure in the form of emotional appeal
- the extent to which the product represents the consumer
- the likelihood of it going wrong and degree of risk.

The Decision-Making Unit (DMU)

Robinson *et al* (1967) coined the term decision-making unit (DMU) or 'buying centre'. They argued it brought together those organisational members involved in the buying process for a particular product or service. Whilst initially a B2B tool, it is also used with B2C. Traditional BAU marketing has always stressed the need to understand the role and influences within the DMU (Figure 3.4).

The DMU stakeholders interact and influence each other, sometimes energising each other, others restricting each other. Post Web 2.0, the DMU still applies, however, different stakeholders not only fulfil differing roles, often contributing to online debates via a forum (or indeed multiple fora), blogs, social network sites or comparison websites. A further complication is that these stakeholders may also use multiple media channels simultaneously; such people are known as media multi-taskers.

Consumers are influenced by external (a.k.a. situational) factors, e.g. family lifecycle, disposable income, education (amongst others). Many products and services are particularly sensitive to socio-cultural differences. Allied to these factors is the question of lifestyle, whether this is what consumers have achieved at a moment in time or would like to achieve. Consumers are influenced by emotional considerations and by how they perceive their place in their families and with our friends and work colleagues. The role of the family has deep meaning and belief for many cultures. Many purchasing decisions often involve more than one member of the family. Families build up portfolios of purchase (or non-purchase) decisions, which may be underpinned by their values. Furthermore, consumers are influenced by friends, colleagues, peers and people they respect for social or technical reasons.

A problem with the DMU in larger organisations is that passivity is implied, i.e. the stakeholders tend to react to events. In SMEs the DMU may be smaller, however different stakeholders often share roles, e.g. initiator and user but not buyer. SME stakeholders in the DMU may have to multi-task, i.e. occupy multiple roles as they may not have, say, dedicated HR or Procurement teams.

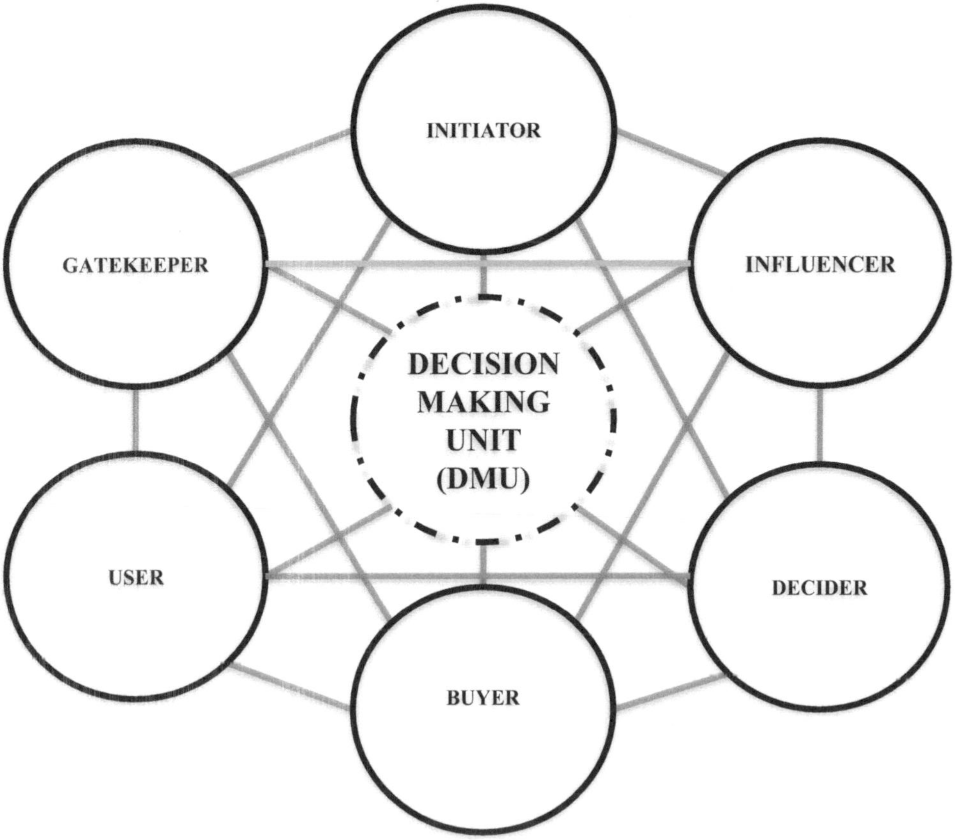

Figure 3.4 The Decision-Making Unit (DMU).

Source: Adapted from Robinson *et al* (1967).

3.2 Organisational Buyer Behaviour

B2B customers are another organisation. Dyson sells through retailers such as Argos. These retailers are Dyson's customers. Dyson are operating initially in the B2B market whereas Argos *et al* are in the B2C market.

The B2B Market

The B2B DMP is shown in Figure 3.5 for a television manufacturer.

Clearly, it differs from the consumer model because of a number of differences in the factors relating to buyer behaviour. Organisational buyers:

- are fewer in number
- are skilled in the art of buying and negotiating

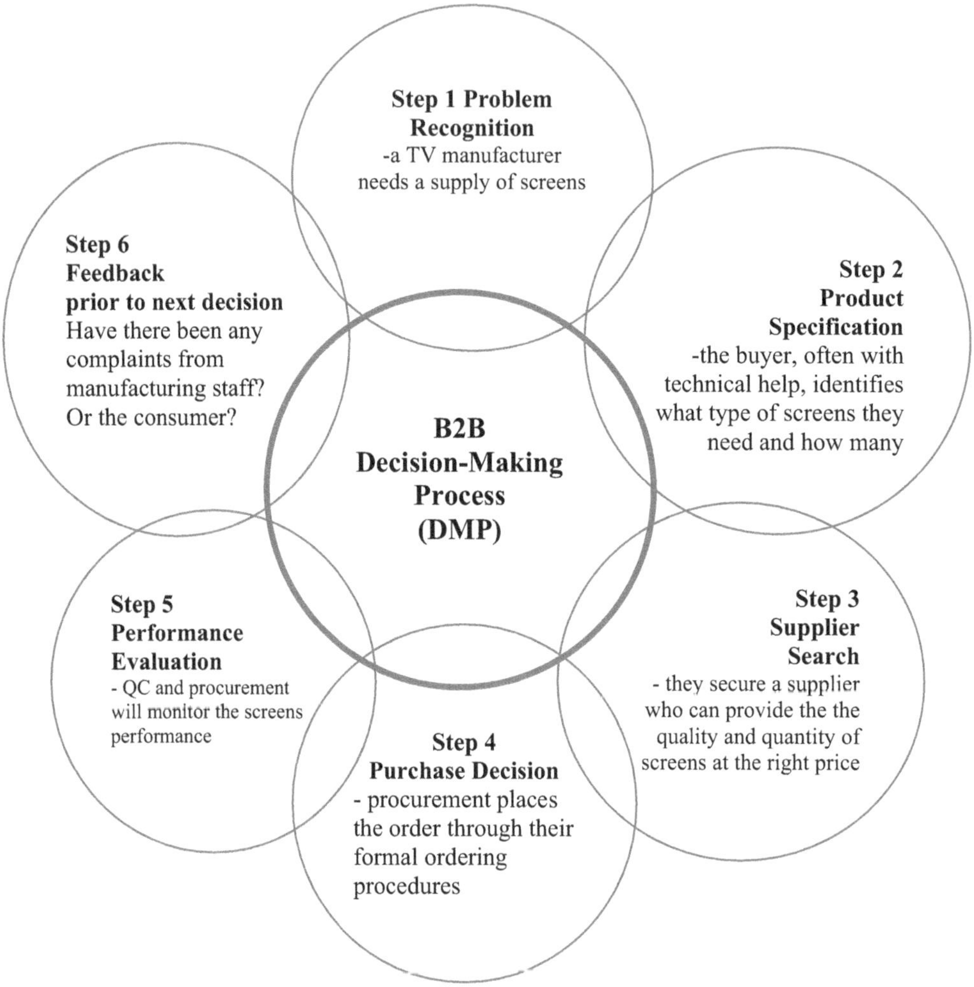

Figure 3.5 Business (B2B) DMP applied to a TV manufacturer.

Source: Author.

- have qualifications from professional bodies such as the Chartered Institute of Purchasing and Supply (see www.cips.org)
- buy in large quantities often over a long timescale
- often seek single-source supply deals.

Influences on Business Buyers

B2B buyers will be aware of Macro factors such as legislation or currency fluctuations (see Table 5.12) and internal/micro-environmental factors such as the organisation's objectives, policies, procedures and systems. On a day-to-day basis B2B buyers are influenced most by a combination of hard (economic) and soft (non-economic) factors. When referring to quantifiable economic factors the emphasis is on a small 'e'. This is not PEST as it is internal to the company. Buyers will always be influenced by price, lead times, quantities, shipment sizes, failure rates, warranty length, payment terms or penalties. These 'hard' figures can be negotiated and are highly visible. The non-economic, soft, interpersonal factors derive from the human nature of B2B buyers. Factors including age, gender, expertise, relationships, prestige, reputation, career stage, ambition or attitude to risk can affect the buying process.

Businesspeople make decisions daily. Some are minor but others may have far-reaching consequences. All decisions are made with an element of fear, uncertainty or doubt (a.k.a. FUD). If there is no FUD, then there is no decision to be made. Rather it is an administrative action that is required. As most managers and leaders make decisions in uncertainty, it is prudent to reduce risk and create more certainty when decision-making. Decision-making is rarely binary, i.e. Option A or Option B. There are often varying answers to questions posed.

3.3 TBL-Based Consumer Buyer Behaviour

Biospheric or Pro-environmental behaviour arises from quite specific value orientations in individuals (Jackson, 2005). Environmental problems stem in part at least from societal values, attitudes and beliefs. Jackson identified three main societal value orientations as

- 'self-enhancement' (i.e. self-regarding)
- 'self-transcendent' (i.e. other regarding) which is prosocial or altruistic
- 'biospheric' (i.e. valuing the environment) (as distinct from other people).

Pro-environmental behaviour involves both purchasing behaviour and non-purchasing behaviour. Green consumers' contexts and values frame the purchase in terms of the motivation to pursue green criteria. It is influenced by the consumer's knowledge of the relevant issues as well as how previous purchase experience influenced the consumer. Primary and secondary green criteria are formed by researching the ethics of a product (and its manufacturer), talking to friends and family or browsing online (Young *et al*, 2010).

Barriers and key factors to facilitate buying 'green' products and factors that could improve adoption are shown in Table 3.1. Tensions are caused by consumers having a range of competing value-types. Such tensions are clearly a barrier to behavioural change. Emery (2012, p 114) develops this suggesting:

> "As citizens the public want to avert the socio-economic and environmental crises by behaving more sustainably but as consumers the public want to drive cars, take flights and buy products which they quickly get tired of only to replace them with more".

Marketers have increasingly sought to identify and communicate with green and ethical consumers with mixed results. There is a real need to understand more about consumers and whether they purchase sustainable goods, services and experiences over the alternatives.

Table 3.1 Contrasting consumer barriers and facilitating factors

Barriers to buying green products	*Key factors that will help green purchases*
Lack of time to research details, e.g. a company's CSR programme	The consumer's sustainable value is strong; Consumer has purchasing experience
The price of a (sustainable) product	Consumer can afford and is prepared for the financial costs
The lack of available information on the environmental and social performance of products	Consumer has time for research and decision-making; to trust certain information sources, labels or organisations providing a shortcut to choosing a more sustainable product
The cognitive effort in researching, decision-making and searching for the products	Consumer has good knowledge of the relevant issues
The prioritising of non-sustainable criteria	Sustainable products are reasonably available; Consumer feels conflicted (e.g. for having other non-sustainable priorities, not prioritising sustainable criteria, not being able to purchase the most sustainable product)

Source: Adapted from Young *et al* (2010, pp 27–29).

Example: In the case of music festivals, consumers are clearly purchasing an 'experience'. That said, food and drink provision are major contributors to the profitability of music festivals. The notion of consumers' values shaping their purchases resonates with the music festival sector. Increasingly, consumers buy food products that are identified as Fairtrade or locally produced. Demand for such goods and services is growing and interest is growing in the ways in which such issues can build and enhance brands. This has led to more festivals stressing the local provision of goods and services.

Consumers do not always differentiate between sustainability issues, e.g. some mix ethical and 'green' issues. Clearly, some consumers regard being ecologically sound as an ethical or even moral matter. For many (though not all) the environment is rated as the most important ethical driver during purchasing decisions, followed by human rights then animal rights/welfare issues. This conflation of issues presents challenges in terms of 'marcomms' (see Section 4.1).

The Elusive Sustainable Consumer

A key component of sustainable consumption is to encourage environmental citizenship which involves asking consumers to reflect on the attitudes that inform their behaviour (Young *et al*, 2010) and may lead to a behaviour change that outlasts more short-term financial incentives. Those strongly committed to causes compatible with sustainability, say green, charitable or ethical, will be more critical (and willing to) undertake more research in the information search and evaluation stages of the DMP (Figure 3.1). Research suggests they are more cynical regarding claims made and buy-in to the notion of green-washing. They also tend to be sceptical about claims made regarding CSR policies. Hence, they go to greater lengths to evaluate whether companies 'practice what they preach'.

As consumers take a greater interest in the environment, driven by the media and better education, the need to consider the environment in a friendly and sustainable manner is increasingly important. Consumers have changing expectations and are increasingly discerning, i.e. are willing to change their spending patterns. The Co-op is the UK's largest seller of Fairtrade wine. Undoubtedly, Fairtrade wines cost more, yet sales grow year-on-year.

Simply depicting consumption as 'bad' is naïve and potentially damaging. According to Mary Douglas (1976 as cited in Jackson, 2005) 'An individual's main objective in consumption is to help create the social world and to find a credible place in it'. In other words, consumption can be viewed as an attempt to improve individual and collective well-being by providing the goods and services necessary to meet people's wants and desires.

The importance of consumer behaviour is reflected in the wide variety of models as identified in the seminal work of Jackson (2005). Professor Tim Jackson produced a detailed review of consumer decision-making from a sustainability perspective. It is comprehensive and should be compulsory reading for marketers. All consumer decisions have the potential to contribute to more or less sustainable consumption (Young *et al*, 2010; Gomez-Trujillo *et al*, 2020). As marketing is about aligning brands with the value sought by customers, it is necessary to define sustainable consumers. Hence for the purposes of this book

> "'sustainable consumers' seek value, enabling decision-making, that complies with the tenets of the Triple Bottom Line. Their decisions are guided by sustainable practices socially and ecologically. In seeking value that chimes with the TBL approach, they recognise that the short-term sacrifice of paying more may be the only way to balance their wants and long-term interests with companies' requirements, society's long run interests and the need for environmental balance".

The challenge lies in the nature of consumers (Table 3.2). The irrationality of consumers often confuses those who expect rational behaviour. Often, they are not only irrational, but downright contradictory.

Emery's identification of five differing aspects to consumption is useful for sustainable marketers. Clearly, a limitation is that consumers can have differing approaches depending on the situation, their disposable income and where they are in the lifecycle. Furthermore, they can display more than one aspect of consumption, i.e. sometimes they are rational whereas other times they may be hedonistic.

As discussed in Chapter 1, the stakeholder concept has informed marketing strategists' understanding of the implications of the sustainability agenda (Belz & Peattie, 2009). To assess stakeholders, consider the power they wield, their legitimacy and their urgency (see Figure 1.3). Drawing on the sustainable consumer literature (Jackson, 2005), Figure 3.6 illustrates how (as with power, legitimacy and urgency) segments can be identified germane to the three elements of TBL namely People, Planet and Profit to produce a Sustainable Segmentation Typology (SST).

The typology in Figure 3.6 identifies potential segments, each of which may need a different 'Comms Mix' (see Section 4.1). Ultimately, in order to meet the needs, wants

Table 3.2 How aspects of consumption relate to sustainably motivated consumers

Aspect	*Consumption Pattern*	*Comment*
Rational consumption	Sustainably motivated consumers make purchases by going through a logical DMP based on reason, having evaluated the product against both conventional and sustainable criteria. The importance and significance of sustainable credentials influences the DMP	Consumer behaviour can always be influenced by marketing efforts which are grounded in logic and provide complete information for the cognitive evaluation of the product choices available. Sustainable consumption results from people being well-informed
Habitual consumption	Routines and habits account for many purchase decisions. The general disinterest that results from habitual consumption results in consumers not bothering to adopt more sustainable routines such as buying more local food produce or reducing meat consumption	For habitual types of purchase the ability, motivation and opportunity of the consumer to gather and process information is low and therefore consumers rely on simple cues to make their decisions
Sociological consumption	Shopping fulfils specific social and cultural needs. Hence, consumption is embedded in the socio-cultural fabric of society, playing a particular role in the lives of individual consumers and in consumer groups	People engage in consumption for the sake of consumption, which contrary to sustainability
Hedonistic consumption	Pleasure may be derived from the very act of shopping itself. The use of goods and services or merely their possession is how some consumers derive satisfaction and personal gratification	If consumers are addicted to consumption because of the enjoyment they derive from shopping itself, this may work against sustainable principles
Self-identity consumption	Consumption solely to satisfy and construct consumers' identities at social and psychological levels. Difficult to resolve with socially responsible and environmentally friendly consumption	A clear contrast exists in attitudes between consumption and sustainability

Source: Adapted from Emery (2012, pp 71–74).

and expectations of customers, marketers need to map how and where value is created, i.e. does it reside with the customers or in the co-creation of a service (see Figure 2.2).

Organisations can support changes aimed at resolving stakeholder conflicts by:

- building understanding by sharing information
- creating plans for SM implementation
- ensuring people are aware of the financial commitment
- demonstrating managerial commitment
- encouraging participation and contributions throughout the company
- sustaining internal marketing (IM) programmes (see Chapter 6), creating healthy responses to sustainability ideas.

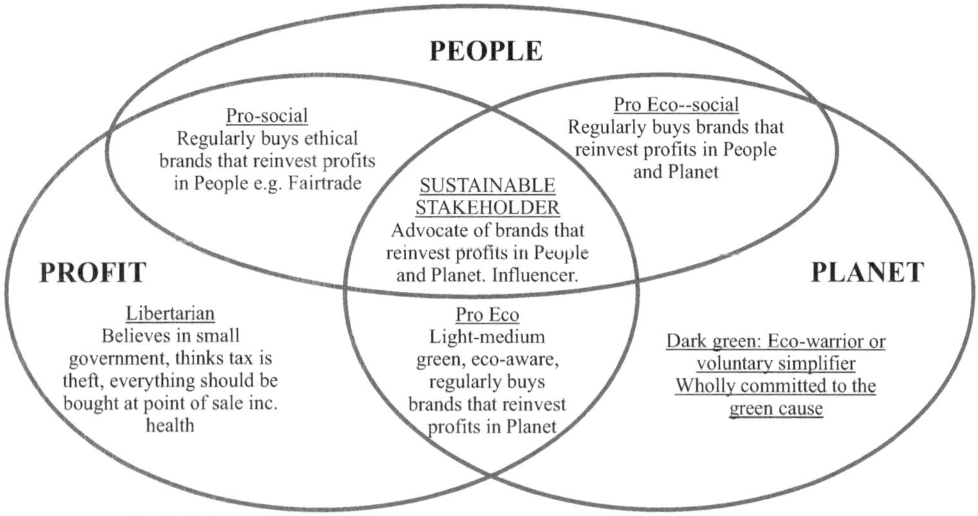

Figure 3.6 Sustainable stakeholder typology (SST).

Source: Adapted from Richardson *et al* (2015, p 83).

A TBL-Based B2C DMP

Belz and Peattie (2009, p 17) insist changing "our production and consumption systems cannot be achieved without changing marketing mindsets and practices". Kollat *et al* (1972) insisted the crux of consumer behaviour researchers' dilemma is that they seek to engage in theoretical and conceptual research and, at the same time to meet the "action" needs of the users. This is made more difficult as consumers increasingly prioritise ethical and green spending (Co-op, 2021). Models and frameworks need to be adapted to incorporate the TBL (see Richardson, 2022). Ashman *et al* (2015) suggest that the BAU DMP model, with some minor tweaks, still provides valuable insights into and explanations of consumer decision making. Minor tweaks are, however, not enough to stop the continuation of BAU. Alvis and Avison (2021) argue against BAU as it assumes little progress on the circular economy. They insist under BAU

- recycling rates will remain at low levels
- there will be little or no growth in remanufacturing, repair or rental services
- there will be minimal growth related to recycling and repair.

Most consumers are unaware that they go through such a process. By understanding the value sought and consumer behaviour, marketers can create the correct materials, environments and additional support across varying touchpoints. Increasingly, Marketers use the DMP to 'support' consumers in their decision making prior to the purchasing decision itself and even before the problem has been recognised (see Figure 3.1). Critical Marketers (see Chapter 2) insist traditional marketing notions such as the 'customer is always right', have always been disingenuous. For BAU marketers, the customer is only right if they buy their brands. A more customer-centric view (see Richardson & Cassop Thompson, 2019, 2023) is that it may be better for the customer not to buy a particular brand at a specific time. Customer-centricity is key component of SM (Richardson *et al*, 2015) and should transform the Marketing Mix (see Chapter 4).

Increasingly, consumers buy products identified as Fairtrade or locally produced. Often, 'locality' is a determinant of higher prices. As discussed, buyers have a complex set of needs, wants and norms that can interact and even conflict (Belz & Peattie, 2009).

Example: Veja is a Fairtrade trainer brand who is also BCorp accredited. They aim to create durable shoes without compromising on sustainability. This meant working with unusual materials like wild rubber from the Amazonian Forest for soles and recycled plastic bottles to create a new kind of mesh (Bellini, 2021). They operate with full transparency throughout their production, from the wages they pay to the way they source their materials. By working directly with small scale producers in Peru and Brazil, they can agree prices in advance for the rubber and cotton, ensuring the producers earn a decent living and reinvest in their farms (*ibid*). Veja are an exemplar of using locality and Fairtrade suppliers. Also, they unapologetically strive to manufacture shoes that will be long-lasting. Demand for such goods and services is growing. Furthermore, interest is growing in how such issues can build and enhance fashion brands. Veja support UN SDGs 3, 8, 9 and 12.

There is often a learning process as consumers move through the DMP. What is learned informs the next cycle and this extends to options post use. These include the Three Rs (see Chapter 1) as well as up-cycling or redistribution. Figure 3.7 portrays a DMP that has been substantially amended to incorporate the TBL into its core.

The TBL DMP raises the importance of Ethical and Environmental support for consumers and marketers. Instead of these key areas being relegated to the internal or external influences (Figure 3.1), they are now core to the DMP. Fashion manufacturers and retailers *must* assume that prospective customers will seek information on ethical and ecological matters.

A limitation of the original BAU DMP (Figure 3.1) is that it is often portrayed without feedback loops between the stages. This implied that it was a linear process that (once started) had to be seen through to completion. Common sense suggests this is not the case. In Figure 3.7, the inter-stage feedback (and feed-forward) loops are represented with dashed arrows. Online retailers face the challenge of prospective buyers disengaging from the process despite putting items into the 'basket'. In stores, customers who try on an item may decide it is not for them. In these cases, they prospective fashion buyer may repeat the step (say 'Information Search' to 'Information Evaluation') several times before progressing. Marketers should analyse such behaviour as it may result from there being inadequate information or customer support. This is particularly problematic for those identified as innovators or early adopters (see Figure 4.8). Once the decision to purchase is made, suppliers must inform consumers how in future their products can be reused, repaired or recycled. The Three Rs should become a key part of the company's IMC.

The BAU DMP largely assumed that the consumer would commit to buying the item. There is little risk to marketers who adopt the TBL-based DMP model. Customers

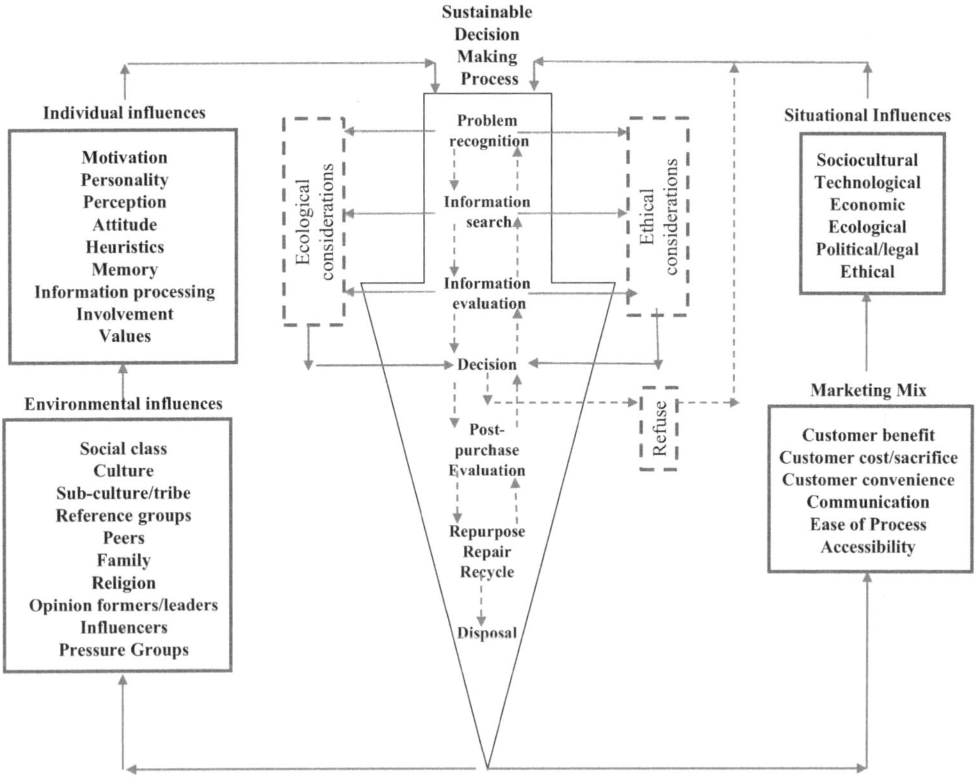

Figure 3.7 The TBL-based DMP for consumers.

Source: Adapted from Richardson (2020).

who have neither interest in Ethics nor the Environment can simply pass through the process as easily as if it was the outdated BAU DMP (Figure 3.1). What is being proposed is to offer support to the increasing number of buyers (see Co-op, 2021) who are concerned about sustainability. Sustainable value cannot be given, rather it can be created and made available for the buyers to take. Value only resides in the mind of the customer (Richardson & Cassop Thompson, 2019, 2023). As is demonstrated herein, being increasingly sustainable can differentiate marketers from their BAU competitors. Such differentiation can justify a higher price (see the Patagonia example in Section 4.4).

TBL Support for 'Information Search' and 'Information Evaluation' DMP Stages

As discussed, the 'Information Search' and 'Information Evaluation' stages (Figures 3.1 and 3.7) are those most impacted by communications. Marketers must support prospects by offering extensive information apropos sustainable practices. This should be explicit as against tacit (see Chapter 6). Consumers have differing degrees of complexity of decision-making owing to their use of information. Information seeking is present to some degree for all consumers. The challenge for sustainable marketers, is to employ a variety of information sources as part of their IMC (see Figure 4.14).

The 'Information Evaluation' stage may involve consumers evaluating an item of clothing on a trial basis before committing to a purchase. This should be encouraged, as a better alternative than the sale being lost. However, if the try-before-you-buy leads to rejected items being unsaleable and sent to landfill, the retailers have a problem. This is neither cost-effective nor ecologically sound practice. Increasingly, online fashion retailers (including H&M, Zara, Boohoo, Uniqlo and Next) are charging for returned goods. Where such trials are not possible, consumers may seek the opinion of others (say influencers) who have reviewed the object in question. At this point the marketer has ceded control, if they ever had it in the first place.

Consumers are increasingly cynical regarding claims made by suppliers and buy-in to the notion of green washing. They also tend towards scepticism regarding ethical policies (see Co-op, 2021). Hence, they go to greater lengths to evaluate whether manufacturers and retailers 'practice what they preach'. This can be done by incorporating the Three Rs. In so doing they will be better placed to support sustainable consumers.

Limitations

Figure 3.7 illustrates how the internal characteristics, that influence the DMP, can be augmented to make them better suited to the TBL. A criticism is that (as with the BAU DMP) these factors are not prioritised and may influence one another. Green consumers do consider environmental factors when shopping (Co-op, 2021) but engage more frequently in (non-purchasing) activities such as switching off lights and recycling paper (daily activities). It is arguable whether seeking sustainable (i.e. societal and/or green) value has anything other than a weak influence on the DMP of many consumers (Young *et al*, 2010). Analysing why corresponding value-types may have a weaker influence on the DMP is key to understanding and changing consumer behaviour towards sustainable consumption. Weaker green influences may result from brand strength, culture, demographic characteristics, finance, habit, lack of information, lifestyles, personalities or trading off between different ethical factors (*ibid*).

Key Findings

1 Buying' is always guided by consumers' thoughts, feelings and actions. Consumers take on attitudes, beliefs, opinions and values of others. Hence companies who are not aware of changes in society run the risk of alienating customers.
2 Providing customers with what they require by anticipating their needs and satisfying them will entice them to come back time and time again. Companies are increasingly seeing 'value' from the customer's perspective.
3 Marketers must understand how customers (B2B, B2C) behave to ensure they are supported throughout the DMP and have the required information to help them make confident and correct decisions.
4 Consumers have complex influences and spend more time searching for information pre and/or post-sales.
5 Organisational buyers are influenced by personal, organisational and environmental factors.

Activities

1 The Chartered Institute of Purchasing & Supply (a.k.a. CIPS) is a well-respected organisation for B2B 'buyers' (see www.cips.org/).
2 Use Google's Customer Barometer to generate insight into how customers use both online and offline information sources (see www.consumerbarometer.com).
3 Visit Google's Zero Moment of Truth (ZMOT) site (see https://thinkwithgoogle). It provides interesting case studies and support materials. Does this differ from the B2C DMP? If so … how?
4 Access the JD Power survey (see www.jdpower.com/). Using a range of different cars, how should marketers respond to issues that arise?
5 Use Trip advisor to review a number of well-known hotel chains (see www.tripadvisor.co.uk/). How should marketers respond to issues that arise?

References

Alvis, S. & Avison, Z. (2021) *Levelling up through Circular Economy Jobs*. Green Alliance policy insight paper August 2021 www.green-alliance.org.uk (accessed 20-10-22).

Ashman, R., Solomon, M.R., & Wolny, J. (2015) An old model for a new age: Consumer decision making in participatory digital culture, *Journal of Customer Behaviour*, 14(2), pp. 127–146. DOI:10.1362/147539215X14373846805743

Bellini, L. (2021) *The Glossary's B Corp Fashion Guide: The Ethical Fashion Brands to Know-From Luxury Fashion Houses to Innovative Footwear Brands, These are the Trailblazing Names Doing Their Bit for the Planet*. 21 October 2021, FASHION https://theglossarymagazine.com/fashion/b-corp-fashion-brands/ (accessed 28-08-23).

Belz, F-M. & Peattie, K. (2009) *Sustainability Marketing — A Global Perspective*. Chichester: Wiley & Sons.

Blackwell, R.D., Miniard, P.W. & Engel, J.F. (2001) *Consumer Behavior*. Fort Worth, Texas: Dryden Press, Harcourt College Publishers.

Brassington, F. & Pettitt, S. (2006) *Principles of Marketing*, 4th Edition. Harlow: Pearson.

Co-op. (2021) *Ethical Consumerism Report 2021 – Can we consume back better*? www.co-operative.coop/ethical-consumerism-report-2021 (accessed 22-08-23).

Dibb, S., Simkin, L, Pride, W.M. & Ferrell, O.C. (2006) *Marketing Concepts and Strategies*, 5th European Edition. Boston: Houghton Mifflin.

Dudovskiy, J. (2022) *Consumer Decision Making Process: A Detailed Analysis*. https://research-methodology.net/consumer-decision-making-process-a-detailed-analysis/ (accessed 25-08-23).

Emery, B. (2012) *Sustainable Marketing*. Harlow: Pearson Education.

Engel, J.F., Kollat, D.T. & Blackwell, R.D. (1968) *Consumer Behavior*. New York: Holt, Rinehart & Winston.

Gomez-Trujillo, A.M., Velez-Ocampo, J. & Gonzalez-Perez, M.A. (2020) A literature review on the causality between sustainability and corporate reputation. *What goes first? Management of Environmental Quality: An International Journal*, 31(2), pp. 406–430. DOI:10.1108/MEQ-09-2019-0207

Herzberg, F., Mausner, B. & Snyderman, B.B. (1959) *The Motivation to Work*. New Brunswick (USA): Transaction Publishers.

Houston, M.J. & Rothschild, M.L. (1978) Conceptual and methodological perspectives in involvement, in Jain, S.C. (Ed.), *Research Frontiers in Marketing: Dialogues and Directions*. Chicago, IL: American Marketing Association, pp. 184–187.

Howard, J.A. & Sheth, J. (1969) *The Theory of Buyer Behaviour*. London: John Wiley.

Jackson, T. (2005) *Motivating Sustainable Consumption- A Review of Evidence on Consumer Behaviour and Behavioural Change*; A report to the Sustainable Development Research Network

January 2005. Funded by the Economic and Social Research Council's Sustainable Technologies Programme (STP).

Kollat, D.T., Blackwell, R.D. & Engel, J.F. (1972) The current status of consumer behavior research: Developments during the 1968–1972 period. in *SV – Proceedings of the Third Annual Conference of the Association for Consumer Research*, eds. M. Venkatesan, Chicago, IL: *Association for Consumer Research*, pp. 576–585.

Margolis, J.D. & Walsh, J.P. (2003) Misery loves companies: Rethinking social initiatives by business. *Administrative Science Quarterly*, 48, pp. 268–305. DOI:10.2307/3556659

Maslow, A. (1954). *Motivation and Personality*. New York: Harper & Row.

Mitchell, V.W. & Harris, G. (2005). The importance of consumers' perceived risk in retail strategy. *European Journal of Marketing*, 39(7/8), pp. 821–837. DOI:10.1108/03090560510601789

Richardson, N. (2022) How new sustainability typologies will reshape traditional approaches to loyalty. *Italian Journal of Marketing. Special issue: "S.I. Sustainable Marketing and Performance Management*, February pp. 289–315. DOI:10.1007/s43039-022-00047-y

Richardson, N. & Cassop Thompson, M. (2019) A new positioning framework for organizational value: Juxtaposing organizational value positions with customer centricity. *Strategic Change. Special edition: Sustainable Business Models*. 28(2) pp. 123–132. DOI:10.1002/jsc.2253

Richardson, N. & Cassop Thompson, M. (2023) How improved understanding of what constitutes 'value' may lead to better underpinning of Corporate Social Responsibility (CSR). *Journal of Global Responsibility*, pp. 2041–2568. DOI:10.1108/JGR-10-2022-0115

Richardson, N., James, J. & Kelley, N. (2015) *Customer-Centric Marketing: Supporting Sustainability in the Digital Age*. London: Kogan Page.

Robinson, P.J., Farris, C.W. & Wind, Y. (1967) *Industrial Buying and Creative Marketing*. Alyn & Bacon: University of Michigan.

Young, C.W., Hwang, K., McDonald, S. & Oates, C. (2010) Sustainable consumption: Green consumer behaviour when purchasing products *Sustainable Development*, 18, pp. 20–31. DOI:10.1002/sd.394

4 The Marketing Mix

Abstract

This chapter considers tactical tools, namely the Marketing Mix. All marketers must understand the fundamentals of communication if they are to gain insights into customers. Customers want easy access to products and services hence marketers must focus on convenience. The basics of product portfolio management are addressed as well as considering how sustainability factors (such as the greening process) are changing marketers' approaches. The key underpinning perspectives on pricing are considered. The chapter concludes by reflecting on the nature of services, the extended Marketing Mix (for services) and related issues.

Learning Outcomes

At the end of this chapter students will be able to

- discuss the nature of communications and associated key models
- examine the attributes of products and how they are managed
- assess how marketers make pricing decisions
- evaluate whether goods are distributed conveniently for the customer
- explain the impact of sustainable consumption on the Marketing Mix
- analyse how services and goods marketing differ.

In the 1960s, Neil Borden and Edmund J. McCarthy laid the foundations for what has become the key framework for tactical marketing (McCarthy, 1960; Borden, 1964). The Marketing Mix (hereafter the Mix) features Product, Price, Place and Promotion (i.e. the 4 Ps). The Mix was originally aimed at goods manufacturers. This manufacturing focus is increasingly outdated, as many countries continue their transition towards being post-industrial economies, deriving their GDP mainly from services. Furthermore, criticism continues to be levelled that the Mix lacks customer centricity (Richardson *et al*, 2015). Hence, customer centric variants are:

Communications	(… Promotion)
Convenience	(… Place)
Customer benefits	(… Product) and
Cost	(… Price).

DOI: 10.4324/9781003434214-5

4.1 Communications (a.k.a. 'Marcomms' a.k.a. 'Comms')

The need to promote a brand is not new. The nineteenth-century showman, entrepreneur and 'icon of American spirit' PT Barnum famously said

> "Without promotion something terrible happens, nothing!"

Marketers prefer the terms 'comms' or 'marcomms'. Promotion represents a one-directional monologue aimed at customers which assumes the customer is listening, engaged or even interested. 'Comms' implies a dialogue where companies seek to 'sell not tell'. Good salespeople know that listening is more important than talking.

Schramm (1955) reflected on the different tasks 'comms' could perform namely sharing knowledge, questioning or instructing. Ideally, 'marcomms' should be simple, where messages are received and understood unambiguously by the intended audience. In reality, this rarely happens.

Figure 4.1 develops the traditional view of 'comms' as a linear process, where a sender 'encodes' a message (using spoken or written language, images, signs or symbols) which is delivered via a source or medium to a receiver. Credibility rises when prospects and/or consumers see products being used by their peers. 'Ads' designed to create awareness of a pair of trainers for teenagers aged 13–16, would probably use models of the same age. The message has been 'encoded' so the receivers will respond positively. The same trainers on a middle-aged man would send a completely different message, even if all other factors were the same. The youth-orientated 'ad' may not appeal to those over

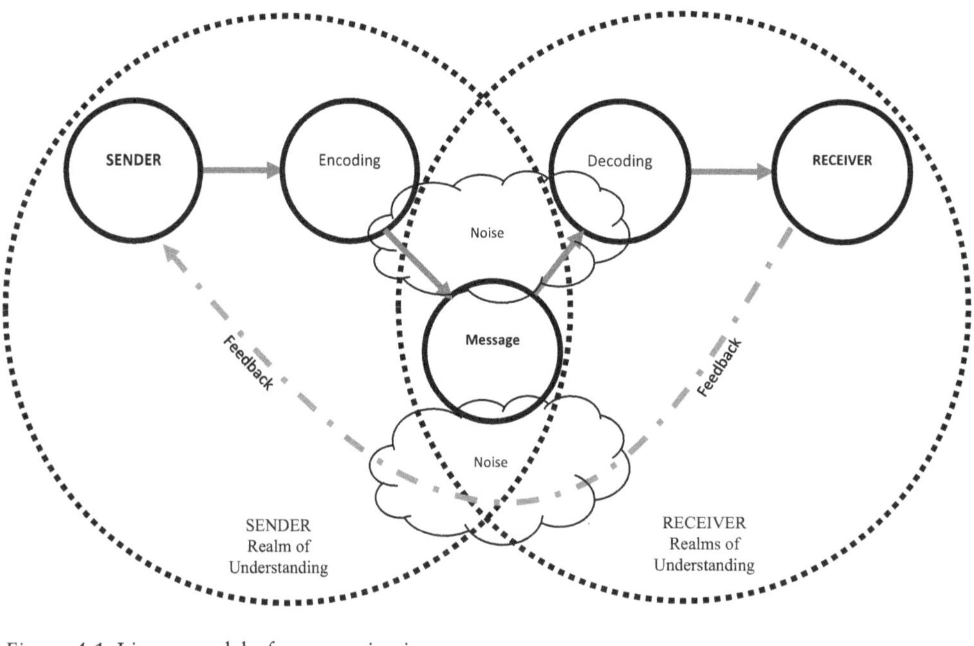

Figure 4.1 Linear model of communications.

Sources: Adapted from Schramm (1955); Shannon and Weaver (1949).

30, which is understandable as they are not the target receivers. With young audiences, messages should be simple and oft repeated. Humour is often used when seeking the attention of younger audiences. Care needs to be taken when using humour, as it does not always translate across generations or beyond cultural boundaries.

Other factors inform the choice of tools and the configuration of the message itself. Marketers must identify the audience/receiver, research their lifestyle choices, reading habits, preferred TV programmes or channels, hobbies and affiliations. The deeper the understanding, the richer and more focused the encoding and message being created. Messages must achieve clear objectives, i.e. raising awareness, selling the product's benefits, stimulating feedback or increasing market share. With focused objectives, the message's development will be more meaningful and easier to convey. What does the brand represent? What is the value offered? The competitors' choices of 'comms' tools (i.e. those used, the frequency and success) inform the message as does whether it relates to products or services. Marketers ascertain, via feedback, whether customers had received the message, understood it and responded appropriately. Memorability can be achieved in numerous ways, e.g. using music, animation, fantasy, imagery and events. Whilst useful, this may not take into account other stakeholders and their realms of understanding. Terms such as CSR and sustainability are easily misinterpreted.

Noise

Messages are subject to 'noise' during encoding (by marketers), decoding (by customers) and during feedback. Indeed, noise itself influences the encoding/decoding (Figure 4.1). It can be anything that impacts receiving the message or distorts its original meaning. Professor Chris Fill, a seminal 'comms' author, warned that consumers may be subjected to several thousand marketing messages daily. Marketers must understand noise and create 'comms' that 'cut-though' the clutter 'bombarding' the consumer.

Noise can involve misinformation (accidentally incorrect messages) or disinformation (deliberately incorrect messages). Automotive manufacturers who deliberately misled consumers regarding the CO_2 outputs from diesel engines engaged in disinformation, which ultimately proved to be hugely expensive. Misinformation arises from the oversupply of information about products or services. Alternatively, it results from language that is not easily understood by consumers, whether from a marketer and/or the competition. It is no surprise that marketer-dominated sources are struggling to gain 'cut-through'.

'Comms' can be inclusive or exclusive. Progressive marketers should practice inclusive communications. Some parties deliberately communicate in a way to exclude others. This is not new. Foucault talked at length about the use of communication as the means of wielding power. Disinformation is also about wielding power. It is often covert where the originator hides their identity. Sadly, governments, as well as unscrupulous organisations, practice such techniques.

Katz and Lazarsfeld (1955) noted that mass media communications often first reach opinion leaders and formers (Figure 4.2). Social communications do not necessarily flow in logical, linear paths. Models should consider the extra directions of communication between parties. Figure 4.2 illustrates how receivers may communicate with the Opinion Leader, other 'receivers' or the original sender of the message. Hence, rather than there just being one or two steps, in the process, there can be a multitude – what is known as 'many-to-many' communication. Opinion formers and leaders cascade messages using their own interpretation and influence the receivers further down the

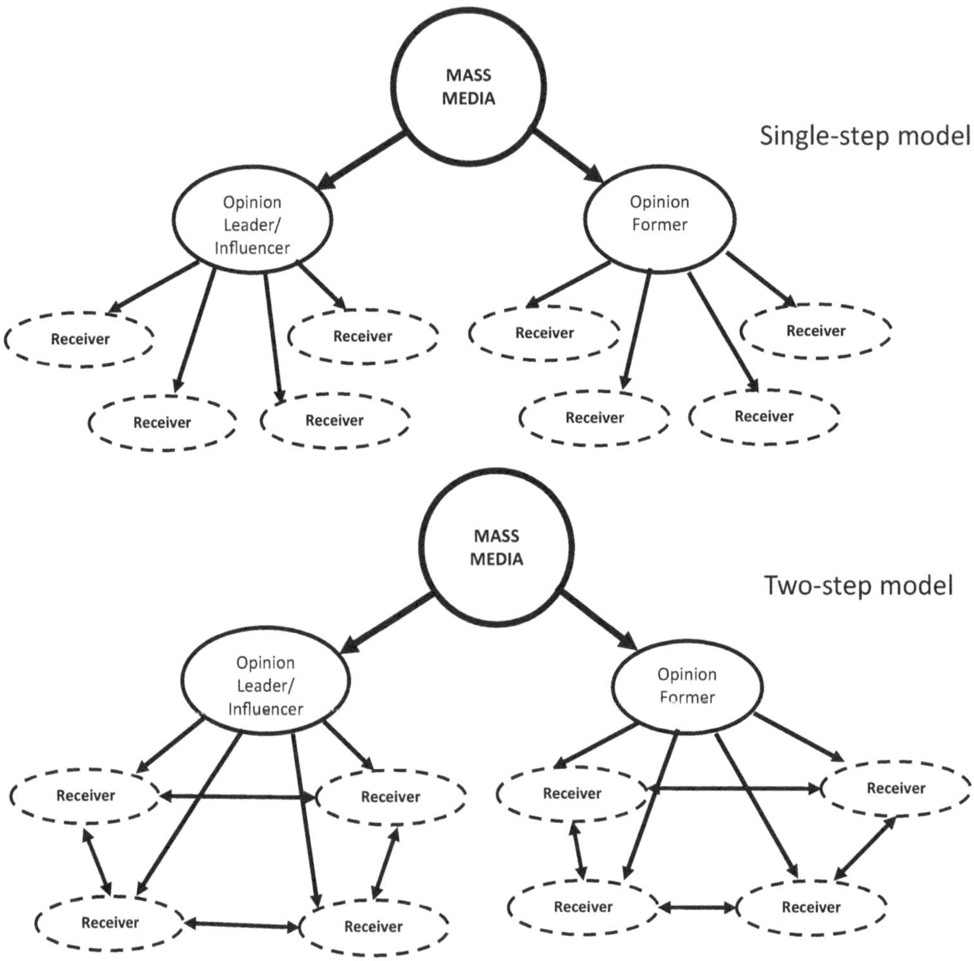

Figure 4.2 One and two-step communications.

Source: Adapted from Katz and Lazarsfeld (1955).

'Two-step Model'. When using such Influencers, marketers must ensure that they are perceived to be credible, sincere and authentic. Furthermore, Influencers will establish a two-way dialogue with their audience. If this is the case, influencers may help to establish trust.

An Opinion Former is somebody who consumers trust because of their education, profession or expertise. They need to be perceived to be independent of any marketing organisation. Jeremy Clarkson is an Opinion Former as he is perceived to be independent of the automotive industry and sufficiently knowledgeable to be considered a maven. Mavens have high levels of knowledge and can be deemed experts in their fields. Using experts supports building trust and credibility into marcomms activities and raising a brand's profile. The Product Adoption Process (see Section 4.3) is a useful model to illustrate how consumers can be influenced by others. Consumers adopt new products at different speeds and junctures. The adoption can be speeded up by using credible influencers.

Opinion leaders (including Influencers) are not necessarily experts; rather they are trusted because of their social standing, closeness or 'relatability'. Influencers have specific interests or passions, e.g. dining, films, technology, gaming, music, fashion, cycling (amongst many others). They create user-generated content (UGC) on blogs and social media. Since the advent of Web 2.0, UGC has increased immeasurably. Some sites have failed to react to changes, e.g. Vine, whilst others are being challenged by newcomers (e.g. Tik Tok). Facebook is still a social networking colossus, however will it be so in, say, 10 years' time? New sites (namely Threads and Mastadon) responded to X (the social media site formerly known as Twitter) post-Elon Musk's acquisition.

Word of Mouth (WoM)

Many linguistics experts argue that written words are more powerful than spoken words. Others insist that imagery is more powerful than text (i.e. a picture is worth a thousand words). Most marketers believe that 'Word of Mouth' is the most powerful means of communication. Particularly when making larger, riskier purchases, consumers need information to make better decisions and often turn to those who offer impartial, credible advice. WoM has now morphed into word-of-mouse (eWoM) or World of Mouth. The latter captures how negative WoM and/or eWoM can pass around the world instantaneously. Marketers must assume that their customers and prospects access 'unbiased' peer comments, pre-purchase. The historical top-down approach is increasingly outdated; marketers must design their marcomms to easily reach Influencers *and* buyers.

Push, Pull and Profile Strategies

Push strategies 'push' stock through the marketing channels from one intermediary to the next. A manufacturer may develop communications, say, encouraging retailers to increase their monthly orders for improved discounts and may be willing to advertise it with posters, direct marketing or via their sales force. 'Comms' will always be a social process. It 'flows' in streams (or certain directions), but there is less acceptance of 'push-based' communications where customers are told what to buy or why. Consumers are less inclined to be told who or what they 'become' through consumption.

A 'pull' strategy involves end-users seeking information, creating footfall or purchasing goods and services. In 'pull' strategies, consumers act of their own volition and are the end users. Manufacturers may develop appropriate 'comms' tactics, i.e. a sales promotion aimed at the end-user by advertising instore and/or on the packaging. It could suggest that if they buy one of the advertised products, they will receive a second free in store (BOGOF – Buy one get one free) or later (BOGOL — buy one get one later).

Many organisations seek to communicate about issues other than their products and services with key stakeholders or organisations identified as having a vested interest in the brand, corporate personality, image or identity. Therefore, 'profile' strategies, the receiver could be any (or even all) stakeholders. 'Profile' strategies can be used when promoting an organisation's stance on sustainability. Promoting companies' ethical and ecological practices can contribute to good WoM. This supports a personalised 'pull' method, where users take active roles. With global levels of networked people, the potential exists for (almost) everyone to communicate with each other. However, marketers must not think customers (and other receivers) are passive. Customers share, create and discuss ideas (Figure 4.2), using social media sites, blogs, forums, and review/price comparison sites. Customers and prospects still talk face-to-face.

The 'Comms' Mix

The 'Comms' mix has sometimes been portrayed with five 'tools' and occasionally six. Herein, six key 'comms' tools are offered (Table 4.1).

Table 4.1 contrasts the strengths and weaknesses of the key 'Comms' mix tools. Marketers must find the right blend of tools and platforms to achieve their marketing objectives. More traditional advertising activities are covered in detail elsewhere (see texts by Shelley Rodgers and Esther Thorson or, alternatively, Chris Fill). Driving the sustainability agenda increasingly uses the internet and other technological developments. Search Engines also provide the opportunity to advertise brands against competitors through organic search results; hence the need for search engine optimisation (SEO). Digital media can also deliver (and support the sharing of) viral ads whose content is more effective when funny, novel, entertaining and contemporary. Advertising is a major battleground where content suppliers are increasingly protective. The battle over whose site should be the gateway (and hence the major beneficiary of advertising and click-through revenues) will intensify.

PR is often construed as being about media relations, i.e. getting a brand in the newspaper, trade magazines, on radio or TV, whether at a local, regional or national level. PR is much more than media relations; the Chartered Institute of Public Relations (CIPR) defines PR as being

> "the discipline which looks after reputation, with the aim of earning understanding and support and influencing opinion and behaviour. It is the planned and sustained effort to establish and maintain goodwill and mutual understanding between an organisation and its publics".
>
> (CIPR, 2023)

The Public Relations and Communications Association (PRCA) suggests it is

> "about the way organisations communicate with the public, promote themselves, and build a positive reputation and public image. The way an organisation is represented in the media has a huge impact on how people perceive it".
>
> (PRCA, 2023)

PR practitioners see publics as being synonymous with stakeholders. Marketers use both terms with stakeholders being engaged whereas publics have interest but no direct engagement. Examples of negative PR can also be seen online, as complaints, poor customer or employee treatment, unethical practices (to name but a few) can be shared. Negative PR has the potential to go viral and reach much larger, sometimes global, audiences causing significant brand damage. Corporate websites can also add PR sections allowing journalists direct access to information, stories and contacts. Social media marketing has revolutionised the way clients want their accounts to be handled. They see PR as being a key tool within the extended marcomms mix (Figure 4.3). In most cases, PR agencies respond to briefs from budget-holding marketers (directors and managers).

Table 4.1 Key 'Comms' mix tools with considerations

Comms Tool	*Examples*	*Advantages*	*Disadvantages*
Advertising Can be used effectively in the B2B and B2C markets. Online platforms offer more targeted, personalised content based on search behaviour and personal profiles.	TV, Newspaper/Magazine, Cinema, Radio, Locational. Online includes Banner ads, pop-ups, interstitial ads. Banner ads can use other platforms/vehicles, i.e. mobile apps and mobile optimised websites. Other areas are paid for display ads, via Pay-Per-Click (PPC), or targeted 'social' ads	• Can be cost effective per person reached. • Repetition of ads aids memory. • Long term image can be created. • Creativity used in some media choices can cut through noise.	• Impersonal • Indirect • Passive • Possibly high upfront costs • Difficult to evaluate
Sales Promotion Can be used effectively in the B2B and B2C market. can be delivered in a more timely, personalised manner and can be linked to loyalty schemes	BOGOF; Competitions; Free Prize Draws; Money off coupons; Loyalty award schemes; Bundles; online-only deals, time limited discounts; the specialist voucher and coupon sites (e.g. Vouchercloud), communities (moneysavingexpert.com), email, SMS, MMS and technologies (e.g. Augmented Reality).	• Can add value. • Can act as an inducement. • Short-term tactical tool. • Everybody likes to think they've got something for less.	• Laws and regulations apply • Credibility • Difficulty forecasting sales • Unsolicited messages can be considered 'spam'
Public Relations Good for B2B, B2C, SMEs & charities. Develops relations with stakeholders; effective in improving stakeholder relations. Supports brands in crisis.	Editorial coverage; Press conferences; Launch themes; Open days; Media Relations; Messages can be shared very quickly and easily online, so crisis response communications can be optimised.	• Cost effective. • Further credibility compared to advertising & sales promotion. • Good for developing relationships.	• Difficult to evaluate. • Difficult if not impossible to control e.g. media
Personal Selling Often face-to-face (F2F) with sales representatives visiting buyers in B2B markets or customer representatives interacting with consumers. Use of KAM in B2B market is crucial. Use in B2C market is extremely effective.	Sales Assistants (retail); Sales Reps, Key Account Managers (KAM). Increasingly organisations engage online using real-time communications i.e. 'online chats' or 'live chats'. Useful with high involvement purchases, whether customer driven (clicking on links), or via a pop-up box.	• Personal • Direct • Aids customer feedback. • Timely feedback • Used to form relationships, particularly in B2B market.	• Expensive • Suffers from 'people problems' • Investment in training and customer service skills required

(Continued)

Table 4.1 (Continued)

Comms Tool	*Examples*	*Advantages*	*Disadvantages*
Direct Marketing Effective tool to use in B2B and B2C market; customers must give permission; needs clarity about the data being used (preferably collected in-house); is the medium appropriate for the target group? is the message appropriate for the medium?	Direct Mail; Direct Response advertising; Telemarketing The key channels are postal, SMS (or MMS), email, Bluetooth and social media.	• Personal • Direct • Easy to evaluate compared with other tools. • Two-way communication process	• Can lack credibility • care required with personal data; • GDPR–Unsolicited messages can be considered 'spam' • Customer can incur costs (which need to be justified and clear in communications)
Sponsorship Fees are paid, usually by companies, to support a person, organization or activity. Can be effective but has risks if those being sponsored act inappropriately	Programmes Events Sports teams Personalities	• Raises brand awareness & corporate image. • Can portray positive associations between sponsored and sponsor	• Difficult to evaluate • What happens if what you have sponsored receives negative press?

Source: Adapted from Gosnay and Richardson (2008, pp 107–108).

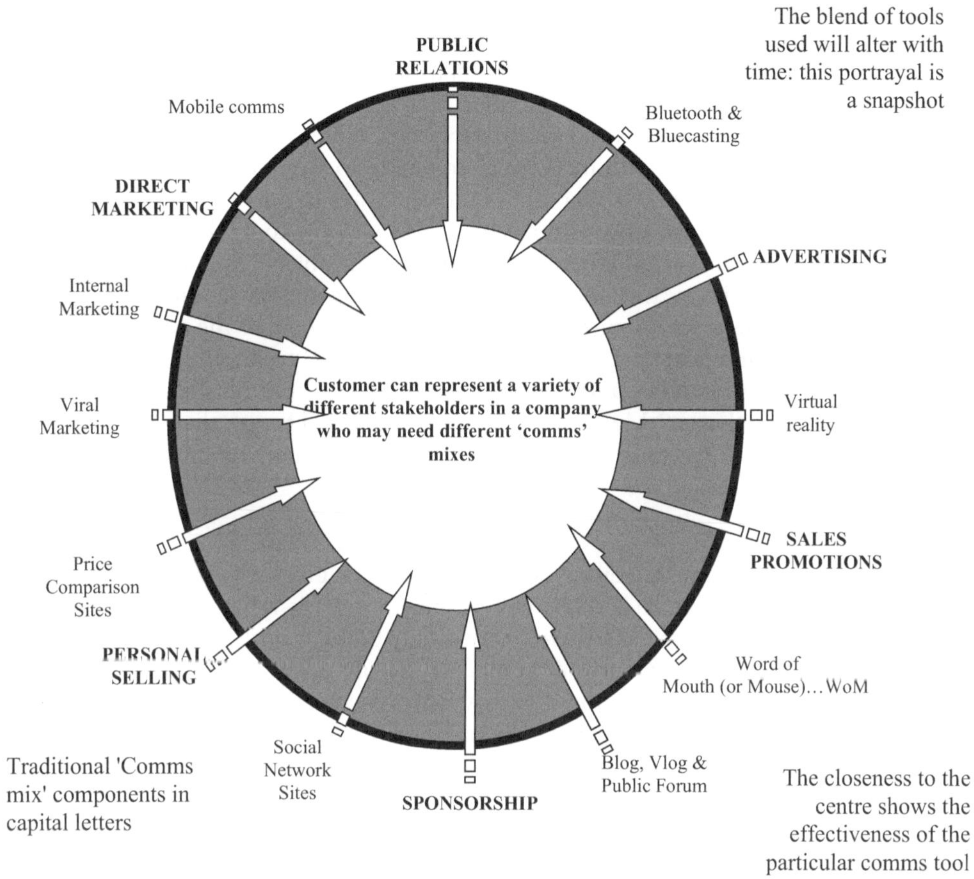

Figure 4.3 Expanded communications mix.

Source: Adapted from Richardson (2010, p 45).

Today organisations develop marcomms campaigns using more tools and vehicles than those captured in Table 4.1. Whilst not exhaustive, Figure 4.3 illustrates some of the tools available to marketers seeking to achieve their objectives.

The differing 'comms' tools (Figure 4.3) do different jobs and blending a selection of them together in an effective campaign generate benefits (i.e. wider audience reach or more consistent messaging). This reduces the confusion of mixed messages whilst increasing the likelihood of 'cutting through' the NOISE and being remembered.

Digital Platforms

An area of communication that has been dynamic in recent years is digital media. It has significantly increased the number of opportunities for marketers when engaging with various audiences. The development of Relationship Marketing (see Chapter 7) had already led to improvements in communications between companies and their suppliers, staff and customers. This has been further improved with the use of two-way communications tools. However, the growth in such two-way communications has driven increasing demands and expectations (within companies and by customers) for more immediacy, transparency and personalised contact. Digital platforms provide opportunities, channels and platforms that can be linked to the Comms Mix.

Mobile devices – Mobile devices, e.g. smartphones, tablets and smart watches, lend themselves to online material with increasing streaming to handheld devices. Marketers can communicate with consumers who are (almost) always in possession of their smartphone which itself is (almost) always on. Smartphones from Apple, Huawei, Sony and Samsung (amongst others) are increasingly bundled with tablets. Tablets (including the substantial iPad Pro with a 12.9-inch screen) are still classed as mobile devices, providing a different experience to smartphones. At the other end of the scale, marketers will increasingly communicate via 'wearable tech' as 'comms' technology becomes more embedded into glasses, watches and clothing. Fifteen to 21-year olds spend more time online than watching 'legacy' Mainstream Media (MSM). They get their news increasingly via their mobiles. That said, it is not all plain sailing as many news-sharing sites are loss-making.

Example: Former fee-paying newspapers have now been given away *pro gratis*, e.g. the London Evening Standard. This new business model is reliant on advertising fees. Free papers such as the Metro are increasingly popular with young consumers despite largely recycling news stories and being heavily reliant on agencies such as Reuters and the Press Association (see www.pressassociation.com). Recent hard times saw long-established, esteemed companies such as Johnson Press struggling to find the right balance of online versus hard-copy content. Monetising websites is a challenge for all newspapers. The *Guardian* asks each contributor to make a donation – effectively, a twenty-first century honesty box for newspapers. By November 2021, the *Guardian* had over 1 million digital subscriptions, from 180 countries, of which half were recurring contributions.

Gaming platforms – Gaming is the most profitable entertainment market in the world. Gaming platforms are evolving, moving from being a niche activity to becoming central to home entertainment. Within gaming networks, such as Xbox Live, marketers can reach and engage with specific markets. Marketers advertise within video games, say FIFA, or offer games for free in exchange for being exposed to advertising messages. As consumers increasingly adopt smartphone technology, there is growth in 'casual' gamers who can be reached by banner and/or in-game advertising. Some organisations, such as Audi, have even created branded 'casual' games delivered via apps.

Indoor and outdoor kiosks – Kiosk's are small, freestanding increasingly sophisticated structures that can provide independent (asynchronous) informational or transactional services. They can be used to provide information in cities or shopping centres, conduct research and provide facilities to purchase or order products. Kiosks can also incorporate a variety of different applications such as Augmented Reality or Facial Recognition making them more interactive and more effective.

Interactive signage – Out of Home (OoH) is another emerging field of outdoor advertising using billboards, posters, bus shelters and street furniture. Traditional billboards are increasingly interactive as technology now allows facial recognition. It is early days, but age, gender and even emotions can be used to influence content.

Example: In 2010 Wall's used interactive techniques when their 'Share Happy' vending machines dispensed ice-cream to those willing to smile and have the pictures uploaded onto Facebook. The success of this project ultimately influenced Wall's partnering with Project Everyone (see www.project-everyone.org/) to launch The Happiness Project in 2023. Their aim is to teach 3 million children a set of happiness habits by 2025, through lessons designed to deliver smiles beyond the classroom (Walls, 2023).

Other fixed connected platforms — Smart TV's allow access to on-demand and online content. They are increasingly using voice commands and incorporating digital assistants, e.g. 'Google' or Alexa. TV service providers like Sky and Virgin also offer these services. One area of emerging interest relates to the 'internet of things' (IoT) where devices and platforms used daily can be connected including cars, TV's, computers, fridges, doorbells, cookers or thermostats. Marketers should work in a sympathetic, ethical way to improve the lives of individuals by providing the right control, the right content, at the right time and in the right place.

Example: In 2021 a legal case was brought between two neighbours over the use of a Ring (i.e. video-enabled) front doorbell attached to domestic properties. The judge ruled that the images and audio files were covered by the General Data Protection Regulation (GDPR). Effectively, the doorbell owner was a data controller and was thus expected to comply accordingly to the data protection principles. Amazon (Ring's parent company) issued a statement to Ring customers following the judgment: "We strongly encourage our customers to respect their neighbours' privacy and comply with any applicable laws when using their Ring product".

The Use of Communications Agencies

Budget shapes the choices of 'comms' tools and the type of agency used by marketers. The use of a 'comms' agency may be the optimal way to achieve marketing objectives. The two agency types available to marketers are

- large full-service agencies, e.g. Saatchi and Saatchi who can create, develop, plan and execute any 'comms' campaign as they employ specialists, have vast resources and can cross-co-ordinate all communication activities; and
- independent specialist agencies are generally cheaper as they do not have the vast overhead to service.

Many 'comms' consultants provide excellent services, often at a fraction of the cost of a full-service agency. Larger companies often employ multiple agencies, say one for design/creative, another for PR and yet another to cross-co-ordinate campaigns. When using agencies, they should be able to provide an analysis of the campaign. The focus may fall on the brief itself. Was the agency given the appropriate information, direction and budget to achieve the objectives? It is the responsibility of the marketer to ensure the brief is 'tight'. Any 'wiggle room' (or contingency) may be used by the agency to avoid being held responsible should a gap arise between what is delivered and what is expected.

4.2 Convenience (a.k.a. Place a.k.a. Distribution)

If companies ship goods, they must establish the cost of transporting products from A to B. The goods must arrive at the right time, in the right place, in the right condition and with the right post-delivery support. This is particularly important when shipping goods overseas. Marketers are expected to reduce the ecological impact (carbon footprint, pollutants or resource usage) whilst delivering goods. Those incapable of performing to high standards may lose customers to others who offer more convenience. 'Convenience' has replaced 'Place' in the Mix, as it is the benefit the customer gains. It links into their values. Simply put, focusing on 'convenience' can help companies to achieve a competitive advantage and to understand it further, it is useful to consider marketing channels and distribution logistics.

Marketing Channels

In the context of distribution, a marketing channel is the route used to deliver goods (and services) to customers. This can be done in different ways, hence channel design is important. Factors include cost, convenience, customer requirements and control. Furthermore, decisions need to be made regarding distributing products directly or indirectly. If indirect, the optimal length of supply channel needs to be used.

Direct distribution uses a Zero Level channel as no other business is involved. This does not include couriers or those delivering the goods. It refers to those who take a proportion of the sales price or profit and has been augmented by the use of technology to such an extent that a wide range of organisations now sell 'direct'. Recording artists are increasingly bypassing retailers and shipping direct to their audience. This increasingly popular option moves the artist (and supplier) closer to the customer AND retains a higher margin. The closer to the customer, the greater the likelihood of forming relationships, receiving timely feedback and, perhaps even more importantly, retaining control over how the product reaches the customer. Websites can attract customers and increasingly support their purchasing. Marketers must have effective postage and delivery systems to achieve complete satisfaction.

A one level channel features one intermediary between the manufacturer and customer. The intermediaries (i.e. retailers, wholesalers, agents or franchisors) move the product from the manufacturer to the customer. They have established networks of outlets to reach certain target markets. Marketers should identify mutual 'marcomms' opportunities with intermediaries and integrate each other's branding information into messages. Two level channels feature two intermediaries between the manufacturer and consumer. Some manufacturers will sell their products to a wholesaler who, in turn, sells the products to smaller retailers and ultimately the end user. The longer the channel, the further removed the manufacturer becomes from the end user. Gaining immediate feedback from the consumer market becomes more complicated. Generally speaking, customers will return faulty or unwanted goods to the retailer. If the customer generates a complaint, this will cascade through the channel until, eventually, it will be filtered back to the manufacturer.

Channel conflict must be avoided at all costs. A key source of conflict is poor communication and 'stepping on others toes'. Evidently, the roles, terms and relationships need to be defined at the outset. When adopting a hybrid approach to distribution (using zero level AND intermediaries concurrently), seek to create a supportive relationship with intermediaries and establish where responsibilities lie. This ensures that channels run smoothly as conflict within channels between intermediaries can be problematic.

Channels significantly influence manufacturers and customers. In the UK the Co-op have been highly proactive in addressing a range of social, ethical and environmental issues. There is concern that the size and price competitiveness of the major retailers can lead to a lack of consideration of sustainability issues such as the working conditions of agricultural labourers or the environmental costs associated with products (CFSD, 2023). That said, most major retailers have at least a CSR platform and increasingly sustainability policies and procedures.

The Use of Intermediaries

There are many reasons for using intermediaries, e.g. their established networks of outlets reach certain customer segments; they offer skills, resources, knowledge, expertise and can share risks. Many organisations (i.e. Danone or Heinz) use retailers (Carrefour, Intermarché or Tesco) to sell their products. If Danone or Heinz had to reach the consumers directly, establishing their own network of stores would cost millions. The major retailers have stores in most cities and towns across Europe. Their customers do not have far to travel to buy goods. Convenience is more than simply location. Intermediaries break down bulk supplies and provide 'allocation' and 'assortment', i.e. they sort them into product groupings that consumers find easier to recognise, e.g. the confectionery aisle in a store. Using existing retailers' resources provides customers with further convenience, e.g. dealing with post-sales services or returns. A large supermarket will stock 50,000 products all of which should be accessible, priced correctly and in good condition.

Manufacturers should concentrate on their core competences (Section 5.2) and leave the distribution to the experts. Let wholesalers support smaller retailers and concentrate on manufacturing the goods. From a sustainability perspective, intermediaries should be treated as partners who also seek value. Marketers must develop and strengthen relationships. Trust and confidence should be central to long-term relationships, but in practice this is not always achievable.

Brick and/or Click

Many organisations sell online and via their own stores. For those selling in the real world (i.e. 'brick') the physical (or task) environment is important. Internal and external appearance of premises, waiting areas, or equipment must be maintained. Customer-facing service deliverers must also pay attention to material aspects such as the appearance of delivery vans or staff uniforms. For those only using online delivery (i.e. 'click') they must ensure that their website is easy to find and navigate.

Retailers with 'brick' and 'click' provision must decide whether it is beneficial migrating 'brick' customers to 'click' (see Figure 4.4). The simple answer is yes. However, the caveat is only migrating customers if their satisfaction can be maintained or improved. The

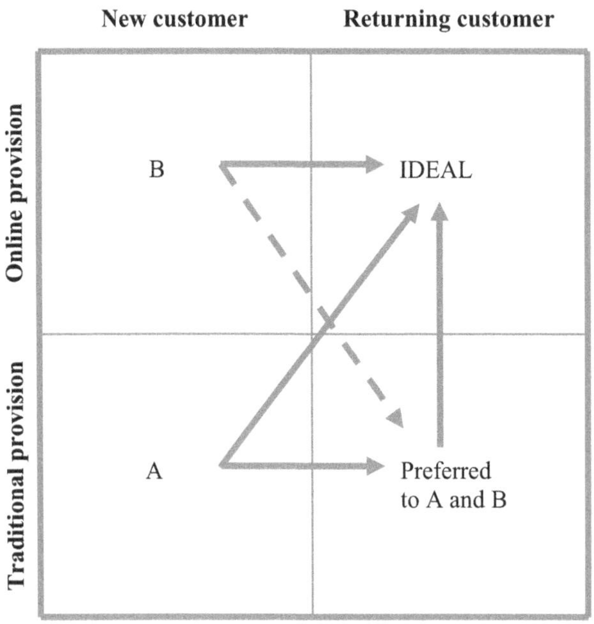

Figure 4.4 Brick versus click distribution.

Source: Adapted from Richardson (2010, p 95).

decision for migrating existing customers to online depends on whether traditional and/or online provisions are offered. Assume a company has converted a prospect into a customer traditionally (A) or online (B). The first transaction (A or B) is fraught with risk and the seller must ensure everything is done to 'get it right first time'. Customers, having repeated their order several times, develop higher levels of trust and may forgive the odd mistake. However, new customers are easy to disappoint. Remember responding to a mistake says more about a company than when things go smoothly.

Not all returning customer positions are equal as overheads are likely to be considerably lower online. Being pragmatic means having repeat customers in any form is 'Preferred' to single transactions (hence the dashed migration from B to Preferred). Ultimately whether through single (A or B to Ideal) or multiple migrations (A or B to Preferred to Ideal) opportunities exist to migrate customers to the 'Ideal' position where they are happy online and the seller 'enjoys' the healthiest margins.

Market Coverage

Marketers must consider the market coverage needed for products. Traditionally the choices of coverage are exclusive, intensive or selective distribution.

- *Exclusive Distribution* involves the deliberate restriction of product availability. This fosters a sense of exclusivity, e.g. Aston Martin cars are usually sold in a single outlet in most major cities.

- *Intensive Distribution* is diametrically opposed to exclusive distribution. It is often used by Fast Moving Consumer Goods (FMCG) companies distributing convenience products such as toilet rolls, milk or potatoes. A wide spread of distribution (intensive coverage) is required as customers require these products often daily.
- *Selective Distribution* is where good coverage is required for products but not to the extent of intensive approach (where horizontal competition may drive prices down) or limiting product availability with the exclusive approach. A small number of select outlets are used, maintaining higher pricing and a degree of exclusivity.

Many organisations store products in warehouses and, as they receive orders, the products are picked, put on board transportation and delivered to customers. The number and location of distribution hubs is key. This can be a costly venture. Many companies have received poor publicity (often as a result of dire working conditions in their warehouses) and governmental scrutiny over perceived poor working practices.

In B2B situations, inventory management and sales order processing (SOP) systems are often required. Stock is costly, particularly if it is finished goods sitting in a warehouse. Insurance and security costs start to increase at this stage. Stock needs to be converted into sales quickly to create income and liquidity for the business. However, managing stock has challenges, i.e. if a key client wants an order fulfilled quickly and the particular item is not available, the customer has little option other than to go to a competitor. However, holding extra stock to accommodate rush orders will lead to capital being tied up. Organisation and time management are crucial skills in this area and marketers must work closely with the warehouse and production functions.

4.3 Customer Benefits (a.k.a. Product)

Marketers often have direct or indirect responsibility for managing products. It is a central task that can generate competitive advantage for companies. Baker (2009) offered useful definitions of key terms.

- *Attributes* define distinguishing characteristics, i.e. a bicycle, car or aeroplane.
- *Features* enable prospects to differentiate between competing products.
- *Benefits* are customer centric, i.e. solve the customer's problem.

A challenge for marketers is that competitors will always seek to replicate successful distinctive features. Always remember that the customer seeks value from the benefits products offer. A common mistake is to simply list features in sales literature. This is poor practice and marketers must sell the benefits, i.e. how the product provides the value sought by the customer.

Consumer-Purchasing Scenarios

It is useful to categorise the different types of decisions or problems that consumers need to solve (Table 4.2)

Kia recognised that customers were concerned about the reliability of their cars (an extended purchasing scenario). This concern could easily contribute to cognitive dissonance. Hence, they adopted a seven-year warranty for their cars. Consider the purchase of a 4x4 vehicle (sometimes known as an SUV). In reality, many are bought by those who

Table 4.2 Purchasing scenarios (a.k.a. problem-solving situations or buy-classes)

Scenario	*Speed of decision*	*Examples*	*Support needed*
Routine problem solving	Can usually be solved quickly as little customer expense and/or risk involved. Little thought goes into purchasing	Fast moving consumer goods (FMCG) items, i.e. bread, vegetables and fruit are in this category, may be habitual purchases	The customer will go through the DMP quickly and little marketing-related support activities are required
Limited problem solving	This type of problem tends not to be as quick to solve as the previous category	Products (i.e. washing machines, new TVs, smartphones) that tend to have a longer customer commitment, i.e. a new washing machine should last several years	Customers spend longer in the 'search' and 'evaluation' steps as purchases involve more risks, mainly financially; customers have less experience of purchasing these products than routine purchases
Extended problem solving	This situation tends to involve the purchase of products and services that require a great deal of consideration before purchase	These 'once in a lifetime/ decade products/ services are high risk (new house, car, wedding dress or holiday apartment). Risks can be financial, social, performance or ego	The customer will therefore take some time moving through the DMP and will need support at various touchpoints

Source: Author.

see them as status symbols. An SUV sends out a message of conspicuous consumption (see Chapter 3). It is a want rather than a need for many. It suggests the driver *could* (but most probably will never) go 'off the beaten track', to get away from the normal combination of work and domestic life.

At its simplest, a product consists of two key components:

- *Tangible factors* can be touched, such as its physical features.
- *Intangible factors* include brand strength, quality or customer care. Customers cannot touch these, nevertheless they enhance the 'product offering'.

Identifying these components can be difficult because the emphasis placed on them differs from product to product.

Example: An Apple iPhone (being a strong brand) may have more emphasis on maintaining brand integrity (an intangible component) than, say, a Huawei equivalent. Since 2003, Huawei has manufactured mobile phones. In 2023 they launched their P60 Pro as a direct competitor to Apple. The P60 Pro is packed with features (i.e. tangible factors) and their advertising has contrasted these with the equivalent iPhone. In most measures, the Huawei equivalent was ahead of the iPhone, the emphasis being on the features of the product (tangible components). The iPhone 14 attracted new customers but was soon criticised on social media for suffering Bluetooth, Face ID and wi-fi problems (amongst others). However, image and usability are intangible factors of the Apple brand and few can compete. Indeed, Apple continues to have an excellent reputation, sector-leading loyalty and high levels of forgiveness from their customer base.

Anatomy of a Product

A model used to develop a better understanding of products is the anatomy of products (Figure 4.5).

Marketers may refer to a product's USP, e.g for Dyson vacuum cleaners, the cyclone technology and the bagless scenario. Very few products offer USPs, most have JNDs. Failure to achieve repeat business is often attributed to factors in the augmented level, where many manufacturers seek to differentiate themselves. Think Apple's image and usability. These sophisticated (intangible) factors are not easy to replicate. The 'future' product alludes to considering the development of the product portfolio. Marketers must research future customer needs and wants, as there is often a need to transform existing products to 'move with the times'. Figure 4.5 provides clarity and understanding of issues requiring consideration and resources, particularly when managing a product portfolio.

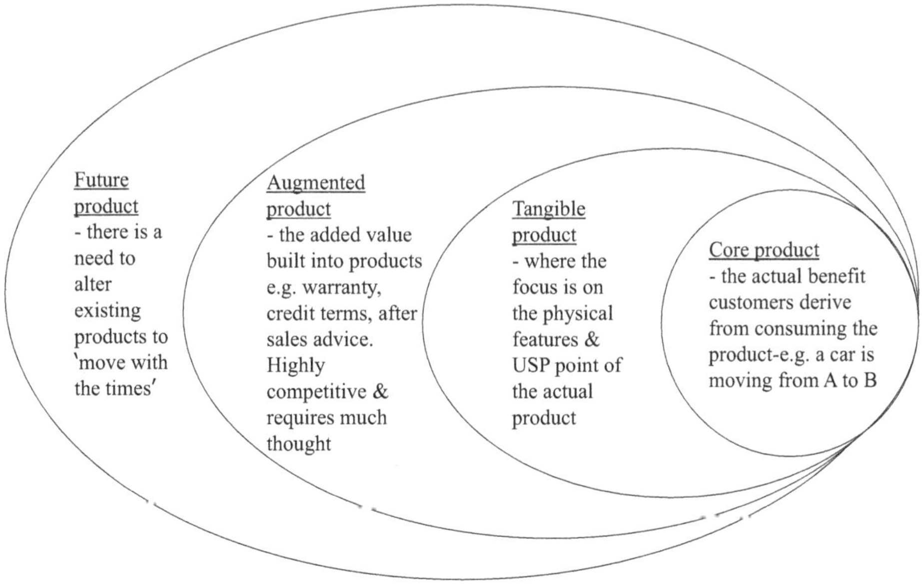

Figure 4.5 Anatomy of a product.

Source: Adapted from Richardson *et al* (2015, p 186).

It encourages reflection on the customer impact rather than simply accepting a product and its features at face value.

Classification of Goods

Marketers must understand how to classify their products. The nature of decision-making varies whether for individuals (B2C) or for organisations (B2B) where goods have distinct classifications (Table 4.3).

From a product perspective, it is necessary to understand how products are categorised so the Mix can be tailored appropriately. If marketers understand the B2C and B2B classifications (Table 4.3) they will better understand how and why customers perceive the product. These shape the amount of resources required and how to support customers in reaching a purchase decision.

Table 4.3 B2C and B2B product classifications

B2C		*B2B*	
Classification	*Comment*	*Classification*	*Comment*
Convenience Goods	Require little consumer time when purchasing goods; little risk (financially, socially or personally) associated, e.g. staple foods such as vegetables, bread or eggs. Often bought as 'routine' or habit	**Installations**	Central pieces of capital equipment, machinery or technology used in production. Critical to the process. Can be expensive
Shopping Goods	Require more consumer time and effort as they incur more risk financially, personally and socially, e.g. a new kitchen suite, a new washing machine. Associated with 'limited' problems	**Accessories**	Part of the production process but not necessarily central. They complement it and create a smoother process, e.g. office furniture
Speciality Goods	Often luxury goods where consumers accept no substitutes. Risk involved as these are often expensive. Branding is important, e.g. designer clothing, expensive perfumes such as Chanel	**Sub-assemblies**	Often B2B customers want suppliers to part-assemble
Unsought Goods	Not anticipated until either they are drawn to customer's attention, e.g. sales promotions, or through unforeseen events, e.g. a flat tyre, burst pipes or a broken window. Customers often highly motivated to buy the goods quickly. May pay higher prices for a rapid solution	**Raw Materials**	Essential for production purposes. The quality and timeliness of raw materials is incredibly important here. They are often supplied in large quantities

Source: Adapted from Richardson (2020, p 104).

Example: Fine jewellery can represent an extended (i.e. substantial) purchase for most consumers (see Table 4.2). Customers are increasingly concerned about the ethical provenance of their jewellery. Fenton is a BCorp-accredited organisation that has, since 2019, given consumers fair access to high quality, responsibly produced, fine jewellery, specialising in ethically and sustainably sourced coloured gemstones as an alternative to traditional diamonds. Customers choose from a variety of stones, metals and cuts to create personalised designs, with all gems sourced directly. In 2023 Fenton was one of only three British jewellers to be BCorp certified, which they earned thanks to their impressive 10-part responsible sourcing manifesto (Bellini, 2021). Fenton only obtains stones from companies that are world leaders in ethical mining, actively supporting the local habitat and environment. Their BCorp accreditation demonstrates their commitment to providing responsibly sourced fine jewellery. Fenton support UN SDGs 8, 9 and 12 amongst others (see Table 1.4).

The Product Portfolio

Sustainable entrepreneurs often start a business with a single product. The entrepreneur can concentrate all their marketing decisions on this product. Once the decision is made to launch a second product, then a new set of decisions are needed, e.g. which product is the most profitable and/or sustainable? At the other end of the spectrum are companies like Procter & Gamble (P&G), a world-class provider of consumer products. P&G has no option other than to practice sound product portfolio management. Some key terms are:

- Product Mix – total sum of all products and variants offered
- Product Line – a group of closely related products, e.g. printers, laptops, PCs
- Product Line Length – total number of items within the product line
- Product Line Depth – number of variants of each item within a product line
- Product Mix Width – number of product lines offered.

The details in Table 4.4 are compiled from P&G's website which is packed with useful information for consumers. The brands are shown (online) with the respective logos and links providing access to further information (supporting the customer's decision-making). There are some interesting insights into P&G's portfolio. First, it is evident that some product lines are longer than others. Indeed 'Baby Care' only features one product: Pampers. The longest product lines feature six different product ranges. Care must be taken in imputing from this that the Pampers provision is weak. It has about 19% of the global market share, making it a substantial product line for P&G. Some products exist to target different segments. Those alluding to luxury target socio-economic groups with more disposable income. Some product lines are more cohesive, e.g. Feminine Care is tightly focused whereas Personal Health Care ranges from pregnancy-testing kits to fixing dentures and the long-established Old Spice. Old Spice is the only product range to feature in more than one product line. Clearly P&G takes a systematic approach to managing its portfolio. The benefits of this are being able to reduce or extend the portfolio by

Table 4.4 Product line mix and depth applied to Procter & Gamble

	Product Mix Width						
	Beauty Care	*Baby Care*	*Feminine Care*	*Fabric Care*	*Home Care*	*Personal Health Care*	*Grooming*
Product line depth	Aussie Hair Care	Pampers Baby and toddler nappies, pants & wipes	Always Feminine Care Pads	Ariel Laundry Products	Ambi Pur Odour Eliminators	Clearblue Pregnancy & Ovulation Tests	Braun Personal Grooming
	Head & Shoulders Anti-Dandruff Shampoo		Always Discreet Light, sensitive bladder protection	Bold 2 in 1 Laundry Products	Fairy Dish Care	Fixodent Denture Adhesives	Gillette Razors & Skin Care
	Herbal Essences Hair Care		Tampax Feminine Care Tampons	Daz Laundry Products	Febreze Odour Eliminators	Oral-B Toothbrushes & Dental Floss	Venus Razors & Shaving Gels
	Olay Face & Skin Care			Fairy Non-Bio Laundry Products	Flash Surface cleaner	Old Spice Hair & Skin Care	
	SK-II Luxury Skin Care			Lenor Fabric Conditioner	Viakal Kitchen and Bathroom Surface Care	Vicks Cough, Cold & Flu Relief	
	Pantene Hair Care			Lenor In-wash scent boosters		Seven Seas Supplements	

Source: Adapted from P&G (2023).

- introducing variations/models
- differentiating the quality
- developing associated items
- developing new products.

However, marketers must reflect on resource allocation, product expectations, brand image and how to co-ordinate the Mix across the portfolio.

Product Life Cycle (PLC)

The PLC reminds marketers that products, like humans, are conceived, develop, are born, grow, mature, decline and ultimately die. Therefore, it helps those managing product portfolios to understand how the stage of a product influences decisions regarding additional marketing-related activities.

Figure 4.6 shows a 'generic' representation a PLC featuring five key stages. If the Development stage is successful, the product may be launched. Growth cannot be assumed. Indeed, it only occurs if the consumers take value. Remember value cannot be given. If enough customers take value, then the company should increase (or hold) market share. During *growth* competitors react by offering their own alternatives. There

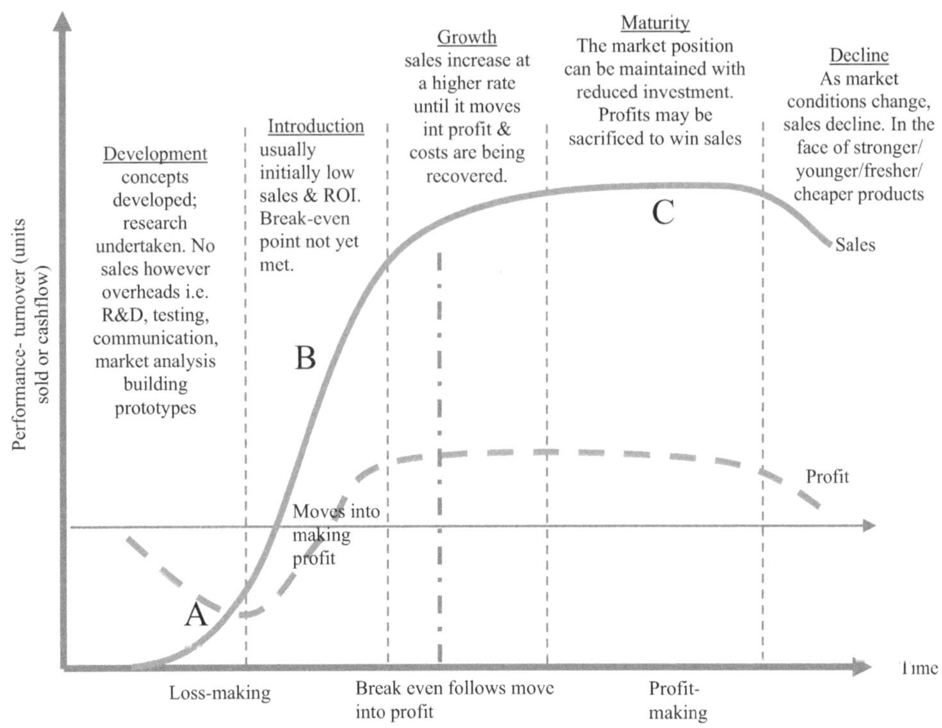

Figure 4.6 The generic product life cycle (PLC).

Source: Adapted from Levitt (1965).

is always a reaction. If the product 'has legs' the market may approach saturation where (akin to Darwinism) only companies that can adapt will survive until the next generation. In *Maturity* growth slows; however, sales may still be high; newer, more contemporary, competitive products have entered the market. Many products spend most of their life in 'maturity', as many marketing decisions relate to extending this stage. For example, Cadburys Dairy Milk has sold in largely the same format for over a century.

Example: Lucozade traditionally was a drink for children recovering from ailments and ailing grannies. Now rebranded with a re-launch featuring phrases such as 'isotonic', it is marketed as a health drink for young athletes and sports people. This not only extended the maturity section but substantially increased sales. It is distributed intensively and is highly visible. Lucozade Sport was adopted as the official sports drink of the Birmingham 2022 Commonwealth Games.

With toothpaste, the delivery mechanism, the toothbrush, has evolved from manual to electric, vibrating and sonic, however consumers still use paste-based products that their great-grandparents would recognise. The toothpaste market has fragmented from the basic product to include protection for gums, reduction in sensitivity and teeth whitening. These new lines have extended the maturity phase and also led to small growth curves in specific, specialised areas.

Companies selling technology products often face shortening PLCs. A consultancy client who sells hubs and routers to the key UK Internet Service Providers (ISPs) argues that PLCs for his goods are now less than 12 months. This highlights the need for good relationships based on regular, meaningful communications because a disgruntled client could simply skip a generation of products with potentially devastating consequences.

Example: A new generation of devices that can be taken apart is creeping into the mainstream. These are designed to be repaired and upgraded by users with the aim of reducing consumerist churn (Guardian, 2023). Framework, a US start-up, has challenged the BAU approach by launching user-repairable laptops. Their Laptop 13 looks like a standard notebook PC running Windows. But it is designed to be easily taken apart with memory, storage and wireless cards that are easily replaceable and upgradeable. The ports on the sides can be easily changed, too. Framework also provides processor upgrade kits so, in theory, consumers can keep the same laptop and just keep changing processor bits to keep them up to date. Build-your-own desktops have always existed; however, Framework is the first to take the niche upgradeable laptop towards the mainstream. The catch is that the Framework 13 is slightly more expensive than equivalent rivals, starting at £1,049, which is around £200 more than Dell, Acer or others (*ibid*).

Some alternative PLCs are shown in Figure 4.7. Some products have mini life-cycles due to the input of further new technology into the product to update it. Smartphone manufacturers are increasingly working with systems integrators who incorporate the phone into their service. This is beyond a simple 'app', e.g. medical instruments are

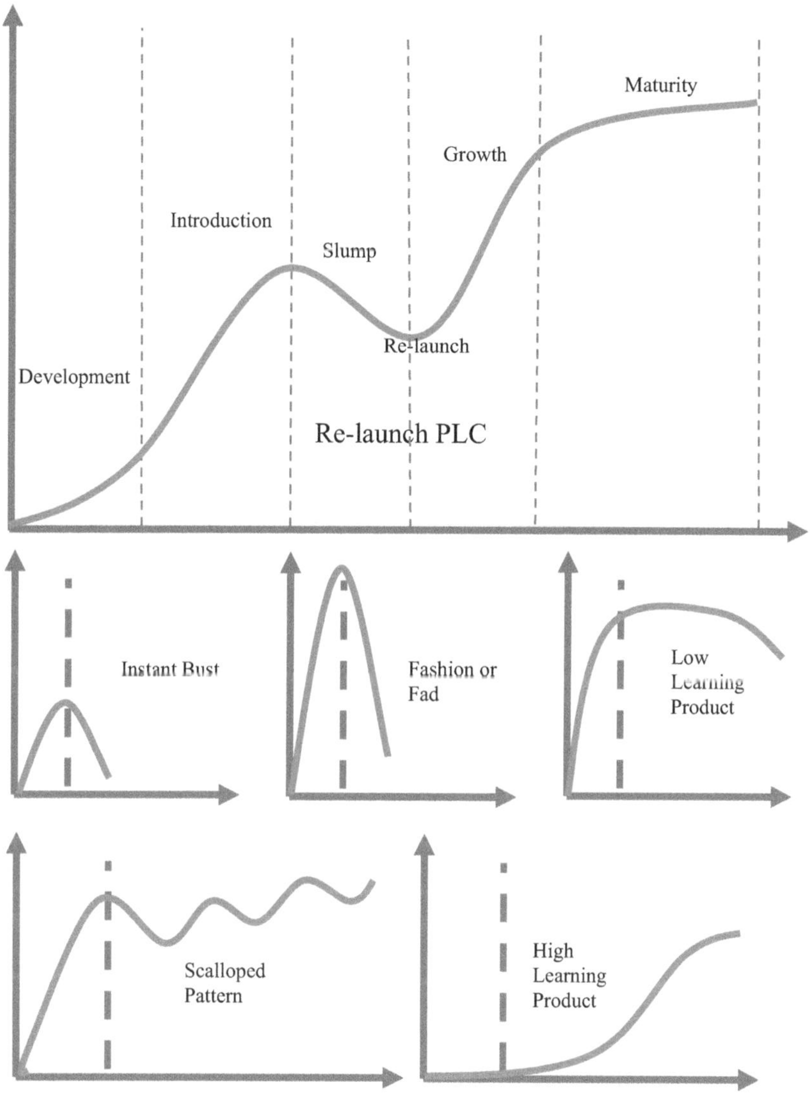

Figure 4.7 Differing PLC scenarios.

Source: Adapted from Lambin and Schuiling (2012).

increasingly using the mobile platform thus enabling remote monitoring of conditions such heart rate and blood pressure. This saves visits and patient stress by providing instant information. Care must be taken when launching the next iteration (Figure 4.7). Launching too early may lead to cannibalisation of the current model; launch too late and sales may have dropped whilst opening the door for the competition. Some marketers seek to extend the maturity stage as their new products may not be ready to launch. There are several different ways to achieve this:

- Re-launch with, say, new colours or packaging
- Find new users, i.e. segments to target, e.g. international markets.
- Find new uses – aspirin is now used because of its blood-thinning properties rather than simply curing a headache.
- Increase the usage/frequency of purchase. Encourage consumers to use products more often by relating the benefits of repeat use of the products (think Sensodyne toothpaste – the more it is used the greater the benefits).

Marketers must decide

- whether to stay in the market (recouping more returns) involving spending precious time, money and other resources on old products
- resourcing newer, more competitive products
- withdrawing the product from the market gracefully.

Example: Danish B Corp accredited beauty company Skandinavisk took the radical decision to adapt their entire product collection only six months after having gained accreditation. For the first time, the majority of their production was now inside Scandinavia. They used sustainably farmed Swedish rapeseed wax for candles. Their Danish-produced cosmetic formulae maximise the amount of certified organic ingredients to the point before they risk compromising its performance on the skin (Russell, 2023). Packaging varies from partially recycled European glass to recyclable bioplastics made in Denmark, from post-consumer recycled metal tubes to FSC-certified paper and card from managed Swedish forests (*ibid*).

It is worth noting that underlying technology 'waves' often influence a given product's PLC? The PLC of VHS recorders was irrevocably affected by the introduction of DVD (see Table 5.7 for substitutes and Section 5.3 for creative destruction). The PLC does have several limitations, namely:

- every product is different, as is every related PLC
- it oversimplifies the real life of a product
- not all products go through all the stages
- it is difficult to pinpoint when products move from one stage to another
- it cannot be used as a predictive tool
- it is inward and myopic as it neglects external factors such as customers' increasing expectations of ethical and/or ecologically friendly products.

Apropos staging (i.e. knowing the stage the product is in and when it is moving from one to another), Marketers can check sales and profitability data, but there are many reasons for such increases or decreases. Consider a product that is subject to 'seasonality'. As soon as the sales and/or profitability dip, this could be taken as a transfer from maturity to decline, but what if it is merely a seasonal blip? Marketers may take unnecessarily drastic action.

The Product Adoption Curve (a.k.a. the Diffusion Curve)

As PLCs of many products shorten, there is a need to access markets quickly, raise awareness and convince customers (and prospects) that the value they seek is better than that offered by competitors. In 1962, Everett M Rogers introduced the Product Adoption Curve (Rogers, 1962), a theory that has helped marketing practitioners over the years. Sometimes it is referred to as the Product Diffusion Curve (Figure 4.8).

This process attempts to explain how a product can be 'adopted' or 'diffused' (spread) throughout a marketplace efficiently. The process is useful as it illustrates how consumers can be influenced by others and recognises that different 'types' of adopters are not evenly spread through society. Marketers can tailor their marcomms to use feedback from 'Innovators' to influence 'Early Adopters' who in turn inform the 'Early Majority'. The 'Innovators' could be knowledgeable opinion formers (see Figure 4.2) whereas the 'Early Adopters' could be influencers or opinion leaders, whose credibility could aid the diffusion of the message through networks and communities.

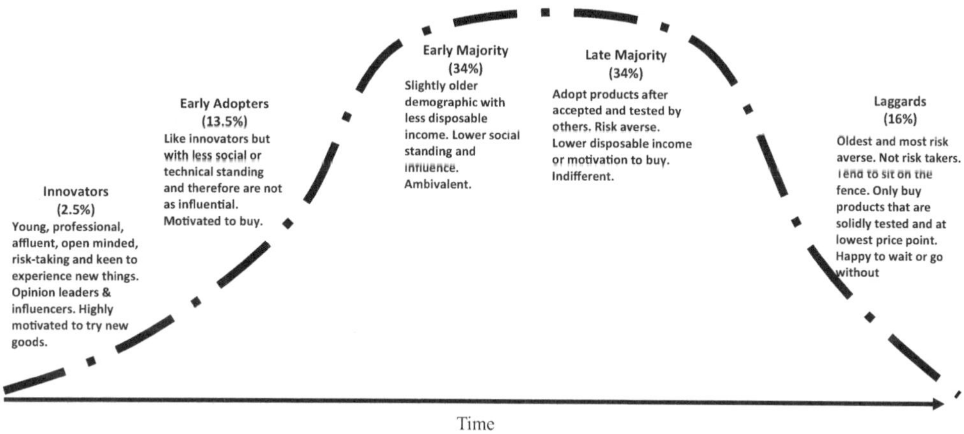

Figure 4.8 Product adoption or diffusion curve.

Source: Adapted from Rogers (1962).

Example: "The Leaf cemented Nissan in the early days of the EV as a real innovator and the first to market," said *AutoPacific* president and chief analyst Ed Kim. It introduced battery-powered mobility to the masses (Motortrend, 2023). According to Kim, its singular status produced an unexpected effect. "The people who ended up buying them were affluent early adopters, because they could afford a discretionary purchase for this technological novelty" he said. Though its estimated range was modest, Nissan's first production proved that ZEVs could feature in everyday driving. Nissan also ensured consumer needs were met on a large scale by establishing manufacturing plants for the Leaf in Japan, the USA and the UK, making it a truly global vehicle. By 2020, over 500,000 Leafs had been sold worldwide. The model's success is measurable not only in sales but in loyalty, as the Leaf claims Nissan's highest owner-retention rate, despite its range remaining behind the curve compared to the latest ZEVs from competitors. Nissan has made consistent improvements in that arena as the Leaf has matured (*ibid*).

The discussion of product diffusion is largely B2C. It is worth noting that the diffusion of new, disruptive technologies applies less in B2B segments.

New Product Development (NPD)

There is an ongoing need to create products desired by consumers. Televisions today look very different and have many alternative features to those of 50 years ago. A 42" (100cm) flat, QLED Sony Bravia TV uses a quarter of the electricity of its 28" (70cm) CRT predecessor. The same can be said of mobile technology. The first mobile phone (Motorola Dyna TAC 8000X) launched in 1983, weighed 1.1Kg, provided 30 minutes of talk time, took 10 hours to charge and cost nearly $4,000. If TV and mobile manufacturers from the 1980s produced the same products today, they would satisfy few customers. They would not survive.

Conversely, a phenomenon with a different direction of travel was triggered by the 2007 global credit crunch. Companies adopted a 'Back to Basics' approach, targeting frugal or nostalgic buyers, i.e. Nokia tapped into nostalgia by re-launching their 3310 model in 2017. That said, it had new features such as a camera, a longer battery life and was nearly half the weight of the original launched in 2000.

Some observers believe that the retail markets and subsequent buying habits have changed permanently. People are buying just enough rather than in excess. This notion of no frills 'sufficiency' chimes with elements of sustainability. Major retailers have increased their 'own-label' offerings as a direct consequence of the impact of the defection of their customers to the discounters, Aldi & Lidl. Perhaps of greater significance, is the view that these 'value-for-money' (vfm) brands represent a longer-term convergence of consumer needs and tastes that can be seen in developed and developing economies. Perhaps consumers are less persuaded or driven by the promise of 'quality' or 'excellence' in return for higher prices. Is this another side of 'sustainable' consumption?

When developing new products, different risks are associated (Figure 4.9). It is worth considering some examples that would fit in the continuum. The pharmaceutical / bio-technology-based industries are key sectors where innovative products dominate. Advances in mapping the human genome are leading to the development of new therapies. A great deal of research, development, testing, resources and time will have been spent on creating and developing these 'new' products. They are initially high-risk ventures, but the returns can be phenomenal. Likewise, if they fail once launched into the marketplace, they can have devastating effects on the investing organisation.

Many governments have legislated for electric cars to replace combustion-engine cars as a means to reducing CO_2 emissions and air pollution. The US sold 1 million battery-driven cars in 2023. Batteries present key challenges in terms of range and the vehicle weight. Furthermore, powertrains may only last 10 years, so the medium-term future will need substantial recycling facilities. In 2023, Toyota claimed it had developed solid-state solution (replacing lithium-ion) for car batteries. A solid-state battery should deliver a greater range for the same weight or a lighter car for city use.

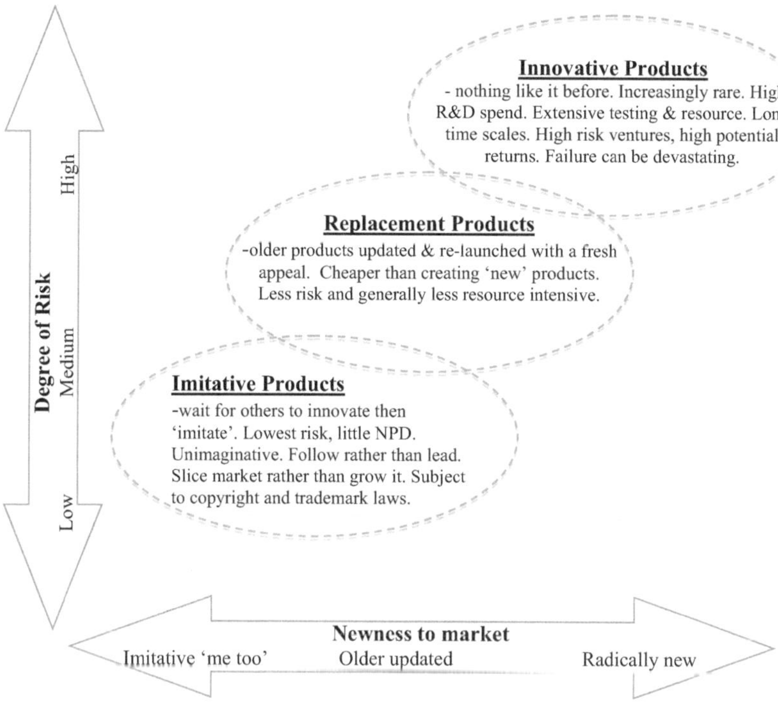

Figure 4.9 New product risk continuum.

Source: Adapted from Richardson *et al* (2015, p 199).

Rather than perpetually creating new products, many companies update existing offerings with 'Replacement' products. There are fewer risks and resource demands. Manufacturers can take on-board comments from customers, stakeholders and the public. Being a 'follower' can, of course, result in substantial sales, e.g. in the energy drinks sector Monster successfully followed Red Bull.

Example: In 1983 Dyson innovatively created a new 'bagless' market by launching the first mass-market 'bagless' DC01 vacuum cleaner with cyclone technology. The inherent risk is that with new successful products, which capture the customers' hearts and minds, imitative followers (perceived to be 'me too' companies) soon follow. Hoover and Electrolux launched 'Imitative' products, typical of some 'Product'-oriented organisations. In 2002, Hoover was forced to pay Dyson over £4 million following a patent-infringement lawsuit. Hoover's Triple Vortex vacuums were deemed a blatant copy of Dyson's design, the same cyclone technology James Dyson had previously offered to sell to Hoover. By 2023, Dyson was the market leader in the UK with over 50% market share compared to Hoover (with circa 30%). It is the top brand in the USA, with 27% of market share. China is now Dyson's second-largest market, after the US.

New products involve higher risks so, to reduce the number of failed 'new' products, organisations have adopted a systematic framework or process in which they develop them. This includes several steps (Figure 4.10).

Large manufacturers can propose hundreds of new products during the Idea Generation stage of the NPD process (Figure 4.10). These are reduced during the Idea Screening stage using a range of filters. Increasingly sustainability has become one of these filters. Focus groups are particularly useful in the Product Development stage as they can actually start to touch, use and feel the product physical prototypes. All Mix-related issues can be tested with focus groups, i.e. using product 'mock ups' to produce insights into their thoughts of the idea/concept, shape, colour, design, proposed pricing or sales channels. This feedback can shape the product launch. At this stage, marketers should be designing the entire marketing strategy, including potential changes to the Mix and how these changes will be controlled.

If the focus group is unreceptive to the new idea, the options are to go back to the drawing board to re-develop the ideas or to abort the process. Historically some marketers, despite receiving negative feedback, pursued the development to the next stage because they believed they knew their brand better than the customer. Often brand marketers are subject to ritualistic or historical pressures, i.e. "we've always done it this way" (the refrain of many failed companies).

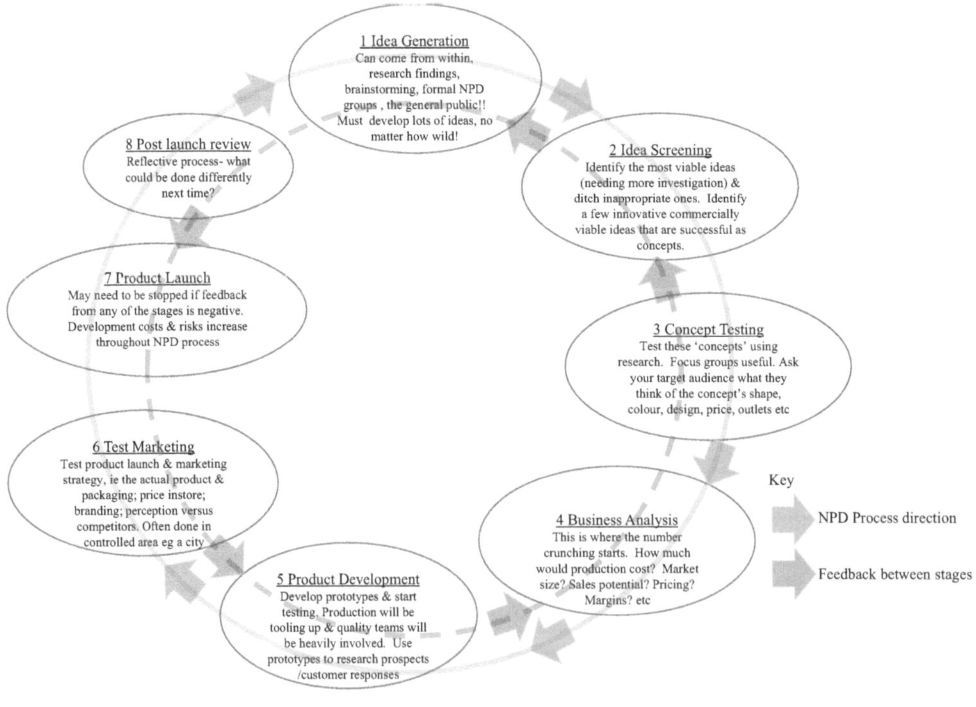

Figure 4.10 New Product Development (NPD) Process.

Source: Adapted from Richardson *et al* (2015, p 201).

Alternatively, genuinely new product ideas such as consumer 'clinics' can produce false, negative results. The Sony Walkman was 'new to the world', i.e. a game changer. However, in test marketing the consumers did not perceive a need for a portable music system, which used headphones, hence they reacted poorly to the concept. Sony ignored the results. Sony may however be the exception to the rule. If prototypes are received warmly, marketers will have sound data upon which to move to the next step in the process.

The 'Business Analysis' stage is where price is seriously considered. Factors such as margins and product viability are considered. Again, the choice is adapt or abort. The latter may be difficult particularly if the prototype has been warmly received. Ultimately throwing good money after bad is rarely a sound choice. Throughout the NPD process, marketers must be aware of the SPC (standard product cost). Procurement and/or accounts teams should be involved in ensuring the latest costings are incorporated. The basic requirement of most pricing decisions is to cover the cost of the product. Furthermore, the marketer must liaise with senior management to ensure the margin of profitability aligns with corporate objectives. This could be based upon the individual requirement of the product, the product range or it could be a historic judgment. Marketers must understand all cost-related issues. The SPC is only one consideration, as marketers must consider the overall development cost, break-even point (Figure 4.1) and pay-back period. As discussed, the PLC length for many products is reducing, therefore creating less time to re-cover the initial development costs and make a profit.

Test marketing is useful to 'test' the entire marketing strategy in a controlled (i.e. less risky) fashion. Negative 'test' feedback will provide the much-needed room to address problems pre-launch. However, caution is needed as testing new products can compromise marketers if the competitors glean key information. They could tweak their own products, pricing, communications or even bring forward a launch to steal some of the limelight.

Even though many companies use a process akin to NPD, many new products still fail in the marketplace. Kotler & Armstrong (2006) refer to research where of 25,000 new consumer food, beverage, beauty and health care products to hit the market each year, only 40% will survive five years. They cite another study which estimates that new consumer packaged products (consisting of mostly line extensions) fail at a rate of 80%. NPD lowers risks, but launching new products can never be a risk-free process. Every judgment call needs knowledge and skill. Often the use of marketing agencies and consultants can help in providing an objective perspective. Moving through this process can take weeks, months and sometimes years. As the environment, marketplace and customers are constantly evolving, this is inherently difficult to manage, as the goalposts are constantly moving.

Example: Danish manufacturer LEGO has an online customer community (LEGO Ideas) where fans can submit ideas for a new LEGO project. When 10,000+ members vote for the idea, LEGO's marketing and design team assess whether it is a viable option. This is a unique take on NPD where fans provide not only the creative idea but also a degree of market analysis. Successful ideas become LEGO sets and sell worldwide. Examples have included LEGO Women of NASA and the TRON Legacy. In 2023 they hosted "A Celebration of 3 Million Fans" which gives some idea of the continuing popularity.

Many organisations fail to invest in research because it may be time-consuming, resource intensive or expensive. Large organisations have the resources available, but many smaller organisations rely on intuition and current knowledge. Some managers are too proud to seek support from internal staff or third parties. Marketers must seek input from colleagues in other functions, especially the sales department. To a certain extent, intuition should not be ignored especially if the marketers have extensive experience in the field and marketplace. However, Marketers must be wary when second-guessing decisions on behalf of potentially millions of customers. They must ensure that the research is conducted and analysed correctly. If the analysis is flawed, the decisions risk being flawed. This leads to (or results from) 'comms' breakdown or misinformation.

Boston Control Group (BCG) Matrix

The PLC acted as a springboard for the Boston Control Group's widely used BCG Matrix (Figure 4.11). In 1970, BCG's founder, Bruce Henderson, suggested:

> "A company should have a portfolio of products with different growth rates and different market shares. The portfolio composition is a function of the balance between cash flows. ... Margins and cash generated are a function of market share".
>
> (Henderson, 1970)

Clearly Henderson's views were shaped by assumptions that were valid in 1970 i.e. marketing investment would create product growth, greater market share generated increased profits and profitability (and cash-flow) increased with larger Economies of Scale (EoS). Products had longer PLCs (see Figure 4.6) and profit could be made during the Maturity stage. Historically, brands sought to dominate their competitors and

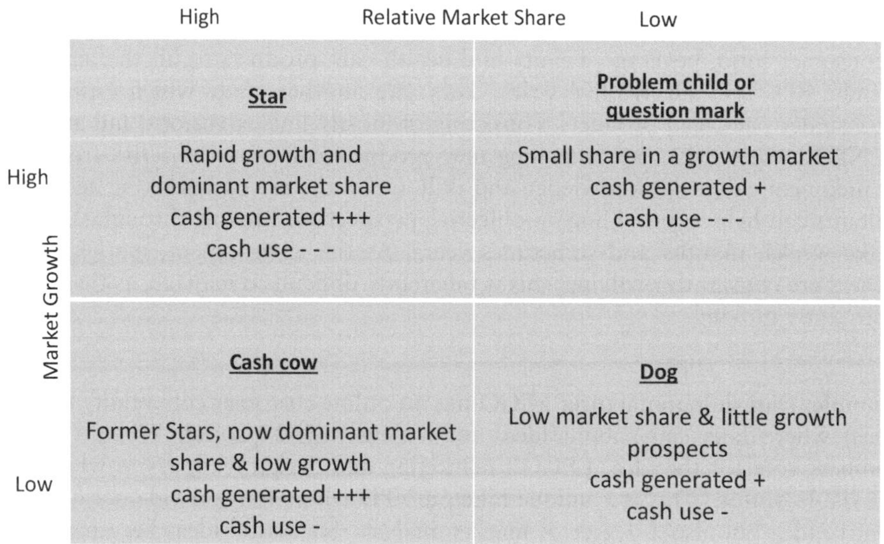

Figure 4.11 Boston Control Group (BCG) Product Matrix.

Source: Adapted from Henderson (1970).

the Growth stage was optimal for creating a dominant brand. So, they invested more working capital into increased production capacities and diverted revenue towards promoting their products. These were the inward focused, top-down behaviours of Product and Production orientated companies (see Chapter 6). Many of these assumptions have been challenged by the changing nature of markets with ESG and sustainability indices being commonly used. It is possible that such tools could have led large manufacturers to prematurely abandon product ranges. Prahalad and Hamel (1990) discuss how US and European TV manufacturers largely abandoned the market, opening the door to Japanese, Korean and Chinese new entrants.

The accepted wisdom is that marketers should invest in Stars to achieve growth. This growth may be at the expense of profit. Question marks (a.k.a. Problem Child) should be evaluated to establish their potential to grow into a Star, a Cash Cow or alternatively decline and become a Dog. Some argue that the optimum cash flow is from Cash Cow to Question Marks. Cash cows should have enough investment to maintain their market share and to provide the investment in other categories. 'Over-milking' the Cash Cows can lead to them being unnecessarily weakened. Dogs, weak Cash Cows and unpromising Question Marks may need to be culled if they threaten the company. Such decisions can be problematic, i.e. Dogs may generate decent profits if not starved of investment.

BCG limitations include being somewhat simplistic, seeing products independently of its peers in the product portfolio. Largely it ignores related accessories e.g. Lazer printers may have a different BCG Matrix to toner cartridges. It does not incorporate external matters i.e. competitors' practices such as predatory pricing or 'dumping'. Successful products provoke reactions from competitors, including new entrants. Unless clearly differentiated from the competition this often leads to lower prices and profits. The BCG's reliance on cash flow neglects the critical issue of profitability. It is neither customer-centric nor sustainable. Customers may choose other brands if their preferred product is lost or adapted to the extant to cause customer attrition.

Example: In 2016 Apple removed the 3.5mm jack from their hugely successful iPhone range. Some customers wanted the facility of the plug-in socket, however they would have to buy a Lightning-to-3.5mm jack adapter or depend on wireless solutions to listen through earphones. Having to buy a separate adapter increases the overall CO_2 footprint of the product and customer cost. Apple's provision of its proprietary Lightning adaptor in Europe was curtailed when the EU common-charger rule came into being in 2023. Most new Apple products, i.e. the iPads were already using USB-C in 2023. Interestingly, all iPhones since 2017's iPhone 8 supported wireless charging. However, the EU insisted the change would (annually) save consumers up to €250m on unnecessary charger purchases and cut 11,000 tonnes of waste.

Finally, like other product portfolio tools, does the BCG apply at product, product line or SBU level? Analyses undertaken at SBU level may conceal significant underlying differences or alternatively ignore synergies between SBUs or products. A BCG, like many simple tools, provides useful insights for marketers. Simple tools are more likely to be used when implementing changes.

Directional Policy Matrices

In the 1970s, General Electric (GE) commissioned McKinsey & Company to develop a portfolio analysis matrix. The GE McKinsey Matrix or GE Matrix succeeded the BCG Matrix. Rather than using single measures of success the GE Matrix or Directional Policy Matrix (hereafter DPM) uses a multivariate approach where market growth rate is replaced by market attractiveness and relative market share by business strength.

If the DPM (Figure 4.12) merely portrays the current 'snapshot', it is purely descriptive. To analytical, it should offer the current product positions and those later in the planning period. This way a DPM better identifies which products need support. The criteria (Market attractiveness versus Business strengths) constitute a range of factors (Table 4.5).

Proctor (2008) insists market attractiveness and business strength are critical success factors (CSFs). The content of CSFs depends entirely upon the organisation and the

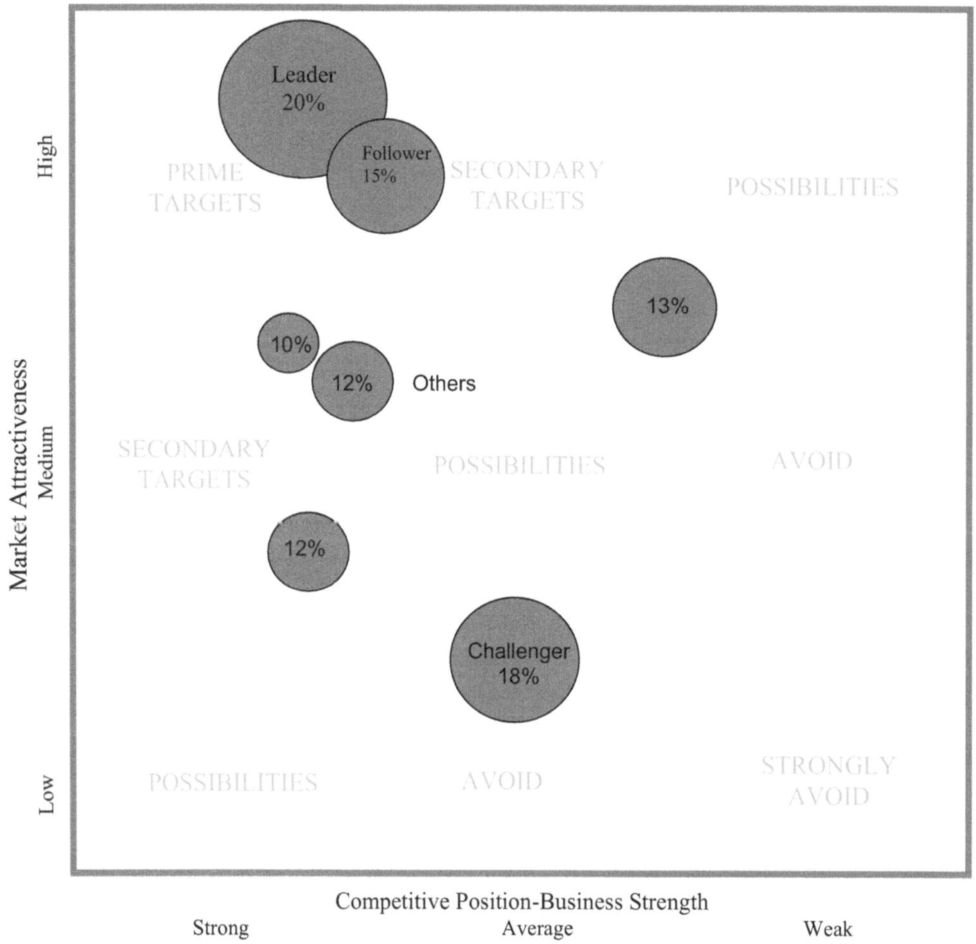

Figure 4.12 Directional Policy Matrix (DPM).

Source: Adapted from Gosnay and Richardson (2008, p 130).

Table 4.5 DPM criteria – industry attractiveness vs business strength

Industry attractiveness	*Business strengths*
size	size
market growth	growth
pricing	share
market diversity	position
competitive structure	profitability
industry profitability	margins
technical role	technical position
social	strengths/weaknesses
environment	image
legal	people
human	size

Source: Adapted from McDonald (1999, p 189).

Table 4.6 Weightings for DPM criteria

		Market Attractiveness criteria			
		Profit potential	*Market growth rate*	*Market size*	*Competition Strength*
Business strengths criteria	Market share	60%			
	Potential for differential advantage		20%		
	Potential cost advantages			10%	
	Brand image				10%

Source: Adapted from Donnelly and Harrison (2009).

competitive environment. Market attractiveness and business strength should be measured by the key criteria marketers must get right to succeed. Business strengths should enable a comparison to be made relative to the major competitors. Donnelly & Harrison (2009) proposed criteria weightings (Table 4.6).

Table 4.6 is useful in reminding marketers that different weightings apply to their selection of criteria. Clearly there is a strong link between profit potential and having a large market share. Furthermore, in growing markets there is potential for differential advantage. Beyond that there are limitations in Table 4.6. In focusing attention on market share and differentiation, it relegates brand image. Clearly it could be argued that the brand image is more valuable to the organisation than the 10% weighting suggests. Tools that refer to markets suffer the problems of (market) definition (see Section 2.1). Products and services may target nascent markets where growth estimates are little more than educated guesses. All these factors (amongst others) can shape the application of internal tools (e.g. PLC, BCG and DPM) and micro-environmental tools (e.g. 5Ms and Porter's 5 Forces). Limitations include

- simplistic visuals, i.e. circle sizes not reflecting the true situation
- positions are largely chosen subjectively

- market growth is a limited description for overall industry attractiveness
- it may not take into account strong buyers and low-entry barriers
- market share inadequately describes relative competitive strength
- other factors, i.e. location or vertical integration may need consideration.

4.4 Cost to Customers (a.k.a. Price a.k.a. Value-for-Money)

> "A cynic is a man who knows the price of everything and the value of nothing".
> (Lord Darlington in Lady Windermere's Fan by Oscar Wilde)

Despite Wilde's play first being performed in 1892, this insight resonates today. Cost (to customers) is preferred to 'Price' as customers experience sacrifices to buy goods. They understand what the cost is to them, seek value for money and often need to justify making a financial sacrifice. This represents a particular challenge for marketers, as there are many different factors to balance. Pricing is an important aspect of the Mix as it:

- is the only variable that creates revenue
- is strategically important being highly visible to senior management
- connects customers with suppliers
- conveys signals about quality and exclusivity
- is highly visible for consumers.

Pricing can establish competitive advantages whereas poor pricing can lead to customer attrition, poor profitability, longer break-even periods, reduced customer satisfaction and employee morale. In past BAU practices, many social and environmental costs of doing business were not met by companies nor reflected in the prices that customers were charged. They were "externalities", or bills for others to pay. Theoretically, these "others" were meant to be governments using the taxes that raised on consumers and producers, but in practice it has often meant passing those costs down to future generations (CFSD, 2023).

Table 4.7 The three perspectives of pricing

Perspective	Comment
Accountant	Pricing should fall within the marketing function, however in some organisations it is determined solely by accountants. The problem with this is long-term, as accountants do not monitor the marketplace, customer requirements/needs, the competition or wider environmental forces. All of which affect the pricing of products and services
Economist	Based on the forces of supply and demand. Where demand exists, a price will be created. If supply and /or demand fluctuate, then so do prices
Marketer	A customer-centric focus. What will the customer pay? Marketers undertake research to determine this e.g. using focus groups to contrast the product with its competition. It is a useful way to gain insights into the customer mindset

Source: Adapted from Richardson (2020, p 120).

Pricing Perspectives

Many academics refer to the three perspectives of pricing, namely *The Economist*, *The Accountant* and *The Marketer's Perspectives* (Table 4.7).

These perspectives illustrate how pricing can be viewed by different stakeholder mindsets. Accountants have a key role in creating correct prices. Indeed, good pricing may only result from involving other functions.

Example: Despite the ongoing greenwashing and ESG claims from BP, Shell and their investors, fossil fuel generates astronomic profits (Corporate Watch, 2023). By 2023, £131bn had been paid to Shell and BP shareholders (i.e. since the 2015 Paris Agreement). If they wanted to help achieve net zero, there are valuable ways they could invest other than providing dividends. As a signatory of the Paris Agreement, the UK has signed up to reduce emissions from heating and powering homes by 68% by 2030 *and* must reach net zero by 2050. Retrofitting insulation to as many homes as possible has never been more crucial however the UK's circa 25 million homes are among the oldest and least energy efficient in Europe. There has been significant research into costing different approaches to retrofitting insulation, e.g. the Climate Change Committee advocates spending £55bn by 2050, giving 15 million households "one of the main insulation measures (loft/wall/floor)" and draft-proofing for another 8 million homes. Alternatively, the New Economics Foundation (NEF), proposed three funding models to retrofit the most critical 8.69 million homes over four years:

- Public-sector finance – £9,484/home = £93.56bn
- Private finance – around £13,801/home = nearly £124.2bn
- Mixed funding approach – average cost £10,461/home = £100.15bn.

Of those three, the NEF report advocates the mixed-funding approach because this creates "a large net gain in government revenue of £25.6bn" over four years, which equates to a return of "£1.74 for every pound spent" (*ibid*).

The above example features hypothetical scenarios of how dividends could be redistributed for only two companies.

Example: Patagonia made headlines in 2022 when it announced that Planet Earth "is now our only shareholder". The founder of the California-based business, Yvon Chouinard, transferred 98% of the company's shares to a new environmental organisation called the Holdfast Collective (BBC, 2023a). Each year Holdfast will receive the profits that Patagonia does not need for reinvestment to "protect nature and biodiversity" and "fight the environmental crisis". The amount of money is expected to be more than $100m (£78m) annually. "We looked at different approaches", says Patagonia's chair Charles Conn. He adds that one option could have been floating the firm on a stock exchange and "then give the money away", but that may have resulted in the company subsequently not being run in such an environmentally focused way. "So we kept coming back to giving shares to environmental foundations, and using it to fight the environmental crisis … It's a radical thing to do, but we're dependent on Mother Earth" (*ibid*).

The numbers involved in these examples illustrate why marketers need economists and accountants to be involved. In reality, all three perspectives offer something. If organisations primarily use one perspective, they may fail in the long term. All three perspectives should be considered. There are, however, a large number of balancing factors which come into play (Table 4.8).

In B2B markets, the situation is slightly different as marketers usually have closer relationships with professional customers. However, getting the pricing correct first time is still important. Marketers must use research to ascertain the pricing points. However, as always, not all organisations have the time and resources to do this. As part of a marketing audit, marketers will conduct a competitor analysis to take a holistic view of the market. They need to know how their brand is perceived by customers when compared to the competition. Costs are incurred when creating products or services. A good grasp of costs is required to be able to undertake ROI, ROMI and ROCE assessments (see Chapter 5).

Pricing can be strategic and/or tactical. In small companies who struggle to survive, problems may arise with cash flow and/or liquidity; pricing can be used to only just cover costs or set to undercut competitors, creating sales volume thus improving cash flow and liquidity. Trying to take all these factors into consideration is difficult. Imagine calculating all the costs for a product, analysing the competition's offerings and setting a price accordingly. A sales price (say £100) is set and the margin being sought is 20% (or £20). But what if the customer is not willing to accept the price? What if they see less value in the offering and suggest lowering prices? If a marketer relents and lowers the price by £10 this does two things. First it puts the brand head-to-head with the established competition. This may be good from a positioning point of view. However, assuming all costs remain the same, the new price has halved the margin. Questions would be raised as to

Table 4.8 Balancing factors germane to pricing

Factor	*Comment*
Customers	How much is the customer willing to pay? What will they demand at that price? Marketers who undertake pricing research are better placed to set the prices as the information is up-to-date and accurate
Competitors	Marketers must reflect on how their brand compares to the competition. Can it command a higher price? Is the brand worth more to the customer than the competitors?
Costs	Marketers usually need to cover costs when setting prices. Costs are made up of fixed costs (e.g. capital, buildings, plant, leases etc.) and variable costs (e.g. raw materials, casual labour, fuel, etc.)
Corporate and Marketing Objectives	The pricing of products and services should be compatible with the corporate objectives. Before creating actual price points, marketers must be aware of the current organisational circumstances

Source: Adapted from Richardson (2020, pp 120–121).

whether the organisation would have launched a new product if anticipating only a 10% gross margin. Lowering prices is easy, however, raising them presents challenges and must achieve objectives. In 2023, Unilever reported a pre-tax profit of €3.9bn (£3.34bn), representing a 21% Y-o-Y increase despite seeing the volumes of goods fall in the same period. Supermarkets, who themselves have been accused of 'greedflation', i.e. exploiting a period of high inflation to increase their profits, have accused suppliers like Unilever excessively raising prices (BBC, 2023b). Clearly, they achieved a ROI objective, however it may have damaged relations with their key outlets.

Once marketers have a sound understanding of the cost mechanisms, the competitive offerings, the requirements and willingness of the customer and the circumstances of the organisation they then need to decide the pricing technique to be used to enter the marketplace.

Pricing Techniques

There are numerous techniques that can be used, each with advantages and disadvantages (Table 4.9). 'Cost Plus' pricing largely ignores issues relating to the quantity of inventory and associated production costs. It is inward focused, looking largely at the product's cost base. It neglects changing customer trends, environmental factors, even the competition. 'Going rate' pricing is another easy, flexible approach to pricing. However, if the offering is superior to the competition, e.g. a more powerful brand name with additional features and benefits, the decision may be taken to price above the competition,

Table 4.9 Pricing techniques

Technique	*Comment*
Cost Plus Pricing	A relatively easy and flexible technique to use. Calculate the total cost of producing one product and add the required margin to calculate the price. Little or no skill is necessary to use this technique
Going rate pricing	Analyse the competition's offerings and prices, then match them. Used if a brand is deemed as good as the competition or marketers prefer to maintain stability in the marketplace.
Pricing techniques that focus on the customers	
Technique	*Comment*
Market skimming	Involves entering the market with a high price and then, as the product/service matures and more innovative products move into the marketplace, the price lowers towards the going rate
Market penetration	Where organisations price their introductory offering below the competition to gain entry to the marketplace. As the brand becomes better known, the prices increase towards the going rate
Even Pricing	Customers psychologically perceive prices set at rounded figures (e.g. \$5, £10, €100) as being a better quality than those set at 'Odd' Prices (e.g. \$1.99, £9.99, €99.99)
Odd Pricing	Odd pricing is used as customers perceive substantial savings when, in reality, they are modest, e.g. a new pair of jeans costs \$49.99 (so no real saving on \$50). However, people often cite the cost in the 40s rather than 50s. Psychologically customers want to be seen as smart shoppers (at least not as having knowingly been ripped off)

Source: Adapted from Richardson (2020, pp 120–121).

i.e. 'Premium Pricing'. If after analysing the market place the offering is perceived to offer less value than the competition, then the decision may be to set a lower price (i.e. 'Discount Pricing'.).

> **Example:** Patagonia, B Corp certified since 2012, is known as an industry leader a propos environmental advocacy and sustainable practices. They were the first California-based company with B Corp certification and passionately advocate for other businesses following suit in what they refer to as a time of 'sustained environmental and social crisis'. Their leaders acknowledge how much work there is still to do in the sector and within their own business. They operate 'Premium Pricing' which enables them to create a Return on Objectives (RoO). For example, they operate a self-imposed Earth tax, through which they donate 1% of their annual sales to grassroots environmental groups. They adopt idealistic CSR and sustainability stances which clearly reflect enlightened self-interest. Their outstanding environmental efforts and entrepreneurial vision, including 70% of its collection using recycled materials, led it to the UN Champion of the Earth accolade in 2019, the UN's top environmental honour. Patagonia once claimed that "The B Corp movement is one of the most important of our lifetime" (Kim & Schifeling, 2022).

Many 'tech' products use the Market Skimming approach. Think about the PLC of a mobile phone – it is short as new technology is continually being used to update the features. Therefore, the time that the manufacturer must recover developmental and capital costs is short. Market penetration is the opposite of market skimming. This is a useful technique for new products where the marketer is seeking to create value for customers, i.e. a reason to choose their product/service rather than the competition that may be more established. It is also a useful technique to use if selling large quantities is an objective. Overall, it is a useful technique to use to become established and to take market share. Market penetration also allows the creation of entry barriers to new entrants because of the relatively low-price set.

As discussed, pricing sends signals to customers and competitors about issues such as quality and exclusivity. It can influence customers 'psychologically'. Quality providers (e.g. Louis Vuitton) generally use even prices to convey the notion of quality or at least the need to avoid such discount techniques. Marketers will carefully draw upon a range of sources to create the necessary price point. Ultimately it is a judgement call and prices must be monitored constantly. The form of the monitoring depends upon the nature (and size) of the organisation, the marketplace and business environment.

Increasingly, smartphones are used as a means of payment.

> **Example:** Paysafecard was launched in Austria and Germany in 2000. By 2007 it had accrued more than 10 million first-time transactions. By 2017 it claimed to be used by over 650,000 sales outlets, in 26 currencies and 46 countries. In the UK it teamed up with BT to enable mobile users to buy online goods and services with the fee simply being charged to their mobile bill. In 2021, Paysafe started trading on the New York Stock Exchange. In the same year Paysafe acquired two major players (eCash and PagoEfectivo) to strengthen their position in Europe and Latin America.

This payment mode (and new market entrants) are likely to increase amongst the younger generations who are increasingly 'cashless'. Marketers should make it easy for customers to spend their money and such technology should be incorporated into marcomms messages and processes when appropriate.

Where there is little differentiation between products, consumers increasingly use smartphone 'apps' to make price comparisons. However, these may direct consumers to disreputable providers. As security is of increasing concern marketers need to ensure that their site is recognised as being secure and displays the padlock symbol. Prospects and consumers should be encouraged to engage with suppliers before buying, as this step will often be beyond the capability of unscrupulous providers. Some sites (e.g. www.trustpilot.co.uk) aggregate reviews into one score

Vouchers and Cashback

Increasingly, consumers are looking to online discount and voucher providers, e.g. myvouchercodes.co.uk. These sites offer promotional codes often for online-only providers. The offers are often store specific, not necessarily the cheapest and usually time stamped. Marketers must ensure that prospects and returning customers are aware of the benefits on offer as the competition prices may be lower but not necessarily better value for money (vfm). Consumers will complement vouchers with cashback deals from sites such as Quidco.com and Topcashback.co.uk who use sales to familiar online stores. The amounts clawed back vary as do payment times (in some cases it can be months). So, again, make sure the product offer is well represented and be aware of the negative publicity of cashback schemes that go awry. Smartphone users are often involved with communities who generate a pool of advice that prospects and community members can access. Hotukdeals.com is such a case where 'best' deals can be found supported by real life advice, which is often up-to-date and impartial. At least, they are perceived to be more impartial.

4.5 Services

A recent, major world trend has been the dramatic growth of services. Services are now the major driver of many economies due to rising affluence, more leisure time and the growing complexity of products that require servicing. It can be argued that too much research relates to the traditional production view of firms rather than services. This manufacturing focus is looking increasingly outdated, as many countries continue their transition from manufacturing economies to being based mainly on services.

Shostack recognised that every time customers interact with service providers a "service encounter" occurs (Shostack, 1984). 'Services' marketing has long been based upon the notion that there is more to service than being served. It is based upon the mutual exchange and fulfilment of promises (Gronroos, 1990). Examples of 'services' are:

- Teaching, tutoring and mentoring
- Price comparison or cashback websites
- Travelling
- Renting a hotel room or Air BNB
- Banking
- Legal representation.

Table 4.10 Benefits sought in service encounters

Sought benefit	*Factors to be measured*
Reliability	Right first time; Consistency (billing, branding, timing)
Competence	Required skills; abilities
Courtesy	Respect; friendliness; politeness
Communication	Information; jargon avoidance
Credibility	Trustworthy; Believability; Honesty; Acts in best interest of client
Security	Risk; danger; doubt; uncertainty
Understanding	Leaning customer requirements; consistency
Access	Approachability; ease of contact; opening times
Responsiveness	Employee willingness; readiness; prompt service

Source: Adapted from Parasuraman *et al* (1985).

These are examples of services marketing as the core 'product' (see Figure 4.5) is intangible. A bank does not manufacture a product in the traditional sense. It simply provides a service with numerous customer 'touchpoints' on what some call a customer 'journey'. All 'touchpoints' provide opportunities to be perceived in a positive or negative way. Before the 'journey' begins, the customer has already built-up expectations and after it, they reflect on the degree to which they were delighted. This reflection can seriously impact customer satisfaction, word-of-mouth and repeat business. That said some issues arise with services, namely

- some are 'unsought' as customers are unaware of their need until a problem arises
- not all consumers can clearly articulate their needs and may become frustrated
- consumers cannot test services before purchase hence there is some risk.

A challenge for service providers is matching supply to demand, whilst creating or co-creating the value customers are seeking (Richardson & Cassop Thompson, 2019). Clearly, consumers seek benefits from service encounters (Table 4.10).

The benefits in Table 4.10 do not have equal weighting nor will they necessarily be sought simultaneously. Customers may seek benefit combinations. Furthermore, in some services the customers may seek differing benefits at different touchpoints. Services take place in a 'task environment', where specific attributes influence consumer decision-making. These attributes reflect tangible characteristics (i.e. spaciousness or layout) or more abstract psychological concepts (i.e., ambience, cleanliness and staff friendliness). Sustainable attributes can include standards, information, authenticity and environmental quality. These can create differentiation between competitors. However, consumer satisfaction is missing from many sustainability studies. The effectiveness of communicating standards or authenticity influences sustainable consumption.

'Services Marketing' Versus 'Marketing Services'

Companies often sell warranties for potentially long-lasting goods. The product is tangible whereas the warranty is intangible and sold (often lucratively) to the client. This is marketing a service. Where the core 'product' is intangible (e.g. online banking), the company engages in services marketing.

> **Example***:* The Co-operative's "Smile" service consistently achieves the highest levels of customer satisfaction. It does this whilst complying with its own strict sustainability protocols. Smile is often followed by First Direct, who consistently out-perform their parent company HSBC in terms of customer satisfaction.

Customer Involvement

A 'servicescape' comes into being when a heightened consumer focus is imposed on the (purely operational) task environment. Those who study the servicescape are concerned with the co-creation of experience between designers, marketers, customers, prospects and consumers (Baker *et al*, 2007). The idea that, on entering a servicescape, people immediately make judgments as to whether they feel welcome, is not new (*ibid*). These judgments have always been shaped by the degree of involvement with the service. Bitner (1995, p 248) cited Disney where

> "each amusement park customer experiences 74 encounters in a single visit and that a negative experience in any one of the 74 can result in relationship deterioration".

The notion of services having differing degrees of consumer involvement is well established (Aldlaigan & Buttle, 2001) with cognitive (think), conative (feel) and affective (do) dimensions varying between consumers, service providers and sectors (*ibid*). The degree of involvement shapes the level of expectations as does whether the service is aimed at people or possessions (Table 4.11).

Not all services have the same degree of customer involvement. A visit to a bank's ATM (cash machine) has a higher degree of involvement than accessing an account

Table 4.11 Contrasting the nature of services being directed at people or possessions

Service Nature	*Directed at People*	*Directed at Possessions*
Tangible Acts	*People Processing* people have to physically present them so that they become immersed within the service process e.g. dentists, airlines, hospitals, haircuts, restaurants, hotels, gyms.	*Possession Processing* objects may breakdown or need maintenance. Here the quality of the repair service is not dependent on the owner or representative of the possession being present whilst the service operation takes place e.g. freight, repair, cleaning, landscaping, retailing, recycling.
Intangible Acts	*Mental Stimulus Processing* People are involved mentally in the service interaction and give time in order to experience the benefits of this service, e.g. education, gaming, broadcasting, consulting, psychotherapy	*Information Processing* (Directed at intangible assets) – Advances in technology have enabled information processing to become quicker, more accurate and more frequent, often at the expense of people processing, e.g. airline bookings, accounting, banking, insurance, legal, research

Source: Adapted from Baines *et al* (2013).

online. Both are relatively low-involvement encounters. Buying a Groupon voucher for a manicure is low involvement, whereas the manicure itself involves a high degree of involvement. Clearly the degree of involvement impacts on the level of customer expectation. This does not mean that customers are happy if the ATM is empty. As Herzberg advises, refilling an empty ATM will not improve customer motivation. If something has gone wrong, simply putting it right does not automatically increase customer motivation (Herzberg *et al*, 1959). They expect it to be right in the first place. Table 4.11 provides a useful template for service providers who can anticipate issues with their delivery. Furthermore, low-involvement services failures can lead to high involvement acts where customers engage with service providers seeking not only correction of the error but also compensation for the inconvenience and, in extreme cases, customers 'switching' providers (Farah, 2017).

In all encounters there are will be some that have a greater impact on relationship building and maintenance than others (Bitner, 1995). When customers interact with service providers for the first time, the initial encounter is vital in creating first impressions. However, often "the importance of the person who creates the organizations' first impression is not recognized" (*ibid*, p 248).

Companies who strive to correct mistakes and then deliver the expected levels of services may benefit from the Service Recovery Paradox (McCollough & Bharadwaj, 1992). Where consumer problems have been satisfactorily resolved, satisfaction levels can be equal to or greater than where no problem occurred (*ibid*). It would be a folly to rely on such phenomena (Michel & Meuter, 2008). The sensible approach is to get it 'right first time' and assume consumers are active (not passive), free to choose suppliers and can switch easily. Changes to regulations and legislation increasingly seek to make it easier for consumers to 'switch' (Farah, 2017). Arguably, if consumers know they can switch service providers easily, they will feel more in control. Ironically, the perception of control may make them less likely to switch, all other things being equal (*ibid*). A way to avoid such dis-satisfaction is to promote value co-creation or seeking for consumers (Richardson & Cassop Thomson, 2019). Either way consumers must feel 'involved'.

Characteristics of Services

Services have characteristics that differ from goods manufacturing (Table 4.12).

Each of the characteristics (Table 4.12) are better thought of as a continuum. Hence Intangibility should be viewed as ranging from 'Tangible' to 'Intangible'. For pure services it will be largely intangible whereas with goods the tangible features are often supported with intangible service features (e.g. warranty). If a company suffers from unacceptable levels of variability the solution lies with standardisation, motivation and/or training. Training is always essential, and marketers must pay particular attention to their relationship with their peers in HR. Recruiting, training and motivating staff is fundamental to marketing success.

The Extended Marketing Mix for Services

Booms and Bitner (1981) created an Extended Marketing Mix for services by complementing the traditional 4Ps with People, Process and Physical Evidence. Traditionally, the extended Mix uses the phrase Physical Evidence; however, it is problematic when considering the digital (i.e. virtual) nature of much modern marketing.

Table 4.12 Characteristics of services

B2C Classification	*Comment*
Intangibility	Services cannot be seen, tasted, felt, heard or smelt before they are bought, e.g. people undergoing cosmetic surgery cannot see the result before the purchase
Inseparability	Services are often inseparable from the providers whether said providers are people (lecturers, hairdressers or doctors) or machines such as cash dispensers
Perishability	Services, unlike goods, cannot be stored for later sale or consumption. A missed flight or doctor's appointment represent missed opportunities for both parties. A key challenge for service providers is matching supply to demand
Variability (a.k.a. Heterogeneity)	The quality of the service is dependent on the person providing it and is therefore variable. This also extends beyond those delivering services to include when, where and how they are provided. Employees need to be motivated to change their behaviour
Ownership	Customers do not own services; rather, they pay for access to the service. Car rental companies allow full use of the car, but the ownership of the car remains with them. iTunes consumers do not own the music, rather they own the right to play the music under certain conditions

Source: Adapted from Richardson (2020, p 125).

Hence, the term 'Presence' is preferred (Richardson *et al*, 2015). The extended Mix is widely accepted amongst marketing academics and practitioners

People

Many commentators argue that the 'People' element is the most important element therein. That said the 'People' element is problematic when interacting online. Marketers must avoid making the service too 'robotic', standardised and soulless. With 'People' being common to the 'Mix' AND the TBL's People-Planet-Profit (or Prosperity) it is difficult to comprehend why sustainability has been largely ignored in the marketing domain for so long. Key sources of conflict are motivation (see Section 3.1), the lack of communication and 'stepping on others' toes' or demarcation. Clearly, the issue of communicating effectively with 'People' is paramount. As discussed, consumers often find themselves 'locked into' making purchases beyond their control. This undoubtedly drives anti-marketing sentiment and unsustainable consumption.

Process

Many service providers use 'Process' as a means of achieving competitive advantage. They seek to make customers' lives easier by providing services that are quicker, more flexible, safer, consistent, easier and with lower risk. Developments in relation to the service and digital technology have greatly improved customer experiences. Governments are investing in 'Process' and are achieving considerable savings by moving online. In the UKm consumers no longer have to possess a physical TV licence. They pay online after the government sends a reminder before expiry. The cost and CO_2 footprint of producing hard copy licences has been removed.

'Online' Process alludes to engagement with websites, social media, email and messaging. Marketers must consider the User Experience (UX) when developing web content. Customer touchpoints must be (perceived to be) quick, easy and efficient. Sites must be easy to use on smartphones. Smartphone users are demanding improved experiences and sensible marketers always make it easy for customers to spend their money. Mobile sites are increasingly efficient and marcomms are becoming more effective as users buy without delay. Many users have their phones with them 24/7.

Operations, a key element of Process, must keep pace with customer changes however some managers lack customer-centricity and have chosen operational effectiveness as the key route to superior profitability (Porter, 1996). This is remiss as without a clear understanding of customer needs, it may be impossible to make the necessary operational changes. What is needed is not change for its own sake, but the right change and many examples now exist of companies who have adopted TBL practices.

All actions and communications online shape the brand's digital manifestation. The other elements of the Mix must support this. Some practical steps specific to smartphone users are:

- segment contacts by heavy or light smartphone usage, time slots, information seekers and whether users can be identified as mobile email readers
- seek permission and use Bluetooth to highlight bargains when users are within range
- use time-related messages to complement their behaviour, e.g. when people are leaving work to remind them to stop on the way home
- keep messages short so that they are easily read
- provide notices, e-vouchers and regular (say monthly) newsletters.
- provide support to extend the product's life. Alternatively provide information to repair/repurpose/recycle.

Presence (a.k.a. Physical Evidence)

A company's digital presence increasingly represents the company, its brands and value sought by stakeholders. Everything online (be it mobile, social, corporate website or anything else digital) must accurately represent the company and brand. Setting standards for logos, text, design or layout encourages a co-ordinated and seamless UX.

> **Example:** The BBC's website is hugely popular. With their iPlayer service they can stream shows around the world. 'Banded' TV schedules are becoming a thing of the past. Consider the enormous amount of content streamed by the BBC of the Glastonbury festival. They send 300 people to Glastonbury who provide highlights on three terrestrial TV channels, cover it extensively on FM and digital radio stations and stream every 'set' via iPlayer. After 30 days much of the content is released via YouTube thus reaching an even bigger audience. The BBC has moved inexorably towards offering a platform where voice, data, TV and mobile (known as quad play) interact seamlessly. This degree of interoperability is a sign of things to come.

Service Quality

Consumers are more discerning and prepared to move if they are not satisfied with services. Sometimes problems occur because of the perception of the service rather than the reality. Hyper-competition means that moving from one provider to another is easy. Competitive advantage can be obtained by delivering consistently higher-quality service than competitors.

Service quality is a value type that resides in the mind of the customer. Value types can combine to represent the value sought by customers. Consumers' perceptions of how well services meet or exceed their expectations inform their decision-making. Three elements that determine service quality experience are Technical, Functional and Expectation, sometimes referred to as the 'triangle of quality perception' (Gronroos, 1984). Technical alludes to aspects of the service, e.g. waiting times for trains; functional refers to how well the service is delivered, e.g. was it provided in a friendly or professional manner? Expectation refers to managing the expectations of the customer and staff delivering the service. Customers may have unrealistic expectations, some of which can be met whereas others cannot. Professor Malcolm McDonald warns against seeking to delight customers to such an extent that the company is no longer profitable. It is no use being a sustainable company which fails because it cannot make a profit.

Competitors can use service quality to differentiate their offering from their competitors, drive customer loyalty and increase satisfaction. Customer satisfaction and loyalty are not the same thing. Satisfaction is an attitude whereas loyalty is behavioural. As mentioned previously, there is more to services than merely being served, particularly if companies seek to create loyalty. Parasuraman *et al* (1985) identified the benefits consumers seek from services (Table 4.10). They then created the SERVQUAL gaps model which became the most widely used model to measure service quality. SERVQUAL (Figure 4.13) identifies customer service gaps between management and customers' perceptions a propos the benefits sought. The gaps model of services encourages companies to develop organisational objectives and tactics to close the gaps (*ibid*).

Marketers must measure the service quality. Service quality can be measured although it is difficult. This will be dependent on learning more about the clients through marketing research, focusing on their expectations and perceptions.

SERVQUAL fails to recognise ICs and BSEs which is remiss (Richardson & Gosnay, 2022). A limitation of all 'gap' models is they do not inform Marketers what steps should be undertaken. Furthermore, not all gaps are equally important so their relevance may differ with time. Research is needed to test the efficacy of the existing gaps. New gaps may be needed. Some approaches to closing the specific gaps are illustrated in Table 4.13.

Marketers should adapt the Mix to ensure the provision of consistently high-quality services. Any changes to service design and delivery should take place in a co-ordinated, planned manner.

4.6 Using the Mix to Coordinate Sustainability Adoption

Part of the ongoing failure attributed to climate conventions (e.g. the 26th UN Climate Change Conference of the Parties (COP26) in Glasgow in 2021) is largely due to a lack of understanding of how consumers behave. The consumerism genie is out of the bottle and cannot simply be put back in. Western consumers are not ready or willing to make the

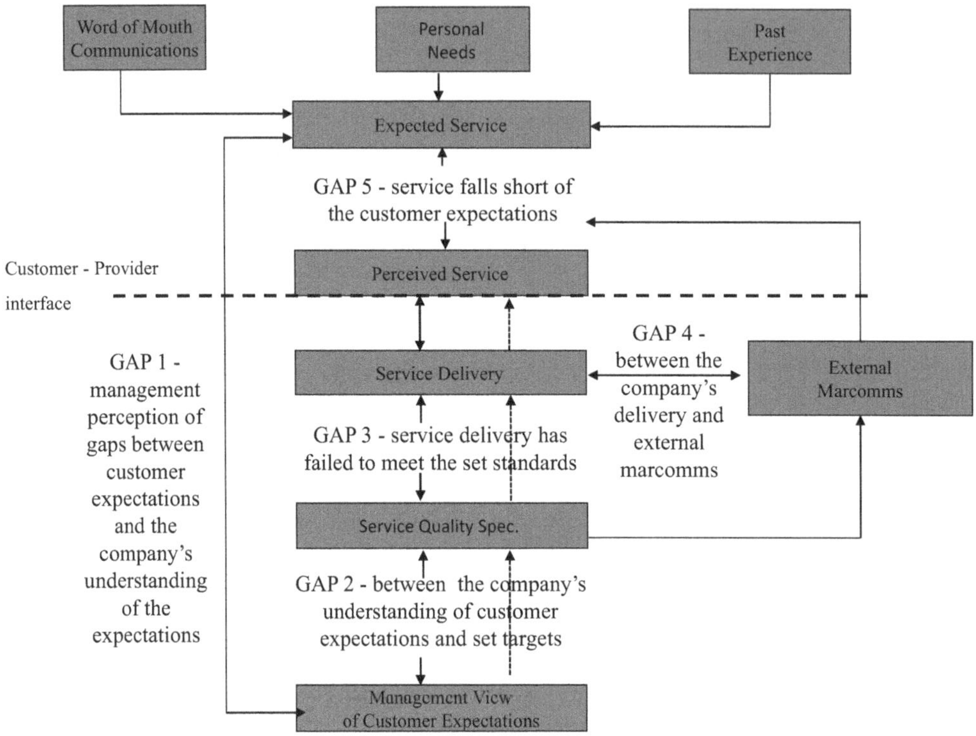

Figure 4.13 SERVQUAL – A gaps model of service.

Source: Adapted from Parasuraman *et al* (1985).

changes necessary to return to pre-industrial levels of pollution or waste or by-products such as CO_2.

If products are not simply the toys of the rich and are to permeate all societies, they need to be better, cheaper and greener. Technological advances may resolve many pressing issues (even global warming) however there needs to be a shift towards replacing older, less efficient products with newer more sustainable equivalents whether cars, televisions, condenser boilers or mobile phones.

Example: Allbirds, a BCorp-accredited shoe brand, addresses issues germane to the environment, i.e. its supply chain and packaging. Often referred to as 'the world's most comfortable shoes', the company uses natural materials, with ranges made from eco-friendly eucalyptus pulp and moisture-wicking merino wool that is ZQ-certified (meaning it meets stringent standards for sustainable farming and animal welfare) and uses 60% less energy than synthetics (Bellini, 2021). The company reimagined their packaging, using 90% post-consumer recycled cardboard that serves as a shoebox and shopping bag all in one, and works with charity Soles4Souls to ensure its gently used shoes find new homes in some of the world's poorest communities. Its Allbirds Flight Plan aims to cut its CO_2 footprint in half by 2025 and to near zero by 2030 (*ibid*). Its packaging aligns with the Re-use and Recycle aspects of the Three Rs (see Chapter 1). Allbirds supports UN SDGs 3, 8, 9 and 12 (amongst others).

Table 4.13 Where the extended services mix and SERVQUAL overlap

Service Mix	*SERVQUAL components and questions*	*Suggestions*	*Approaches to closing gaps*
Process	*Reliability* Can the company perform the service, accurately, dependably and consistently? Does the delivery 'fit' the instructions given?	Set agreed, quantifiable, attainable standards for service delivery. Create systems to measure and monitor success	**GAP 1** – Hold regular team meetings and briefings to ensure they are customer focused **GAP 2** – Improve interaction between management and staff to establish realistic targets for staff **GAP 3** – Use internal marketing techniques to ensure customer facing staff are clear on their roles, targets and expectations **GAP 4** – Service delivery standards need to be maintained and improved whilst managing customer expectations **GAP 5** – Ensure the highest levels of customer service are achieved and a customer-centric approach is adopted
People	*Responsiveness* Can the company offer a timely service that meets customers expectations?	Establish clients' requirements Analyse internal implications – e.g. training needs, restructuring. Develop training programmes	
	Empathy Does the company focus on the individual?	Determine client care objectives	
	Assurance Does the company convey trust and confidence?	Ensure adequate internal education and communication. Consider performance-related pay and recognition systems. Set up/revise systems for service delivery	
Physical Evidence or Presence	*Tangibles* Does the company project itself in a professional manner?	Ensure look and feel of tangible attributes (offices, cars, reception etc.) are excellent. Create a culture where staff want to present themselves in the best possible manner. Ensure online presence is easy to find, navigate and monetise	

Source: Author.

A number of forces underscore the emerging opportunities to proactively adopt sustainable practices including networked communications, extended (and interconnected) supply chains and rapidly changing markets (Moore & Manring, 2009). The development and launch of new sustainable products can generate success stories for organisations and create a real sense of achievement for those involved in its conception and development. Successful new sustainable products can:

- Enhance an organisation's reputation and standing in the marketplace
- Bring prominence to the brand
- Increase turnover, profit and market share
- Enhance customer satisfaction and build loyalty.

Choice Editing

The shift towards sustainable consumption will influence the choices available to consumers. Increasingly choice editing will take place where manufacturers and/or retailers limit the consumers' options. Manufacturers will bias their product mix towards sustainability if they see long-term cost reductions or new ethical and/or green markets. Sometimes the choice editing will be imposed by government, as is the case with diesel cars being banned in the UK from 2030.

Choice editing is not new. In 1995, the DIY store B&Q set a target for its timber to be certified sustainable by the Forest Stewardship Council (FSC) by 1999. Consumers at B&Q would be given the simple choice of buying sustainable timber (from B&Q) or shopping elsewhere. Some retailers prefer to offer sustainable and non-sustainable goods then leave the choice to the customer. In the long run, customers are becoming more ethical and green 'savvy'. More non-sustainable options will be removed from the shelves. Sainsbury was amongst the first major retailers to offer pole and line caught tuna. 'Pole and line' inflicts much less damage on the marine environment and eradicates cast-off, i.e. the catching of unintended fish that are returned to the sea, sometimes after perishing. Nowadays, most major retailers offer pole and line and often Marine Stewardship Certification (MSC) as well.

The various Mix tools can be used to coordinate the adoption of TBL-based practices. The PLC can support co-ordination of other tools in the Mix.

> **Example:** At Alpro, environmental accountability is key. In turn, having robust data is indispensable for achieving and maintaining the BCorp certification. Therefore, Alpro is committed to the continuous evaluation of the impact its products have through an extensive life-cycle analysis. This analysis will also support environmental labelling on Alpro's products. Empowering consumers to make more sustainable food choices by providing additional information about the environmental impact of food products is an integral part of the transition to more sustainable food systems (Alpro, 2023).

This Alpro example illustrates how the 'comms' mix may have to change as the product moves through its life cycle. It can also provide insights into strategic changes necessary. Consider three scenarios depicted in Figure 4.6.

Zone A: Involves spending money developing and testing products prior to release. Here research could involve sustainability opinion formers (eg George Monbiot) who, in turn, could inform the early adopters (particularly with high-value sustainable products such as Fenton's jewellery). The research could lead to a teaser campaign to raise awareness pre-launch.

Zone B After a successful launch, rapid growth can quickly recoup more R&D costs. Some may extend the growth period or allow it to evolve into the maturity stage. Marketers may use social media or mobile email campaigns to involve sustainable segments e.g. voluntary simplifiers. Testimonials could help to explain the sustainable benefits or value taken. Positive feedback can be cascaded via the mass media, informing existing customers of new sustainability developments. Remember, advertising is expensive and its impact may be diminished as people expect marketers to say good things about their own products. That said, they gladly accept the word of real customers or other opinion formers.

Zone C It is often desirable to maintain sales in 'maturity' for as long as possible. Marcomms can be used to extend maturity, e.g. using PR to explain the product's reliability. Customers should be supported in terms of repairing their products (see Chapter 3). Good feedback from third parties, i.e. Which? social media sites, user forums and/or price comparison websites should be utilised. Any PR should be seeded into the mass media.

Have no doubt that consumers are more discerning and prepared to move if they are not satisfied. Sometimes problems occur because of the perception of the service rather than the reality. The BCorp accreditation process stresses the need for transparency with customers and suppliers.

Competitive advantage can be obtained by delivering consistently higher-quality service than competitors. Marketers should strive to provide a consistent high-quality service. Rigorous marketing research should focus on the sustainable value they seek, their expectations and perceptions.

Integrated Marketing Communications (IMC) and Sustainability

Today's technologies offer exciting 'comms' choices and challenges. Marketers are often expected to achieve a Return on Marketing Investment (ROMI) or, alternatively, a Return on Objectives (RoO). Whenever creating 'comms' campaigns (say using PR, sales promotions, ads and direct mail letters), marketers must have the means to monitor the 'comms' effectiveness. Lessons must be learned and adopted in future campaigns. Failing marcomms need to be analysed to ascertain the flaws, i.e. Is the message unclear? Is the digital media chosen to carry the message working? Is there too much noise? Does the encoding work?

Effective marcomms can provide considerable success for brands and companies. However, if they go wrong, they can have devastating effects. Not only can precious time, money and resources be wasted, but brand equity (the value of the brand) and the reputation of the company can also suffer. As marcomms activities are highly visible, key stakeholders may witness mistakes. It is important to remember that within any marketing mix, the 'comms' mix should be integrated (not separated) and used to create customer value.

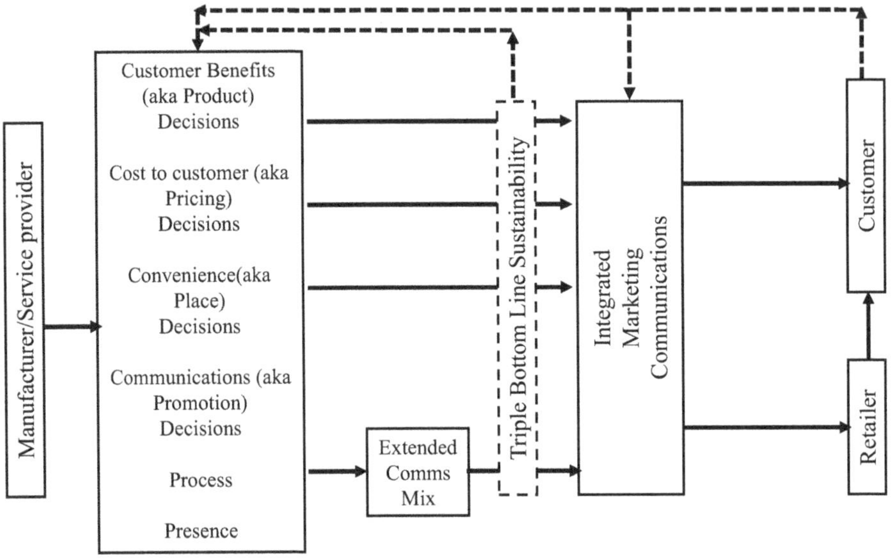

Figure 4.14 Using IMC to co-ordinate sustainability adoption.

Source: Author.

Companies often use marcomms techniques without fully understanding the impact of individual activities, never mind the collective impact of using a range of tactics. Marketers are responsible for the adoption of Integrated Marketing Communications (IMC) which can facilitate 'buy-in'.

IMC is predicated on message consistency, interactivity, being stakeholder-centric and having a strategic focus. The effectiveness of the Mix components must be understood and feedback loops must exist regarding the overall coordination and/or how individual aspects perform (Figure 4.14). Taking a holistic approach increases the likelihood that, say, the 'comms' tactics used, from sending press releases to communicating with customers, prospects and other stakeholders are most effective. IMC can be delivered on a range of platforms.

Different consumers have differing degrees of complexity of decision-making owing to their use of information. Information seeking is present to some degree for all consumers. The challenge is to employ a variety of information sources as part of the IMC. This is an opportunity to use 'marcomms' positively as historically it "has been a focus of social criticism for its role in promoting conspicuous consumption" (Belz & Peattie, 2009, p 178). Instead, it can be used to inform consumers about how their products can be reused, repaired or recycled in future. The Three Rs should become a key part of the company's IMC. Eco-warriors (see Figure 3.6) distrust marketer-dominated 'comms' therefore the IMC could use testimonials from green customers, 'independent' third-party information (say from Greenpeace) and/or credible celebrities (Young *et al*, 2010; Richardson *et al*, 2015). Marketers should target responsive segments with sustainability appeals and interventions should be tailored to reflect the specific needs and motivations, barriers, and benefits of the target consumer (White *et al*, 2019). Marketers must tailor

Table 4.14 Adoption vs adaptation of mix components to target sustainable segments

		Product		
		Adopt	*Adapt*	*NPD*
Comms Mix	Adopt	Sell to new market using existing product & comms mix (Lowest risk.)	Sell to new market using next iteration of same product and existing comms mix (Medium risk)	Develop and launch new product with new comms mix (Highest risk)
	Adapt	Sell to new market using existing product with a new comms mix (Medium risk)	Sell to new market using next iteration of same product and adjusted comms mix (Medium-High risk)	

Source: Author.

their 'comms' to their audience which may involve different 'comms' mixes for the sub-segments (see the SST in Chapter 3).

IMC can facilitate Internal Marketing (IM). Managers must use IMC to ensure information flows (well) and is shared across departmental boundaries and even organisational frontiers (Porcu *et al*, 2020). This applies to all organisational types and sizes, including SMEs and micro-enterprises where marketing is often allocated to a multi-tasking individual. Adopting good IM practices involves continuous dialogue with stakeholders.

Marketers wanting to improve their sustainable positioning can adopt and/or adapt their Marketing Mix for new markets. Table 4.14 illustrates how Customer Benefits (Product) and Comms could be adapted to influence sustainable product adoption.

Marketers must choose which option will have the highest likelihood of success. FMCG products have a high failure rate. Higher risk options would involve adaption or launching a new product to target a sustainable segment.

Example: Finisterre is a BCorp-accredited outdoor clothing label providing innovative waterproof and windproof fleeces designed to warm surfers. They use sustainable supply chains and resurrected the British merino wool industry in 2005 to bring manufacturing closer to home. It has a flock of over 300 Bowmont sheep, the only breed capable of producing a fine merino wool with the hardiness to survive the British climate (Bellini, 2021). The impact on the environment is taken into account, including its garment bags, which are part of their 'Leave No Trace' initiative. Taking over a year to develop, the water-soluble bags were adapted to be recyclable, biodegradable and break down harmlessly into non-toxic biomass in soil and sea. They created a special sea suit, designed to overcome barriers to surfing in countries where modesty laws make access to the ocean difficult for women and young girls (*ibid*). Finisterre aligns with 'biospheric' value-types of consumers by drastically reducing its supply network's CO_2 footprint and with 'self-transcendent' value-types having addressed different cultural approaches to female bathing. Finisterre supports UN SDGs 3, 5, 9 and 12.

The question of 'adopt versus adapt' presents different challenges when coordinating changes across the whole Mix. Adoption, sometimes referred to as standardisation, will create economies of scale. As the same product is adopted in differing markets companies will benefit from improved inventory management, shorter replacement lead times and less capital tied up in goods.

Example: Stuart Kirk, HSBC Asset Management's global head of responsible investing, questioned the risk climate change plays in financial markets (Investment Week, 2022). Presenting a speech '*Why investors need not worry about climate risk*' he asked: "Who cares if Miami is six metres under water in 100 years? Amsterdam has been six metres underwater for ages and that is a really nice place. We will cope with it". He went on to add that he does not "doubt the science at all" and acknowledged "there will be fires" but argued this should be solved through adaption. "One of the tragedies of this whole debate, which we obsess about at HSBC, is that we spend way too much on mitigation and financing and not enough on adaption financing". His speech was shown to HSBC Asset Management, whose CEO, Nicolas Moreau, stated remarks made by Kirk

> "do not reflect the views of HSBC Asset Management nor HSBC Group in any way ... (we are) ... committed to driving the transition to a sustainable global economy and have a fiduciary responsibility to ensure its clients' monies are managed for positive long-term environmental and social outcomes ... HSBC regards climate change as one of the most serious emergencies facing the planet, and is committed to supporting its customers in their transition to net zero and a sustainable future and, like HSBC Asset Management, is committed to achieving net zero by 2050".
>
> (*ibid*)

This is a typical response from a MNC regarding its ESG position. Kirk undoubtedly adopts a maverick position in respect to his views on climate change. That said, Kirk's comments about the lack of finance for adaptation ring true.

Sustainable Distribution

Distribution Logistics alludes to managing the practical realities of physically moving products often over great distances. The trend for manufacturing goods in the Far East and Pacific rim is going to continue for the foreseeable future. Hence, the process of logistically manoeuvring the freight around the world to markets in the west has increased in importance and significance. Distribution of products is an area where much of the sustainability impact of products occurs through the burning of fossil fuels to transport products throughout global supply chains. There are also social implications to distribution in terms of the accessibility of products, particularly in markets such as financial services where there are concerns about the exclusion of disadvantaged customers through the closure of bank branches and post offices (CFSD, 2023).

Example: Bird was the UK's first certified BCorp eyewear brand and it has addressed the ecological impact of manufacturing its glasses. Dedicated to designing beautiful glasses, its frames are created using the highest quality sustainable materials, including certified woods, bio-based acetate, renewable cork and recycled aluminium, and come with cleaning cloths made from recycled plastic bottles (Bellini, 2021). For every pair bought the company distributes solar light to families in Zambia and Malawi, replacing the use of fossil fuel burning lamps, through their Share Your Sun partnership with SolarAid. In supporting SolarAid they also support UN SDG 3. All their bamboo and wooden frames are compostable, while their laminated wood and aluminium frames can be recycled (Bellini, 2021). Bird only use sustainably sourced materials, including the accessories (i.e. cleaning cloths), thus supporting UN SDG 12 by adopting responsible consumption and production. Clearly, it reinvests profits into People- and Planet-friendly activities.

Poor distribution can negatively affect customer satisfaction. From a B2B perspective, poor delivery may lead to attrition of key accounts as professional buyers seek alternative suppliers. Sustainability needs to be viewed in terms of involvement within the wider context of stakeholder relationships. Reputations are easily tarnished by supply-side scandals with emotive issues such as child labour. Hence, with organisational success often depending on suppliers, it is important to ascertain whether the supply network (a term preferred to 'chain') operates in a sustainable manner. Retailers, for example, are undoubtedly inter-dependent, networking organisations and will need to trust their partners. Trust can be shaped by previous experiences and co-operative efforts and on the more general reputation a firm has built up through its earlier behaviour (Haberberg *et al*, 2010). Adopting sustainable practices may engender trust in consumers, which can be grown, say, through positive word of mouth. The role of packaging is important, as complaints will often arise from goods damaged in transit. Therefore, the packaging needs to be robust enough (to stand the journey and mode of transport used) and recyclable. For an organisation to trust its suppliers it must assume they will comply with its sustainability policies. However, suppliers comply for a range of reasons, e.g. being enlightened, coerced or mimetic amongst others (*ibid*). Organisations who are highly motivated may adopt idealistic CSR stances or even ones of enlightened self-interest whereas stakeholders on whom they rely may only do so when coerced.

Example: Seat's main manufacturing facilities are located in Martorell, 30 km northwest of Barcelona. They produce 500,000 cars annually in what is regarded as one of the most efficient car plants in the world. Seat may want a supplier to provide a complete head-light assembly rather than the constituent components. This generates higher revenue and profit for the supplier, however quality control is paramount as any failures will impact the whole sub- assembly. Often Original Equipment Manufacturers (OEMs), say the bulb manufacturer Lucas, will happily supply to the third party as it wants to keep the end-user (in this case Seat) happy.

Products can be transported using airfreight, cargo ships, railways, lorries, cars, or motorbikes. Hence careful consideration is needed regarding the mode of transport from one intermediary to another. Cost, convenience, capability and carbon footprint all need to be taken into account. When purchasing space on container vessels, wagons, or trains, whatever the mode of transport, there are inevitable costs. Customers are increasingly expecting suppliers to use 'green' logistics. So, a balance may be needed, e.g. when shipping goods from China to the EU, as sea-containers are cheaper and have a lower carbon footprint per item. However, it can take several weeks for the goods to arrive. Using airfreight dramatically increases the carbon footprint and cost but dramatically reduces the delivery time.

Example: The madness of thousands of tonnes of basic foodstuffs, passing each other in the sky, by rail, sea or roads, has been well documented. For example, in 2021, the UK exported 352,400 tonnes of poultry meat (Statista, 2023a). However, also in 2021, the UK imported 408,000 metric tonnes of poultry (Statista, 2023b). This lunacy is repeated in many countries.

The notion of a return to greater local production is not new. In 1936 John Maynard Keynes (one of the greatest economists of the twentieth century) said:

> "Ideas, knowledge, art, hospitality, travel – these are the things that should of their nature be international. But let good be homespun wherever it is reasonable and conveniently impossible, and above all let finance be primarily national".
>
> (Keynes, 1936, cited in Porritt, 2005, p 77)

As discussed, consumers can develop different types of involvement with activities, objects, ideas or even social issues. Higher involvement results from stakeholders being committed to causes or alternatively being affected such as the local community. People belong to a local economy, which differs from the global economy and is extremely important to the welfare and quality of life in their locality (Tilley & Young, 2009). Sourcing locally is a clear way of acting in a more sustainably responsible way. Companies using local suppliers may engender trust in consumer communities *and* supplier networks.

Hence it is logical to recognise the case for measuring and developing trust within supply networks across a range of issues. Marketers must evaluate whether they can trust the stakeholders in their network to act in recognisably sustainable ways. Misplaced trust poses risks for companies and relationships need to be managed carefully. More progressive companies seek to establish relationships with local firms, consumers and regulators. Rather than simply complying with the minimum expectations, marketers need to be more inclusive and sensitive to stakeholders. This itself may generate improved PR with the community. Not to mention enhancing the chances of success by favourably influencing the opinions of planners who receive positive feedback from the local community. Transparency is key to sustainable trade. Many companies are developing sustainability policies and practices and looking closely at their supply chains. Increasingly the onus is

> "on companies to be proactive rather then reactive, to anticipate inevitable change, to fill the space available to them for much more environmentally and socially responsible actions, and to lobby government for faster change".
>
> (Porritt, 2005, p 240)

Considering that 'government' covers local, national and international government it is safe to assume that marketers' remits are becoming increasingly complex. It is not enough to compete, but they are expected to lobby as well.

Key Findings

1. Marcomms campaigns need to consider the customer journey. The 'comms' mix needs to be integrated into a seamless, consistent experience from the customers' perspective.
2. 'Convenience' involves getting the right products to the right place at the right time in the right condition. Failure to do so can result in customer dissatisfaction.
3. Intermediaries provide skills, knowledge and access to markets. Increasingly, organisations are seeking to 'green' their supply network.
4. Logistics includes decisions relating to warehousing: number, size and location, transportation, internal ordering systems etc.
5. A product is formed by tangible and intangible factors. Consumer and industrial goods can be categorised.
6. The PLC highlights products have lives.
7. The Adoption/ Diffusion curve identifies those who help diffuse the product and support acceptance amongst prospects.
8. Introducing new products helps organisations remain competitive, increase profitability, sales, market share, customer satisfaction and loyalty. Developing new products involves risks. The NPD Process provides a more controlled, organised process.
9. Customers experience sacrifices to buy goods. Pricing connects with customers' values, e.g. value for money, quality, exclusivity, etc. Factors when setting prices include the costs, competition, customer motivation, corporate objectives and legal/ regulatory issues. Lowering prices is easy, raising prices presents marketers with challenges.
10. Service industries drive economic growth. Service quality can be used to achieve competitive advantage. Marketers must establish clients' requirements and then set internal standards for service delivery.

Activities

1. Research online into social media 'fails' – examples of where organisations have tried to implement online campaigns via social media with no success.
2. For OoH advertising see https://oaaa.org/.
3. Imagine you are developing a newer, fresher version of a household product. Using the NPD Process, write down what is involved in each of the steps.
4. Using Table 4.3 classify recently bought B2C goods. Were they unsought? How could the categorisation inform the DMP?

5 Exhibitions provide insights into products, often running seminars. One such UK show is the Technology for Marketing show (see www.t-f-m.co.uk).
6 Draw the PLC for a product, what steps are needed to extend the maturity stage? How could the tools from the extended marcomms mix be used?
7 EFQM is another widely used model to measure service quality (see https://efqm.org/).
8 Representative PR bodies (i.e. the CIPR and PRCA) provide useful information as does the European Public Relations Confederation (see www.cerp.org/)

References

Aldlaigan, A.H., & Buttle, F.B. (2001) Consumer involvement in financial services: an empirical test of two measures. *International Journal of Bank Marketing*, 19(6), pp. 232–245.

Alpro. (2023) *Alpro: Promoting Healthier Eating and Sustainable Living*. https://bcorporation.eu/case_study/alpro-promoting-healthier-eating-and-sustainable-living/ (accessed 29-08-23).

Baines, P., Fill, C. & Page, K. (2013) *Essentials of Marketing*. Oxford: OUP.

Baker, M. (2009) *Aided Recall and Marketing Mnemonics* Guest Lecture presented by Professor Michael Baker to Leeds Business School, November 2009.

Baker, S.M., Holland, J. & Kaufman-Scarborough, C. (2007) How consumers with disabilities perceive "welcome" in retail servicescapes: A critical incident study. *Journal of Services Marketing*, 21(3), pp. 160–173.

BBC. (2023a) *The Firms Giving Nature a Stake in Their Businesses*. www.bbc.co.uk/news/business-66132669 (accessed 19-09-2023).

BBC. (2023b) *Magnum-Maker Unilever's Profits Higher after it Raises Prices*. www.bbc.co.uk/news/business-66299138 (accessed 20-09-23).

Bellini, L. (2021) *The Glossary's B Corp Fashion Guide: The Ethical Fashion Brands to Know-From Luxury Fashion Houses to Innovative Footwear Brands, These are the Trailblazing Names Doing Their Bit for the Planet | 21st October 2021* FASHION. https://theglossarymagazine.com/fashion/b-corp-fashion-brands/ (accessed 28-08-23).

Belz, F-M. & Peattie, K. (2009) *Sustainability Marketing — A Global Perspective*. Chichester: Wiley & Sons.

Bitner, M.J. (1995) Building service relationships: It's all about promises. *Journal of the Academy of Marketing Sciences*, 23(4), pp. 246–251.

Booms, B. & Bitner, M. (1981). Marketing strategies and organisation structures for service firms in *Marketing of Services: 1981 Special Educators' Conference Proceedings*, Donnelly & George, (Eds), Chicago: AMA, pp. 46–51.

Borden, N.H. (1964) The concept of the marketing mix. *Journal of Advertising Research*, 4 June, pp. 2–7.

CFSD. (2023) Centre for Sustainable Design. Pricing & Distribution https://cfsd.org.uk/smart-know-net/links/pricing.htm (accessed 06.08.23).

CIPR. (2023) About PR. www.cipr.co.uk/CIPR/About_Us/About_PR.aspx#:~:text=Public%20Relations%20is%20about%20reputation,and%20influencing%20opinion%20and%20behaviour (accessed 04-08-23).

Corporate Watch. (2023) *Carbon Cash Machine: What If Bp & Shell Dividends Were Used for the Common Good?* https://corporatewatch.org/how-carbon-profits-could-solve-crises-rather-than-create-them/ (accessed 18-09-23).

Donnelly, R. & Harrison, G. (2009) *CIM Coursebook: The Marketing Planning Process*. Routledge: London. DOI:10.4324/9780080961231.

Farah, M.F. (2017) Application of the theory of planned behaviour to customer switching intentions in the context of bank consolidations. *International Journal of Bank Marketing*, 35(1), pp. 147–172. DOI:10.1108/IJBM-01-2016-0003.

Gosnay, R.M. & Richardson, N. (2008) *Develop Your Marketing Skills*. London: Kogan Page.

Grönroos, C. (1984) A service quality model and its marketing implications. *European Journal of Marketing*, 18(4), pp. 36–44. DOI:10.1108/EUM0000000004784

Grönroos, C. (1990) Relationship approach to marketing in service contexts: The marketing and organizational behavior interface. *Journal of Business Research*, 20, pp. 3–11. DOI:10.1016/0148-2963(90)90037-E.

Guardian. (2023) *Say Hello to Longlife Tech That Can Challenge Our Throwaway Culture.* www.theguardian.com/money/2023/jul/30/say-hello-to-longlife-tech-that-can-challenge-our-throwaway-culture?CMP=Share_AndroidApp_Other (accessed 18-09-23).

Haberberg, A., Gander, J., Rieple, A., Martin-Castilla, J-I. & Helm, C. (2010) Institutionalizing idealism: The adoption of CSR practices *Journal of Global Responsibility*, 1(2), pp. 366–381. DOI:10.1108/20412561011079443

Henderson, B. (1970) *The Product Portfolio.* www.bcg.com/publications.aspx (accessed 03-02-19).

Herzberg, F., Mausner, B. & Snyderman, B.B. (1959) *The Motivation to Work.* New Brunswick (USA): Transaction Publishers.

Investment Week. (2022) *HSBC AM Global Head of Responsible Investing: 'Who Cares If Miami Is Six Metres under Water in 100 Years?'* www.investmentweek.co.uk/news/4050010/hsbc-global-head-responsible-investing-cares-miami-metres-water-100 (accessed 18-09-23).

Katz, E. & Lazarsfeld, P.F. (1955). *Personal Influence: The Part Played by People in the Flow of Mass Communications.* New York, NY, US: Free Press.

Kim, S. & Schifeling, T. (2022) *Good corp, bad corp, and the rise of B corps: How market incumbents' diverse responses reinvigorate challengers. Administrative Science Quarterly*, 67(3), pp. 674–720. DOI:10.1177/00018392221091734

Kotler, P. & Armstrong, G. (2006). *Principles of Marketing, 11th Edition.* Upper Saddle River: New Jersey: Prentice-Hall.

Lambin, J.J. & Schuiling, E. (2012) *Market-Driven Management – Strategic and Operational Marketing,* 3rd Edition. Basingstoke: Palgrave McMillan.

Levitt, T. (1965) Exploit the product life cycle-to convert a tantalizing concept into a managerial instrument of competitive power. *Harvard Business Review*, June 1965.

McCarthy, E.J. (1960) *Basic Marketing: A Managerial Approach.* Indiana: RD Irwin.

McCollough, M.A. & Bharadwaj, S.G. (1992) The recovery paradox: An examination of customer satisfaction in relation to disconfirmation, service quality, and attribution based theories. in *Marketing Theory and Applications*, Chris T. Allen, (Ed.), 119. Chicago: American Marketing Association, 1992. ISBN 0877572240

McDonald, M. (1999) *Marketing Plans – How to Prepare Them, How to Use Them.* 4th Edition. London: Butterworth-Heinemann.

Michel, S. & Meuter, M.L. (2008) The service recovery paradox: True but overrated? *International Journal of Service Industry Management* 19, pp. 441–457. DOI:10.1108/09564230810891897

Moore, S.B. & Manring, S.L. (2009) Strategy development in small and medium sized enterprises for sustainability and increased value creation. *Journal of Cleaner Production*, 17(2), pp. 276–282.

Motortrend. (2023) *Nissan Leaf History: The EV That Launched a Movement- Nissan's Trailblazing EV Paved the Way for the Japanese Automaker's Electrified Future.* www.motortrend.com/features/nissan-leaf-ev-history-pioneerfuture/#:~:text=But%20the%20carmaker's%20groundbreaking%20move,produced%20electric%20vehicle%20in%20history (accessed 08-08-23).

P&G. (2023) *Brands.* www.pg.co.uk/brands/ (accessed 26.07.23).

Parasuraman, A., Zeithaml, V.A. & Berry, L.L. (1985) A conceptual model of service quality and its implications for future research. *The Journal of Marketing*, 49(4), Autumn, pp. 41–50.

Porcu, L., del Barrio-García, S., Kitchen, P.J. & Tourky, M. (2020) The antecedent role of a collaborative vs. a controlling corporate culture on firm-wide integrated marketing communication and brand performance. *Journal of Business Research*, 119, pp. 435–443. DOI:10.1016/j.jbusres.2019.10.049

Porritt, J. (2005) *Capitalism as if the World Matters*. London: Earthscan.

Porter, M.E. (1996) What is strategy? *Harvard Business Review* 74(6), pp. 61–78.

Prahalad, C.K. & Hamel, G. (1990) The core competence of the corporation. Harvard Business Review, 68(3), pp. 79–91.

PRCA. (2023) What is PR? www.prca.org.uk/careers/what-is-pr#:~:text=Public%20Relations%2C%20or%20'PR',on%20how%20people%20perceive%20it (accessed 04-08-23).

Proctor, T. (2008) *Public Sector Marketing*. Harlow: Pearson Education.

Richardson, N. (2010) *A Quick Start Guide to Mobile Marketing*. London: Kogan Page.

Richardson, N. (2020) *Sustainable Marketing Planning*. Abingdon: Routledge.

Richardson, N. (2022) How new sustainability typologies will reshape traditional approaches to loyalty. *Italian Journal of Marketing. Special Issue: "S.I. Sustainable Marketing and Performance Management*, February. DOI:10.1007/s43039-022-00047-y

Richardson, N. & Cassop Thompson, M. (2019) A new positioning framework for organizational value: Juxtaposing organizational value positions with customer centricity. *Strategic Change. Special edition: Sustainable Business Models*. pp. 1–10, DOI:10.1002/jsc.2253.

Richardson, N, James, J. & Kelley, N. (2015) *Customer-Centric Marketing- Supporting Sustainability in the Digital Age*. London: Kogan Page.

Rogers, E.M. (1962) *Diffusion of Innovations*. New York: Free Press.

Schramm, W. (1955) How communication works in *The Process and Effects of Mass Communications*, W. Schramm (Ed.), Urbana, Illinois: University of Illinois Press, pp. 3–26.

Shannon, C.E. & Weaver, W. (1949). *The Mathematical Theory of Communication*. Urbana, Illinois: University of Illinois Press.

Shostack, G.L. (1984) Designing services that deliver. *Harvard Business Review*. 62(1), 133–139.

Statista. (2023a) *Volume of Poultry Meat Exports from the United Kingdom (UK) from 2003 to 2021*. www.statista.com/statistics/316393/poultrymeat-export-volume-in-the-united-kingdom-uk/ (accessed 10-08-23).

Statista. (2023b) *Poultry Meat Import Volume in the United Kingdom (UK) 2003–2021*. www.statista.com/statistics/316405/poultrymeat-import-volume-in-the-united-kingdom-uk/ (accessed 10-08-23).

Tilley, F & Young, C.W. (2009) Sustainability entrepreneurs – Could they be the true wealth generators of the future? *Greener Management International*, Iss 55, pp. 70–92, Greenleaf Publishing. DOI:10.9774/GLEAF.3062.2006.au.00008

Walls. (2023) *Wall's Looks to Bring Happiness Lessons to 3 Million Kids*. www.unilever.com/news/news-search/2023/walls-looks-to-bring-happiness-lessons-to-3-million-kids/ (accessed 10-08-23).

White, K., Habib, R. & Hardisty, D.J. (2019) How to SHIFT consumer behaviors to be more sustainable: A literature review and guiding framework. *Journal of Marketing*, 83(3), pp. 22–49. DOI:10.1177/0022242919825649.

Young, C.W., Hwang, K., McDonald, S. & Oates, C. (2010) Sustainable consumption: Green consumer behaviour when purchasing products. *Sustainable Development*, 18, pp. 20–31. DOI:10.1002/sd.394.

5 Sustainable Marketing (SM) Planning

Abstract

This chapter reflects on how marketing planning can drive the adoption of sustainable practices. It is wise to have a degree of structure when planning, hence some widely used frameworks are discussed. Students need to be clear about the terminology, e.g. the difference between objectives, strategies and tactics as this is the lexicon of marketing practitioners. The role of audits is considered with practical examples and many tools/frameworks are critiqued. Students are shown how to create marketing objectives and how to choose the appropriate strategy. Matters relating to implementation and control are addressed. The chapter concludes by considering the barriers to adopting SM planning.

Learning Outcomes

At the end of this chapter students will be able to

- differentiate between objectives, strategies and tactics
- examine the nature of the internal, Micro and Macro environments
- assess which tools and frameworks are optimal for analysing the business environments
- appreciate how a SWOT summary provides the platform for a TOWS analysis
- evaluate the role of Segmentation, Targeting and Positioning (STP)
- identify the correct strategy to achieve the key objectives
- explain how tactical implementation can be controlled and monitored
- reflect on the barriers to implementing SM planning.

Professor Stephen Brown (an influential critical marketer) argued that the traditional, linear, step-by-step marketing model of analysis, planning, implementation and control no longer seems applicable, appropriate or even pertinent to what is actually happening on the ground (Brown, 1995). This is interesting as a critique; however, extensive interaction with practitioners has shown that they want some form of structure to implement planning. Implementation is everything beyond the ivory towers of academia.

DOI: 10.4324/9781003434214-6

Increasingly companies need to reflect on their positioning and the extent to which they are willing to adopt sustainable practices. Managers have to implement planned changes and must reflect on

- efficiency versus effectiveness
- relational communications (RC)
- balancing organisational needs with customer (and stakeholder) satisfaction
- their long-term focus
- value-creation
- corporate culture.

Directors often insist they have the right strategies; however, few think they are implementing them well. Drucker argued that Efficiency is doing things right, whereas Effectiveness is doing the right things. Clearly organisations need to be Efficient AND Effective regarding sustainability adoption, improved implementation and higher productivity.

The language of strategy is largely influenced by military terminology (Table 5.1). Low-cost airlines have used flanking strategies. The rapid growth of airlines such as Ryanair and easyJet were based upon flanking attacks on the established national carriers, especially British Airways (Baines *et al*, 2013) who served broad markets with a differentiated service (see Figure 5.12), ignoring the low cost, niche segment Ryanair spotted the flanking opportunity and became the market leader in the new market. A propos a 'Position defence', resistance can be built around a product, distribution channel or geographic area, e.g. Procter and Gamble (see Table 4.4) developed a portfolio of hair care brands to protect their key hair care brand, Pantene. Head & Shoulders and Wash & Go act as flanker brands to protect market share and divert challengers to Pantene (Baines *et al*, 2013).

The use of militaristic language (Table 5.1) is incongruent with a modern, more progressive approach to business. Similarly, a degree of hubris would suit many managers who think they are 'in control'. Ultimately companies are allowed to ply their trade if they have the blessing of society (van Dam & Appledoorn, 1996). Clearly the TBL is predicated on social justice and societal collaboration, i.e. with people. Sustainability and conflict are mutually exclusive.

Planning Frameworks

Assuming marketers know their strategic direction, the next challenge lies in achieving it. Planning frameworks makes it easier to implement plans. Kotler (1967) introduced his APIC planning framework to a wider business audience. Since then, other BAU corporate planning models have been offered (Table 5.2).

This list is not exhaustive. In reality, no framework is better than any other. Increasingly authors are reframing models and frameworks to be more appropriate for the twenty-first century (Table 5.2). The REACH NEW framework does this by using better language (Table 5.3). Its use of positive, collaborative, inclusive terminology is much more suited to sustainability today.

There are similarities across corporate and functional (e.g. marketing) planning frameworks. Ultimately, planning frameworks can be distilled into the following stages:

Table 5.1 Militaristic origins of strategic language

Attack	*Explanation*	*Defence*	*Explanation*
Frontal Attack	A head-on assault on a rival, used where low customer loyalty exists, poorly differentiated products and easy of customer switching	**Position defence**	Building fortifications to 'sit tight', i.e. defend current position amid resistance around a product, distribution channel or territory area
Flanking	Pressurising a rival's vulnerable or unguarded areas, e.g. segments not served well by incumbents, open territories, weak products, or inappropriate distribution channels	**Mobile defence**	Creating elusive moving target by introducing regular new or replacement products, changing segments and target markets. Supported by constant repositioning
Encirclement	Involves attacking a rival on all sides, literally encircling the target rival. The goal is to disrupt the competitor's strategy causing them to reorganise resources and to create panic as market share is taken from many sides. Works when the target market is loosely segmented or segments lack substantially resourced firms	**Flanking defence**	Protecting the rear and the flanks by strengthening the competitive position in these segments, with new products, product lines and repositioning existing product
Bypass	Introducing 'game-changing' substitute products avoiding direct conflict with rivals	**Counter-offensive defences**	Retaliation once an attacker engages. Hit the attacker's weakest spot, quickly and ruthlessly using various attacking options
Guerrilla	Irritating, slow erosion of a rival's market share through a series of unpredictable attacks on their weaker areas. Useful for SMEs with fewer resources when the target is able to defend itself relatively easily from a frontal or flanking attack. Typically, guerrilla attacks involve heavily promoted price discounting, followed by differing lengths of inactivity	**Contraction defence**	Some markets or segments are too weak to be defended so the best action is to withdraw and concentrate resources around protecting core products. A strategic withdrawal strategy was used by Diageo when the company sold off Burger King in order to withdraw from the fast-food market and concentrate on the premium drinks market
Pre-emptive defence	Assumes best form of defence is attack, e.g. by dropping product prices the overall perceived value of a market can be reduced, detering investors and diverting attackers to other markets. Alternatively, launching a heavyweight advertising programme or several new products may deter attacks		

Source: Adapted from Baines *et al* (2013).

Table 5.2 BAU planning process models and frameworks

APIC Planning Framework	*Parallel Corporate Strategy Model*	*Sequential Marketing Strategy Framework*	*SOSTAC Sequential Marketing Strategy Framework*	*Sequential Corporate Strategy Model*
Analyse (Environment, resources, expectations, objectives and culture)	*Strategic Analysis* (Environment, resources, expectations, objectives and culture)	*Situation Review* (Marketing Audit, SWOT Analysis)	Situation Analysis	Environmental Analysis (e.g. marketplace, customers) Resource Analysis (e.g. human, financial)
Plan (generation and evaluation strategic options; forecasts)	*Strategic Choice* (generation and evaluation of options)	*Goal setting* (mission, corporate objectives)	Objective setting	Vision, mission and objectives
Implementation (resource planning, Tactical implementation)	*Strategic implementation* (resource planning)	*Strategy formulation* (objectives, plans and mixes)	Strategy	Strategy Development
Control (ROI, KPIs, budget)		*Resource allocation and monitoring*	Tactics Actions Control	Strategy Implementation

Sources: Adapted from Kotler (1967); Johnson and Scholes (1999); McDonald (1999); Smith *et al* (1999); Lynch (2000).

Table 5.3 REACH NEW heights planning framework

'REACH NEW'	*Steps to marketing success*
Reflect on	• the role of sustainability and your company • your readiness to change • your orientation/approach to marketing
Enable change	• by recognising and removing barriers to adoption of good marketing practices • by putting the TBL into your Marketing Mix
Actively communicate	• by managing your message in a considered manner • using tools and techniques that help your customers • by getting your staff to 'buy-in' to promoting internal change • your brand to your customers by tailoring your 'comms' tools to be fit for purpose
Consider your situation	• so you know your strengths and weaknesses • and be able to exploit future opportunities • to understand how those around you impact your progress
Harvest Knowledge	• to know you're achieving what you want • to identify where you want to be
Nurture growth	• by acquiring and satisfying new customers • through developing relationships
Embrace co-ordination	• by planning your marketing campaigns • through monitoring your success in reaching your goals
Where do you stand?	• on the key issue of sustainability • when technology keeps changing

1 Goal Setting – Mission (or Purpose) statement, corporate objectives & scenario planning.
2 Situation Review – The Internal, Micro and (External) Macro environments.
3 Strategy Formulation.
4 Implementation – Monitoring, evaluation and control.

It is appropriate to consider each of these key stages.

5.1 Goal Setting – Mission (or Purpose) Statements, Corporate Objectives and Scenario Planning

When adopting a long-term focus, planning (potentially) years ahead, the issues of balance, value-creation and corporate culture arise. The transition to being sustainable is more likely to be successful if it is well-planned, i.e. considered, planned, implemented and evaluated.

Mission and Purpose Statements

A mission statement expresses a company's overall purpose. They vary widely from a few lines to comprehensive statements concerning wide-ranging factors, i.e. why the company exists, how it operates, what sort of company it seeks to be. Often (most importantly) they define the customers, the value sought and the benefits offered. Ideally, mission statements should fit the values and expectations of key stakeholders. The core elements of a mission statement are as follows:

- Raison d'être – essence – purpose
- Long-term view – strategy
- Area of company involvement – products or services
- Core competences – key strengths
- Benefits to customers
- Policies – standards (e.g. CSR, ESG)
- Value systems, attitudes, e.g. ethical and/or green.

A caveat is that such lists can be misconstrued as 'one-size-fits-all'. Certainly, managers should strive to influence purpose statements to serve the company's interests *and* to inform the customers of the value being created for them. Mission statements that lack customer centricity need to be reviewed and revised to ensure that they are still relevant. Whittington *et al* (2019) argue that the key influences on mission statements are:

- Corporate governance
- Whom the organisation should serve
- Accountability and regulatory framework
- Stakeholders
- Business ethics.

With customers increasingly concerned about ecological and ethical practices, overtly sustainable organisations (including those B-Corp accredited) often prefer Purpose Statements to Mission and/or Vision statements as they are better aligned with the key stakeholders' values and expectations. Companies lacking clarity in their purpose, often have employees who lack direction (Richardson, 2020). Employees need to engage with a progressive, aspirational, grounded vision of the company if they are to be fully motivated to drive through any changes.

Corporate Objectives

Too often terms are used loosely in marketing. Such poor use of terminology causes problems when implementing plans. Three common terms that marketers must understand are objectives, strategies and tactics. Objectives and strategies can be organisational or functional (e.g., marketing, HR, production etc.) whereas tactics are always a matter for the functions.

Larger organisations' corporate objectives often relate to profit, Return on Investment (RoI) or Return on Capital Employed (RoCE), since these satisfy the demands of governance and (usually remote) shareholders. Richardson (2020) advocates complementing financial returns (RoI) with Returns on Other Objectives (RoO). This will meet with some resistance, say from institutional investors. Companies with weak marketing departments or no marketing representation at Board level may see the customer insights marginalised (*ibid*). With small businesses, it is the manager/proprietor that needs to be satisfied (see Section 8.4). Hence, it is appropriate to clarify some of the key terminology apropos objectives, strategies and tactics. Simply put, a strategy is what an organisation uses to achieve its objectives (Figure 5.1).

The POST model reminds us that when moving from the Purpose statement to the Objectives, managers should not lose sight of how they are going to achieve this whilst remembering why they are doing it. It is effectively a reflective circle in the hermeneutic tradition. The same applies when moving between the objectives and strategy and then strategy and tactics. The functions within companies (e.g., marketing, sales, HR, accounting, production, logistics) will have their own functional objectives (Figure 5.2).

Functional objectives do not stand in isolation; in most cases, functional objectives support the corporate objectives. To do otherwise is to adopt a maverick position. This is highly risky. Shareholders like mavericks when their schemes work, however when they go wrong, and dividends are cut, it is a different matter. At this juncture the maverick is sacrificed. Functional objectives should support corporate objectives particularly in periods of change by

- communicating messages and the business mission/vision/values
- raising awareness of business issues and priorities
- maintaining managerial credibility
- improving employee motivation whilst allowing for staff to feedback
- improving the communications skills of management.

Objectives are shaped by the organisational attitude to risk. Whether change should be incremental, transformational (or somewhere in between), risk-averse organisations should not set demanding objectives (i.e. for growth) as they usually incur greater risks. Aggressive approaches may result in blurring of the distinction between organisational strengths and weaknesses. Marketers use a TOWS analysis to create marketing objectives (see Table 5.15).

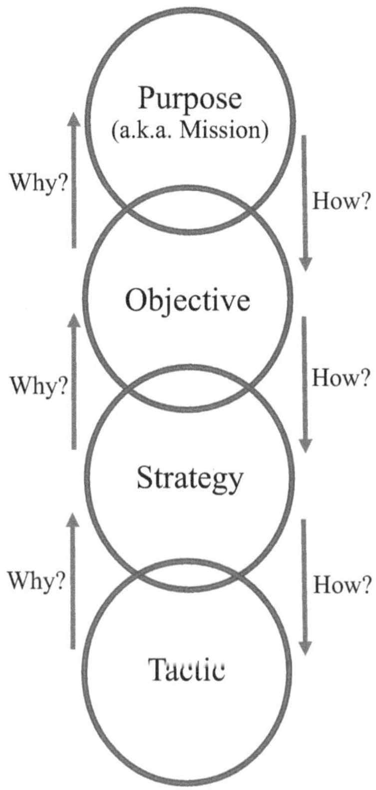

Figure 5.1 The POST model.

Source: Author.

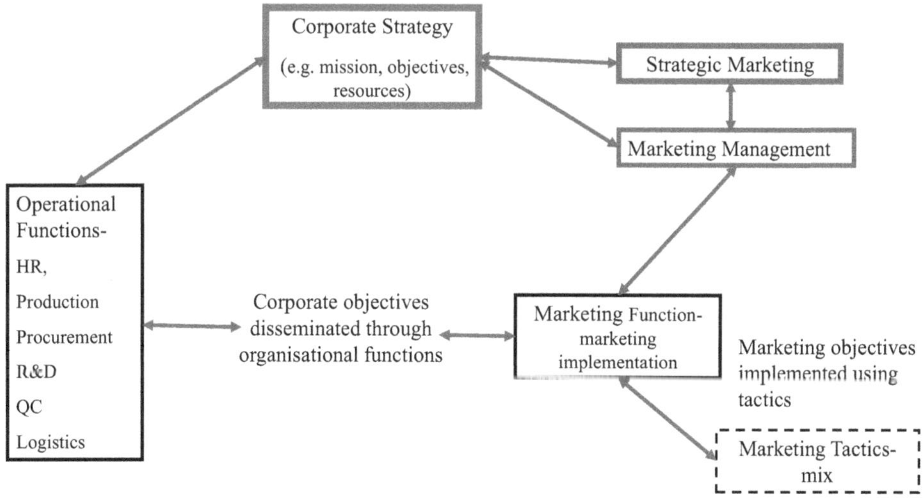

Figure 5.2 Relationship between corporate and functional objectives.

Source: Adapted from Donnelly and Harrison (2009).

Scenario Planning

Successful marketing plans consider the potential problems and identify solutions to deal with them. This underpins the ability to respond to change. The 'What if?' approach serves well here. Some examples are 'What if'...

- the oil price hits $200 per barrel?
- Turkey joins the EU?
- female representation at board level becomes mandatory?
- our competitors start to incorporate graphene into their products?

'What if' scenarios are diverse. Clearly the spread of outcomes of each scenario is potentially wide. Good planning improves understanding of the drivers of change and how implementation occurs. It encourages marketers to

- prioritise – ensure that time is not wasted on unnecessary activities
- avoid unplanned activities
- be cohesive – in short, medium and long-term activities
- reflect on activities that will influence achieving objectives
- be cost effective – use ROMI to demonstrate past achievements
- engage stakeholder groups – identifying their needs and potential to contribute
- control the agenda – work proactively to identify issues and corrective actions.

Plans can be short term, say based around a specific event, or a long-term programme of activities affecting the whole business. Strategic timescales vary depending on the organisational circumstances. Strategic 'horizons' are usually expressed in years, i.e.

- Short term 1–3 years
- Medium term 3–5 years
- Long term 5+ years

Managers must ascertain which horizon is appropriate. If PLCs are under pressure (see Section 4.3), moving to a shorter strategic horizon may be prudent. Volatility in the macro-environment, whether political, economic or legal will shorten planning horizons. The key is to look as far forward as is sensible and then consider the different scenarios. Too many managers do not spend enough time looking to the future. They stay within their comfort zones by focusing on internal rather than external issues. This is understandable as thinking about how markets will develop over the next 10 years is challenging. They often fail to meaningfully consult with colleagues in order to build consensus on the shape of future markets. Those that do tend to look 2–3 years into the future rather than 10–20 years. They adopt the simple approach of predicting the future by reflecting on current situational trends that (they hope) will continue into the future. Marketers do not have this luxury; they must consider short, medium and long-terms changes to the market. They should seek to understand, better than their competitors, the Macro-environmental trends (and disruptions) that may transform sectors and create new opportunities.

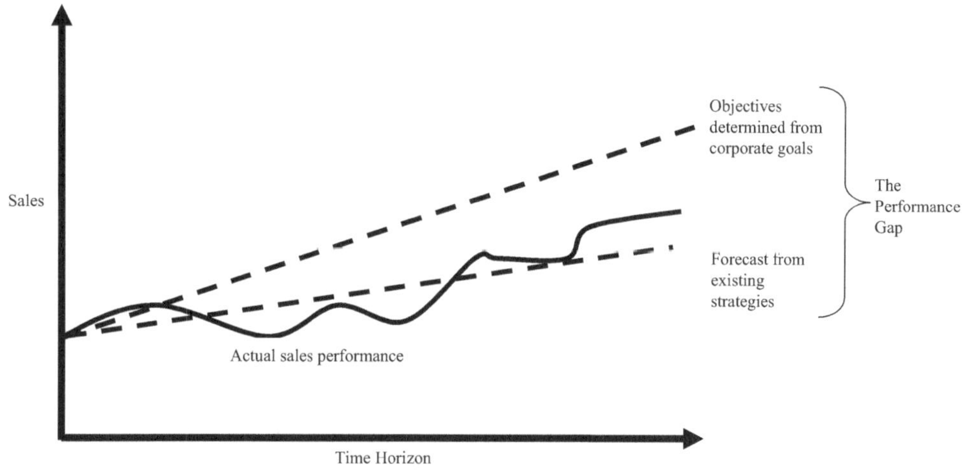

Figure 5.3 Gap analysis.

Source: Adapted from Richardson *et al* (2015, p 111).

A common approach (in the Goal-setting phase) is to undertake a gap analysis to illustrate the brand's current position and extrapolate (or forecast) its future performance (Figure 5.3).

Gaps can be operational or strategic. In larger companies, gaps are often measured in terms of turnover; however, caution is needed. If turnover is up 50% in a market that has grown 100% in the same timescale, the company has lost market-share which could have dramatic effects. Growth in profit is often safer (than turnover) but market share is better. This applies to most companies irrespective of size, profit making, third sector or charity. This means considering alternatives, i.e. revisiting the objectives or seeking to raise performance. Some marketers measure success against other criteria such as brand awareness (see Chapter 8) or customer satisfaction. These can be measured but some skill is needed. Gaps have to be addressed if the organisation is to achieve its potential. This is achieved by reviewing the opportunities available (Table 5.4).

Operational (i.e. tactical) gaps can be addressed by improving organisational productivity, reducing costs, increasing prices, stimulating sales or finding alternative uses for existing products. The strategic choice of selling new products to new markets (known as diversification) carries higher risks, e.g. during the financial crisis of 2007–2008 Northern Rock in the UK and Lehman Bros in the US both failed. In 2009 Virgin's make-up diversification, Virgin Vie, was divested in a management buyout which subsequently failed.

5.2 Strategic Decisions: STP and Strategy Formulation

Before marketers can identify strategies, they must assess the foundations that will support any decisions. They must continually monitor the factors operating externally and internally, i.e. the 'Marketing Environments' (see Figure 5.4) which influence a company's ability to transform its inputs (think ITO models) into value-creating outputs.

Table 5.4 Operational versus strategic gaps

Gap	*Solution*	*Comment*
Operational	Improving organisational productivity, reducing costs or increasing prices	Links to extending the PLC maturity stage by stimulating sales or finding alternative uses. The company's core competences should be determined, where managers link internal skills with resources such as technology.
Strategic	Finding new user groups, entering new segments, geographical expansion, new product development and/or diversification	The company's attitude to risk must be considered. The strategic choice of selling new products to new markets (known as diversification) carries higher risks

Source: Adapted from Richardson (2020, p 141).

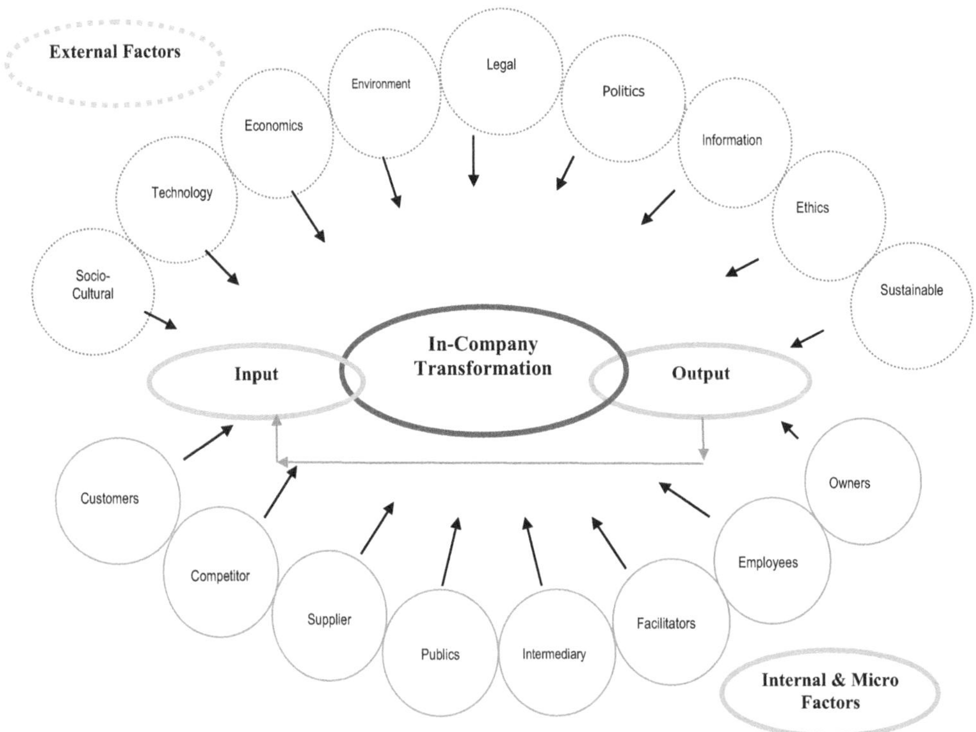

Figure 5.4 Marketing environments influencing value creation.

Source: Author.

In Figure 5.4, 'External factors', beyond the organisation's control, are known collectively as the Macro (or Situational) Environment. With Macro analysis marketers look to identify future trends. 'Internal' factors, shaped by particular industries or organisations, involve degrees of control (see Figure 1.2). These reside in the 'Internal' and 'Micro' environments, featuring recent or current strengths and weaknesses amongst, say, the target segments, suppliers or competition. Too little detail will lead to a lack of action whereas too much could lead to 'analysis paralysis'. A lack of skills and resources are key factors that lead not only to poor marketing planning but also to ineffective implementation (Mintzberg, 1990).

Marketing Audits

An audit is a key component of most planning frameworks (see Table 5.2). Environmental scanning feeds into the Marketing Audit, which should be:

- Comprehensive
- Apolitical
- Structured
- Timely.

CAST is useful as it provides a degree of structure; however, it leaves a number of matters to be judged, e.g. How comprehensive? What degree of structure? Is an apolitical audit achievable without external input and the timing of audits? Each needs careful consideration. ALL audits are inherently political. They can suffer from clashes within organisational power bases and functions. The findings may not be palatable to non-marketers, however the focus on the customer should be unrelenting. This underpins the need for healthy dialogue between the functions. Otherwise, those carrying out the audit may be exposed to hostility. Ultimately the message has to be conveyed that customer satisfaction matters. Furthermore, it is not enough to carry out a marketing audit and then fail to act on the findings. This risks the audit simply becoming a ritual, an onerous task, which is unlikely to have the required impact.

Example: In 2011 the Cass Business School produced a report entitled 'Roads to Ruin'. The report found that poor corporate governance led to many organisational failures. The Non-Executive Directors (NEDs) were found to be unwilling or incapable of monitoring and controlling the activities of those at Board level, i.e. the executives. In part, this inability resulted from nepotism, i.e. NEDs had existing connections or relationships with the CEO. Alternatively, some of the NEDS simply lacked the knowledge and skills necessary to perform their duties in a meaningful manner. This was demonstrated by the organisations' core values and/or principles being ignored in practice. Some of the companies had adopted a 'group think' mindset where directors and employees conformed to the expectations of the CEO. Some conformed because they did not know any better, because they benefitted from it or they feared sanctions for non-compliance.

Increasingly companies are recruiting NEDs who specialise in aspects of sustainability. UK beauty products company Faith in Nature, founded in 1974, now has two directors who are "give nature a voice and a vote on how Faith In Nature is run" (BBC, 2023d). These NEDs come from two environmental organisations – Earth Law Centre and Lawyers for Nature. "It's about how to make business better, so less damage is done ... we didn't want this to just be marketing. We wanted to create a formal and legal structure with a practical framework" says Anne Hopkins, creative director at Faith in Nature. Fellow director Simeon Rose suggests "the biggest difference is now it enables other board members to see what decisions nature makes, and it helps them make further conscious decisions" (*ibid*).

Internal Environment Analysis

Three widely used internal analysis frameworks are McKinsey 7S, Porter's Value Chain Analysis (VCA) and the 5 M frameworks (Table 5.5). Marketers should draw on these (amongst others) to create an internal 'blend' that really suits the circumstances.

The 7S, VCA and 5M frameworks (Table 5.5) help Marketers to have a holistic view of organisations. These frameworks have advantages and disadvantages (Table 5.5) however (essentially) they largely distinguish between hard and soft factors. Waterman *et al* (1980) created the McKinsey 7S framework to assist managerial analysis by portraying the interconnectedness (and need to align) the seven factors. It was one of the earlier frameworks (drawing on academic research) to inform managerial practice. It sought to promote organisational change, shape new strategies and (if nothing else) act as a checklist. They concluded that businesses that have these seven elements aligned and mutually reinforced are more likely to achieve competitive advantage. This applies to all of the frameworks (*ibid*).

In 1980, Michael Porter introduced the VCA framework, comprising primary and secondary value-creating activities. The value-creating activities provide a 'value' flow through the organisation; ultimately value is 'given' to the customer in a profitable way. Whittington *et al* (2019) suggest VCA describes the activities within and around an organisation which together create a product or service. They describe how the primary activities are linked to the support activities. Indeed, it is the interaction between the value-creating activities that determines the success of achieving organisational objectives.

Like many of the tools used today, it drew on the experiences of large, manufacturing companies and was shaped by the economic situation of the time where relatively stable market structures endured. It can be applied to SMEs, however there are limitations (see Chapter 8). Porter's models rely on being able to know an organisation or being able to predict behavioural outcomes of third parties. The more dynamic the environment, the more the organisation needs to collaborate internally hence Internal Marketing (see Chapter 6) plays an important role. That said, VCA has a role in the modern marketers' environmental analysis toolkit.

The primary versus secondary nomenclature is problematic. To say that Marketing and Sales are primary whereas procurement and/or HR are secondary is questionable. These professional functions have their own bodies (CIPS and CIPD respectively). Clearly all of the functions have to be customer-centric if the organisation is to prosper. Internal barriers can impact on the ability to satisfy customer needs. A common issue for a number of the tools is that they have separate 'elements' to be benchmarked. These 'elements' are not isolated and success is dictated by their interaction. In VCA, Sales

Table 5.5 BAU 'Internal' frameworks

Framework factors	*Advantages*	*Disadvantages*
	McKinsey 7S	
Structure: the way the organisation is structured including reporting structures **Strategy:** the plan(s) devised to maintain and build competitive advantage **Staff:** the employees and their general capabilities **Style:** the style of leadership adopted **Systems:** the daily activities and procedures that staff members engage in to get the job done **Skills:** the actual skills and competencies of the employees **Shared values:** organisational core values of evidenced in the corporate culture and the general work ethic	• Comprehensive internal review • Highlights the need to consider soft and hard factors • Underpins how strategy implementation is shaped by other factors, which in turn influence each other • Develops historical over-reliance on only considering strategy and structure when reviewing organisational effectiveness • Emphasises coordination and planning • Early model linking academic research with managerial practice	• May not consider SBUs – gaps in strategy conception or execution may occur. • Little practical support for the model particularly with SMEs • Difficult to properly assess the degree of fit ... relies on judgement calls. Only works within a blend of other tools • Does not provide solutions to improve implementation and control • It is a static model in an increasingly turbulent environment • Although interlinked not all are equal and will be subject to the usual politics • Neglects external stakeholders (especially customers) and macro-environment. • Whose values are shared?
	Porter's Value Chain Analysis	
Firm Infrastructure: organisational structure, control systems, company culture, etc. **Human Resource Management (HRM):** employee recruitment, training, development, and compensation **Technology Development:** capital machinery, IT, analysis & test equipment, websites, systems, etc. **Procurement:** managing suppliers; buying materials, supplies, and gear **Logistics (inbound and outbound):** receiving & storing raw materials; distribution to manufacturing when needed distribution of finished goods to channel or direct to customer **Marketing, Sales & Service:** identification of customer needs and the generation of sales	• Comprehensive internal review • Highlights the need to consider soft and hard factors • Underpins how implementation is shaped by functions, which in turn influence each other. • Can be used as a template to 'fit' suppliers and other companies (e.g. mergers and acquisitions • Emphasises coordination and planning • Early model linking academic research with managerial practice.	• Each SBUs (in large companies) may need its own VCA • Designed with large manufacturers in mind. Less useful for SMEs • Assumes customers only the concern of Marketing and Sales • Relies on judgement calls • Only works within a blend of other tools. • Does not provide solutions to improve implementation and control • A static model in an increasingly turbulent environment • Assumes linear supply chains – networks and constellations are more apt • Assumes value can be created and given • Functions not all are equal and will be subject to the usual politics • Neglects macro-environmental concerns.

(*Continued*)

Table 5.5 (Continued)

Framework factors	*Advantages*	*Disadvantages*
	5 Ms	
Materials: receiving & storing raw materials; distribution to manufacturing; distribution of finished goods to channel or customer **Manpower:** employees and their general capabilities; recruitment, retention, training, development, and compensation **Money:** company finances, profitability, cashflow, leveraged, supported by lenders, and/or shareholders; ROCE, ROI, yields, dividends etc. **Minutes:** linked to planning process and strategic horizons; process efficiency and effectiveness; time to launch products; reaction time to market changes **Machines:** capital machinery, IT, analysis & test equipment, websites, systems, etc.	• Comprehensive internal review • Highlights the need to consider soft and hard factors • Underpins how implementation is shaped by functions • Functions influence each other. • Can be used as a template to 'fit' suppliers and other companies (e.g. mergers and acquisitions) • Emphasises coordination and planning • Early model linking academic research with managerial practice	• Each SBU (in large companies) may need its own VCA • Designed for large manufacturers. Little use to SMEs and micro-enterprises • Assumes customers only the concern of Marketing and Sales • Relies on judgement calls • Offers no solutions to improve implementation and control • A static model in an increasingly turbulent environment • Assumes linear supply chains – networks and constellations are more apt • Assumes value can be created and given • Functions not all are equal and will be subject to the usual politics • Neglects macro-environmental concerns.

Sources: adapted from Porter (1980); Waterman *et al* (1980); Donnelly and Harrison (2009); Richardson (2020).

& Marketing are integrated whereas in practice this is often not the case. Marketing is separated from HR whereas, in reality, the role of HR is crucial for marketers. They must recruit, train, motivate and reward the marketing and/or sales teams. The relationship with 'Procurement' is important internally and externally. Internal buyers manage relationships with key suppliers, from whom they gather relevant competitor intelligence.

Areas for potential inter-functional conflict (with marketing) exist. Production wants to standardise products and demand accurate forecasts. They are often risk averse and resist the demand to change products. Quality want to influence product specifications. Procurement can be short-termist, seeing necessary spending as 'costs' rather than investment. Finance set corporate budgets, measuring the Return on Marketing Investment (RoMI) through a short-term lens rather adopting a longer-term (say sustainable) perspective. Many of these arguments have merit, however only Marketing garners customer insights into value, which only resides in the mind of the customer. It cannot simply be added up and given. This is a key flaw in VCA.

VCA is essentially an internal framework but it can be used to assist in micro-environmental analysis such as benchmarking frameworks or in mergers and acquisitions (M&A). It can be used to compare and contrast organisations or SBUs. This can support strategic decisions, say regarding internal restructuring. Managers would seek to identify synergies, overlaps or gaps.

5Ms is one of the CIM's preferred environmental tools however many cite it as having Money, Men, Machines, Materials, Markets and Minutes. If Markets are to be included this effectively becomes a Micro framework. For the purposes of this text Markets is covered elsewhere. The inherent sexism in the M=Men factor must be addressed. It is an old model which really should be non-gender specific; however, 4Ms and a P (for People) may reduce its memorability. Furthermore, 'Men' is duplicated with HRM in Porter's VCA and Staff in McKinsey's 7S framework. Those who (rightly) object to the use of the term Men, should use these alternatives. There is no place for sexism in marketing, or anywhere else.

Micro-Environment Analysis

Two widely used 'Micro' frameworks are Porter's 5 Forces and Kaplan's Balanced Scorecard. (Table 5.6). In 1979 Professor Michael Porter introduced a model based on the 5 'Forces' (hereafter P5F) to be evaluated when assessing competitive (i.e. micro) environments (Porter, 1979). It is widely used by marketers when evaluating an organisation's industry structure. P5F assumes that a corporate strategy should meet the opportunities and threats in the organisation's micro-environment. Essentially, competitive strategy should be based on an understanding of industry structures and the way they change (*ibid*). The evaluation of these features is subjective and again marketers will have to make judgment calls. Where possible utilise credible sources of information and remember competitors are unlikely to provide the information willingly. Hamel & Prahalad were fairly critical of the P5F model. They argued that the core competences of company should not be underestimated and suggested that "in the long run, competitiveness derives from an ability to build core competence, at lower cost and more speedily than competitors" (Prahalad & Hamel, 1990).

Competition does not equal substitution; historically, academics argued that steel suppliers from China entering the UK market would be substitutes for the incumbents. This is a flawed logic. All marketers are global marketers. Chinese steel (or American steel for that matter) is a Competitive Rivalry force. Substitution is akin to creative destruction where a new paradigm is created (see Table 5.7).

Within some of the substitute categories, existential competition can take place. With video tapes, VHS succeeded where Betamax failed, despite the latter using superior technology. Substitutes may have first-mover advantage but they will have to react to a competitive response. Sky were hugely effective at rolling out their technologically inferior analogue satellite dishes whilst BSB toiled to perfect their digital alternative. In the end Sky won the battle and BSkyB emerged. Of course, today all satellites are digital so whilst BSB were the visionaries, Sky had the better marketing plan.

Whether cigarettes predate chewing tobacco or vice versa is a moot point. Both have been around for centuries. Some cigarette substitutes are regional, e.g. Snus is a form of chewing tobacco used in Scandinavian countries since the mid-nineteenth century. It's popularity rose dramatically in the 1970s. Users place a pea-sized portion under their top

Table 5.6 BAU 'Micro' frameworks

Framework	*Advantages*	*Disadvantages*
Porter's 5 Forces **New Entrants:** Economy of scale (EoS); Differentiation; Switching costs; Convenience for customers; Cost leadership; Market type (duopoly, oligopoly, fragmented etc.); Capital requirement **Supplier Power:** Differentiation; Switching costs; Availability; Status; Attraction to competitors **Buyer Power:** B2B or B2C; Differentiation; Switching costs; Profitability; Loyalty; Scale; One-off or repeat **Substitute products or services:** Switching costs and risk; Approvals; Reputation; Quality; Lead times; Post-sale support **Competitive Rivalry:** Concentration; Nature (aggressive, collaborative etc.); Sector characteristics (growth rate, profitability etc.); Diversity	• Comprehensive internal review • Highlights the need to consider soft and hard factors • Underpins how strategy implementation is shaped by other factors, which in turn influence each other • Develops historical over-reliance on only considering strategy and structure when reviewing organisational effectiveness • Emphasises coordination and planning • Early model linking academic research with managerial practice.	• May not consider SBUs where gaps in strategy conception or execution may occur • Little practical support for the model with SMEs • Difficult to properly assess the degree of fit ... relies on judgement calls • Does not provide solutions to improve implementation and control • It is a static model in an increasingly turbulent environment • Although interlinked not all are equal and will be subject to the usual politics • Neglects external stakeholders (especially customers) and macro-environmental concerns • Whose values are shared?
Balance score card **Financial:** Profitability; Managing Key stakeholders; Return on Capital; Net profit margin; % of turnover; ROCE; Cash flow (Suppliers, Clients); Organisation growth v Industry growth. **Customer:** Value for money; Willingness to pay; Competitive pricing; Client satisfaction; Supplier Satisfaction; Conversion rates; Satisfaction; Pricing index; Mystery shop ratings; Client meetings; Customer attrition; Recommendations; % repeat business; % new business; retention; attrition. **Internal:** Operations management; Service development; Employee Motivation; Accountability; Low work duplication; Effective MkIS system; co-operation between departments; Staff churn; Level of responsibility; ownership **Innovation & learning:** Time to market; Creative workforce; Learning organisation; Forward looking; Transparent NPD cycle time; Enabled & empowered workforce; 360 degree reviews; Continuous environmental monitoring; Staff input valued.	• Comprehensive internal review involving finance/accounts function • Highlights the need to consider factors other than financial metrics • Underpins how implementation is shaped by functions (to create customer value), which in turn influence each other • Can be used as a benchmarking template • Emphasises coordination and planning • Early model linking academic research with managerial practice.	• Each SBUs (in large companies) may need its own Balanced Scorecard • Designed with large manufacturers in mind Less use to SMEs and micro-enterprises • Relies on judgement calls • Does not provide solutions to improve implementation and control • few companies utilise 360/540-degree reviews • Assumes linear supply chains when networks and constellations are more contemporary • Assumes value can be created and given • Functions not all are equal and will be subject to the usual politics. Who will lead teh review? Ownership issues • Neglects macro-environmental concerns • Assumes leadership, management and workforce can unlearn old habits.

Source: Adapted from Porter (1980); Kaplan and Norton (1992); Richardson (2020).

Table 5.7 Original offerings and related substitutes

Incumbent	*Substitute A*	*Substitute B*	*Substitute C*	*Substitute D*
Cigarettes	Chewing tobacco	Nicotine patches	Vaping	
Vinyl record	Cassette	CD	MP3	Streaming
Cinema	Video tape	DVD/Bluray	MP4	Streaming
Television	Satellite	Cable	Streaming	Podcasts

Source: Author.

lip. Snus, like all tobacco products, is carcinogenic, however it is still popular amongst younger Scandinavians. Within regions of South Asia variations of chewing tobacco include Betel quid (used in India) or paan (Bangladesh) where tobacco is blended with areca nut and flavourings. Chewing tobacco use may be higher than for cigarettes because of cost and relative lack of regulation compared to cigarettes. In England, the highest self-reported use of chewing tobacco products is among Bangladeshi women followed by Indian men, Pakistani men and Pakistani and Indian women (Longman *et al*, 2010). This presents a challenge for Social Marketers who want to promote healthy lifestyles.

Some substitutes evolve from posing an existential threat to being complementary, e.g. movie producers have shortened the gap between a film's release and its launch on streaming platforms and DVD. This maximises the impact of the film's original marketing campaign for streaming and DVD sales, both major income generators.

Example: Record companies now release on multiple formats accepting that there are segments who want to buy vinyl (often at substantial prices), or CDs for convenience. Increasingly vinyl albums include a code for downloading the MP3 code. Vinyl has seen a resurgence built on marketing events such as Record Store Day. That said vinyl sales will never recapture the magnitude of the 1970s. Streaming is the greenest option with virtually no CO_2 footprint or raw materials. However, ethical issues exist around whether artists are paid fairly for their creative content. Artists are increasingly adopting marketing tactics such as having 'merch' stalls at gigs and providing opportunities to buy via their websites.

The Balanced Scorecard framework aims to not only link objectives with performance measures but also to provide a more holistic view than merely financial measures (Kaplan & Norton, 1992). It combines qualitative and quantitative measures to evaluate the different expectations of stakeholders and relate assessments of performance to strategic decisions (Whittington *et al*, 2019). It is a useful framework as it challenges the hegemony of the financial functions, making accountants think about customers and marketers think about accounts. If applied meaningfully it can identify hidden, complex inter-functional relationships by reviewing the organisation from four perspectives (Table 5.8). Companies use it to set (more consistent) objectives and to focus on how organisational operations interact. Hence it provides a platform to monitor effectiveness and efficiency. Furthermore, it can include those in the supply networks and constellations. Like all frameworks, it is only useful if it helps to create value that the customer is willing to take.

Table 5.8 Balanced scorecard showing typical strategic objectives, measures and information sources

Perspective	*Strategic Objective*	*Strategic Measure*	*Information Source*
Financial	Profitability Managing key stakeholders Return on Capital Cash Flow Organisational Growth	Net profit margin; % of turnover; ROCE; Cash flow (Suppliers, Clients); Organisation growth v Industry growth	Annual audited accounts; Management Accounts; Industry information; publications; benchmarking using industry standards; Competitor analysis
Customer	Value for money Willingness to pay Competitive pricing Client satisfaction Supplier Satisfaction Tender to success ratio	Satisfaction survey; Pricing index; Mystery shop ratings; Client meetings; Customer attrition; Recommendations; % repeat business; % of new business; Non/ Late payments	Satisfaction Survey; Marketing information; Review of competitor pricing; Complaints; Customer ranking survey Competitor Benchmarking; Social media analysis
Internal	Operations management Service development Employee Motivation Accountability Ownership	Low work duplication; Effective MkIS system; Effective co-operation between departments; Client feedback; Client engagement time; Staff churn; Level of responsibility and ownership	Departmental function updates; Work schedules; CRM System; Account Management meetings; HR database Job satisfaction survey
Innovation & learning	Time to market Creative workforce Learning organisation Forward looking Transparent	NPD cycle time; Enabled & empowered workforce; 360-degree reviews; Continuous environmental monitoring; Staff input valued	Research in NPD – focus groups; Idea generation from shop floor, Can unlearn old habits; Clear strategic horizon; Employee motivation

Sources: Adapted from Kaplan and Norton (1992); Donnelly and Harrison (2009).

There should be clear links between any control measures and the objectives (Figure 3.18). This should engender improved employee engagement. The Balanced Scorecard requires involvement with (and by) employees, which should improve employee 'buy in' to strategic objectives and measures. Any inter-functional synergies within organisations can only have positive effects on value creation internally and throughout the supply network.

Limitations include being difficult to operate in practice as objectives are set in different functions, at different levels and with differing timescales. Whilst it has a customer-centric component, it only tacitly recognises the influence of other stakeholders. It is the most complex micro-environmental tool to use. Companies must invest sufficient soft and hard resources for it to be meaningful. It will have to reside in the Management Information System (MIS) as it has to access functional systems (e.g. the MkIS for customer insights). This limits the extent to which some staff will be allowed to engage. It is predicated on complementing financial returns (RoI) with returns on other objectives (RoO). Finally, in common with all internal and micro-environmental analysis frameworks, it ignores the impact of the turbulent, tumultuous, uncontrollable macro-environment.

Table 5.9 shows how internal and Micro factors could be applied. Assume the others have been captured elsewhere or are deemed irrelevant. Finding information on competitors is never easy. Markets are not always easy to define and their behaviour cannot be predicted. That said, Table 5.9 clearly provides insights that would complement those of the other tools (and vice versa). These can be mapped to core competences. Marketers should draw on the internal and Micro frameworks to identify the organisation's strengths and weaknesses. No one tool is sophisticated enough to capture the data whereas using several tools creates as many problems as it solves. Marketers should prioritise the 'blend' (Table 5.9) by entering their judgement on the 'Impact' (whether High, Medium or Low) and whether the impact is positive or negative. This will facilitate a ranking (or prioritisation) that will feed into the creation of the marketing objectives in the TOWS analysis.

Example: The 'BCorp Beauty Coalition' is a collective action initiative of BCorps committed to working together to change the beauty industry for good. They have a governance framework and actively seek to recruit other BCorps. Their manifesto sought to broaden the meaning of the word 'beauty' itself, from one traditionally focused on improvement of the external self to one that represents a proper balance with the natural environment (Russell, 2022). In other words, for soil as much as skin, nature as much as natural, evidence as much as ego, and impact as much as performance. Skandinavisk CEO Sean Russell believes his "25 motivated individuals in Copenhagen can now work alongside, and benefit from, the combined experience and talent of more than 40 B Corps across five continents, representing thousands of people and millions of customers. It means we all finally have the scale to challenge the status quo and be confident of success" (*ibid*).

Core Competence

In 1990 Prahalad and Hamel introduced the notion of organisational 'Core Competence'. They suggested a company's competitiveness derives from its core competences based on its (collective) knowledge, skills and attitude. Can it learn when coordinating diverse skills and technological platforms? (Prahalad & Hamel, 1990). Those interested in 'learning organisations' should seek out the work of Burgoyne and/or Sprenger and ten Have. Prahalad and Hamel's seminal paper, focused on large, manufacturing companies as was often the case in marketing.

Clearly core competence extends to services. They involve promoting behavioural changes in order to create value for customers. Value-creating behaviours should become the company's foundation. Companies should adopt behaviours that apply to

Table 5.9 Internal and Micro summary for Biffy – A fictional dog grooming products importer

Factors from 5M, Porter's 5F, VCA & McKinsey 7S audits		*Impact (H/M/L)*	*Positive or negative*	*Rank*
Materials	• Imports dog grooming products so no manufacturing materials needed • Graphic design company provides range of services including photography, videos and the production of literature for new products			
Money	• Biffy has experienced a 33% growth in turnover between 2016 and 2018, which is projected to rise further to 38% in 2020 despite the Brexit instability (Confidential Report 1, Biffy) • Due to increased turnover pressures GM% has declined from 21% (2014) to 18% YTD 2018 (Confidential Report 2, Biffy)			
Sales & Marketing	• Despite the growth of sales in most product categories, some areas are behind budget for 2018. (Confidential Report 2, Biffy). • Sales targets have increased by 24% between in 2016 and 2018 (Confidential Report 3, Biffy) • Biffy does not utilise SEO for the website to analyse web traffic on new products. • Biffy has a weaker brand than its biggest competitors, as it is a younger company which entered the market later (Biffy US, About Us).			
Strategy	• Biffy now launching more new products than any of its competitors (Biffy Market Research Report, 2018)			
Competitive rivalry	• Due to the extensive competition and well-established brands, new entrants selling quality products are sporadic • More than (41%) UK companies including Biffy's competitors are using social networking sites to win new business • The oligopolistic market where Biffy operates has a clear leader – Bodger Petfoods with a 34% marketshare • Biffy does not currently undertake any audits to assess the marketing environment			
Buyer power	• A recent customer survey suggested Biffy needed to provide a better range of Dog Shampooing Aids (Biffy Customer Survey, 2015)			
Machines	• Telecommunications are utilised when launching new products within the market to increase sales quickly and recoup initial investment costs • MKiS suffers due to a lack of functional integration and information sharing due to departmental silos			

Source: Original diagram.

all stakeholders. They can be values-based, reflecting the organisation's core values and culture. Marketers must communicate these to all key stakeholders across organisational boundaries (see Figure 1.2).

Competences are a key resource and will have to be 'managed'. There will be multiple competences within an organisation; too many will lead to confusion and inertia, whereas too few implies a lack of meaningful reflection. The competences must be memorable, typically no more than five with each being broken down into (a maximum of) five behaviours. These limits make the successful implementation and control of the core competences more likely. Core competences should be chosen with care. They should meet the following criteria

1 providing potential access to a wide variety of markets,
2 creating value for customers and prospects,
3 differentiating the organisation whilst being difficult to imitate,
4 reflecting the organisational values,
5 crossing organisational boundaries internally and externally via collaborations,
6 being resilient, i.e. not diminishing with time.

Table 5.10 compares and contrasts core competences for a large organisation with those of a smaller marketing agency. Ultimately marketing students will work client-side and/or agency-side, hence this exercise is useful. The large company would build on

Table 5.10 Core competencies – client versus agencies

	Core competencies	*Measurable behaviours*
Client-side	Leadership	Communication; Clarity; Foresight; Commitment; Values
	Conscientious	Focus; Detail; Efficiency; Resilience; Initiative; Excellence
	Service	Responsiveness; Reliability; Credibility; Courtesy; Consistency
	Collaboration	Advocacy; Flexibility; Representative; Compliance; Personal Development
	Professionalism	Understanding organisational purpose; environmental awareness; knowledge of structure, process flows, profit centres and cost controls
Agency-side	Digital expertise	Social media management; Direct marketing skills; Content design; Control measures; Lead conversion
	Marketing experience	Branding; CRM skills; segmentation analysis; positioning knowledge; Marcomms abilities; Internal marketing
	Procedural	Project management; Accountability; Reporting; Brief creation; Presentation
	Insightfulness	Customer-centricity; Feedback opportunities; Tailoring service; Creativity; Responsiveness
	Tenacity	Self-motivation; Resilience, Problem-solving; Adaptable; Flexible

Source: Original diagram.

the strengths that derive from its size, structure and resources. Leadership is crucial in large companies. The agency would look to use its strengths deriving from its ability to service niche markets, its speed of response and being able to adapt to create value. For example, its digital marketing expertise could be used to exploit growing social media opportunities as it has lower overheads. Akin to the notion of USPs, core competences are unlikely to be unique to all companies. Many will share similar behaviours, as is the case in Table 5.10. In both cases the core competences should be tested against the aforementioned 6 criteria.

Core competences are the engine for NPD (see Section 4.3) and as such should be nurtured. This necessitates 'buy-in' from senior management as does marketing planning generally. Each competence (and behaviours therein) will have to be measured and monitored over a long timescale. Indeed, Prahalad & Hamel suggest competences can take decades to develop in a process of continuous development. That said, companies seeking to refine their competences could see immediate benefits on the first steps of their 'journey'.

A product is not a core competence rather it is the output (of core competences). Apple should not see itself as an iPhone or iMac manufacturer. Clearly it has a proven ability to design, develop and launch (successfully) highly stylised user-friendly devices. Design, development and marketing are amongst their core competences. First Direct offers bank accounts, credit cards and mortgages, however its competences relate to its award-winning customer-centric services featuring ease of use, 24-7 access and a sector-leading use of technology. Many online banks have call centres, apps and online facilities but few can replicate the long-term customer satisfaction garnered by First Direct.

Prahalad and Hamel refer to 'competence carriers' who are effectively the champions of the concept. These people should be supported by senior management and operate across functions. They should create core competence communities and in travelling regularly, talking frequently to customers, and meeting with peers, competence carriers may be encouraged to discover new markets (Prahalad & Hamel, 1990)

Competence is not a permanent state, rather it can be lost. Companies that suffer staff turnover will lose much of their tacit knowledge (see Chapter 6) when the employees leave. Wherever possible this knowledge should be made explicit, i.e. recorded in a format than can be communicated in future. The costs of losing competences can be substantial and only partly calculated in advance (*ibid*). Hence it is prudent to consider some of the barriers, as follows

- not all competences are equal
- to be effective they must interact
- different competency sets may be needed for different groups of people
- rigid SBU structures limit sharing best-practice and resources
- Identifying competences that will be relevant in 5–10 years is challenging.

Even now, the building of core competences is considered ambitious by some commentators. Many managers take easy decisions such as changing company structures. It is much easier to change structure than culture and behaviours. That said if core competences are supported at a corporate level, marketing objectives and strategies should seek to offer support.

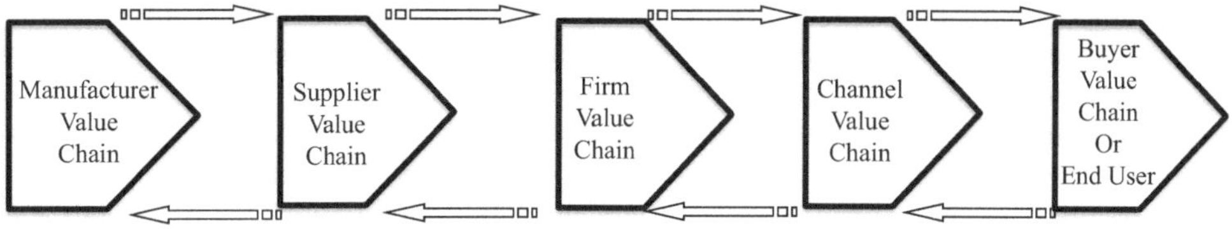

Figure 5.5 Porter's value system.

Source: Adapted from Porter (1980).

Value Systems

Marketing channels represent all of the organisations involved in delivering goods and services to customers (see Section 4.2). There can be several intermediaries between a manufacturer and the customer. Porter suggested value can be created (or destroyed) at the interfaces between upstream suppliers and downstream channels and customers (Figure 5.5).

There are issues with the value system. Clearly there needs to be feedback reflecting on the interactions. The term chain is problematic, first because it alludes to companies being chained to their customers which is anachronistic; second, modern companies use networks of suppliers, many of whom provide similar services and products. The structure of the organisation also plays a role. Those with high degrees of vertical integration may be better able to coordinate upstream and downstream activities. Those with little vertical integration will still have access to a vast, global, online array of potential suppliers. Manufacturers often encourage their suppliers to be in the same proximity in order to improve the creation of value. Being closer suggests improved communication (including feedback), reduced lead times and more progressive inventory management approaches (e.g. Kanban). Kanban is a supply approach in lean manufacturing systems. The suppliers often play active roles in stock management taking responsibility for monitoring stock levels and replenishing inventories. This has led to the increased use of one-stop shopping by manufacturers. The supplier must be local and have access to all of the necessary items. It is a highly integrated value system where some boundaries are becoming blurred.

Traditionally commentators argued that a company's competitive advantage derived from its own value chain and ability to manage the value system. This suggests a degree of control, which is often illusory. Many product recalls have resulted from a lack of control. Mattel famously had to organise global recalls of children's toys because their manufacturing sub-contractor used lead-based paint.

Communities and Networks

Pressure is increasing on companies to act sustainability. This involves engaging with communities whether inside or outside of the organisation. Communities are groups of people that come together due to a common interest. They are often based upon trust and shared values. Larger organisations are more likely to have numerous communities residing internally or in the microenvironment, each with different interests or roles. Some may be hostile, antagonistic groups whereas others may be supporters or advocates. Some communities may be special-interest groups, interested in, say, customers, processes or design. Marketers must consider the role of internal communities and the benefits they can offer as they can create value and bring many benefits.

All communities are networks of individuals, but not all networks are communities. Essentially, networks are a series of connections (between individuals, organisations or groups) which can be used to co-ordinate differing campaigns. This often happens with large political events such as the G20 Meetings (e.g. Delhi, 2023 or Bali, 2022). Communities can network with each other to achieve mutually beneficial objectives, i.e. Greenpeace supporters concerned about the environment network with union representatives concerned about workers' rights. Communities develop around a shared, collective purpose or interest whereas networks may not have that. They are (however) often sympathetic towards each other's causes. There are 1,400 environmental pressure groups in Britain alone. Any one of these could create a 'bad news' story. The 13 largest green UK groups have over 5 million members who exert pressure through lobbying, PR campaigns & direct action.

Relational communications (RC) refer to the affective or expressive group communications which contribute to creating and maintaining a social fabric promoting positive relationships amongst different organisational groups (Ramjaun, 2021). Managers must consider the role of communities and the benefits they can offer as they can create value and bring many benefits. Communities communicate using tools such as websites, social networks, email, messaging apps, even text messages. Social media can be used by marketers to link various communities of stakeholders into networks. Communities provide opportunities for marketers to undertake research, generate insights, test new ideas and/or engage in dialogues. Marketers should ensure that members of the community are enthused, passionate, informed and supported. The community should feel embraced, valued and rewarded. Benefits will accrue from the community's influencers and advocates, opinion leaders and innovators. To ascertain whether the community is part of the brand's audience …

- Has the community been developed for a particular *purpose*? If so, impartial advice and support can be offered.
- Does the community exist for people in the same *position*? For example, people at the same lifecycle stage (say new parents) or health issues.
- Is the community there for people with common *interests*? Possibly involving a shared hobby, passion or enthusiasm. Marketers could seek to improve their experience by providing knowledge, information or even reward.
- Has the community linked to a particular *profession*? Professional communities may relate to specific industries. The CIM, however, has a community of marketing practitioners across all sectors. Content could include information regarding jobs opportunities, roles, skills or current issues.

If these criteria are met, marketers can be confident they are aligned with the community. The key theme here is based around providing the communities with meaningful content and information, that helps them, offering specific benefits to meet their current needs. Organisations can develop their own communities. Chaffey and Ellis-Chadwick (2012) suggested organisations can develop four different types of communities – purpose, position, interest and profession. These provide a degree of structure for marketers.

Different communities have different rules. Marketers must understand the culture of the communities and seek out opportunities for conversations. It presents opportunities to intervene if there is negativity towards the brand and provides mechanisms for mutually agreeable resolutions. Marketers cannot control communities (nor networks) and must not seek to shape them into something else. Communities exists in their own right, for their own purposes. They are not sales platforms, rather they provide opportunities to develop awareness and positive sentiment with those who may want to take value. When people search for information from online communities, they trust their opinions on companies, brands and products. This is useful as often marketer-dominated information (say adverts) generates less trust than non-marketer-generated information (say WoM).

> **Example:** Mumsnet is the UK's biggest network for parents, with over 8 million unique visitors per month, over 100 million page views and 20,000 daily forum posts (Mumsnet, 2023). Whilst it is not overtly political (i.e. party political) it is a lobby group and has instigated a number of campaigns that have influenced retailers such as Primark, Next, Tesco, John Lewis to change practices in relation to selling clothes that sexualised young girls and moving magazines with overtly sexual covers out of children's eyelines in stores. This is just an online community, but one that has developed significant influence within the marketing environment.

Godin (2008) developed the idea of online communities by seeing them as 'tribes' and focusing particularly on the leader. Communities, or tribes, are no longer merely 'local' and marketers are privy to new social behaviour on a global scale. There are only two requirements to turn a group of people into a tribe, a shared interest and a way to communicate (*ibid*). Hierarchies exist within online tribes. Communities brought together through shared interests may have leaders. Members can be opinion leaders for outsiders, as can the leaders within the tribe. Marketers should identify the value sought by the tribe and whether they see value in the brand. If aligned, marketers can try to become part of the tribe's narrative. That said tribes do not always share the same narrative.

> **Example:** Climate sceptics often rely on feuding activists to tear each other's ideas apart; activists often spend more time attacking one another than battling climate falsehoods (Richie, 2023). Nuclear 'zealots' want to go all-in on building new power stations, whereas renewable 'zealots' want no nuclear at all. Such behaviour plays into the hands of the deniers, the oil companies, the anti-climate lobbyists. For some it is not about the specific technology deployed, rather that technology is a solution at all. Some believe technology will fix everything. Their detractors think this techno-optimism is naive. The American economist Michael Munger described how the world is split into "directionalists" and "destinationists". Directionalists back any solution that moves towards the final goal. Destinationists are less flexible, preferring an ideal outcome. They block and reject anything that does not fit their idealistic vision. Those who want a car-less world, push against electric vehicles (EVs), even if they cut emissions. Destinationalism is problematic. No solution is a panacea – ZEVs, lab-grown meat, renewable energy, nuclear power – all have some

impact. Transparency is needed about the impacts (*ibid*). To improve narratives Richie (2023) suggests those disposed towards aspects of sustainability need to be:

- less fixated on the ideal pathway
- generous when dealing with our rivals
- honest about what is and is not true about unpalatable solutions.

In short, becoming better directionalists, focusing on moving towards our goals, rather than pinning our hopes on an ideal means of getting there.

Social networks and online communities compete for online time, searches, clicks and patronage. Because of this the audience may be spread across platforms with some individuals on multiple-platforms. Marketers can

- strive for an omni-channel presence, being present on every platform
- adopt a multi-channel presence, being present on key platforms used by the majority of the target audience
- build their own community.

Marketers could use combinations of these three approaches. Most use options 2 and 3. Existing social networks offer marketers the ability to create their own, managed community. There are millions of local business pages on social media sites covering SMEs, places, large organisations, brands, products, public figures and more. Social media is an essential tool for marketers whether targeting audiences directly as a B2C company, building awareness and preference as a B2B, or even facilitating new channels such as C2B, G2B or G2B.

Micro-social media sites (X, Threads or Mastodon) allow organisations to build positive profiles of the organisation, brand or product and then build audiences of interested followers with whom they can engage. Engagement is key. The followers can form an invaluable community who choose to follow, are interested in and potentially passionate about the brand. Marketers who invest resources in engaging with communities will be expected to provide a RoMI. This is challenging as much of the interaction is qualitative in nature. Marketers can use analytics tools to track where traffic originates and whether it is from the communities. Furthermore, in page 'pop-ups' can pose questions such as 'How did you hear about us?'.

Mendelow Grid

Stakeholder mapping was introduced in Chapter 1. The Mendelow grid, whilst less useful than the approach used in Figure 1.4, is more widely used. Whilst mapping tools, such as those contained in Table 5.11, are merely snap shots, they can provide insights into relationships that can contribute to refined stakeholder communications. Power sources may be identified, however relationships may not be evident from the grid. Marketers should consider where the stakeholders may be in the future and (be prepared to) act accordingly. However, stakeholders may only have interest in aspects of an organisation's activities, say a project.

Table 5.11 Mendelow grid featuring sources of Power

		Interest	
		Low	*High*
Power Sources of power: Positional; Resource; System; Expert; Personal. Within organisations Hierarchy (formal); Influence (informal); Possession of knowledge & skills; Control of human environment; Involved in strategy implementation.	High	A	B
External power sources Control of strategic resources; materials, labour, money; Through internal links; Possession of knowledge & skills; Involved in strategy implementation	Low	C	D

Source: Adapted from Donnelly and Harrison (2009).

Macro (External) Environmental Analysis

The Macro environment is volatile, ever changing and can profoundly affect companies. Marketing objectives, strategies and tactics are subjected to these external forces. Hence, marketers must identify trends that will continue into the future which is when (after all) new products or services will be launched.

Macro forces do not operate in isolation. They can constrain or alternatively energise each other. Businesses need to take advantage of any opportunities that arise and avoid any threats. Unless of course the threats provide a radical new direction. At some point Apple (at the time a computer hardware/software manufacturer) saw the potential for portable music players even though the company had little experience in the sector. It can be argued that the diversification towards the iPod laid the foundations for much of Apple's subsequent success.

Remember, a trend is a phenomenon that (over time) maintains the status quo, increases or decreases. Once identified, it is necessary to recognise whether the trend is gathering momentum. Furthermore, marketers must establish whether the trend has a neutral, positive or negative effect on achieving objectives.

Table 5.12 PEST and other macro frameworks

Political/legal	S	P	S	E	S	P
Economic	Legal	E	T	P	T	L
Sociocultural	E	S	E	Informational	E	Access
Technological	P	T	E	S	E	T
	T	Environmental	P	T	L	Finance
		L	L	L	P	Ores
			Ethical	E	I	Regulations
					E	& reform
					Sustainable	Manners

Sources: Adapted from Gosnay and Richardson (2008); Stead *et al* (2003).

PEST has acted as the springboard for most commonly used frameworks (Table 5.12). There are some aspects worth considering before choosing a framework ...

- some use Educational in STEEPLE ... this could be covered by Informational which refers to knowledge and knowledge management
- charities and not-for-profits could use STEEPLE's ethical component
- technology companies may prioritise Information and use EPISTLE
- only STEELPIES covers all of the factors and specifies 'Sustainability'

Richard Stead developed PLATFORM in the 1990s. Whilst not widely used, it may be useful for those who seek access to raw materials in other countries. Many raw materials are depleting and irreplaceable, presenting problems for future generations, e.g. Helium is not only used for party balloons, but also in MRI scanners. Another way to audit the use of raw materials (including Ores) is to use the Materials aspect of the 5Ms framework.

Example: The Chinese government's 'Belt and Road' policy involved many African nations being offered substantial developments in infrastructure developments in return for granting access to sources of ores for decades to come. The host nation sees it as an opportunity to boost their economy using infrastructure as an economic multiplier.

Economics

'Economics' covers factors such as national growth/decline, interest rates, exchange rates, inflation rate, balance of trade, wage rates, minimum wage, working hours, unemployment (local and national), credit availability, cost of living, levels of disposable income or import tariffs. Combinations of these substantially impact consumer confidence. A country's economic performance is traditionally measured using Gross Domestic Product (GDP). In 1948 Simon Kuznets introduced GDP as a means to compare the economic wealth of nations (Kuznets, 1949). Since then, GDP has been used extensively as the yardstick for economic growth. However, the underlying factors are complex and include many unsavoury contributors. A sad reality is that war often boosts GDP for some countries (though not necessarily those involved in the conflict). No sane person would advocate war as a means of economic growth.

Furthermore, headline GDP figures hide wide variations within countries. Consider the potential impact on GDP of Brexit. There are only two absolutes regarding the economic impact: first, there are winners and losers; second, the impact is not spread uniformly across the UK. Many factors that shape GDP are beyond the control of national governments. After the global credit crunch of 2007–2008, the UK GDP reduced by 7% – the biggest fall in living memory. The UK economy technically 'recovered' most of the losses by 2013; however, by 2018, wages (when allowing for inflation) were lower than pre-crunch.

Organisations such as the OECD are seeking more meaningful ways of measuring economic growth. Their Better Life Index (see www.oecdbetterlifeindex.org) compares well-being across countries using 11 measurements considered to be essential regarding material living conditions and the quality of life. The measures clearly correlate with sustainability and in future GDP will have to be complemented (or replaced by) such approaches.

Politics

There are three levels of Politics namely local, national and international. The three levels cover design and implementation of tax policy, employment law, environmental regulation, trade restrictions or reform, tariffs and political stability (among others). The EU may introduce a new environmental law to cover all member states. However, when it comes to policing the implementation, it falls to local government officers. Local government has enormous power, as transgressors are likely to be prosecuted (and jailed) by local government representatives. It is not all about illegality. Companies seeking to physically expand will need planning permission, which is provided through local government facilities. At times there are tensions between the differing Political levels.

Example: Swelled by the rise of fast fashion, the clothing industry is one of the most wasteful sectors, with three-quarters of clothing ending up incinerated or in landfill (WEF, 2020). Clothing production doubled from 2000 to 2015 while there was a 40% drop in the amount of time clothing was worn (MacArthur, 2017). In 2020, Amsterdam declared itself the first city in the world to commit to building a circular economy, focusing on food and organic waste streams, consumer goods and the built environment. By 2030, Amsterdam plans to have halved its use of new raw materials. By 2050, the ambition is to be fully circular – relying only on used and recycled materials (BBC, 2023e).

Governments impact marketers' activities and intentions. Change, or potential change in governments (before or after general elections) bring uncertainty, changes in emphasis or, occasionally, dramatic policy reversals. Many governments are accused of 'greenwash' as they claim to be green and yet reduce support for renewable micro-generators such as solar panels (Ethical Consumer, 2022). Government action "is not necessarily as effective as we would like" (Tadajewski & Hamilton, 2014, p 81). This has to be seen in the context of post-credit crunch 'austerity' programmes where many national governments (often at the behest of central banks) cut social budgets in response. Increasingly national governments are 'delegating' responsibility for social causes to the third sector. Hence marketing is inherently political though not necessarily party political. Local governments, along with communities, institutions and individuals may need to take part in longer-term, SM projects to create society-wide changes.

Example: Since the UK national governments introduced charges for plastic carrier bags, the number issued by retailers has reduced dramatically. In 2022 the English reduction in bags being issued was greater than 95%. Before the law was introduced in 2015, more than 7.6 billion single-use carrier bags were given to customers by major supermarkets in England. The 'average person' (whatever that means) now uses 19 bags per year compared to 140 before the charge. The bag levy raised £58 million in 2017 alone which was given to good causes. Subsequent studies suggest plastic-bag-based marine litter had reduced by 50% around UK shorelines. Other single-use plastic items are now under scrutiny, e.g. plastic straws, stirrers, cotton buds and coffee cups.

Apropos plastic bags, in 2018 Friends of the Earth (FoE) argued: "A 5p charge may not have sounded like much, but the plummeting number of single use plastic bags demonstrates the difference that can be made by effective legislation. Companies and governments must do more. It's time legislation was extended to cover all other unnecessary single-use plastics, from straws to coffee cups". Similarly Greenpeace insisted "the success of the plastic bag charge shows that a smart and well-aimed government intervention can change behaviour … but we need to go further, faster".

Socio-Cultural

A common mistake is to confuse 'socio-cultural' with 'social'. Indeed, 'social' trends may be of interest, however they only represent one facet of this huge, diverse area. Socio-cultural includes cultural norms and expectations, health consciousness, demographics (e.g. population growth rate, age distribution, family size, lifecycle, divorce rates etc.) career attitudes, emphasis on safety, attitudes to global warming, lifestyle choices, hobbies to name but a few.

Marketers must remember that such trends transcend national borders. It is worth noting that because of film, broadcast media and, of course, the internet, attitudes, fashions and pastimes are evolving. What is unacceptable now may not always be the case. Alternatively, things tolerated in the past are no longer acceptable. An example is drink driving. Behaviour tolerated in the 1970s is simply not acceptable in the twenty-first century. It is difficult to predict how future media consumption habits will change. Younger generations already read fewer hard copy newspapers, preferring to get their news online. Similarly, television-viewing habits are changing with more 'on demand' options becoming available. It is hard to see how the credit card industry can survive (in its current form) as users increasingly use mobile phones as their preferred choice of payment device. The banking industry will increasingly incorporate smartphones that provide greater security, into their processes. The development of Chip and Pin dramatically reduced credit card fraud. It is a moot point, but eBay's purchase of Paypal was undoubtedly a shrewd business acquisition; their auction business may have peaked online and mobile payment is only going to grow. Marketers must ensure that goods and services can be paid for (easily) using a mobile platform to reflect the socio-cultural changes of the younger segments.

Technology

As technological change accelerates, marketers need to adapt to achieve their corporate and marketing objectives. Samsung, Panasonic and Sony launched internet-enabled TVs in 2009. Around the same time in the UK Channel 5 announced that most of its key output was to be shown on You Tube thus creating a virtuous circle of converging technologies. This interoperability continued with Netflix and Amazon (amongst others) commissioning and offering exclusive TV shows 'online', e.g. Tim Burton's *Wednesday* series. Musicians such as Bjork provided projects (e.g. Biophilia) where an app was integral rather than merely complementing the usual formats (e.g. CD, download or streaming). Where the creative industries lead, traditional businesses often follow.

3D Printing will become more significant as the technology becomes more accessible and affordable. Consumers will have the ability to print in plastics, powder (achieving a much higher resolution), resin, metal, ceramic and even foodstuffs. Future marketers and customers will be able to produce their own bespoke products. Manufacturers may have to evolve from making goods to providing the blueprints (or at least printing instructions) and raw materials for smartphone cases, simple toys, clothes or even food. Undoubtedly consumers will be more sophisticated with 3D printing in future. If a product breaks or a part is lost, it could be printed and replaced locally, significantly extending its longevity, environmental footprint and making a major contribution to the circular economy.

Example: Consumers often have a limited choice of makeup, hair or skincare products and resort to buying items where the shade is not quite right. Manufacturers may resort to overproducing products, so stores may be left with terminal stock (i.e. items they cannot sell before their expiry dates). Consumers often dispose of partially used cosmetic items. It is difficult to quantify how much waste is created as these products end up in landfill and are included in general household waste statistics. Plus, beauty companies are often tight-lipped about how much of their stock is wasted (BBC, 2023c). Ellure was founded by Selah Li, a Chinese entrepreneur, who has a Masters in human robot interaction at the Royal Institute for Technology in Stockholm. Ellure aims to cut waste in the beauty industry by enabling customers to design their own products, which are then produced on demand. Li insists "you have the added benefit of consumers considering this product to be more personal, and thus they are going to use it more". They launched their own lipstick brand in 2022. Ellure's customers first upload a selfie or pick a photo model with a similar skin tone. Then they use an online colour wheel to pick from more than 10,000 shades, which they can try on virtually. Their choice is sent to a 3D printer which adjusts the consistency, as some shades need to be thicker than others. The finished product is typically available in three to five minutes, packaged in a recyclable glass tube. While Ellure's 3D make-up printing is still a niche product, it fits into a growing trend for increased personalisation in the beauty industry. Priced at around £21 (295kr, $27), Ellure's customised lipsticks are not budget products (*ibid*).

Legal

Legal frameworks regulate business and ensure it operates, legally, ethically and fairly. A number of UK Acts have provided a framework for. The Libel Act of 1792, the Data Protection Act 1998, the Freedom of Information Act 2000 and the Privacy Law of 1987 are crucial to protect the activities of many practitioners as well as act as a boundary for ethical practice. The EU Directive on Information and Consultation of Employees (2004) gives employees of 'undertakings of 50 or more employees' rights to be informed and consulted about issues that affect their employment and the prospect of the business. This, in turn, has increased the need for employers to embrace Internal Marketing (see Chapter 6) in order to communicate more effectively with staff via internal communication strategies that are increasingly designed and delivered by marketers rather than HR departments. Other forms of legislation allude to employment, access to materials, quotas, resources, imports/exports, taxation, pricing etc.

Marketers now have access to a staggering amount of information. In 2016 the EU passed legislation to create the EU General Data Protection Regulation (GDPR) to harmonise privacy laws across Europe from 2018. The GDPR was introduced to reverse institutional bias and to give subjects more control over how organisations use their personal information, or data. It sets out seven key principles:

- Lawfulness, fairness and transparency
- Purpose limitation
- Data minimisation
- Accuracy
- Storage limitation
- Integrity and confidentiality (security)
- Accountability.

It is likely that Marketers will face more requests for personal information from consumers. They need to ensure they act in accordance with GDPR and have the correct systems and procedures in place (Figure 5.6).

Personal information means anything that identifies a living person, directly or indirectly, including their name, address, location, phone number, IP addresses or even internet cookies. The GDPR covers data classed as 'sensitive', i.e. DNA, ethnicity, sexual orientation, religious belief or trade union membership. Such 'sensitive' data is expected to be given more protection and any breach must be reported within 72 hours. Breaches are extensively covered in mainstream media, causing reputational damage. The GDPR allows the ICO to issue fines to anyone failing to comply up to £17.5m, or 4% of a company's global turnover, whichever is higher. Since 2021, heavy fines have been issued for misusing data, data breaches, or failing to process an individual's data correctly (Table 5.13).

The fine imposed on TikTok (Table 5.13) was retrospective, i.e. imposed three years after the breach. Interestingly, the EU fine was considerably larger than the £12.7m imposed by the UK data watchdog earlier that year for allowing children under 13 to use the platform in 2020 (BBC, 2023a). It should be noted that most of the fines in Table 5.13 marked with an * were imposed by the Irish Data Protection Commission (DPC) often after lengthy legal proceedings, which in themselves would have incurred costs for the miscreants.

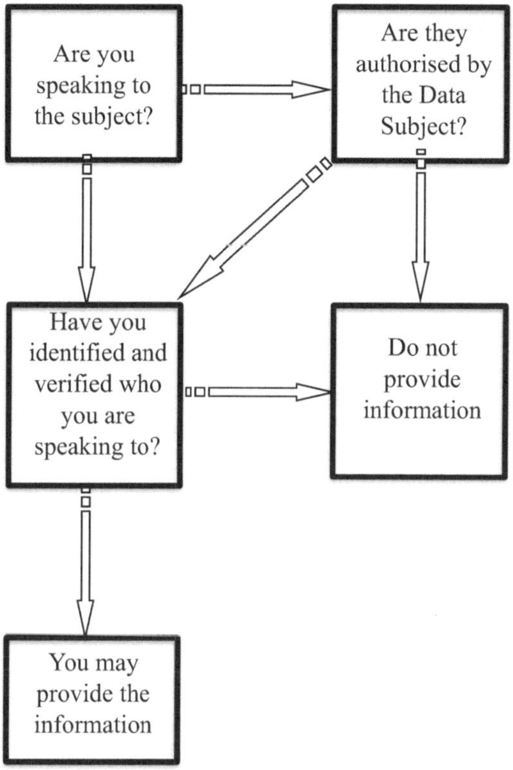

Figure 5.6 Flowchart for information requests under GDPR.

Source: Adapted from ICO (2018).

Subjects must actively 'opt in' to having their data used and they can withdraw consent at any time. They can request information regarding the nature of data being collected, how companies use their data and why. Companies must respond in language that is easy to understand. Subjects have the right to be provided with a copy of the information – as well as the rationale for collecting their personal data and who has access. The response must be provided pro gratis, in an accessible way and within 30 days. On receipt of the information subjects can insist on inaccurate data being corrected.

There are two key stakeholder groups namely data 'controllers' who determine how and why personal data is processed and 'processers' who collect the data. Larger companies (i.e. > 250 employees) who sell into the EU will have to comply with the GDPR irrespective of where their HQ is located. They must document the data they are processing, including how customers opted in, who has access and their security measures. The GDPR also applies to sole traders, entrepreneurs and SMEs. Indeed, any organisation who (say) collects customers' email addresses must comply. SMEs need only document sensitive data or data that is used regularly.

People have the right to be forgotten which means they can ask for their personal data to be deleted, assuming it is no longer relevant. Employers can reasonably hold relevant

Table 5.13 GDPR fines

Company	*Fine*	*Year*	*Cause*
Meta*	€1.2 billion ($1.3 billion)	2023	Facebook violated GDPR laws related to their standard contractual clauses (SCCs) for data transfers between the EU and the US
Amazon	€746 million ($781 million)	2021	Amazon Europe were fined by Luxembourg's National Commission for Data Protection (CNPD) for not getting user consent before storing advertisement cookies
Instagram*	€405 million ($427 million)	2022	Instagram for violated children's privacy online, including publishing children's phone numbers and email addresses
ByteDance*	€345 million ($349 million)	2023	TikTok mishandled children's data in 2020 – particularly around age verification and privacy settings
Meta*	€265 million ($275 million)	2022	Personal Facebook data was found on an online hacking forum
Meta*	€225 million ($247 million)	2021	WhatsApp failed to properly explain its data processing practices in its privacy notice

Sources: Adapted from Enzuzo (2023); BBC (2023).

information such as emergency contacts. Companies who may share data are obliged to inform others that the subject has requested the right to be forgotten. The data, links (to it) and copies (of it), must be deleted. Social media companies will have to delete any posts made when the subjects were children.

Further to the GDPR, the EU's Data Act 2025 aims to promote data sharing and regulating how data can be shared, in relation to IoT-connected devices. It largely applies to manufacturers, suppliers and users of IoT devices/related services. It also applies to 'data holders' in the EU, some public sector bodies and data processing service providers including cloud service provision. The Act requires companies to share data collected with others in the value chain, and sanctions will be imposed to ensure compliance.

Environment

For the purposes of macro-analysis, the term environment refers to the broader, ecological environment. As consumers take a greater interest in ecology, Marketers must see the environment in a friendly and sustainable manner. All things being equal, where consumers have a choice, they choose green. What is worth noting is that since the 1960s many of the 'green' initiatives that have been adopted globally, started in the US. California was at the forefront of introducing legislation on Zero Emitting Vehicles (ZEV) and creating an infrastructure for hydrogen as an energy source. A dozen other US states adopted the Californian initiative constituting a third of the US domestic car market. President Trump challenged the autonomy of the individual states to set their own emission targets. Indeed, in 2018, California was one of 17 states to file a lawsuit challenging the US Environmental Protection Agency who had declared the US vehicle emissions to be inappropriate. This coincided with President Trump ending US participation in the 2015 Paris Climate Treaty. Whether this was right or wrong is beyond the scope of this book. Irrespective of who is in the White House, Californians will continue to develop and adopt new 'green' products.

In August 2022, US President Joe Biden implemented the $369bn Inflation Reduction Act often referred to as the 'Green deal'. The US is the world's second largest emitter of greenhouse gases and the Act was forecast to slash these emissions, by up to 48% before 2035. It is described as

> "the largest investment in clean energy in American history, and I would argue in world history, to tackle the climate crisis".
>
> (John Podesta, Biden's chief clean energy advisor)

Podesta identified an "enormous response" in take-up for the tax credits, directed at zero-carbon energy projects (i.e. solar, wind and nuclear), grants to bring renewables manufacturing to the US and consumer incentives to purchase electric cars, heat pumps and electric stoves (Guardian, 2023). By September 2023, around $278bn had been invested in new clean energy creating more than US 170,000 jobs. The Act included rebates of up to $7,500 for electric vehicles (EV). US EV sales exceeded 1 million for the first time in 2023. Moreover, over half of US drivers were (then) considering an EV for their next purchase. The Act contributed to more than 80% of new US electricity capacity (in 2023) coming from wind, solar and battery storage (*ibid*).

Ethical

Consumers' changing expectations and spending patterns are repeated with ethical purchases, for example the Co-operative is the largest seller of Fairtrade wine in the UK. Undoubtedly, Fairtrade wines cost more and yet sales grow year-on-year. Attitudes to ethics are socio-cultural in origin, however they are often intertwined with environmental concerns.

Privacy campaigners are concerned about the implications of the data and information available on mobile platforms downloaded from sites, intranets, confidential meetings etc. Increasingly technology is enabling unethical behaviour (e.g. upskirting, clandestine audio/video recording etc.). Whilst most commercial technology is used respectfully, the information could be used in an unethical manner for commercial purposes. Many professional bodies provide Codes of Conduct to address such behaviour. As discussed in Chapter 1, ethical issues are prevalent and the need for ethical behaviour is paramount, so marketers must use sound judgement (see Table 1.3).

Issues with the Environmental Tools and Frameworks

Marketers must assess an organisation's strengths and weaknesses before implementing any marketing-related changes. It should be noted that the tools are not sacrosanct and can (or even should) be adapted. Some of the issues relating to the internal, micro and macro tools are:

- having differing degrees of complexity, e.g. the 5Ms tool is easier to apply than, say, undertaking a Balanced Scorecard exercise
- larger organisations work in Strategic Business Units (SBUs) often addressing different markets (think of the Virgin empire and its enormous range from music to trains to planes to credit cards)
- information is not easily available from competitors. Look for trade bodies to give a market overview
- with matrices and grids (e.g. Mendelow, BCG, DPM) the findings rarely fit neatly into a pigeon-hole
- with staged models (e.g. the PLC) it is not always easy to know which stage the product is in, nor when it should move from one (stage) to another
- far too many micro-tools lack customer centricity
- not all Macro factors are of equal weight.
- some Macro factors overlap in the PEST framework, e.g. disposable income (Economic) and leisure time (Socio-cultural) have changed the platforms used to communicate (Technological).

Marketers should not be fooled by the vast array of internal and/or micro-tools compared to the simple PEST analysis. The external analysis is vital and must be carried out diligently.

The SWOT Summary

A SWOT summary juxtaposes the Internal/Micro analysis in the form of recent strengths and weaknesses (SWs) with future macro-opportunities and threats (OTs). It should be detailed and include trends rather than snapshots (Table 5.14).

In Table 5.14, SWs reflect the organisation over recent years and up to the current time. They provide meaningful information that alludes to the organisational core competences. OTs represent the marketer's perception of the issues that may impact on the company over the planning horizon. Some findings could go in differing sections, e.g. a competitor's strength could go into a company's weakness section, unless the finding involves opening a new market. Apple did not invent either tablet computers or MP3 players. However, their iPad and iPhone were game changers that opened markets. They certainly benefitted from first-mover advantage however the competitors, e.g. Samsung and Huawei soon caught up.

The SWOT informs strategic planning (e.g. acquisition opportunities or investment opportunities) or marketing planning (e.g. product development, launches or research). To be effective it needs to be regularly undertaken so organisations may spot trends before others thus providing competitive advantage. However, SWOT summaries capture data at one specific time.

Often students produce SWOTs with single words of short phrases for example "disposable income". The phrase is meaningless unless qualified, i.e. is it increasing, decreasing or staying the same? In other words, trends are needed rather than snapshots. Having carried out a 'meaningful' SWOT, marketers should be in a better position to create marketing objectives. To be 'meaningful' the SWOT should feature findings from recognised, reputable sources. If it is comprised of guesses it reduces the credibility of the exercise. It is often wrongly called a 'SWOT analysis', which is a misnomer as (so far)

Table 5.14 Generic SWOT summary

Strengths (Internal/Micro) Resources, Assets, People Experience, knowledge, data Financial reserves, likely returns Market reach, awareness Innovative aspects Location Price, value, quality Accreditations, qualifications Processes, systems, IT Cultural, attitudinal, behavioural Management qualities Market developments Competitors' vulnerabilities USPs (or JNDs) Tactics – surprise, major contracts Business and product development Information and research Partnerships, agencies	**Weaknesses (Internal/Micro)** Gaps in capabilities Lack of competitive strength Reputation, presence and reach Financial strength Timescales, deadlines and pressures Continuity robustness Effects on core activities Reliability of data Morale, commitment, leadership Accreditations Processes and systems, IT Competitor intentions Market demand Sustaining internal capabilities Insurmountable weaknesses Loss of key staff Sustainable financial backing Volumes, production, economies New or niche target markets
Opportunities (Macro) Industry or lifestyle trends Technology development and innovation Global influences Geographical, export, import Seasonal, weather, fashion influences	**Threats (Macro)** Political effects Legislative effects Environmental effects IT developments New technologies, services, ideas Economy – home, abroad Seasonality, weather effects

Source: Author.

no analysis has taken place, rather a collection of findings has been presented. Finally, a SWOT does not provide answers, rather it informs the creation of objectives.

Generating SM Objectives

The creation of marketing objectives starts by judging where the internal/Micro (S&W) fit with the macro (O&T) in such a way that marketers can create marketing objectives.

Figure 5.7 shows the SWOT summary for a restaurant chain that is contemplating diversifying into vegan outlets. In a form of test marketing, they are investigating Leeds as a potential first location. The success of the first 'flagship' store could provide the platform for expansion across the country. Figure 5.7 illustrates how the components of the SWOT impact upon one another. Generic areas for marketing objectives may include raising a brand's profile, shaping the opinions of key stakeholders or increasing the market share. SMART objectives were developed by Doran (1981) who suggested SMART stands for (his version in italics)

- *Specific* – Avoid being either too vague or too tightly focused.
- *Measurable* – Ensure objectives can be measured and compared with previous results. This raises the credibility of marketing objectives in other functions.

Strengths	Weaknesses
1. High customer/prospect population 2. Strong Core Competency among staff 3. Premier facilities available in Leeds. 4. Strong marketing expertise 5. Experienced serial entrepreneur with good attitude to risk 6. Leeds has a substantial student population with 5 degree awarding institutions 7. Parent company has strong track record of digital development for start ups	1. No existing corporate presence in Leeds 2. Millenials harder to target as predominantly seek information online 3. Entrenched/outmoded working practices of many suppliers/retailers 4. Increasing red tape when starting businesses 5. Potential partners have poor online footprint, i.e. website or social media presence 6. High city property rates and rents
Opportunities	**Threats**
1. Obesity is on the rise with the UK having one of the worst rates in the EU 2. Graduates can't get on the housing ladder so increasingly living with non-vegan parents 3. Leeds is the 3rd largest city in the UK and will grow to nearly 1 million over next 20-25 years 4. Yorkshire has increasing demand for vegetarian and vegan enterprises 5. The trend for increasing fragmentation of the food market is set to continue 6. Consumers are increasingly demanding healthier foods and choosing to 'eat out'	1. Vegans perceived by some to be "tree huggers" & obsessed with worthy causes 2. Vegans attracting negative perceptions due to death threats being issued 3. Vegans associated with aggressive pressure groups/extremists 4. Increasing conflict between consumer perception of taste and health concerns when food is deemed desirable (taste) and undesirable (high calorie/fat content of meat) 5. Reducing funding from government agencies, including councils 6. Economic uncertainty after Brexit

Figure 5.7 SWOT summary for a restaurant chain opening a vegan outlet in Leeds.

Source: Author.

- *Attainable* – (Accurate or Aspirational or Achievable) – Do not set unachievable targets (a.k.a. wish-lists) as imposing targets that cannot be met demotivate staff.
- *Realistic* – Will the objective deliver the required changes? Will senior management buy-in?
- *Timely* – (or Targeted) – Are the resources available to achieve the objectives in the timescale? Is the objective targeting the appropriate segment?

Not all elements of SMART are equal. S&M are fundamental as objectives must be specific (not vague) and measurable. Marketers are often persuading colleagues from other functions who may be sceptical. Hence, offering measurable objectives, which can be judged, goes some way to defusing inter-functional objections.

TOWS Analysis

TOWS analysis was introduced by Heinz Weirich in 1982. A TOWS analysis is a creative process that can easily generate 20–30 objectives which need to be evaluated against 'Probability' (that senior management will buy-in to the idea), 'Urgency' and 'Impact' on client perception. 'Impact' ensures the TOWS must be customer-centric irrespective of the function. These BAU factors are widely used however there is no reason why 'Sustainability' could not be incorporated at this juncture. Weirich's TOWS approach is used widely today however it did not provide a method of prioritisation nor did it specifically relate to sustainability. As such it is yet another BAU framework from that period.

The marketing objectives in Table 5.15:

- clearly spring from the SWOT (by identifying the specific SWOT factors, e.g. S_2)
- are evaluated against criteria and therefore can be prioritised
- are SMART … at least S&M
- have timescales.

In Table 5.15, the inclusion of 'S' as a prioritising element influences the TOWS. Without 'TBL', SO_1 is the highest-ranking objective. Whereas with 'TBL', SO_2 overtakes it. These rankings are not 'fixed in stone', rather they are designed to improve marketers' decision-making. Identifying 'key' objectives provides a platform for achievable marketing goals; they are most effective if few in number, concise and prioritised (Table 5.15). The aforementioned vegan restaurant's key marketing objectives have been ranked in a TOWS analysis. Ultimately the TOWS must be customer centric. Remember marketing objectives do not stand in isolation. Hence, having identified SO_1, SO_2 and ST_1 as the key marketing objectives, the marketer must first ensure that they 'fit' the corporate objectives and then identify which components in the Mix (i.e. the 7Ps) need to be adapted. It is useful to map the marketing objectives against the Mix (Table 5.16).

Table 5.16 should act as the springboard for control tools such as KPIs or Gantt Charts, which are useful for detailing implementation.

5.3 Strategy Formulation and Tactical Implementation

Prior to implementing changes to the Mix, Marketers must identify first, the segmentation, targeting and positioning (STP) and the correct strategy for the marketing objectives. Whether STP precedes strategy, vice versa, or they are done simultaneously is a matter of taste. Herein, STP is considered first then strategy.

Segmentation

Any assessment of the segment undertaken during the audit stage of a marketing plan will have to be revaluated. Marketers cannot assume that the original segment (whether B2B or B2B) will be appropriate for marketing objectives developed in the TOWS. Furthermore, the means of communication (with the segment) may also need to be reviewed.

Segmentation involves customer analysis. Organisations must be proactive in gathering information about consumers' interests (Mercadé-Melé *et al*, 2018). Under BAU, segmentation largely gathers data on the economic value garnered from customers. This shapes the organisation's communications and is remiss as 'Sustainability' can enhance not only corporate reputations but also stakeholders' acceptance and perceptions of companies' activities (Gomez-Trujillo *et al*, 2020).

Segmentation involves breaking down a heterogeneous population into smaller homogenous segments. This is a challenge for many marketers; indeed, Professor Malcom McDonald describes the segmentation chapter in his practitioner text as "the only difficult chapter in this book" (McDonald, 2017, p 63). He implores readers to read the chapter as segmentation really is the key to commercial success. He cites research in the

Table 5.15 TOWS analysis with detailed objectives for vegan restaurant

TOWS	*Marketing Objective*	*Urgency*	*Probability*	*Impact*	*TBL*	*Total*
SO_1 ($S_1S_4O_3O_4O_6$)	Create a profile in the local media over the next six months	3	3	3	1	10
SO_2 ($S_2S_7O_2O_5O_6$)	Offer discounted vegan meals to students in existing branches to test recipes by year end	3	3	2	3	11
ST_1 ($S_1S_4S_7T_4T_6$)	Start teaser campaign with advertising hoardings around Leeds over next six months	3	2	3	1	9
ST_2 ($S_1S_4T_3T_4T_6$)	Create a mobile platform to engage with Vegans in Leeds in the next fiscal year	2	2	2	2	8
WT_1 ($W_1W_2T_3T_4T_6$)	Develop social media campaign to target existing customers in region by the end of the quarter	2	2	1	1	6
WO_2 ($W_1W_4W_5O_3O_4O_6$)	Buy an existing vegan restaurant and rebrand by year end	2	1	3	3	9

Source: Author.

Table 5.16 Mapping the Mix against marketing objectives from the TOWS analysis

Mix	*Marketing Objectives*		
	SO_1	SO_2	ST_1
Customer benefits (aka Product)	•	•	•
Cost to customer (aka Price)			•
Convenience (aka Place)	•	•	•
Comms (aka Promotion)	•		•
People	•	•	
Process	•	•	•
Physical Evidence or Presence	•	•	•

Source: Author.

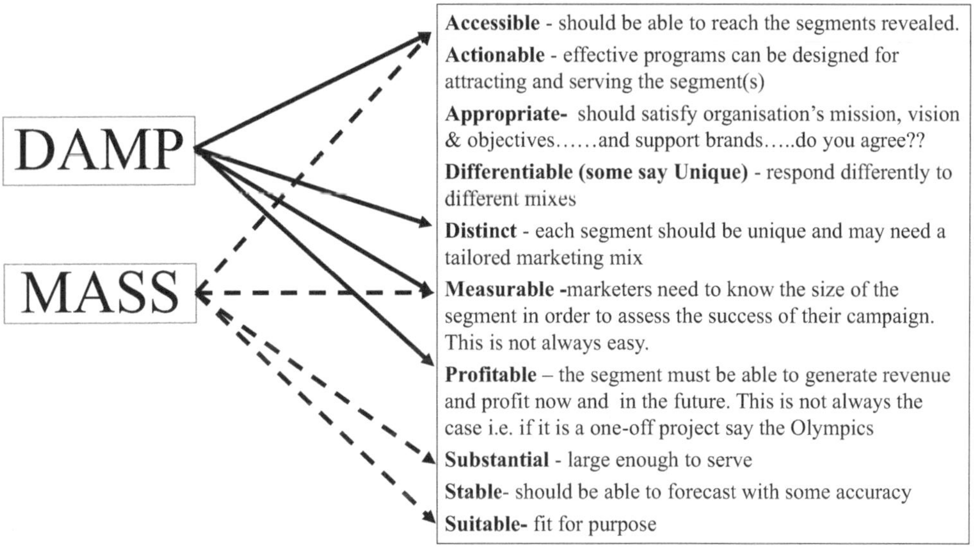

Figure 5.8 Two widely used BAU segmentation frameworks.

Source: Author.

Harvard Business Review "where 85% of US product launches had failed simply because of poor market segmentation" (*ibid*, p 74). Surely a scientific approach (to segmentation) would be able to address this. However, some marketers insist on reducing everything to data sets. They think marketing is a science whereas in reality it is as much art and philosophy as it is science. Consumers are often emotional and irrational when buying goods. They are often driven by the value they seek. Two well-known BAU (economic focus) segmentation frameworks are 'DAMP' and 'MASS' (Figure 5.8).

As illustrated, some bases are common to both frameworks. Furthermore, Figure 5.8 shows other potential (BAU) bases. Segments have to be constructed judiciously when considering multiple values and motivations of individual consumers (Guido *et al*, 2020).

If the segment is too broad it may dilute the impact of communications campaigns. If it is too narrow, it may not provide the RoI or RoMI.

There is more to being a sustainable consumer than is covered in the BAU segmentation frameworks. Table 5.17 offers an SM appropriate segmentation framework entitled APPROVES. 'Return' helps to prioritise investments in business actions intended to promote segment growth. For instance, two consumer segments may both be highly involved in a category in terms of attitudes and volume of purchases, but one may value time over savings and typically pay full price. It is worth noting that segments may be split into sub-segments. These sub-segments still have to be large enough to target. Using the aforementioned vegan restaurant, the marketing consultant would undertake research and identify sub-segments (Table 5.18).

Having identified the sub-segments the marketers could apply the APPROVES framework (Table 5.17) to identify those worth targeting. The Mix could be tailored for each segment to attract most of the sub-segments to the restaurant, though probably not the 'Carnivores'. Marketers cannot keep all of the people happy all of the time.

Ultimately in order to meet the needs, desires and expectations of customers, marketers should map how where value is created, i.e. does it reside with the customers or in the co-creation of a service.

Figure 5.9 shows how four possible behaviour patterns of festivalgoers enable segmentation based on their approach to minimising the ecological impact of attending music festivals. It alludes to possible strategies each interested party may support. Each option presents government, business and society with possible scenarios. The left side, labelled *sacrifice*, suggests some stakeholders will have to give up something in order to behave

Table 5.17 APPROVES – a sustainable segmentation framework

Factor	*Comment*
Accessible	The marcomms campaign must be able to access buyers/prospects/influencers whether B2B, B2C, B2G or C2B
Profitable	The segment must be large enough (or in smaller segments where customers have sufficient disposable income) to provide revenue, profit or ROI
People and Planet	The segment must be willing to pay for products or services where some profit is invested in People and Planet related objectives. Linked to achieving other objectives, e.g. charities may seek to recruit volunteers (ROO)
Return	Marketers should differentiate consumers by their profitability and their involvement in a category
Opportunity	The segment must have long-term prospects unless it is for a specific project. Opportunity also considers frequency or depth of use, knowledge or expertise and the amount of money spent (or available). Takes into account the time customers spend thinking, researching, learning, talking about and shopping for brands
Values	Assesses the degree to which consumers consider a product category important given their needs, emotional makeup, attitudes, perceptions, values, and interests
Estimable	Each segment should be measurable and distinct. It will need a tailored marketing mix
Size	Relevant to market needs marketers need to know the size of the segment in order to assess the success of their campaign. This is not always easy

Source: Adapted from Richardson (2020, p 183).

Table 5.18 Segments for meat-eating versus plant-based eating

Segment	*Comment*
Fruitarian	Lives mainly or exclusively on fruits. Some only eats fruits that have fallen
Ultra-vegan	Eats, wears, uses no animal related products. Like voluntary simplifiers actively seeks information to ensure they abide by their principles. Accepts limited choice as way of life
Vegan	Eats, wears, uses no animal related products largely – will compromise occasionally
Vegetarian	Eats no animal related products under any circumstances but may consume dairy products
Flexitarian	A plant-based diet with the occasional addition of meat. Sometimes referred to as flexible vegetarianism, casual vegetarians or vegivores
Omnivore	Eats meat and veg with little distinction
Conscious consumer	Eats meat and veg but insists on minimal animal suffering or environmental damage. Will take vegan option when offered. Subscribes to notion of TBL-based sustainability
Carnivore	Predominantly consumes meat as part of a high protein diet

Sources: Adapted from Flexitarian (2023); VeganSociety (2023); Vegsoc (2023).

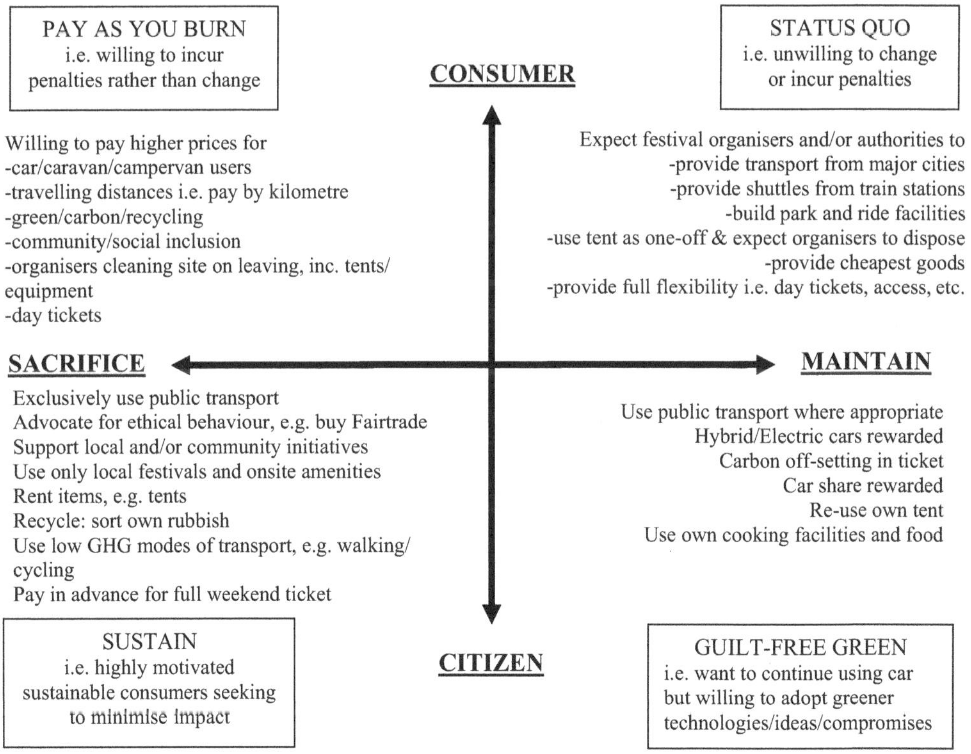

Figure 5.9 Possible sustainability behaviours of consumer versus citizen 'segments' attending festivals.

Sources: Adapted from Emery (2012); Richardson *et al* (2015).

as they wish. Some consumers will '*pay as they burn*' accepting financial disincentives (say higher duties, tolls, vehicle tax). Where governments bring in such 'taxes' a criticism is that it allows the wealthy to behave as they please whereas those with less disposable income will have to change behaviours. The *sustain* quadrant shows the most radical option for the highly motivated sustainable citizen wishing to avoid the impacts of car usage as much as possible. This behaviour chimes with highly committed groups such as eco-warriors or voluntary simplifiers.

Good, meaningful segmentation efforts will be wasted unless the whole organisation embraces it. Too often, critical insights are not realised, because of a lack of senior-management buy-in. Furthermore, other functions that are not directly involved may feel disconnected or lack engagement.

Ethical Targeting

Oddly some texts refer to targeting as identifying the target market or segment. This seems like a duplication of effort, as clearly the task of segmentation is to identify the people or companies to approach. Targeting simply refers to the intended means of communicating the benefits on offer so value-seeking customers can take value. There are four traditional modes of targeting namely

1 *Undifferentiated* – for mass markets, e.g. British Gas servicing 22 million UK homes. They do offer differing levels of service however on the whole their communications are targeted using undifferentiated means.
2 *Differentiated* – where markets can be broken down into clear segments to target. Hence, Toyota has Hilux trucks, family saloons, green cars (e.g. the the Prius) all of which need different marketing mixes and 'comms'.
3 *Concentrated* (a.k.a. niche) – this can be in the luxury end of the market, e.g. in 2014 Astbury launched unique bejewelled handbags for a select audience who were invited to the London store. At over £3,000 per bag, it was a bold attempt to target a niche market.
4 *Focused* (a.k.a. customised) – in B2B markets a company may provide a Service Level Agreement (SLA) for a specific customer. This comes with a high degree of risk if the customer is 'let down'. In B2C markets bespoke solutions can be targeted in this way, e.g. artisan wood carvers will make a piece of furniture to specification.

Good targeting will help a company to achieve its positioning, i.e. how it is perceived by the customers and prospects. This clearly involves communication (rather than segment identification).

CRM systems are widely used and this is a key challenge for marketers when complying with GDPR. Marketers should adopt a default position where data protection is designed into all systems. ICO (2018) refer to seven principles of privacy by design. These should underpin targeting.

1 *Proactive not reactive; preventative not remedial* – evaluate risks by anticipating privacy issues. Use good systems design to embrace a culture of 'privacy awareness' across organisations.
2 *Privacy as the default setting* – design systems, services, products, and/or business practices to protect personal data automatically. With privacy 'built in', individuals do not have to take steps to protect their data.

3 *Data protection as the default setting* – embed data protection into the design of systems, services, products and business practices.
4 *Full functionality-positive sum, not zero sum* – seek 'win–win' scenarios rather than trade-offs. Seek privacy AND (rather than OR) security. Incorporate all legitimate objectives whilst ensuring compliance with obligations.
5 *End-to-end security – full lifecycle protection* – Introduce strong security measures from the beginning, and extend this throughout the 'data lifecycle', i.e. process the data securely and destroy it securely when not needed.
6 *Visibility and transparency – keep it open* – Ensure all practices and technologies operate accordingly, in an independently verifiable way.
7 *Respect for user privacy — keep it user centric* – Keep the interest of individuals paramount in the design and implementation of systems or services.

When planning 'ad' campaigns, choices have to be made regarding which customers to target, the method of 'comms' and the personal details to use. In this case the Marketing Director cannot also be the company's Data Protection Officer (DPO) as there is a potential conflict of interests between the campaign's aims and the company's data protection obligations. The Marketer makes the decisions regarding the processing of the data whereas the DPO ensures information rights compliance takes place.

Sustainable Positioning

Positioning alludes to how consumers, customers and prospects perceive the position companies adopt in comparison to competitors. Products and services can be positioned by focusing on specific factors which themselves can be subject to differing positioning approaches (Table 5.19).

Features can be used when they provide differentiation, e.g. the bagless Dyson devices. Problem solving is at its best when a company has a USP, though few do. All toothpastes will clean teeth, however Sensodyne took market share by stressing the use for sensitive users. Competitive positioning can be linked to class positioning to gain market share by implying similar quality – think how Lexus is compared to Mercedes Benz. Alternatively, it can be linked to cost leadership (see Huawei's adverts comparing features with Apple's iPhone). Once marketers have established the necessary factors, they must then choose which approach to adopt. A single approach is always the preferred option.

Table 5.19 Contrasting differing positioning factors and approaches

	Positioning Factors					
	Features & design attributes	*Benefits, problems & solutions or needs*	*Specific usage & applications (or occasions)*	*Competitive positioning against other product*	*Class association*	*Cost leadership*
Positioning approaches	Distinctive – a clear, unambiguous brand position Unoccupied – where the competition is absent, under-represented, under-performing, inefficient or generating dissatisfaction Repositioning – products and services may need to be adapted ... may involve finding new uses for products					

Source: Author.

To determine the strategic position of brands, marketers often use mapping devices (see Figure 4.11 BCG and Figure 4.12 DPM). A common approach is to use perceptual mapping featuring 'plots' with two axes. The most common format is plotting price versus quality. This is useful, but it can be misleading, as price is clearly not the same as value for money. Some products may be the cheapest in their category and yet deemed poor value. Conversely the owner of an Aston Martin may consider it extremely good value for money despite its six-figure cost.

Ultimately four attributes underpin positioning, namely

1 *Credence* – Damage to credibility can taint the whole organisation as was proven in the Diesel Emissions scandal of 2017 where VW Audi lost $30 billion resulting from false environmental claims.
2 *Competitiveness* – the value taken should be unique, i.e. not imitated by competitors. Rolls Royce cars have a unique position in the luxury car market that derives from a 100-year history of satisfying their clients.
3 *Consistency* – The Cooperative Retail organisation has consistently promoted ethical behaviour and is the UK's largest seller of Fairtrade products
4 *Clarity* – Companies must be transparent in their dealings with the public and other stakeholders. Increasingly, companies are accused of greenwashing. Sustainable consumers will avoid such companies.

To build sustainable brands that consumers associate with social and environmental values, challenging decisions have to be made involving sustainability brand positioning (Belz & Peattie, 2012). Historically, the track record of many companies has been dubious as they have lacked transparency and credibility regarding adopting sustainability. Governments have failed to legislate preferring to delegate responsibility for sustainability to the largely voluntary organisational mechanisms such as CSR. This has contributed to consumer awareness of greenwashing and scepticism regarding ethical claims.

Kotler's competitive positioning strategies (Table 5.20) is often cited as a useful tool. As with all such BAU tools, care has to be taken when using labels. 'Superbargain' may be difficult to differentiate from, say, 'Bargain' in the customer's perception. Furthermore, only a minority of companies will be able to adopt a 'Premium' positioning strategy. Individuals consider and/or adopt the attitudes, beliefs, opinions and values of others. This influences their decision-making. Companies need to appreciate how they are perceived apropos sustainability.

Hart's "Beyond Greening" introduced sustainability positioning by offering the Environmental Sustainability Portfolio (Table 5.21).

Table 5.20 Positioning strategies contrasting price and quality

		Pricing strategies		
		High	*Medium*	*Low*
Quality	High	Premium	Penetration	Superbargain
	Medium	Overpricing	Average Quality	Bargain
	Low	Hit and run	Shoddy goods	Cheap goods

Source: Adapted from Kotler *et al* (2009).

Table 5.21 Hart's Environmental Sustainability Portfolio

	Internal	*External*
	New environmental technologies	*Sustainability vision*
Tomorrow	Many organisations that have made good headway in pollution prevention and product stewardship are still limited by existing technologies. To develop fully sustainable strategies, they will need to develop new technologies	The company's products and services, processes and policies must evolve and what new technologies must be developed to get there. This vision of sustainability provides a framework for pollution control, product stewardship and environmental technology
	Pollution prevention	*Product stewardship*
Today	Involves more than pollution control –cleaning up waste after it has been created means eliminating or minimising waste before it is created 'green marketing' programmes – developing ecologically safer products, recyclable and biodegradable packaging, better pollution controls and more energy-efficient operations.	Minimising not just pollution from production but all environmental impacts throughout the full product life cycle, and all the while reducing costs. Many companies are adopting design for environment (DFE) practices, which involve thinking ahead in the design stage to create products that are easier to recover, reuse or recycle. DFE not only helps to sustain the environment; it can be highly profitable for the company

Sources: Adapted from Hart (1997, p 74); Kotler *et al* (2009, p 90).

Most companies focus on the lower-left quadrant of the grid, investing largely in pollution prevention (Kotler *et al*, 2009). This is often the case for large manufacturers. Some progressive companies practice product stewardship and develop new environmental technologies; however, few have well defined sustainability visions, which may be owing to the inherently product-orientated nature of Hart's portfolio. It lacks customer centricity, which critical marketers suggest applies to many marketing models and frameworks.

There is debate around implementing SM practices. Some suggest SM practitioners will need to challenge existing assumptions and alter traditional marketing practices. Others argue that SM has evolved from the 'marketing orientation' and largely uses the same frameworks and tools as conventional marketing (Richardson *et al*, 2015). To address this paradox, Armstrong & Kotler (2013) positioned SM in relation to other concepts (Table 5.22).

This is problematic as it implies that companies adopting the 'Marketing concept' are only interested in 'now' and not the future. Companies who adopt the 'Marketing concept' are deemed to be marketing orientated (see Chapter 6) and clearly are interested in the future needs, wants and desires of customers (and prospects). The framework is simplistic, as is often the case, limiting discussion of stakeholders to the business and its customers, thus ignoring key 'actors' such as the local community. It provides no indication of how organisations should migrate between orientations. It is not detailed enough

Table 5.22 Sustainable Marketing Matrix

	Business needs (Now)	*Business needs (Future)*
Customer needs (Now)	Marketing Concept	Strategic Planning Concept
Customer needs (Future)	Societal Marketing concept	Sustainable Marketing concept

Source: Adapted from Armstrong and Kotler (2013, p 509).

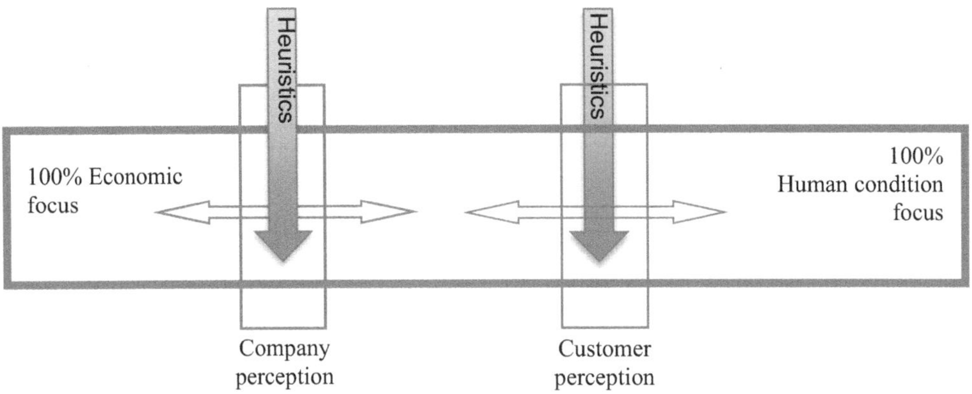

Figure 5.10 Sustainability Perception Continuum influenced by heuristics.

Source: Author.

to be a benchmarking framework. Kotler himself counters the legitimacy of the grid in arguing that marketers cannot rely on the behaviour of consumers to provide the market signals to shift to SM. Some

> "are committed to ethical consumption and many enjoy the warm glow of doing good when they buy, but consumers are confused and there is little sign that they will buy ethical products that cost more or perform less well than the norm. It is a free-rider problem: most wealthy consumers are enjoying being free riders where their immediate descendants and the world's poor pay".
>
> (Kotler *et al* 2009, p 112)

As service providers need to be able to position themselves within their markets in order to make effective decisions it is prudent to assume that they (knowingly or otherwise) are located on the sustainability continuum (Figure 5.10). Organisations need to be aware of how customers perceive their sustainable position. Those not aware of changing consumer attitudes, such as the increasing consumer demand for green and ethical practices (Ethical Consumer, 2022), risk alienating customers.

The continuum illustrates the influence of heuristics on the company and the customer Marketers understand that customers use heuristics to simplify decisions and ultimately perceive companies in simplistic terms, e.g. good company vs bad company or sustainable vs unsustainable. This diagram improves positioning as it highlights how decision-making is simplified for companies and consumers alike. Prioritisation must take place, e.g. whether to invest in People and/or Planet and to what extent? Two issues arise, first, whether 'Profit' (i.e. 100% economic focus) alludes to the company's profitability or rather the profits re-invested in the People and Planet foci. Second, whether outputs or perceptions should be benchmarked.

Belz and Peattie (2012) suggest challenging decisions have to be made involving sustainability brand positioning. Historically the track record of many companies has been dubious. They have lacked transparency and credibility regarding adopting sustainability. Sustainability and CSR are inherently value-based concepts (Richardson & Cassop Thompson, 2023). Governments have failed to legislate preferring to delegate responsibility for sustainability to the largely voluntary organisational mechanisms. This reflects on the perceived values of organisations, contributing to consumer awareness of greenwashing and scepticism regarding ethical claims. Sustainability should be central to organisational culture and beliefs whereas some maintain it may simply be an 'add on' feature to their business operation, an afterthought (Jones *et al*, 2009) or deemed voluntary in nature (Barkemeyer, 2009). Strategic decision-making is aided by plotting the three foci of TBL (Figure 5.11).

Figure 5.11 assumes that companies must not only reinvest Profit but should also be seen to do so. The degree of reinvestment depends upon the company and its circumstances. Consider three scenarios, first, a company is profitable but only invests a small amount of profit into People (position C). It could simply invest more to improve its social/ethical position. Another invests a high amount of its profit into green projects but nothing in People (position D). In which case it could maintain the status quo, invest some profit into People or invest more in its existing green projects. Finally, a company invests profits into People and Planet with a bias towards green projects (position B/A). It may want a more balanced sustainable positioning and thus may sacrifice some green

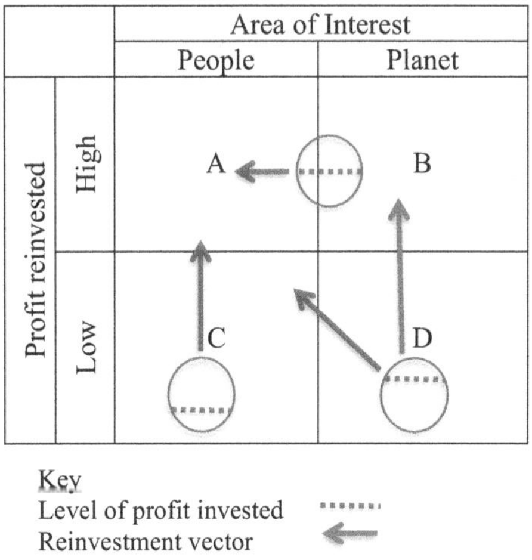

Figure 5.11 TBL positioning grid.

Source: Adapted from Richardson (2020, p 193).

projects to invest in ethical alternatives. The options suggested for the scenarios are far from exhaustive.

Strategy Formulation

Marketers may identify a wide range of strategic options hence they will need to prioritise which ones best suit their company. Three 'grand' corporate strategies are Stability, Expansion or Concentration

The origins of the Grand Strategies (Table 5.23) are unclear. The term was used as early as 1834, possibly by Jacques Antoine Hippolyte, Comte de Guibert. More recently Basil Liddell Hart alluded to grand strategy in his 1925 '*Paris, or the Future of War*' publication. Grand Strategies apply predominantly to large organisations as they may take many years (even decades) to achieve. Hence a degree of stability is necessary.

Table 5.23 Three 'Grand' generic strategies

Strategy	*Approach*	*Risk level*	*Comment*
Stability	Seeks to maintain the status quo using incremental improvements	Suits risk-averse organisers who may struggle to develop alternatives	Creates 'buy-in' from risk-averse stakeholders. good for low growth, stable markets with minimal opportunities
Expansion	Involves business redefinition	Transformational leaders seek dramatic returns and appeasing investors.	Redefine the organisation by adding services and products to meet their economic objectives
Concentration	Exploiting existing resources often when companies have relatively small market shares	Lower risk. They do not need to take risks to grow. They simply need to outperform the competition	This may reap short-term rewards; however, in the long-term it may be more effective to be proactive

Source: Original diagram.

Example: By 2023, China had cornered the market in electric vehicle batteries and were on course to overtake Tesla. Many of the new car companies (i.e. Byd), started off as battery manufacturers. BYD, long-backed by legendary US investor Warren Buffett, attended the 2023 Munich motor show with six Europe-bound models. In total, China had already overtaken Germany and Japan for overall global car exports by 2023. This is no accident according to Andy Palmer, the former Aston Martin and Nissan boss. "Twenty years ago, I was sitting on the board of (Chinese carmaker) Dongfeng. It was the decree of the Chinese government that Chinese car companies needed to leapfrog over western companies and the best way of doing that was to adopt new energy vehicles, as they called them at the time. That ultimately, of course, meant battery-electric vehicles" (BBC, 2023b). That strategic planning for dominance in this sector meant China carved up capability on batteries, motors and the raw materials supply chains stretching across the world. Palmer also suggested the scale, combined with subsidies, mean Chinese manufacturers are able to undercut other global players (*ibid*).

A grand strategy may be used to co-ordinate normal strategies. Since the 1970s the Japanese Kaizen approach has influenced manufacturing in Europe. Kaizen, akin to a Stability strategy, involves implementing incremental changes across a wide range of metrics, i.e. be 1% better at 100 things rather than 100% better at one thing. If maintained over a period of time, dramatic changes result. Clearly Stability and Concentration strategies are similar in approach. The differences are nuanced. A Concentration strategy may involve marginally more risk. It simply needs to outperform the competition.

Sustainability represents a nascent branch of social science that some consider a form of creative destruction (Sandberg, 2010), which could ultimately render the traditional ways of operating businesses redundant. Alternatively, others suggest organisations find their strategic intentions may be deflected (Mintzberg, 1990) by failing to react to changes in consumer values, e.g. the growth in demand for ethical and/or green goods or services. Hence, it is sensible to consider these two schools of thought.

Schumpeter's Creative Destruction

'Creative destruction' describes the process where incumbents' competences and perceptions are challenged by new paradigms (Schumpeter, 1950). To be Schumpeterian, TBL's step change would have fundamentally changed service providers' knowledge base leading to new opportunities and in turn market growth. Market boundaries would be redefined as companies sought to differentiate product offers or to create and target new segments. New entrants to the enlarged market would have a greater incentive to innovate. Sustainable entrepreneurs may discover new opportunities and stimulate change in society whether this is a production method, technological development, product/service, distribution system or even a new organisational form (Tilley & Young, 2009).

A key point is that sustainability (and its subsequent potential for creative destruction) applies to services as much as production of goods however in services the innovation is in process. Some warn that the fears formed by the innovation resulting from

> "the entrepreneurial process of 'creative destruction' can bring out the worst among the 'modernisation losers' (industries that are intrinsically unsustainable). This conflict with vested interests can affect non-innovative people and organisations leading to resistant, evasive and disruptive behaviours".
>
> (Tilley & Young, 2009, p 82)

Studies have identified a significant increase in the media coverage of (corporate) sustainability-related concepts since 1990 (Barkemeyer *et al*, 2009). This increase seems to be of an incremental nature, rather than distinctly associated with a certain number of events. This could be argued to counter those in the Schumpeterian school.

Mintzberg's Deflected and Realised Strategies

Mintzberg (1990) argues that due to the turbulent business environment, companies cannot foresee impacts on their strategies. Managers reacting to events and trends adapt existing strategies; they create 'realised' strategies rather than those originally intended. A risk is this could lead to strategic drift (*ibid*).

Figure 5.12 illustrates how strategic drift may result from failure to adopt or react to emergent elements of TBL, macro-environmental changes, and/or changes in consumer values, e.g. growing demand for ethical or green goods. To militate against such outcomes, organisations may need to be benchmarked in terms of their sustainability. As discussed in Chapter 1 consumers consider many of society's problems to be beyond the capacity of government alone to solve. They expect companies to contribute significantly to solving these problems, some of which they have aggravated. However, inertia or fear of change is often cited as a reason for businesses to be conservative or risk averse.

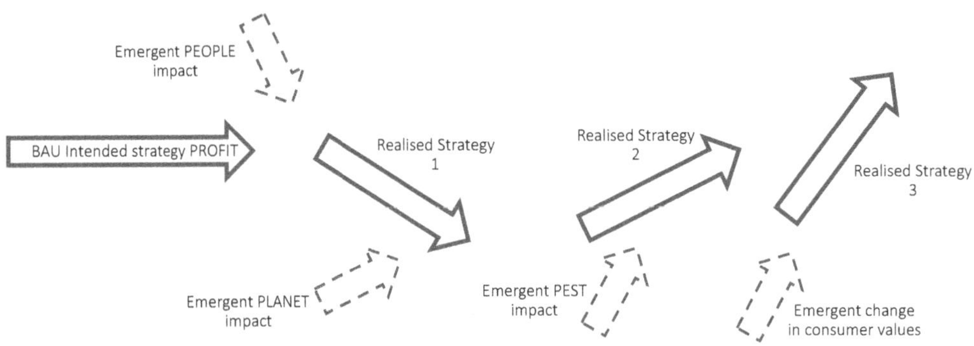

Figure 5.12 Mintzberg's realised versus intended strategies.

Source: Adapted from Mintzberg (1990).

Example: Big brands are also slowly improving the sustainability of mainstream products. The batteries are lasting longer, with many maintaining their useful life for in excess of 1,000 full charge cycles, or roughly five years' charging, if done once every two days. Battery life is the number one cause of phone replacements (Guardian, 2023), so progress is essential. These slow, but needed, changes have been driven, in part, by increasing consumer awareness, with a growing percentage of buyers actively seeking out more sustainable, or longer-lasting, devices. But it is the EU's upcoming new rules on eco-design that will force the issue. The overhaul of regulations for batteries, device durability, longevity and repairability will come into force in 2027, ensuring that any device sold in the EU will have to be designed to be easier to repair, more durable, have much longer software support and user-replaceable batteries. The big firms are likely to be able to make such design changes, but phones may become thicker and more expensive as a result. Either way, the Android or Apple phone of 2027 may have a battery (replaceable with simple tools), be durable and supported for up to five years after the device is discontinued. But the question is whether longer-lasting phones will stop yearly or biannual upgrades. A side-effect may see a booming secondhand phone market. A phone with a longer useful life has more value to a second or third owner, which is beneficial to wallet and the environment alike (*ibid*).

Strategies may change with time as progress is made. The change may not be voluntary. No objective, strategy or tactic is cast in stone. Leaders must reflect on strategic choices and be prepared to make changes. A trend is a phenomenon that (over time) maintains the status quo, increases or decreases. Once identified, it is necessary to recognise whether the trend is gathering momentum, neutral or has a positive or negative effect on achieving objectives. Strategies are subjected to these external forces as are objectives and tactics. Hence, the need to identify trends today that will continue into the future which is when (after all) new products or services will be launched.

Two commonly cited generic strategic options are Porter's Generic Strategies and Ansoff's growth related strategies. Porter's work has influenced much of the debate on strategy. Porter (1980) proposed three strategic choices, namely cost leadership, focus or differentiation (Figure 5.13).

Traditionally, the danger faced when adopting Porter's Generic Strategies was becoming "stuck in the middle". Subsequently this risk has dissipated as Focus has increasingly been considered just another form of differentiation. Hence, there is a straight choice between cost-leadership and differentiation. The customer should regard the brand as offering good value-for-money (VFM) or should be able to take value that justifies paying more. Good VFM is offered rather than simply saying 'the cheapest' which simply is not the case. Consumers rarely buy the cheapest product available. They do, however, constantly strive to find the best VFM. A Porsche 911 can be argued to provide excellent VFM.

British retail is recognised as being world class. The choice is wider than ever and the high street is under pressure from changing consumer behaviour coupled with macro influences such as Brexit. Figure 5.14 shows how some retailers could be mapped using Porter's Generic Strategies. Some have broad segments whereas others are cost leaders

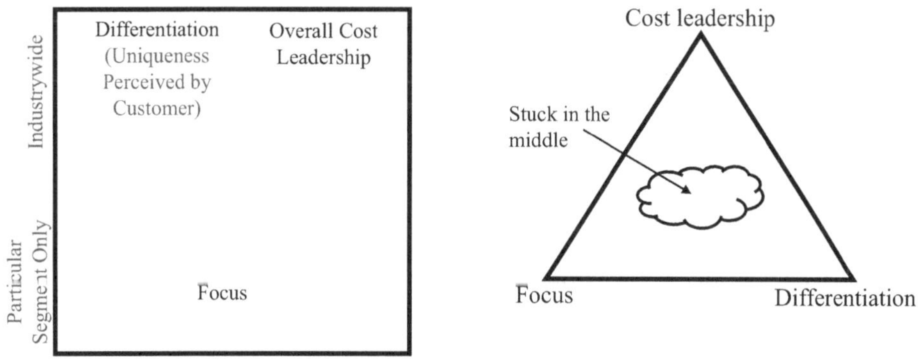

Figure 5.13 Two ways to portray Porter's Generic Strategy.

Source: Adapted from Porter (1980).

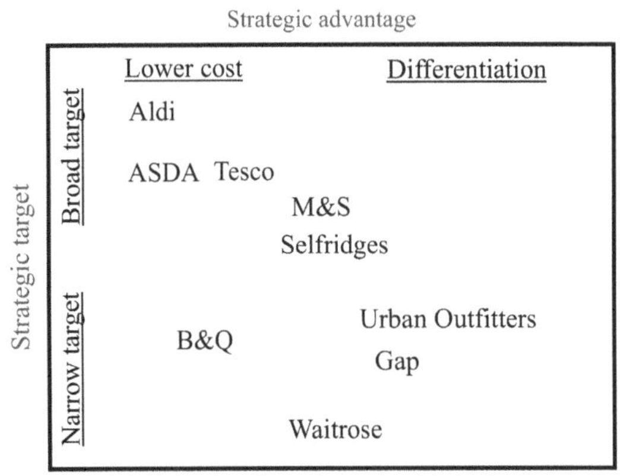

Figure 5.14 Porter's Generic Strategy applied to retailers.

Source: Adapted from Porter (1980).

Table 5.24 Ansoff's strategy matrix

	OLD PRODUCTS	*NEW PRODUCTS*
OLD MARKETS	*Market Penetration* Low risk – seeks increased sales for its present products in its present markets through more aggressive promotion and distribution.	*Product Development* Medium risk – seeks increased sales by developing improved products for its present markets. Can lead to diversification if product taken to a new market
NEW MARKETS	*Market Development* Medium risk – seeks increased sales by taking its present products into new markets. Can lead to diversification if followed by a new product.	*Diversification* High risk – seeks increased sales by developing new products and new markets. Can be achieved by Concentric or Conglomerate diversification or via Vertical or Horizontal integration

Source: Adapted from Ansoff (1957).

with narrow segments (e.g. B&Q). This is useful at a corporate level, but limited for marketers who are naturally concerned with products and markets.

Ansoff (1957) recognised that company growth is linked to the relationship between products and their markets (see Table 5.24). He proposed that companies should reflect on whether new or existing products are to be delivered in new or existing markets. His matrix is widely recognised as a useful tool in choosing a marketing strategy.

Ansoff's matrix is preferred by many marketers to Porter's Generic Strategy as it links strategy to the two key marketing areas: product and markets. Also, it introduces the recognition of risk into the strategic decision. If a company is risk averse (say a charity or social enterprise) then Diversification (with high risk) is probably not appropriate. Seeking growth by selling more to the existing market (i.e. Market Penetration or concentration) is the strategy for many companies who have small market shares and / or limited resources. If the company culture is inclined towards taking risks (say growth through aggressive mergers and acquisitions or even simply highly resourced) then immediate diversification is an option. Those in the middle ground (i.e. willing to take some risks, however analysis suggests that in the long run they need to diversify) have two options. They can take the following two-step approaches:

- Market penetration – Market Development – Diversification
- Market penetration – Product Development – Diversification

It is important to remember that these strategies are not mutually exclusive. Indeed, the successful firms often pursued two-step strategies in parallel and that following combinations of new products and new markets frequently resulted in diversification (Richardson, 2020). Ultimately theory without implementation is futile. Managers need to translate objectives into strategies that can be implemented.

If the company culture is inclined towards taking risks (say growth through aggressive mergers and acquisitions or even simply highly resourced) then immediate diversification is an option. Think of Microsoft spending $3billion developing the first Xbox knowing they would never recoup the investment. Those in the middle ground have two options. They can take the following two-step approaches:

Example: Brexit was an act of economic national self-harm. The Institute of Fiscal Studies (IfS) estimated that by 2023 the UK economy had reduced by 4%, a substantial drop for a $2 trillion economy, dramatically lowering the tax revenue. In 2022, the UK Government used it's 'freedom' to sign bilateral trade agreements with Australia and New Zealand. The IfS estimated that the Australian bilateral agreement would add 0.08% to the UK's GDP. Many UK farmers (who largely voted for Brexit against the advice of the National Farmers Union) should now be planning for different scenarios. Why? Australia and New Zealand are major exporters of beef and lamb respectively. The UK Government insisted on a 15-year taper before full zero-tariff imports to the UK could happen. Australia and New Zealand have economies of scale which mean they can land their meat products cheaper than many UK farmers. The UK has few problems with Country of Origin (CoO) effect as has been proven by their willingness to buy Danish bacon for decades. For the UK livestock industry this represents an existential crisis. They have until 2037 to plan alternative strategies. Many farmers are cash-poor but asset rich. Diversification (see Table 5.24) will create opportunities to use their land in different ways, e.g hosting events, opening farm-shops (with online provision), glamping or rare-breed collections.

As discussed, a strategy is what an organisation uses to achieve its objectives. A sustainable strategy addresses the three foci of the TBL (Figure 5.15).

With a TBL-based (i.e. sustainable) strategy, Profits must be reinvested in Planet and People. Strategies may change with time as progress is made. As Mintzberg suggests, the change may not be voluntary. Individuals consider and/or adopt the attitudes, beliefs, opinions and values of others. This influences their decision-making. Companies need to

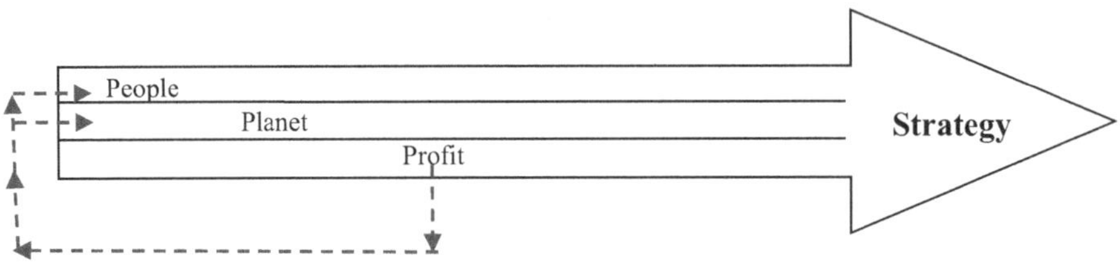

Figure 5.15 A TBL-based sustainable strategy.

Source: Author.

appreciate how they are perceived apropos sustainability to build sustainable brands that consumers associate with social and environmental values.

A number of objectives can be achieved with a clear strategy; however, too many objectives (and strategies) can lead to confusion. Within functions, managers must reflect on whether a strategy helps them to achieve their objectives. Is it the best fit? How will tactics be implemented to achieve the marketing objectives? Hence corporate strategies achieve corporate objectives and marketing strategies achieve marketing objectives.

5.4 Implementation – Monitoring, Evaluation and Control

Ultimately theory without implementation is futile. The Institute of Directors (IoD) were asked if they had the appropriate strategies for their organisations. Over 80% responded that they did. When asked if they felt they implemented their strategies well, the figure plummeted to 14%. This raises major concerns about productivity and organisational effectiveness.

Tactics are the short-term measures implemented by functions to achieve the objectives and subsequent strategies. In marketing, tactics relate to the marketing mix. Tactical implementation can be measured. Organisations can undertake a gap analysis (see Figure 5.3) to contrast the current position with a future forecast. What is needed is not change for its own sake, but the right change and many examples exist of companies who have benefited by moving towards adopting TBL. Third-party codes of conduct can be useful. They provide credibility to the argument for being more sustainable whilst acting as valuable sources of information in their own right. The FTSE4Good index, for example, includes human rights criteria. Marketers can sell the concept of sustainability to cynics by highlighting how the public's mounting concerns are partly driven by

- growth in prosperity
- expansion of media coverage
- notable disasters
- greater scientific knowledge
- longer-term cultural shifts
- PR & celebrity endorsements.

Most of these have increased as a direct result of social media. With billions of internet users worldwide, avoiding reputational damage is increasingly difficult. The following are increasing daily.

1 Levels of environmental awareness/concern leading to demand for eco-friendly products, adoption of green product substitutes, reuse/ redesign /recycling of products.
2 Consumer values are shifting from consumption to conservation.
3 Demand for less industrial pollution with more conservation of resources and energy saving.
4 Greater governmental regulation with businesses charged for environmental impacts.
5 Demand for, and availability of, information on environmental issues with companies expected to conduct and publish ecological audits.
6 Opportunities to develop protection of the natural environment, animal rights and endangered species.

There has been a sea-change in consumer opinion regarding TBL and it is likely that marketing academics are trailing consumers, progressive organisations and other disciplines. Kotler argues that marketer's lives will become more complicated. Meeting 'Planet' costs may necessitate raising prices. This does not automatically mean that the product will be harder to sell, however the focus will need to be on the benefits and value for the customer. Increasingly companies will need to reflect on their position on the 'Sustainability Perception Continuum' (Figure 5.10) and the extent to which they are willing to adopt sustainable practices.

Control and Measuring Value

Throughout the ensuing implementation of changes to the Mix there should be scheduled opportunities to reflect on the plan's effectiveness. All stakeholders should be aware of the timescales and the need for feedback. Marketers must act on these reflections. Simply put, a marketing plan without control is not a marketing plan. The issue of control is key. There must be a period of measurement and review of any marketing plan. Controls must be established to assess how well it is being put into practice. Key factors are:

- objectives must exist
- outputs must be measurable (some use KPIs)
- a predictive model of the outcomes is required (to enable measurement)
- capability to take action must exist.

Key Performance Indicators (KPIs)

On KPIs, the most important element is 'Key'. Far too often companies produce dozens of KPIs and then are puzzled when they underperform. KPIs should be few in number and sufficiently important that all stakeholders buy into achieving them. There are many examples of frivolous KPIs often where the company culture promotes managerialism or box-ticking rather than genuine innovation.

The controls should reflect the organisation's culture. Hence scenario planning and forecasts for an organisation with an aggressive growth culture should reflect this. Simplistic sales analysis, say actual versus budgeted turnover, is only the first step. Further analysis, e.g. by product/service type, region or customer, may be needed. In a hotel, marketers should identify the activities needed to support each guest by category and the cost drivers of these activities. Thus, the cost of a one-night midweek stay by a businessperson could be distinguished from that of a one-night stay by someone visiting a cultural event.

If analysing market share, it must be done in context, i.e. related to the market type (duopoly, oligopoly etc.), condition (static, growing, declining), size and your role (e.g. market leader, challenger or follower).

540° Feedback

The organisation's capacity to react to changes needed to get the plan 'on track' should have been considered during the internal audit. There should be scheduled opportunities to reflect on the plan's effectiveness. Marketers must recognise the need to get feedback from the staff. Sustainable marketing involves undertaking 540-degree feedback. 360-degree feedback features staff providing feedback on their line managers whereas the 540-degree alternative encourages inviting consumers, customers, suppliers and other stakeholders to provide inputs. They will provide key insights into areas such as a lack of staff knowledge, training, vision, skill or security. In short, 540-degree feedback should go beyond monitoring and become a platform to promote learning within organisations.

Hard and Soft Controls

Controls can take many forms. They can be 'hard' (i.e. number based) or 'soft', which is to say qualitative. Examples of hard (quantitative) metrics are:

- cost level
- units produced per week – sales levels and costs
- delays in delivery time
- zero defects/returns
- customer service complaints
- market share – market penetration by product/service type
- customer retention and acquisition.

One benefit of digital marketing is the ability to quickly review marcomms campaigns using 'hard' data (Table 5.25).

The effectiveness of a campaign can be viewed in real-time and, if necessary, amended. Reports can be produced in a simple spreadsheet and can cover key metrics.

Examples of soft (qualitative) measures are

Table 5.25 Key mobile metrics

Metrics	*SMS*	*MMS*	*WAP*
Messages sent	☺	☺	
Messages delivered	☺	☺	☺
Messages bounced		☺	☺
Stop messages	☺	☺	☺
Replies	☺	☺	
Downloads & value		☺	☺
Opens and click throughs		☺	☺

Source: Author.

- brand image, awareness and perception
- employee motivation and welfare
- customer satisfaction
- social responsibility performance.

To be clear, there is no ranking between 'hard' and 'soft', they are equally important. Many companies will use a blend of 'hard' and 'soft' measures.

Budget

In an SM plan there should be a detailed budget for the first year. The budget should follow the SMART objectives. Indeed, budgets need to be related to what the whole company wants to achieve, which makes the resulting budget more likely to be realistic. The results can be broken down into the different market segments, therefore allowing analysis of how well the marketing mix has worked on specific target sectors. Ideally, the company should use the budget to contribute to knowing the RoMI. It makes sense to know the marketing costs associated with differing strategies.

Many costs are driven by customers (delivery, discounts, marketing, after sales service, etc.). Costs and targets must always be measured against operating conditions. A company may have a corporate objective to boost its profitability by attracting new business. The TOWS analysis generates a prioritised marketing objective of using direct marketing. After the audit the strengths and weaknesses lend themselves to using mail as against telesales or personal selling. The marketing function posts 10,000 mail-outs at a cost of £1,000. This seems good value at a cost of £0.10 per mail-out. The mail-out has a 5 % response rate (which is considerably better than the industry norm) generating 500 responses. Typically, the pipeline suggests converting 25% of the responses. Each sale generates a nett profit (surplus) of £12. Hence you have £12 x 125 or £1,500 profit. This generates a number of metrics that may be useful for control/evaluation purposes:

- cost per response – £1,000/500 responses = £2 per response
- cost per sale- £1,000/ 125 sales= £8 per sale
- ROI- (£1,500-£1,000)/£1000 = 0.5 which equates to a 50% gross ROI.

Whether these metrics are acceptable will depend on a number of factors both internal (aims, objectives etc.) and external (competitors, market share, market growth etc.). Larger companies use more complex feedback control indicators such as the Return on capital employed (ROCE). ROCE factors in the use/depletion of capital assets to give an overview of the whole company not just the sales/marketing functions. There are issues, i.e. ROCE may be

- justifiably different in different parts of the supply chain
- impacted by geography
- influenced by the age of a department/division (and its assets)
- inappropriate to products early in their PLC
- driving (short-term) investment in old products, rather than new (and more productive) assets.

Naturally operations have to keep pace with customer change and the move to SM could be one such change.

SM Benchmarking

Benchmarking can be used to instil best practice into companies across a range of issues. It should be a continuous, iterative process that measures gaps between what the marketer thinks the brand offers and the customers' perceptions of the offering. Benchmarking compares and contrasts perceptions of value(s) with recognised competitors. As previously discussed, value can be created (or destroyed) by anyone in the Value System (see Figure 5.5). Hence benchmarking should be applied to all aspects of the value-creation process across departments, suppliers and distributors. If done in a meaningful (rather than tokenistic) manner, it will provide the springboard for planning and marketers must address the issues highlighted within the benchmark report. To promote the adoption of SM practices for companies of all sizes and types marketers can use the Sustainable Marketing Benchmarking Framework (see Figure 5.16).

This framework deliberately chimes with Mintzberg's realised/deflected strategies (see Figure 5.12). Marketing strategies, like any other, can be deflected. It clearly shows the areas to be benchmarked and the areas where marketers must scan (i.e. the Macro environment and other disciplines). The factors portrayed can impact on multiple TBL elements for example adopting a CSR policy could impact on People and Profit. Most of the benchmark areas are self-explanatory.

Environment Social and Governance (ESG) Benchmarking

European firms with more than 500 employees are expected to to collect environment, social and governance (ESG) data on every company in their supply networks and constellations. By 2025, these rules apply for companies with 250 staff; SMEs will have to meet SG obligations by 2026.

ESG has its critics. The former HSBC Asset Management global head of responsible investing Stuart Kirk undoubtedly adopted a maverick position in respect to his views on ESG. He suggested the ESG has three fatal flaws (FT, 2023) namely

- moral high grounds invariably crumble – mostly due to changes in scientific knowledge, attitudes, money or politics
- knowing where to stop
- everyone has their own view on what is good and bad – resulting in "Death by fatuous and incomparable data ... somebody has to arbitrarily decide the relative weightings between 'E', 'S' and/or 'G' (*ibid*)

His comments resonate with those of Friedman, Jensen (see Chapter 1) and their libertarian supporters. He claimed to have accepted the scientific communities' findings on climate change but railed against the EU's steps to address abuse by introducing ESG measures. This is often the way with critics.

Marketers may use outside support from environmental or sustainability consultants or agencies. They can be employed on a one-off or ongoing basis. SM is a long-term orientation and changes may take time. Having carried out a sustainability audit, 'comms'

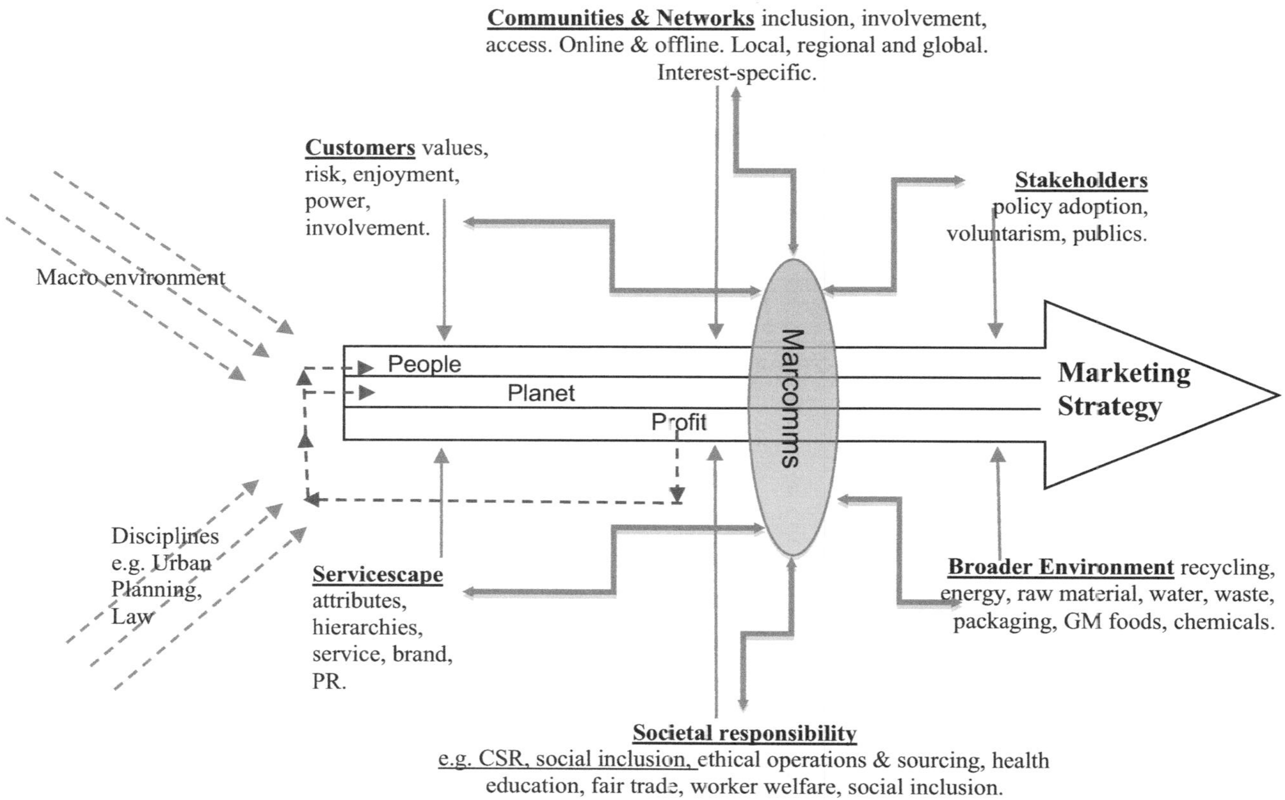

Figure 5.16 Sustainable Marketing (SM) Benchmarking Framework.

Source: Adapted from Richardson (2015).

should be used to publish the results in a format that is easy for people to assess (see Figure 5.17).

The 'comms' should explain how the new measures may satisfy more than one element of People-Planet-Profit, e.g. reducing their CO_2 footprint by holding meetings and/or conferences 'virtually'. Hence these meetings could be a considerable environmental improvement undertaken at little cost with greater convenience for the stakeholders.

Example: A useful online tool is offered by B Corporation (see https://bimpactassessment.net) who are a US-based not-for-profit organisation. Their approach is similar to Kotler's APIC planning framework (see Table 5.2). It provides limited options regarding choosing the sector, i.e. users are asked to choose 'Service with minor environmental impact' or 'Service with major environmental impact'. This is a judgment call and some stakeholders in organisations may not know the answer unless directly involved in environmental auditing. It poses questions on governance, workers, community, environment and customers. These again are limited, i.e. there is little on suppliers. That said, it is a useful tool if US centric and really more suited to large manufacturers. This is a common complaint; indeed, far too many marketing texts make the same mistake. That said, some of the questions it posits should make marketers think about their relationships with the community and the environment.

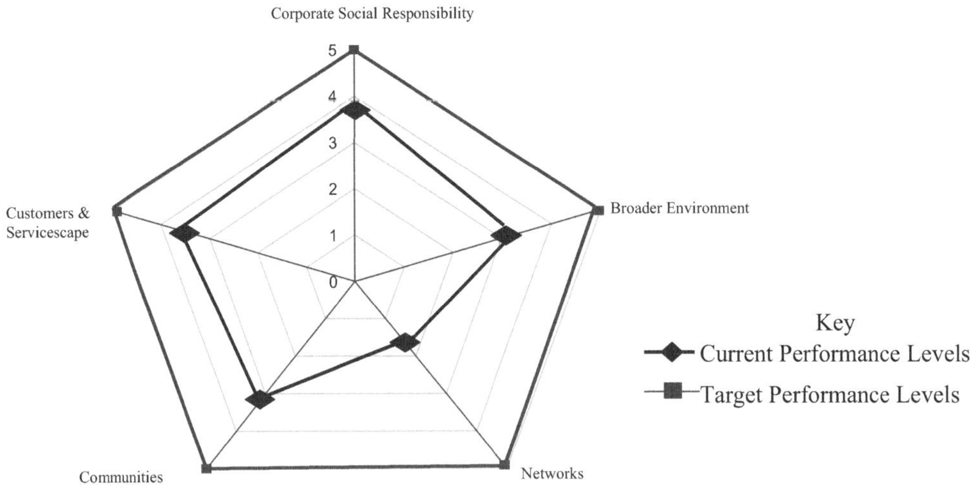

Figure 5.17 Polar diagram plotting sustainability results against targets.

Source: Author.

5.5 Barriers to Adopting SM Planning

As discussed, SM must be adopted more widely and with more conviction. However, many companies fail to implement successful marketing planning with the added challenge of adopting sustainability. Many managers have chosen operational effectiveness over customer-centric strategies, particularly in scenarios like retail where constant improvement is often seen as the route to superior profitability. This may be because of having a disproportionate internal organisational focus rather than external factors such as customers and competitors. Retailers like Wilko did not react to external (and-competitive) changes and lost their fight for survival.

Often size is cited as a justification, however many studies have noted the positive link between having a marketing plan and business performance in SMEs. Also, many large well-resourced organisations fail to plan or fail to implement well as a result of their planning. Certainly, organisational culture (rather than size) has a lot to do with successful planning. One of the key causes of corporate failure is 'bad management' and this also applies to marketing planning. This can take the form of weak direction from senior management. Simplistic forecasts with unachievable target are problematic. Too often the sales target is a wish list, i.e. 'it's where we need to be'. In future marketers will need to operate in an increasingly sustainable fashion and will need to identify and remove barriers to adopting sustainability. Richardson *et al* (2015) identified the barriers as.

- Responsibility for ownership
- Shareholder dominance – monitoring management
- Predominant sales orientation
- Dividends versus investment
- Crisis management
- SMEs don't plan
- Self-interest shareholder groups
- Definitional problems
- Short-termism
- Multiple stakeholder interests.

This list is not exhaustive but provides insights into the challenge of adopting sustainability. The REACHNEW framework (see Table 5.3) should support those undertaking an SM plan. That said, it is appropriate to consider some of these barriers in detail.

Planning in a Crisis

Marketers cannot plan for all identifiable eventualities (e.g. fire, flood, contract breaches, financial mismanagement, disrupted customer services etc.). Hence it is prudent to consider crisis as a risk element that can either be anticipated or not. Often managers are judged on how they deal with crises. Many PR agencies (see Chapter 4) provide crisis management support to organisations who may suffer reputational damage. Marketers can take steps to plan for a crisis, e.g. they can run simulations and test different scenarios.

If a damaging scenario is flagged (say regarding exposure in the media of unsustainable practices) this can inform senior management's strategic decision making. Any stakeholder mapping analysis will shift dramatically during a crisis. Dormant stakeholders may become active and consideration must be given to whether they will be a positive or negative influence and to what degree. It is better to communicate with key stakeholders proactively rather than wait until they read about the problems elsewhere. Ignoring some stakeholder groups could result in extending or escalating the crisis. Too many organisations adopt the unethical stance of denying any wrongdoing and demanding proof. They refuse to acknowledge the story until sufficient time has passed that (when raised again) they can dismiss it as 'old news'. This leads to further scrutiny and the media (and other audiences) will be more sympathetic to the brand if the response is sincere, sympathetic and authentic. Demonstrating sincerity may require further evidence that the issue is not only being addressed but measures are being implemented to ensure it does not reoccur. In crises, brand reputation is limited if the company is open and transparent.

Responsibility for Ownership

Sustainability 'ownership' can be fuzzy in some companies and hotly contested in others. Ethical matters (e.g. CSR) are often controlled by Human Resource departments. Some organisations recognise the importance of CSR with elements in their mission statements (a strategic management decision) which may include 'green' issues (possibly a Quality Control issue), ethical supply policies (the purchasing department) and charitable links (all of the above). This corporate 'bun-fight' is reflected on the larger stage where proponents of sustainable development differ widely in terms of emphases, e.g. what to sustain or to develop and when? In B2C sectors responsibility lies with the service provider, the consumer, the community, the regulator and/or even the government. An example of governmental influence is the Companies Act 2006 which heavily impacts CSR. Increasingly the environment will be used as a launch pad for governmental initiatives and legislation. Marketers must use a blend of 'comms' tools to inform the different parties and manage their expectations.

Undoubtedly when things are going well everyone wants to stake their claim however when it goes wrong where does responsibility lie? As discussed in Chapter 1, CSI has led to organisations seeking competitive advantage through misinformation and/or disinformation. It is no wonder consumers are increasingly sceptical of environmental claims, hence the rise of accusations of greenwashing. Ultimately marketers must act in an ethical way and communicate transparently with the stakeholders.

Shareholder Dominance – Monitoring Management

Principals (i.e. shareholders and institutional investors) are aware that agents (i.e. Directors and Managers) may act out of self-interest and position the company in such a way as to reduce returns and share value. Hence the principals incur the cost of monitoring the directors via annual audits, which are obligatory for most large companies. Too often agents only communicate with their shareholders in the run up to the AGM. This approach should be avoided and replaced by engaging shareholders in the same way as customers, i.e. using 'comms' to build relationships, keep stakeholders informed, build loyalty and enhance shareholder satisfaction.

In larger companies, or those with 'active' shareholders who seek maximum return on their investment, there are many tensions some of which are exacerbated by the (mis)use of the word sustainability itself. For some, shareholder sustainability is the main corporate driver featuring returning dividends and maximising share value for owners. Principals demand regular stable dividend payments however funds needed to pay dividends detract from the agent's ability to undertake new (sustainable) projects; principals want to sustain dividends to maintain market value. Shareholders concerns (having funded the company through investment) should be acknowledged in conjunction with those stakeholders who enable the company to continue and thrive. Progressive managers should naturally cater for the lives and well-being of their micro-environmental stakeholders, e.g. employees, suppliers and the community in which the company is located. Hence, for most commentators, shareholder sustainability does not equate to 'Sustainability'.

In some companies, shareholders had influence but were largely deemed to be passive. Increasingly shareholders actively participate in the running of AGMs. Some acquire shares specifically to affect the company's direction, which would usually be the domain of the directors. This may lead to strategic shift and/or drift not to mention the potential for diminishing returns. Recently shareholders have formed well-organised pressure groups in order to maximise their influence on corporate policy. These groups often use PR and digital 'comms' as key tools in promoting their agenda.

Multiple Stakeholder Interests

The terms used so far, i.e. 'business', 'company' or 'organisation' are somewhat nebulous. There are many differing types of multi-stakeholder businesses, e.g. single proprietorships, partnerships, co-operatives, non-profit enterprise, social enterprises, private limited companies and public limited (Plc) enterprises. Each of these differ in terms aims, objectives, vision, culture, structure and so on.

Organisations do not exist in isolation. Simply put, companies affect the lives and well-being of their stakeholders (see Chapter 1). Managers must interact with employees, unions, suppliers, intermediaries, government and most importantly customers. Each may have an agenda and/or be motivated by self-interest. Shareholder 'value' may come at the expense of customer 'value' and satisfaction. Companies could certainly use 'comms' to address issues, i.e. diminished job security, higher unemployment and poorer (perceived) products and services. At a higher level it is a concern that 'customers' rarely feature in sustainability models discussed at the highest levels, e.g. the UN, EU or UNCTAD. Many of the contributors lack understanding of consumer behavior.

Short-Termism

The economic difficulties of 2008/2009 and the COVID-19 pandemic illustrated clearly that many institutions do not operate in a free market where they can do as they wish. Governments will always rescue financial institutions if the alternative is economically damaging. Cases such as Northern Rock should serve as an invaluable lesson in the danger of short-term approaches. In Northern Rock's case the business model was changed (after demutualisation) to a more aggressive model, which strove for higher returns than had been the case in the company's long history as a mutual 'friendly' society.

In some cases, managers may wish to adopt policies beyond those demanded by legislation or regulatory bodies, such as being listed on the FTSE4GOOD index. This could incur costs that diminish market value or returns. Such action is often watered down if not prevented outright by fear of an over-reaction by the short-termist markets. Hence those with vested interests (such as institutional investors and free marketeers) encourage managers to ignore investments in longer run drivers of success such as sustainability. Many investors lost substantial funds in Northern Rock who (ironically) could have had a different trajectory if they had adopted a more sustainable approach.

Overcoming Barriers to Adoption

In future, marketers will need to operate in an increasingly sustainable fashion whilst being able to identify and remove barriers to adopting sustainability. Key issues are

- Costs
- Technical and organisational
- Conflicts between objectives
- International implications
- Lack of visibility
- Timescale
- Lack of certainty about the nature of the problem
- Concerns regarding proposed remedies
- Tokenism
- Moral fatigue.

These can prevent adoption, particularly as some issues, say costs, can combine with others (say timescales) to generate inertia. What is needed is a marketing campaign that regularly updates stakeholders with measurable evidence of improvements. Do not expect them to make huge leaps in the dark. Instead, gently nudge them over a period of time and steady progress will be made.

As well as Codes of Conduct a range of 'standards' are available to assist in measuring sustainability, e.g. ISO 20121 provides a specification for a sustainable events management across Europe. As service industries generate the majority of GDP in developed countries, it is fair to assume that some of the support materials for the Event Management sector will chime with other areas. ISO 14001 is an internationally accepted standard that provides organisations with a planned set of criteria required for implementation of an effective Environmental Management System (EMS). Trade bodies and special interest groups will have their own codes.

Key Findings

1 'Mission statements' are increasingly replaced by Purpose Statements based on a company's core value-types. Value types must reflect the value sought by stakeholders and influence sustainable business models. Mission statements should be customer centric and reviewed periodically.
2 A marketing strategy (e.g. Ansoff) should achieve specific marketing objectives. Marketing objectives must support corporate objectives. Objectives must be specific and measurable.
3 Efficiency is doing things right; effectiveness is doing the right things. Clearly sustainability involves being efficient AND effective.
4 The situation review must feature 540-degree feedback from consumers, customers, suppliers and other stakeholders.

5 It is not enough to carry out a marketing audit and then fail to implement changes. If it has simply become a ritual, an onerous task, it will fail.
6 Customers should be central to *all* business decisions and activities. Organisations should continuously scan all business environments, looking inward *and* outwards to understand/react to changing customer behaviours.
7 The SWOT summary collects internal, micro and macro findings. Too little detail will lead to a lack of action whereas too much could lead to 'analysis paralysis'. However, it is the TOWS that generates marketing objectives.
8 A marketing plan without control is not a marketing plan. KPIs should be few in number but sufficiently important that stakeholders 'buy' into them.
9 Companies must know their sustainability position to make good strategic and tactical decisions. Benchmarking is a practical and proven method to help measure (sustainability) performance against competitors.

Activities

1 Access the various outputs of Professor Malcolm McDonald. Though not without critics he has written more on planning than most.
2 For an overview of Core Competences see Prahalad and Hamel's article at http://hbr.org/1990/05/the-core-competence-of-the-corporation/ar/1 (accessed 01.09.2023).
3 Regarding the benefits of treating staff well, seek out the works of Pfeffer from Harvard, Michael Armstrong and the CIPD in the UK.
4 See Chaffey's thoughts on developing online communities at www.smartinsights.com/customer-engagement/customer-communities/social-engagement-for-business/ (accessed 01.08.2023).
6 Further to the Dow Jones Sustainability and FTSE4Good indices, investigate the Global Reporting Initiative and Better Business Bureau.
7 Faith in Nature has an online guide for those interested in following its example (see www.faithinnature.co.uk/pages/avotefornature).
8 Access the following 'standards' to identify useful information and practices relevant to adopting sustainability:

- ISO 20121:2012 *Event sustainability management systems.*
- ISO 26000 – *Social responsibility.*

References

Ansoff, H.I. (1957) Strategies for diversification. *Harvard Business Review*, 35(5) 113–124.
Armstrong, G. & Kotler, P. (2013) *Marketing: An Introduction,* 11th Edition. Boston: Pearson.
Baines, P., Fill, C. & Page, K. (2013) *Essentials of Marketing.* Oxford: Oxford University Press.
Barkemeyer, R. (2009) Beyond compliance – below expectations? CSR in the context of international development. *Business Ethics: A European Review*, 18 273–289.
Barkemeyer, R., Figge, F., Holt, D. & Hahn, T. (2009) What the papers say: Trends in sustainability – A comparative analysis of 115 leading National Newspapers Worldwide. *Journal of Corporate Citizenship*, 33, Spring, pp. 69–86.
BBC. (2023a) *TikTok Fined €345m Over Children's Data Privacy* www.bbc.co.uk/news/technology-66819174 (accessed 18-09-23).
BBC. (2023b) *Chinese Electric Cars Will Reduce UK Emissions but what about Rivals Here?* www.bbc.co.uk/news/business-66820791 (accessed 18-09-23).

BBC. (2023c) *The Firms Hoping to Cut down on Wasted Cosmetics* www.bbc.co.uk/news/business-66585299 (accessed 18-09-23).

BBC. (2023d) *The Firms Giving Nature a Stake in Their Businesses* www.bbc.co.uk/news/business-66132669 (accessed 19-09-2023).

BBC. (2023e) *Can Amsterdam Make the Circular Economy Work?* www.bbc.co.uk/news/business-65696083 (accessed 19-09-2023).

Belz, F-M. & Peattie, K. (2012) *Sustainability Marketing – A Global Perspective,* 2nd Edition. Chichester: Wiley & sons.

Brown, S. (1995) *Postmodern Marketing.* London: Routledge.

Chaffey, D. & Ellis-Chadwick, F. (2012) *Digital Marketing: Strategy, Implementation and Practice,* 5th Edition. Harlow: Pearson Education.

Donnelly, R. & Harrison, G. (2009) *CIM Coursebook: The Marketing Planning Process.* London: Routledge. DOI:10.4324/9780080961231

Doran, G.T. (1981) There's a S.M.A.R.T. way to write management goals and objectives. *Management Review*, 70(11), pp. 35–36.

Emery, B. (2012) *Sustainable Marketing.* Harlow: Pearson Education.

Enzuzo. (2023) *51 Biggest GDPR Fines and Penalties So Far (Updated!)* www.enzuzo.com/blog/biggest-gdpr-fines (accessed 20-08-23).

Ethical Consumer. (2022) *Ethical Consumer Markets Report 2022.* Downloaded from www.ethicalconsumer.org/research-hub/uk-ethical-consumer-markets-report (accessed 02-06-23).

Flexitarian. (2023) *The Flexitarian Website* https://theflexitarian.co.uk/the-flexitarian-diet/ (accessed 10/09/2023).

FT. (2023) *Rebranding ESG Won't Save It From Its Internal Contradictions* www.ft.com/content/86e91a73-62fb-45f6-852e-2da659505d86 (accessed 18-09-23).

Godin, S. (2008) *Tribes: We Need You to Lead Us.* London: Penguin.

Gomez-Trujillo, A.M., Velez-Ocampo, J. & Gonzalez-Perez, M.A. (2020) A literature review on the causality between sustainability and corporate reputation. *What Goes First? Management of Environmental Quality: An International Journal*, 31(2), pp. 406–430. DOI:10.1108/MEQ-09-2019-0207

Gosnay, R.M. & Richardson, N. (2008) *Develop Your Marketing Skills.* Kogan Page: London.

Guardian. (2023) *Say Hello to Longlife Tech That Can Challenge Our Throwaway Culture.* www.theguardian.com/money/2023/jul/30/say-hello-to-longlife-tech-that-can-challenge-our-throwaway-culture?CMP=Share_AndroidApp_Other (accessed 18-09-23).

Guido, G., Amatulli, C., Peluso, A.M., De Matteis, C., Piper, L. & Pino, G. (2020) Measuring internalized versus externalized luxury consumption motivations and consumers' segmentation. *Italian Journal of Marketing*, pp. 25–47. DOI:10.1007/s43039-020-00002-9

Hart, S.L. (1997) Beyond greening: Strategies for a sustainable world. *Harvard Business Review*, Jan/Feb1997, 75(1), pp. 66–76.

ICO. (2018) *Guide to the General Data Protection Regulation (GDPR).* https://ico.org.uk/for-organisations/guide-to-the-general-data-protection-regulation-gdpr/ (accessed 13-08-23).

Johnson, G. & Scholes, K. (1999) *Exploring Corporate Strategy,* 5th Edition. London: Prentice Hall.

Jones, B., Bowd, R. & Tench, R. (2009) Corporate irresponsibility and corporate social responsibility: Competing realities. *Social Responsibility Journal*, 5(3) pp. 300–310.

Kaplan, R.S., & Norton, D.P. (1992) The balanced scorecard- measures that drive performance. *Harvard Business Review.* January–February Issue. 1992.

Kotler, P. (1967). *Marketing Management: Analysis, Planning and Control.* Englewood Cliffs, NJ: Prentice-Hall.

Kotler, P., Wong, V., Saunders, J. & Armstrong, G. (2009) *Principles of Marketing,* 5th European Edition. Harlow: Prentice Hall.

Kuznets, S. (1949). *Suggestions for an Inquiry into the Economic Growth of Nations, in Problems in the Study of Economic Growth.* New York: National Bureau of Economic Research, pp. 3–20.

Longman, J, Pritchard, C., McNeill, A., Csikar, J & Croucher, R. (2010). Accessibility of chewing tobacco products in England. *Journal of Public Health* (Oxford, England), 32, pp. 372–8. DOI:10.1093/pubmed/fdq035

Lynch, R. (2000) *Corporate Strategy*. London: Prentice Hall.

MacArthur. (2017) *A New Textiles Economy: Redesigning Fashion's Future* (2017). Ellen MacArthur Foundation https://ellenmacarthurfoundation.org/a-new-textiles-economy (accessed 20-09-2023).

McDonald, M. (1999) *Marketing Plans- How to Prepare Them, How to Use Them*, 4th Edition. London: Butterworth-Heinemann.

McDonald, M. (2017) *Malcolm McDonald on Marketing Planning-Understanding Marketing Plans and Strategy*, 2nd Edition. London: Kogan Page.

Mercadé-Melé. P., Molinillo, S., Fernández-Morales, A. & Porcu, L. (2018) CSR activities and consumer loyalty: The effect of the type of publicizing medium. *Journal of Business Economics and Management*, 19(3), pp. 431–455. DOI:10.3846/jbem.2018.5203

Mintzberg, H. (1990) The design school: Reconsidering the basic premises of strategic management. *Strategic Management Journal*, 11, pp. 171–95.

Mumsnet. (2023) *About Us* www.mumsnet.com/info/about-us (accessed 28.01.2019).

Porter, M.E. (1979) How competitive forces shape strategy. *Harvard Business Review*

Porter, M.E. (1980) Industry structure and competitive strategy: Keys to profitability. *Financial Analysts Journal*, 36(4), pp. 30–41. DOI:10.2469/faj.v36.n4.30

Prahalad, C.K. & Hamel, G (1990) The core competence of the corporation. *Harvard Business Review*, May–June, pp. 79–91.

Ramjaun, T.A. (2021) Corporate brand management in a charity context: The internal communications challenge. *Corporate Communications-an International Journal*, 26(2), pp. 296–310. DOI:10.1108/CCIJ-05-2020-0083

Richardson, N. (2010) *A Quick Start Guide to MOBILE MARKETING: How to Create a Dynamic Campaign and Improve Your Competitive Advantage*. London: Kogan Page.

Richardson, N. (2015) *The Adoption of Sustainable Marketing Practices within the UK Music Festivals Sector*. PhD thesis. University of Leeds https://etheses.whiterose.ac.uk/13578/ (accessed 06-07-23).

Richardson, N. (2020) *Sustainable Marketing Planning*. Abingdon: Routledge.

Richardson, N. & Cassop Thompson, M. (2023) How improved understanding of what constitutes 'value' may lead to better underpinning of Corporate Social Responsibility (CSR). *Journal of Global Responsibility*, pp. 2041–2568. DOI:10.1108/JGR-10-2022-0115

Richardson, N., James, J. & Kelley, N. (2015) *Customer-Centric Marketing: Supporting Sustainability in the Digital Age*. London: Kogan Page.

Richie, H. (2023) *The Big Idea: Why Climate Tribalism Only Helps the Deniers*. www.theguardian.com/books/2023/jul/10/the-big-idea-why-climate-tribalism-only-helps-the-deniers?CMP=Share_AndroidApp_Other (accessed 19-09-2023)

Russell, S. (2022) *If You Want to Go Far, Go Together- Beauty B Corps Join Forces to Raise the Bar*. https://bthechange.com/if-you-want-to-go-far-go-together-988b78378963 (accessed 28-08-23).

Sandberg, M. (2010) *The Greening of the Swedish Innovation System*. Paper presented at the International Schumpeter Society Conference 2010 on INNOVATION, ORGANISATION, SUSTAINABILITY AND CRISES Aalborg, 21–24 June, 2010.

Schumpeter, J.A. (1950) *Capitalism, Socialism and Democracy*, 3rd Edition. New York: Harper & Bros.

Smith, P.R., Berry, C. and Pullford, A. (1999) *Strategic Marketing Communications: New Ways to Build and Integrate Communications*. London: Kogan Page.

Stead, R., Curwen, P. & Lawler, K. (2003) *Industrial Economics – Theory, Applications and Policy*. London: McGraw Hill.

Tadajewski, M. & Hamilton, K. (2014) Waste, art, and social change: Transformative consumer research outside of the academy? *Journal of Macromarketing*, 34(1), pp. 80–86. DOI:10.1177/0276146713509631

Tilley, F & Young, C.W. (2009) Sustainability entrepreneurs — Could they be the true wealth generators of the future? *Greener Management International*, 55, pp. 70-92, Greenleaf Publishing. DOI:10.9774/GLEAF.3062.2006.au.00008

van Dam, Y.K. & Apeldoorn, P.A.C. (1996) Sustainable marketing. *Journal of Macromarketing*, 16(2), pp. 45–56. DOI:10.1177/027614679601600204

VeganSociety. (2023) *What is a Vegetarian?* www.vegansociety.com/go-vegan/definition-veganism (accessed 10/02/2023).

Waterman, R.H., Peters, T.J. and Phillips, J.R. (1980) Structure is not organisation. *McKinsey Quarterly in-House Journal*, pp. 14–26. New York: McKinsey & Co.

WEF. (2020) *These Facts Show How Unsustainable the Fashion Industry Is*. World Economic Forum report www.weforum.org/agenda/2020/01/fashion-industry-carbon-unsustainable-environment-pollution/ (accessed 20-09-2023).

Weirich, H. (1982) The TOWS matrix: A tool for situational analysis. *Long Range Planning*, 15(2), pp. 54–66.

Whittington, R., Regnér, P., Angwin, D., Johnson, G. & Scholes, K., (2019) *Exploring Strategy: Text and Cases*, 12th Edition. Harlow: Pearson.

6 Internal Marketing (IM)

Ruth M. Gosnay[1]

Abstract

Internal Marketing (IM) is essential however, despite being a well-established concept it is often poorly practised. Appropriate definitions are offered. To understand IM's role, Marketers must recognise the orientation of their company. An Internal Marketing Orientation (IMO) derives from a Marketing Orientation (MO) the benefits of which are identified herein. The chapter concludes by considering IM's influence on the Mix, strategic decisions and barriers to implementation.

Learning Outcomes

At the end of this chapter students will be able to

- appreciate IM's origins and link to services
- differentiate between BAU orientations and more customer-centric versions
- examine the nature of IM and its associated orientation (IMO)
- reflect on the role IM plays in the Marketing Mix
- assess how IM influences strategic decision making
- better understand issues around implementing IM including barriers.

A key reason for the lack of awareness is that Internal Marketing (IM) is rarely taught and (therefore) many managers today have simply not been educated or trained in the mechanics of practice. Hence, it is prudent to first look at what is meant by IM.

Anderson and Smith (2017) suggest Heider (1958) first identified the relations among three parties (e.g. customer, firm and employee) and the effects of their interdependence on the service experience. Carson *et al* (1997) developed Heider's Balance Theory to produce the 'service triangle' which Kotler developed further (Figure 6.1) by incorporating three modes of marketing, namely 'External', 'Interactive' and 'Internal'.

Figurer 6.1 portrays a refined version of Kotler's services triangle illustrating the internal dyadic (i.e. two-way) relationships. A positive or negative sign is used to represent the relations among the parties. A plus sign '+' denotes a positive relation, whereas a minus sign '-'signals a negative relation (Anderson & Smith, 2017). A triadic relationship is either balanced or unbalanced according to the relations among the parties (*ibid*). The ideal state occurs when all three parties (i.e. the service organisation–service provider, service organisation–consumer and service provider–consumer) have good relationships. Here, relationships are harmonious as no tension exists (Carson *et al*, 1997). Figure 6.1

DOI: 10.4324/9781003434214-7

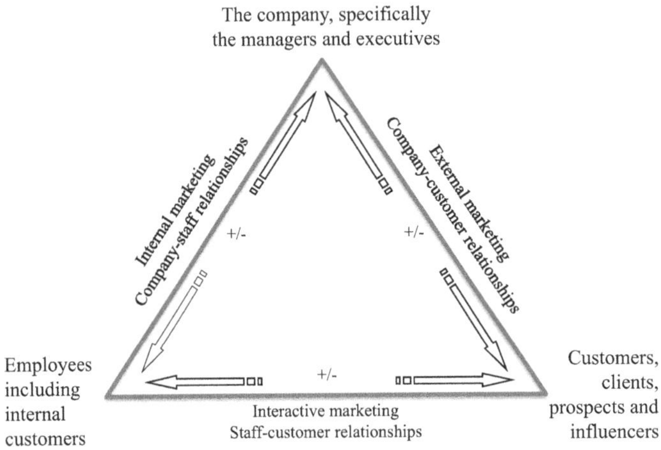

Figure 6.1 Kotler's service profit chain.

Source: Adapted from Kotler *et al* (2009).

shows how IM applies within large service providers where the Executive are responsible for leadership and strategy, whilst Managers (who report to the Executive) have department heads or supervisors reporting to them. The internal customers (ICs) of senior management teams are the staff they 'line-manage'. The supervisors supply their skills and knowledge to the staff (i.e. the supervisors' ICs) who come into regular contact with external customers. ICs regularly interact with external customers and prospects.

6.1 Organisational Orientations

To better understand IM, it is necessary to understand the orientation adopted by companies. A Marketing Orientation (MkO) involves understanding current and future customers' needs in order to develop offerings where customers can seek and take distinctive value compared to the competition; companies with an MkO undertake ongoing research to improve relationships with customers. The different business orientations (Table 6.1) have strengths and weaknesses.

Production orientation is the oldest form; Henry Ford is attributed with introducing new manufacturing techniques when he launched the Model T Ford in 1908. The old adage of 'you can have any colour you want as long as it's black' is often attributed to Henry Ford. This is clearly far from being customer-centric and yet Ford sold 15 million Model T Fords whilst revolutionising car manufacturing. Ford did not invent the automobile. They were not necessarily the best car available, however they were affordable and led to the democratisation of independent transport in the United States. It was a similar story with the Honda C90. Launched in 1958, by 2017 over 100 million units had been sold with the latest iteration (the Honda Super Cub) still being sold.

If a market exists, why introduce radical, costly changes? Production-orientated companies focus upon production techniques, reducing costs, marginal gains and efficiencies. Typically, involving high-volume, lower-margin businesses with less R&D or innovation,

Table 6.1 Attributes of pre-sustainability organisational orientations

Orientation	*Nature*	*Driver*	*Motivation to change*	*Marketing Activities*	*Marketing Oriented*
Production	High volume, Low margin, little risk, minimal R&D and innovation. Imitates first movers.	Internal (In-Out; top down)	Take share by cost leadership. Towards end of extended product life cycle (PLC). Often target late majority and laggards. Little NPD. Low risk. Products often cash cows.	Yes	No
Product	Adds to existing ideas. Market follower of new products. Some tailoring of product offer. Medium volume, occasional high margins.	Internal (In-Out; top down)	To improve existing product or adapt/ develop rivals' offering. Target early majority, niche or new overseas markets. Risks trademark and intellectual property infringements.	Yes	No
Sales	High focus on advertising. Seek high brand awareness and recall. Not always the first, the best nor the cheapest. Can take market share.	Internal (In-Out; top down)	Take share from competitors by having higher awareness. Single transactions. Heavy reliance on promotion – some use of mass media, others through sales teams. Strong branding. Can miss changing customer patterns.	Yes	No
Marketing	Sell what customers want. Seek to innovate with products and services. Customer central to all business decisions.	External (Out-in; bottom up)	Seek to identify customer needs that are not satisfied by rivals and provide solutions. Look to develop customer relationships. Heavy reliance on market research. Promote loyalty schemes. Sell benefits and create customer value.	Yes	Yes
Market	Sell what customers want. Gather insights internally (from other functions) and externally (from micro-environment). Often market leaders. Seek to innovate with products and services.	Internal + External (Out-in; In-In; bottom up)	Adopts all aspects (and accepts benefits) of a marketing orientation. Complements customer-centric approach with full understanding of markets (i.e. competitors, suppliers, pressure groups, trade bodies etc.) and focus on developing inter-functional relationships. Uses internal marketing techniques.	Yes	Yes

Source: Original diagram.

they are inward looking, which is problematic as markets, competitors and customers change. Some changes are legislative, e.g. governments banning the sales of disposable vapes. Organisations following this 'Inside-Out' approach (Table 6.1), may not recognise the need for change as they operate in fast-paced marketplaces. Blackberry smartphones were 'technologically superior' products, but the company struggled to react to changes in a post-iPhone world.

Product orientation is not new. It can be argued that Thomas Chippendale's 1754 publication 'The Gentleman and Cabinet Maker's Director' is one of the first sales/marketing catalogues. His batch-making approach fits most (Product orientation) definitions as he focused on developing existing product features or offering improvements on competitor's products. Chippendale did not invent chairs, but he knew to improve the product and market it (using his Director) to individuals with high disposable income. The Apple iPad is a brilliant concept, but many of its components have existed for decades (displays, solid state storage or touch screens). It was not the first tablet to market; however, it was the first to have substantial customer take up. Apple is a unique company, some might argue the exception to the rule, as most product-orientated organisations adopt an inward focus at their peril. Most are successful initially, but when newer, more innovative and competitive products appear, they suffer. Apple remains a technological force.

Sales orientation focuses on selling products (and/or services) with little regard to the market. This approach relies on above-the-line communications (see Section 4.1) and sales techniques. Originating in the 1950s, customers were offered a greater choice of products and services but were often subjected to hard-sell techniques to persuade customers to buy a particular product or service. Today, hard selling is considered unethical though not necessarily illegal (see Table 1.3). Recent scandals highlighted aggressive selling techniques in banking and other financial services, energy, cosmetic surgery and, reprehensibly, in sales of pension products and services to the elderly.

Example: Consumers and prospects see Dell's massive investment in advertising. Dell did not invent the PC, they may not be the cheapest unit in the market, but few companies advertise their products more effectively. In 2023, Dell was shipping 60 million units per annum, taking 17% of the global market share (up from 11% in 2011) behind HP and Lenovo.

Production, Product and Sales orientations are transactional. The focus is (more) on closing deals rather than building relationships. Furthermore, there may be limited feedback from customers, let alone any longer-term relationship beyond these individual transactions.

MkO-oriented companies recognise that the customers are their most important 'assets'. Irrespective of whether a company is product or service based or, indeed a charity, they must place the customer at the heart of *all* decision-making and planning. Where customer needs drive all the business decisions, a marketing philosophy has been adopted and implemented. This is achieved by entering into regular, honest dialogue with customers. Each time marketers receive customer feedback, their company (and brand) is strengthened. All employees must be customer centric, not merely those who interact with the customers. This is generally known as the 'marketing concept'. Organisations who adopt the marketing concept are said to be marketing orientated (MkO). Drawing on Doyle and Stern (2006), an MkO can be defined as

> "understanding current and future customers' needs and wants in order to develop products and services that offer value for the customer, distinctive from the offers of other companies, which can be profitably produced. Hence companies must recognise the importance of continuing research in the marketplace and ongoing relationships with customers".

Market Orientation (MO) – A Definition

The term Market Orientation (hereafter MO) is preferred as it develops the MkO by signalling the importance placed on an organisation's approach to its customers and (unlike an MkO), its competitors (Kohli & Jaworksi, 1990) and stakeholders in the micro-environment. All staff are responsible for supporting the MO. Customers are key information sources, as are suppliers, distributors, intermediaries, representative bodies and trade associations. Formal and informal research methods must be used when adopting an MO. The dialogue should be ongoing and undertaken within their wider networks. The intelligence gathered by sales staff is particularly important, however there may be internal politics when extracting information on the market. Good IM practices encourage non-customer-facing functions (R&D, Production or QA) to contribute, as their insights are valuable. There are, however, no quick or cost-free options when developing an MO.

Kohli and Jaworski (1990) defined MO as the organisation-wide generation of market intelligence pertaining to current and future customer needs, dissemination of the intelligence across departments and organisation-wide responsiveness to it. They insist intelligence gathering cannot (solely) be the responsibility of the Marketing function. However it *is* logical for Marketing to lead data collection, processing and dissemination across the organisation. Fang *et al* (2014) insist there must be an active, responsive IM activity within organisations that seeks, gathers and disseminates information from and to employees. Their research suggests a strong link between effective IM and *external* market capabilities in what they term 'market sensing', i.e. identifying the dynamics of the market place and external environment then 'customer linking', i.e. analysing current and prospective customer behaviour and building relationships ('bonding').

'Buy-in' from senior management reduces the risk of inter-departmental competition and politics. Information must not remain in functional 'silos' and best practice must be shared. It must be embedded through formal contractual means and through reward systems (with input from the HR function) that recognise MO's importance. All employees must embrace the MO. It is naïve to assume that adopting an MO will guarantee success. As discussed, many successful companies do not follow this approach and are unlikely to do so in future. They have, however, taken unnecessary risks and may struggle to adapt.

Benefits of Adopting an MO

There is a positive correlation between adopting an MO and organisational success. The benefits of adopting a market orientation are

- increase in market share, turnover and profitability
- improved customer acquisition, satisfaction, retention and loyalty
- lower customer attrition
- improved staff morale, motivation and lower churn
- improved WoM, reputation and competitive advantage.

Satisfied customers do more than simply return to purchase, they also tell their friends, families and colleagues. Conversely, if they have a poor experience, they tend to tell even more people about it. There is an ongoing debate regarding whether the advent of Web 2.0 (featuring consumer-generated tools such as blogs, vlogs, price-comparison websites etc.) has changed how marketing fundamentals are applied. Undoubtedly, the power of consumers has grown prior to making purchasing decisions and companies must adopt a more customer-centric approach if they wish to "*sell not tell*". Companies of all sizes can now reach millions of new customers on a global scale that until recently was available only to major corporations. It is the most exciting time there has ever been for starting and growing smaller companies (see Section 8.4). Marketers can tap into this as long as they recognise changing consumer behaviours.

Marketers must avoid becoming overly internally focused, say analysing and crunching sales and market share figures, focusing upon staffing issues or buying-in new capital equipment. Companies certainly need excellent production techniques, products and sales initiatives but the need for customer awareness and understanding factors in the wider environment is paramount. Wherever and whenever markets or environments change, marketers must change and adapt or they risk being left behind. An MO can be embraced and implemented in any size or type of organisation. Indeed, it is arguably more important that small firms monitor the market forces which can impact on the customer.

Marketing's Role in Supporting the MO

All interactions or 'touchpoints' in the consumer's 'journey' provide opportunities to portray the service provider in a positive or negative light. Senior management must reflect on how ICs, particularly Boundary Spanning Employees (BSEs), create value and simultaneously why value must be created. Therefore, effective relationship bridges between managers and employees must be supported by underpinning culture and behaviours. Marketers (the specialists in customer research and communications) can assist with these activities particularly where cross-coordination is required.

Example: Throughout its B Corp journey, Alpro learned some valuable lessons, three of which are germane to IM:

- *Becoming a B Corp is quite time-consuming.* When taking the B Impact Assessment, make sure to have (human) resources in place to support the certification – a dedicated team and time to engage key internal stakeholders.
- *Celebrate your B Corp certification.* Take the time to celebrate and make employees proud to be working in a company that is B-Corp certified. You can also use this momentum to start building an improvement plan for your next re-certification which will be due 3 years later.

- *Internal engagement during the process but also after is key.* Alpro created many ('comms') resources to increase awareness internally. "For instance, we built an internal B Corp Q&A including explanations of the B Corp values but also our journey as Alpro. We explained what is behind our score for each of the 5 impact areas but also already identified areas for improvement and clear future actions to take. In parallel, we had a live session with all Alpro employees to engage around the B Corp values and also to present the results and analysis of our re-certification" Juliane Greff (Alpro, 2023).

6.2 IM and Its Associated Orientation (IMO)

Marketing can be seen as an internal service provider for other functions/departments and should lead because marketers can:

- act as a catalyst for change by communicating changing customer needs
- use IM to disseminate corporate culture
- brief HR on the skills required for customer service
- liaise heavily with all functions (or departments), say, regarding product launches.

IM is conceptual whereas an Internal Marketing Orientation (IMO) is more practical. A distinction is needed between the two (Gounaris, 2006). Gounaris suggests an IMO represents the synthesis of specific beliefs with specific marketing-like behaviours; these focus on the needs and expectations of the employees (*ibid*). IMO can be traced back to the 1990s when a focus upon relationship marketing (RM) and subsequently IM became more prevalent. (Berry & Parasuraman, 1991; Piercy & Morgan, 1990).

Rafiq and Ahmed (2000, p 449) suggest there

> "is a great deal of confusion in the literature as to exactly what IM is, what it is supposed to do, how it is supposed to do it and who is supposed to do it".

This confusion, combined with limited information available to practitioners, may explain why IM is still not widely adopted in organisations (Boukis *et al*, 2014). There is no single accepted definition of IM; indeed, Yu-ting and Rundle-Thiele (2014, 2015) cite 43 different definitions over the last 30 years. Furthermore, they argue that most studies in IM have neglected the views of employees, which is a serious omission given the nature of the research. For the purposes of this book, IM is defined as

> "a planned effort using a marketing-like approach to overcome organisational resistance to change and to align, motivate and inter-functionally co-ordinate and integrate employees towards the effective implementation of corporate and functional strategies in order to deliver customer satisfaction through a process of creating motivated and customer orientated employees".
>
> (Rafiq & Ahmed, 2000, p 454)

This definition is cited widely. Ruizalba Robledo *et al* (2015) identify the seminal work being specifically developed by Lings (2004), Lings and Greenley (2005) and Gounaris

(2006). Others also recognise the work of Lings and Greenley (2005) including Ruizalba Robledo *et al* (2014), Tortosa-Edo *et al* (2009), Kaur *et al* (2009) and Sahi *et al* (2013).

IM can be viewed from a behavioural perspective whereby companies create job opportunities that satisfy employee (especially IC) needs, which ultimately are designed to achieve organisational objectives. It is also viewed as a mechanistic perspective where the employees (ICs) are merely parts of an organisation's internal service value chain. In practice, a holistic approach is adopted, blending the behavioural and mechanistic perspectives; organisations see the internal market as a place where jobs are created and various processes lead to value creation, ultimately leading to external customers taking value.

IM is valuable in helping cross-coordination within and around the internal environment. Developing effective modes of communication internally and liaising across functions supports the cascading of the corporate culture and objectives. This shapes the organisation internally by producing a cohesive, professional image and approach to the external marketplace, satisfying customers and earning their loyalty.

Dimensions of IMO

Qui *et al* (2022) found many studies ignore the Marketing Orientation (MkO) platform on which an IMO is based. Kohli and Jaworski's seminal work developing an MO, underpins the dimensions of an effective IMO (Lings 2004; Lings & Greenley, 2005, 2009; Gounaris, 2006, 2008; Ruizalba Robledo *et al*, 2014, 2015; Ruizalba Robledo & Vallespín-Arán, 2014). Organisations should develop a robust IMO prior to pursuing an external MO (Piercy, 1995; Lings & Greenley, 2010). Lings (2004) developed three sub-dimensions of IMO behaviour to reflect the three broad sets of behaviour relating to organisations who are successfully implementing IM programmes and initiatives. The three sub-dimensions, often referred to as pillars, are: -

- *Internal market research* – the investment and communication required to collect and generate information pertaining to the internal market; what is of value to the employees, the internal environmental and market conditions.
- *The dissemination of the intelligence* – the communication between different managers and employees both vertically and horizontally throughout the organisation; identifying and responding to the employees' needs regarding requirements from their managers; communicating the organisation's vision, objectives and strategies to the employees through internal mass media initiatives.
- *The design of job creation* – providing the skills, abilities, tools and motivation to deliver (Bitner, 1995) by meeting the needs of the employees via reward, motivational and training schemes (Lings, 2004).

Whilst investment in each of the three pillars of IMO is required, the actual culture of the organisation needs to support this, supported by an appropriate managerial culture. Indeed, Lings implies that the recruitment of managers needs to be considered carefully and that they recognise the need to place employees at the heart of their decisions, strategies and actions. If the relationship bridges are built, then interaction, integration and communication and cross-functional cooperation should follow.

A critique is that the ownership of pillars 1and 2 normally resides within the marketing department. Whereas pillar 3 is predominantly the responsibility of the Human Resources

(HR) department. There has been considerable debate about whether IM is based in HR, Marketing or a combination of both functions (Huang, 2020). Many authors (Sahi *et al*, 2013; Kaur *et al*, 2009; Tortosa-Edo *et al*, 2015) have directed their readers to Lings (2004), whilst others use the model to underpin their own studies. Huang *et al* (2020) incorporated three dimensions and 18 sub-dimensions. Qui *et al* (2022, p 56) identified "six overarching dimensions".

1 Internal Market Analytics.
2 Internal Communication.
3 Employee Development.
4 Employee Rewards and Recognition.
5 Job Design and Empowerment.
6 Leadership and Organisational Culture.

Clearly Qui's Dimensions 1 and 2 reflect Ling's Pillars 1 and 2. Dimensions 3, 4 and 5 are overtly under the auspices of Lings 'Responsiveness' pillar. Apropos dimension 6, it is the role of 'leaders' to establish an appropriate organisational culture. Campaigns without senior level support experience a greater degree of difficulty in terms of user acceptance (Huang, 2020). IM has featured in marketing and HRM debates as it must "embed the strategy of the overall organizational operation" (*ibid*, p 166). Hence, Leadership and HRM can be conflated with Ling's work to produce a more appropriate framework for IMO (Figure 6.2).

The extra dimensions in both Huang *et al* (2020) and Qui *et al* (2022) 'fit' within Figure 6.2 which encourages marketers to take a holistic view of the organisation. Businesses where the (marketing) pillars support Leadership and HRM are more likely to achieve competitive advantage. Henry Mintzberg has long recognised that system overlaps often dictate organisational success. For good IM to thrive, the Executive, HRM and Marketing systems must overlap and integrate meaningfully. The 'pillars' and

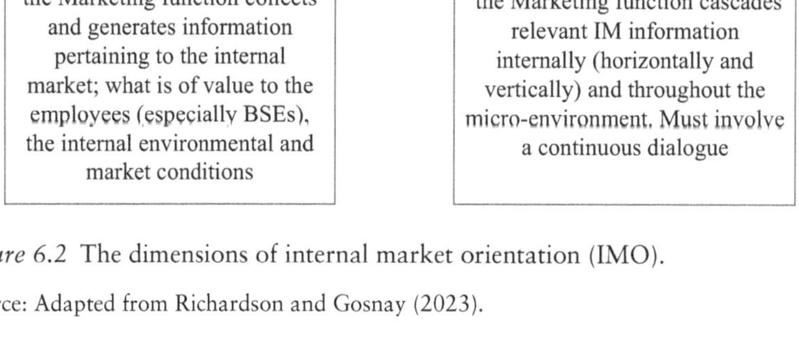

Figure 6.2 The dimensions of internal market orientation (IMO).

Source: Adapted from Richardson and Gosnay (2023).

supported activities are not isolated. HR, crucially for marketers, recruit, train, motivate and reward the marketing and/or sales teams. However, marketers should be recognised as the specialists apropos communication and market research. In many workplaces, employees need to understand industry jargon and subtle differences in organisational culture to communicate effectively and efficiently (Huang, 2020). There is a need for fluency in communication between managers and employees (*ibid*). The purpose of pillars 1 and 2 are to communicate the organisation's vision, objectives and strategies to employees and to report their needs apropos requirements from managers (Lings, 2004). The organisational culture must support this (Lings & Greenley, 2005, 2010; Gounaris, 2008; Ruizalba Robledo *et al*, 2014) along with effective horizontal and vertical IC (see Chapter 4).

Chen *et al* (2021, p 1216) suggest dimensions should include "value of needs, authorised autonomy, internal communication and rewards" (*ibid*, p 1223). Clearly these align with Figure 6.2 where vision, values and autonomy are the responsibility of the leadership. IMO is an important aspect of the employees' work environment; it reflects the firm's emphasis on creating value for internal stakeholders (Boukis *et al*, 2017). Value, however, cannot be given to employees, it can only be taken by them. Internal value only resides in the minds of those seeking it.

6.3 IM and the Marketing Mix

To better understand IM, it is useful to consider how it influences the interpersonal aspects of the Marketing Mix.

Internal Supplier–Customer Relationships (ISCRs)

The IC is a key asset to any organisation irrespective of its size. The ICs of senior management teams are the staff they 'line manage'. The supervisors supply their skills and knowledge to the staff who come into regular contact with external customers. These staff are the supervisors' ICs including those who regularly interact with external customers and prospects, i.e. 'boundary-spanning employees' (BSEs). It is necessary to ensure that BSEs are well trained, motivated and rewarded. They need to be fluent in the organisation's culture and objectives and have the key information necessary to perform effectively and efficiently. The underpinning processes required to do this are key and ultimately the responsibility of the management team. Communication is instrumental in furnishing the internal market with up-to-date, timely information furnished by effective 'comms' systems. Such processes link the various management teams with the BSE's and become part of the key ISCR.

In large, highly structured organisations such as supermarkets, complex networks of ISCRs operate daily. The board of directors are responsible for leadership and strategic management led by the CEO. The personnel rely upon the Board's strategic ability and skills to lead the organisation. The CEO may visit various supermarkets on a regular basis but will rarely work on the shop floor. Then there are Area Managers (AMs) who report to the Board of Directors and Store Managers (who report to the AMs). These, in turn, have department heads reporting to them, who in their turn, supply their supervisorial abilities to the BSEs (i.e. customer-facing shop floor staff). Clearly there are many layers of staff who have other employees as ICs and ISCRs exist.

In SMEs, the structure will be flatter, however ISCRs will still exist. For example, a creative design agency employs a designer, a copywriter and an account manager (AM). The Copywriter and Designer are reliant on the skills and ability of the AM to win accounts and brief them correctly on customers' requirements. The Copywriter and Designer are ICs to the AM (the commercial supplier). Likewise, the AM (the IC in this scenario) relies on the abilities of the Designer and Copywriter (the creative suppliers) to fulfil the design requirements of the client's brief, ensuring that the AM has the proofs of work ready to meet the required deadlines at the agreed points in the brief's development. To enable this internal chain of events to unfold in an effective and efficient manner, effective systems and processes are required.

People

Organisational success is usually predicated on the way the internal stakeholders perform. An organisation is an intricate web of functions that marketing transcends in its inter-functional approach. Within those functions people strive to fulfil their role and the overall strategic objectives of the organisation. Marketers must be willing to ask

- Do the staff feel valued by the management and to what extent?
- How motivated are they to fulfil their role to the best of their ability?
- Does the organisation reward their staff well?
- How does the company 'benchmark' against the sector regarding delivering rewards for employment and the exchange of skills and knowledge?

Many managers struggle to answer these questions and are surprised when staff surveys generate negative outcomes. Those who advocate IM recognise their colleagues not just as employees but as valued 'ICs'. Once this change in perception is established, the attitudes and responsibilities of senior management must change. In larger, highly structured organisations it is easy for the management team to become divorced from the 'shop floor'.

To facilitate ISCRs, systems and operations should be designed to enable and empower the 'people' performing their duties within a company and throughout the supply network. Marketers must identify the ISCRs that are formed, developed and used daily. This can ultimately affect the quality of the final product or service that reaches the external customer. Fang *et al* (2014) argue that there must be active, responsive IM activities within organisations that seek, gather and disseminate information from and to employees.

Boukis *et al* (2017) insisted service success is largely determined by front-line employees (i.e. BSEs). The term 'front line' is somewhat outdated. Success is also derived from other ICs, particularly in services where 'People' are the key component. Hence, the recruitment, training, motivation and rewarding of staff is critical to ultimate success. Even with product-based marketing, the role of the staff involved in its development, testing, production, marketing, distribution and post-sales support are all central to success. Marketers must ensure that ICs are satisfied and focused on value-creation particularly BSEs (Richardson, 2020; Richardson & Gosnay, 2022).

These 'BSEs' (Figure 6.3) often work daily with external customers and every touchpoint or interaction provides an opportunity to portray the organisation in a positive or

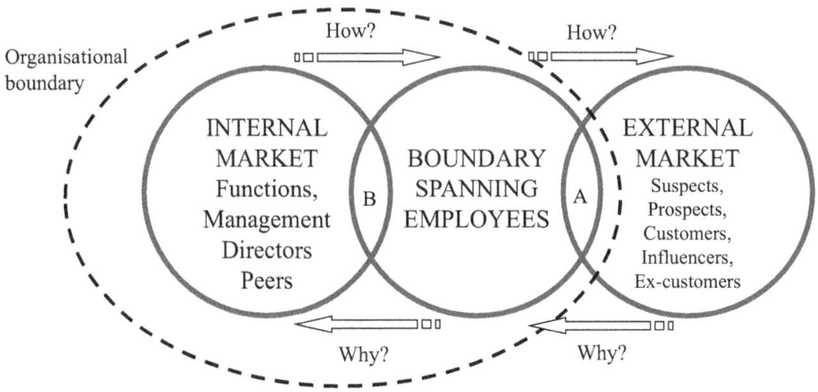

Figure 6.3 Boundary spanning employees (BSEs) at the internal–external markets interface.

Source: Adapted from Richardson and Gosnay (2023).

negative light. As such senior management must reflect on how BSEs create value whilst the staff should always reflect on why value must be created. This applies at

- the BSE: customer interface (A) and
- the BSE: colleague interface (B).

Internal feedback is not solely the responsibility of the HR department as marketing has a unique inter-functional responsibility that transcends formal structural boundaries. The need to train or inform staff throughout the organisation should drive the value-creation and improve the external customer's brand perception. Marketers should inform decisions made by the HR function when recruiting staff.

Communication

Good engagement takes account of staff views and suggestions. Marketers can influence the 'comms' media and messages used to inform, persuade and gain support of ICs for the marketing plan. The message and language will have to be adapted to the needs, concerns and understanding of the target audience. A key concern of staff (particularly in larger organisations) is that they have not been made aware of major issues. This could relate to the strategic objectives, mission or values of the organisation as a whole. Marketers must reflect on the effectiveness of the organisation's IC processes and be willing to speak 'truth to power' apropos how middle and senior management communicates.

Internal and External Communication

IMO adoption entails the internal 'comms' element "necessary to develop brand knowledge among the company's employees" (Boukis *et al*, 2017, p 692). Internal 'comms' feature the interactions and relationships between various internal stakeholders across and throughout an organisation. Indeed, they are so important that they are deemed to be operational AND strategic value (Lemon & Towery, 2021). Managers require strong communication to deliver the organisation's vision (Huang *et al*, 2020, p 57). Excellent 'comms' can assist teams to work better and improve their relationships (*ibid*).

ICs can range from the explicit and formal to the implicit and informal. They can be conveyed by both the written word and actions. Explicit communication is directed to employees through training programmes and formal organisational directives. Whilst managerial behaviours present implicit communications to employees, providing the framework in which employees receive and interpret explicit communication. Previous studies suggest explicit communications tend to be used to deliver messages to employees to emphasise their role in delivering quality services or customer satisfaction; however, implicit communication (often more consistent with the underpinning culture of the organisation) may be at odds with the explicit message. Too often organisations communicate that employees are the most valuable asset of the organisation, whilst in reality treating them as expendable. Inconsistencies in the approach of explicit and implicit communication can create a mistrust of explicit messages, reducing their effectiveness, resulting in employee cynicism or dysfunctional behaviour. This is a key issue as commitment and trust are central to the development of relationships and therefore an effective internal marketplace.

Internal 'comms' disseminate tacit and explicit knowledge across the organisation (Lings & Greenley, 2005), forming effective vertical and horizontal interpersonal relationships, inter-functional integration, cooperation mechanisms (Conduit & Mavondo, 2001) and shared vision, comprising a comprehensive dimension of intelligence exchange and network interactions (Qui *et al*, 2022).

Tacit (or Implicit) Communication

Employees receive tacit (implicit) and explicit organisational messages through their working conditions, treatment from supervisors (and co-workers) and customer feedback. All of these messages communicate different elements (Boukis *et al*, 2017). Arnett and Wittmann (2014) argue that implicit knowledge (and its transfer) is paramount for BSEs. They refer to this as 'tacit knowledge', a term first coined by Polanyi (1958). Their research found tacit knowledge improved financial performance, potentially improving efficiency throughout an organisation. Arnett and Wittman (2014) posit that BSEs are vital sources of knowledge, as they create and explore external social networks, providing mechanisms for information and knowledge transfer (say between sales and marketing) throughout the entire organisation. When co-worker trust is higher, tacit knowledge exchange also tends to be higher. When salespeople have more opportunity to liaise directly with the marketing team, again the exchange of tacit knowledge tends to be higher; furthermore, when senior management is seen to support the exchange of tacit knowledge, again, trust tends to be higher (*ibid*). ICs may not be fully aware of the value of their tacit knowledge or how valuable it is to others. The value of tacit knowledge (often based on experience) internally is a key asset; indeed, it is a core competence (see Table 5.8) that cannot be easily imitated or replicated by competitors. Therefore, organisations should actively satisfy ICs, as when they leave, not only is this valuable asset of the person leaving, but also their knowledge.

The Internal Brand Champion and Becoming a Brand Ambassador

An IMO is integral to ensuring employees understand and 'buy into' the promises that the firm makes to its customers. Positioning IMO as a key enabler of internal branding programs (Boukis *et al*, 2017; Richardson & Gosnay, 2023). Many organisations today invest in building internal brand champions/advocates (Ramjaun, 2021), ambassadors (Andersson, 2019) or informal spokespersons engaging in communicative actions (Lee & Kim, 2021). Lohndorf and Diamantopoulos (2014) suggest that a close identification by employees with their organisation constitutes a powerful motivational force. The stronger an employee identifies with their employer and the organisation's identity and values, the more internally motivated employees are to engage in behaviour (both internally and externally) to support the organisation's brand building efforts. These employees also demonstrate a better performance overall, engage in voluntary citizenship behaviours and tend to express less negative behaviour (*ibid*). As ambassadors, employees internalise the organisational/brand identity (and values) and deliver them as part of their own identity in interactions with stakeholders (Andersson, 2019). An employees' personal words or messages are often perceived as credible by external parties, their advocacy can shape corporate reputation (*ibid*) and create a competitive advantage (Lee & Kim, 2021). Indeed, studies suggest that employees are now seen as 'active communicators' who can both create and/or destroy value. Simply put, when employees trust, feel committed and are satisfied with their company and management team, they are likely to create and distribute favourable messages about their company voluntarily. Therefore, the active communication that employees are engaged in both internally and externally are important.

Managers who communicate organisation values well, make organisational brands easier to identify with and more transparent for employees (Boukis *et al*, 2017). As brands become increasingly hard to control, managers should "empower" employees to take responsibility for the brand. Employees who understand the brand can create relevant value for other stakeholders (Andersson, 2019). This develops early IMO conceptualisations where employees are merely mechanistically involved in value creating activities (Gummesson, 1987). Value creation has moved from the factory to communication processes (Andersson, 2019) and increasingly employees are considered important communicators, encouraged to think of themselves as ambassadors (*ibid*). Their words may greatly influence organisation-to-public relations and corporate reputation (Lee & Kim, 2021). Employees (who feel trusted, committed and satisfied with their company) may distribute favourable messages voluntarily whilst engendering self-enhancement, altruism or enjoyment resulting from positive, pleasant and satisfying experiences (*ibid*).

Practical Steps Towards Implementing IM

Naturally, the other Mix ingredients should also be viewed through the prism of IM. When changing the benefits of a 'Product', ICs (especially BSEs) must have input into the marketing plan, objectives and strategies. They have valuable insights into customer values, attitudes and behaviours. Changes in customer perception of the value available from a brand can be shaped by pricing. There may be costs and benefits for ICs who may be asked to make sacrifices as a result of a new marketing plan (e.g. lost resources, lower status, new (harder) ways of working). Changes to the convenience of the service consumption can influence the achievement of marketing objectives. Marketers must choose the most effective way to engage with the ICs directly or indirectly.

IM can be implemented (or at least introduced) by adopting the following practices:

- *Information generation* — ensure that the organisation is providing timely and accurate information to all staff.
- *Communicate* relevant information to the correct ICs in a timely manner.
- *Reflect* on how well the company responds to its internal market's needs. Are ICs well rewarded for their skills, time and abilities? Is the company a competitive organisation regarding pay, pensions, holiday entitlement? Flexible working? Or do they lose valuable staff due to their lack of competitive ability in this area.
- *Gather data* from performance reviews. Too many managers merely appraise staff in a top-down manner.
- *Acting on the findings*. To be effective, IM needs 'buy-in' from senior management, which, (sadly), is not always the case. Too often marketing audits (whether internal or external) are rendered ineffective by the lack of management commitment. Changing structure within organisations is often easy as is evidenced in the early days of new senior management appointments. Often a cultural shift is required which can take time, skill, resilience and resource. However, the benefits that can be achieved both internally with a greater number of satisfied, motivated and skilled ICs, will inevitably affect their ability to create value for the external customer and achieve key performance metrics for the organisation.

6.4 IM'S Influence on Strategic Decision-Making

A critique of the behavioural pillars (Figure 6.2) is employees are deemed homogenous. Internal staff are not homogenous (Huang *et al*, 2020) for example more experienced workers will place higher demands for IMO research apropos exploring and understand their needs (*ibid*). With internal staff being heterogeneous, they need be segmented appropriately. Segmentation is strategic part of the planning process (see Section 5.3).

IM and Segmentation

A critique of the behavioural pillars (Figure 6.2) is employees are deemed homogenous. However, what is communicated to BSEs is not necessarily the same as that to the back-office staff. Internal staff are not homogenous. (Huang *et al*, 2020). More experienced workers will place higher demands for IMO research apropos exploring and understand their needs (*ibid*). Lings (2004) suggests IM segmentation represents a dimension of the organisation's ability to collect intelligence regarding the employees' market. However, Gounaris (2006, p 436) insists internal intelligence is a "precondition for segmentation that follows ... the same is true for the dimension of developing strategies for specific segments". Huang (2020) identifies five groups namely 'Stakeholders', 'CEO', 'Manager', 'Employees' and 'Customers'. They do not differentiate between BSEs and other ICs. Furthermore, 'Stakeholders' and 'Customers' normally reside in the 'micro-environment' (see Figure 5.4) whereas ICs reside in the 'internal' environment. Herein, only those in the internal environment are considered for IMO segmentation purposes including, internal line managers, team peers, project-to-peer (Lemon & Towery, 2021).

Value should be created for all internal staff (e.g. senior executives, back-office staff, middle-level managers) (Qui *et al*, 2022). Marketers are experienced in developing techniques to target and obtain feedback from external customers. However senior

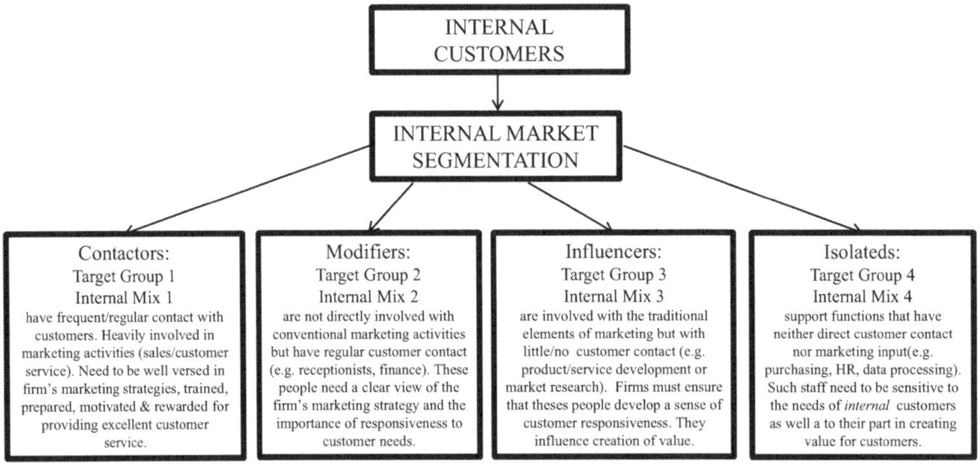

Figure 6.4 Internal marketing (IM) segmentation.

Source: Adapted from Christopher *et al* (1991); Jobber (2007).

management rarely uses this expertise to secure feedback from their ICs on how well they, the management team, are performing. All marketers understand the concept of segmentation (see Section 5.3) and should be capable segmenting internally (Figure 6.4).

Figure 6.4 provides useful differentiation between differing types of ICs. Clearly 'Contactors' and 'Modifiers' should be treated as 'full-blown' BSEs where managers strive to enable and empower them (Brown, 2020) to keep the promises made to customers (Bitner,1995). Modifiers could for example be modern IT departments who increasingly talk about satisfying 'customers' (Richardson, 2020). 'Influencers' have a small degree of BSE activity whereas 'Isolateds' are largely in support functions. Clearly parallels can be drawn between this form of Influencer and those identified by Marketers in social media communications (Hanlon, 2019).

As with 'External Marketing' (Figure 6.1) research should be undertaken and each target segment should have a tailored Mix applied. Particular emphasis should be placed upon communications and process. Companies like First Direct have happy customers and (unsurprisingly) happy staff. It is a Yin and Yang situation where they both feed into each other to the benefit of all parties.

6.5 IM Benefits and Criticisms

Organisations that fail to explicitly use IM at a strategic, tactical or operational level, incur risks as there are many benefits that can accrue. Research has identified that employee engagement is central to organisational success (Gode *et al*, 2020) and encouraging employees to express their voice can engender positive attitudes, enhance corporate well-being, increase the quality of relationships overall and encourages the likelihood of employees sharing positive information about their organisation. There is consensus in the IMO literature that 'external' success is partially due to having motivated, satisfied staff, particularly BSEs (Lings & Greenley, 2009; Berry & Parasuraman, 1991).

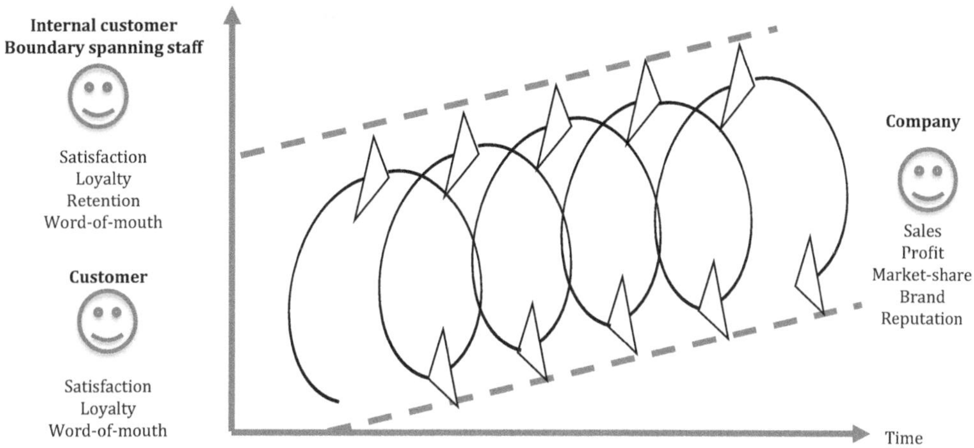

Figure 6.5 Benefits of IM expressed as organisational performance indicators.

Source: Author.

Research has demonstrated that effective IM practices increase business performance overall (Figure 6.5).

If ICs are engaged (Figure 6.5), they are more likely to be motivated and satisfied; they will feel valued which in turn leads to increased work output, higher quality and attention to detail in their work. Richardson (2020) suggests this can lead to:

- increased sales and market share
- improved reputation and brand integrity
- greater employee knowledge, satisfaction and retention
- better trained, motivated staff being more involved with corporate objectives
- breaking down 'them and us' cultures and reduction of the silo effect
- improved communication and organisation
- product/service innovation from ICs
- as a core competence it offers a competitive edge that is hard to 'imitate'

ICs, particularly BSEs, should be providing meaningful feedback on their line manager's ability to provide them with the resources, skills, time and rewards. Performance reviews should involve 360-degree appraisals. Satisfying ICs increases the likelihood of creating value and delighting external customers (Bitner, 1995), which leads to the improved business performance indicators (Figure 6.5). This is particularly important in a service-based organisation where BSEs are in direct contact with the external customer often daily. That said good customer service needs constant reinforcement. An additional benefit of meaningful IM practices is that increased inter-functional cooperation may improve alignment of SBUs or divisions. The 'silo' effect may be lessened as best practice is shared (Richardson & Gosnay, 2022, 2023).

Many employees, particularly in large organisations, complain of the lack of joined up thinking in terms of inter-functional operations and communications. As an organisation grows and functions and employees become more formally structured, quite often into formal departments or functions, the cross-functional links between these departments can fracture. Often job descriptions and general responsibilities do not formally recognise the inter-functional collaboration that is required.

As IM is based upon viewing the IC as part of the internal supplier and customer process, it generally starts to bond employees and managers throughout the organisation in a more robust manner, creating much better cross functional relationships and operational efficiencies. Richardson and Gosnay (2023) identify key areas that benefit from the effective implementation of IMO practices, namely Voice of Employee (VOE), Corporate Communication (CC), communications channels, change management, trust and HRM-marketing relations.

There are criticisms of IM. Lings and Greenley (2005) insist different 'sectors' have unique characteristics and, therefore, results are not generalisable across all service-based environments. Furthermore, manufacturing (ironically) is only studied infrequently (Qui *et al*, 2022). Many IMO studies' results are not generalisable as the national contexts therein may exert influence. IMO cannot be truly understood without being related to actual organisations or persons involved (Ahmed *et al*, 2003). Therefore, further studies with national, sectoral and more in-depth organisational perspectives, may provide insights to this field (Richardson & Gosnay, 2023).

Whilst some researchers recognise the synergy between an external and internal orientations, others view it as contradictory. Piercy (1998) warned against 'internal euphoria' whereby employees can become so cohesive and social that they focus upon serving the needs of the organisation, diverting the focus and resources away from the external customer. IM can

- create sub-servient internal relationships with power struggles arising throughout and across various functions of the internal market
- develop 'internal euphoria' when the ICs become so cohesive as a unit, it is to the detriment of the external customer relationship.
- lead to inter-functional conflict with power struggles being created as a result of shifting internal responsibilities and resourcing
- highlight many internal aspects of managerial weakness, particularly from operational, resource and communication perspectives. This is inherently political.
- create problems for managers may wish to preserve the status quo, who are resistant to change or are not well versed in change management

The Future of IM

IM is worthy of its own Chapter in this book as it is an antecedent of adopting sustainability. IM is wholly congruous with Sustainable Marketing (SM). Good, meaningful implementation of IM will facilitate the adoption of sustainable practices. Poor IM implementation could easily become a barrier. There is still sustained interest (even if smaller than Marketing and MO) in IM and IMO (Richardson & Gosnay, 2023). The interest in the technical constructs (i.e. MO and IMO) is less than the concepts. It is fair to describe it as a niche area (*ibid*). Considering the potentially widescale impact of poor IMO implementation, the paucity of studies seems counter intuitive. Indeed, IMO research should be expanded. This Chapter aligns with Boukis *et al* (2017, p 699) who see IMO as an inside-out dynamic organisational capability, reflecting the ability to modify service delivery by reconfiguring internal resources (i.e. employees). This contrasts directly with previous studies, which largely saw IMO as a set of normative marketing activities with an internal focus. IMO is more than this. Like MO it is an orientation, a mindset, a philosophy that should permeate the whole organisation. IMO adoption has been found to have benefitted many organisational aspects such as employee satisfaction (Chen *et al*, 2021) and internal branding (Boukis *et al*, 2017). There is a wealth of IMO-related material available in the marketing communications (marcomms) literature journals and databases (Richardson & Gosnay, 2023).

The Chapter posits the notion that the full resources of the organisation should be channelled to empower and enable BSEs to create the maximum value for the external customers. This resonates with current thinking regarding value creation in that it can be created (by BSEs) and taken (by external customers) but not given. However, too many IMO studies focus upon 'managers' or one level of employee. Future studies could include a better cross section of employees going beyond senior managers, including BSEs. More understanding is needed apropos how an IMO should adapt to organisation's nature.

Note

1 Ruth M. Gosnay is a senior lecturer in Marketing at Leeds Business School who has taught on higher education programmes for over 20 years. Previously, Ruth worked for leading brands such as Morphy Richards and Spear and Jackson. She has co-authored two books and numerous academic articles relating to internal marketing. Her key areas of teaching interest include core marketing and communications. Ruth has received commendations from the Chartered Institute of Marketing for delivering core marketing and integrated communications modules. She is a senior fellow of the Higher Education Academy.

Key Findings

1 IM is an old concept, which is poorly practiced by most companies and has low awareness amongst academics.
2 IM uses a marketing-like approach to align, motivate and inter-functionally co-ordinate employees towards achieving corporate objectives
3 IM will enable adoption of sustainability as it ensures ICs see the benefits of sustainable brands.
4 A Marketing Orientation (MkO) involves understanding current and future customers' needs. A Market Orientation (MO) develops this by including micro-environmental stakeholders.
5 Production, Product and Sales orientations are transactional, with In-Out top-down foci whereas MO and MkO have Out-In bottom-up foci.
6 An IMO encourages employees to 'buy into' the value created and promises that the firm makes to its customers.
7 BSEs interact regularly with external customers and every touchpoint provides an opportunity to portray the organisation in a positive or negative light
8 ICs and BSEs receive tacit (implicit) and explicit messages from supervisors (and co-workers) and customer feedback.

9 Internal staff are not homogenous. IM segmentation needs to be part of the organisation's intelligence gathering regarding the internal market.

Activities

1 What techniques would you use to support IM in an organisation of your choice?
2 For an organisation of your choice, identify the barriers to IM adoption. How would you overcome them?
3 Studies into IM predate IMO. See Varey (1995) for an early review of the IM literature. Other insightful literature reviews include Huang (2020), Qiu *et al* (2022) and Richardson & Gosnay (2023)
4 Drawing on Figures 6.3 and 6.4, segment an organisation and ascertain whether other segments are needed. If so, where would they fit in the diagrams?
5 Using a selection of organisations, which of the orientations (Table 6.1) apply? Are they In-out or Out-in? Top-down or bottom-up?
6 Review user review websites (see www.imdb.com https://www.kelkoo.co.uk/ or https://www.moneysavingexpert.com/). How do they contribute to adopting good IM practices?

References

Ahmed, P.K., Rafiq, M. & Saad, N.M. (2003) Internal marketing and the mediating role of organisational competencies, *European Journal of Marketing*, 37(9), pp. 1221–1241. DOI10.1108/03090560310486960

Alpro. (2023) *Alpro: Promoting Healthier Eating and Sustainable Living*. https://bcorporation.eu/case_study/alpro-promoting-healthier-eating-and-sustainable-living/ (accessed 29-08-23).

Andersson, R. (2019) Employees as ambassadors: Embracing new role expectations and coping with identity-tensions. *Corporate Communications: An International Journal*, 24(4), pp. 702–716. DOI:10.1108/CCIJ-04-2019-0038

Anderson, S. & Smith, J. (2017) An empirical examination of the services triangle. *Journal of Services Marketing*, 31(3), pp. 236–246. DOI:10.1108/JSM-12-2015-0369

Arnett, D.B. & Wittmann, C.M. (2014) Improving marketing success: The role of tacit knowledge exchange between sales and marketing. *Journal of Business Research*, 67(3), pp. 324–331. DOI:10.1016/j.jbusres.2013.01.018

Berry, L. & Parasuraman, A. (1991) *Marketing Services: Competing through Quality*, New York: Free Press.

Bitner, M.J. (1995) Building service relationships: It's all about promises. *Journal of the Academy of Marketing Sciences*, 23(4), pp. 246–251.

Boukis, A., Gounaris, S. & Lings, I. (2017) Internal market orientation determinants of employee brand enactment. *Journal of Services Marketing*, 31(7), pp. 690–703. DOI:10.1108/JSM-07-2016-0272

Boukis, A., Kostopoulos, G., & Katsaridou, I. (2014) IMO and different fit types as key enablers of employee brand-supporting behaviour. *Journal of Strategic Marketing*, 22(2), pp. 117–134.

Brown, D.M. (2020) *Internal Marketing – Theories, Perspectives, and Stakeholders*. Abingdon: Routledge.

Carson, P.P., Carson, K.D., Knouse, S.B. & Roe, C.W. (1997) Balance theory applied to service quality: A focus on the organization, provider, and consumer triad. *Journal of Business and Psychology*, 12(2), pp. 99–120.

Chen, Q., Huang, R., Pak, K.Y & Hou, B. (2021) Internal marketing, employee satisfaction and cultural congruence of Gulf airlines. *Tourism Review*, 76(6), pp. 1214–1227. DOI:10.1108/TR-06-2019-0266

Christopher, M., Payne, A. & Ballantyne, D. (1991) *Relationship Marketing: Bringing Quality Customer Service and Marketing Together*, Oxford: Butterworth Heinemann.

Conduit, J. & Mavondo, F.T. (2001) How critical is IC orientation to market orientation? *Journal of Business Research*, 51(1), pp. 11–24. DOI:10.1016/S0148-2963(99)00044-2

Doyle, P. & Stern, P. (2006) *Marketing Management & Strategy*, 4th Edition. Harlow: FT Prentice Hall.

Fang, S, Chang, E., Chueh-Chu, O. & Chia-Hui, C. (2014) Internal market orientation: Market capabilities and learning orientation. *European Journal of Marketing*, 48 pp. 170–192. DOI:10.1108/EJM-06-2010-0353

Gode, H.E., Johansen, W. & Thomsen, C. (2020) Employee engagement in generating ideas on internal social media – A matter of meaningfulness, safety and availability. *Corporate Communications: An International Journal*, 25(2), pp. 263–280. DOI:10.1108/CCIJ-03-2019-0024

Gounaris, S. (2006) Internal market orientation and its Measurement. *Journal of Business Research*, 59(4), pp. 432–448. DOI:10.1016/j.jbusres.2005.10.003

Gounaris, S. (2008) The notion of internal market orientation and employee job satisfaction: Some preliminary evidence. *Journal of Services Marketing*, 22(1), pp. 68–90. DOI:10.1108/08876040810851978

Gummesson, E. (1987) Using internal marketing to develop a new culture. The case of Ericsson quality. *Journal of Business Industry Marketing*, 2(3), pp. 23–28. DOI:10.1108/eb006032

Hanlon, A. (2019) *Digital Marketing: Strategic Planning & Integration*. London: Sage Publications Limited.

Heider, F. (1958) *The Psychology of Interpersonal Relations*. London: Psychology Press.

Huang, Y.-T. (2020) Internal marketing and IC: A review, reconceptualization, and extension. *Journal of Relationship Marketing*, 19(3), pp. 165–181. DOI:10.1080/15332667.2019.1664873

Huang, Y.-T., Lee, T.R. & Jiang, Y.J. (2020) Applying grey relational analysis to evaluate internal marketing practice: A cross-cultural case study in Taiwan and Mainland China hotels. *Contemporary Management Research*, 16(1), pp. 55–75. DOI:10.7903/cmr.19552

Jobber, D. (2007) *Principles & Practice of Marketing*. London: McGraw-Hill.

Kaur, G., Sharma R.D. & Seli, N. (2009) Internal market orientation in Indian banking: An empirical analysis. *Managing Service Quality*, 19(5), pp. 595–627. DOI:10.1108/09604520910984391

Kohli, A.K. & Jaworski, B.J. (1990) Market orientation: The construct, research propositions and managerial implications. *Journal of Marketing*, 45(2), pp. 1–18. DOI:10.2307/1251866

Kotler, P., Wong, V., Saunders, J. & Armstrong, G. (2009) *Principles of Marketing*, 5th European Edition. Harlow: Prentice Hall.

Lee, Y. & Kim, H.K. (2021) Enhancing employee advocacy on social media: The value of internal relationship management approach. *Corporate Communications an International Journal*, 26(2), pp. 311–327. DOI:10.1108/CCIJ-05-2020-0088

Lemon, L.L. & Towery, N.A. (2021) The case for internal communication: An investigation into consortia forming. *Corporate Communications an International Journal*, 26(3), pp. 541–556. DOI:10.1108/CCIJ-07-2019-0093

Lings, I.N. (2004) Internal market orientation constructs and consequences, *Journal of Business Research*, 57, pp. 405–413. DOI:10.1016/S0148-2963(02)00274-6

Lings, I.N. & Greenley, G.E. (2005) Measuring internal market orientation. *Journal of Service Research*, 7(3), pp. 290–305. DOI:10.1177%2F1094670504271154

Lings, I.N. & Greenley, G.E. (2009) The impact of internal and external market orientations on firm performance. *Journal of Strategic Marketing*, 17(1), pp. 41–53. DOI:10.1080/09652540802619251

Lings, I.N. & Greenley, G. E. (2010) Internal market orientation and market-oriented behaviours, *Journal of Service Management*, 21(3), pp. 321–343. DOI:10.1108/09564231011050788

Löhndorf, B. & Diamantopoulos, A. (2014). Internal branding: Social identity and social exchange perspectives on turning employees into brand champions. *Journal of Service Research*, 17(3), pp. 310–325. DOI:10.1177/1094670514522098

Piercy, N.F. (1995) Customer satisfaction and the internal market: Marketing our customers to our employees. *Journal of Marketing Practice: Applied Marketing Science*, 1, pp. 22–44. DOI:10.1108/EUM0000000003878

Piercy, N.F. (1998) Barriers to implementing relationship marketing: Analysing the internal marketplace. *Journal of Strategic Marketing*, 6(3), pp. 209–222. DOI:10.1080/096525498346630

Piercy, N.F. & Morgan, N. (1990) Internal marketing: Making marketing happen. *Marketing Intelligence & Planning*, 8(1), pp. 4–6. DOI:10.1108/EUM0000000001069

Polanyi, M. (1958). *Personal Knowledge: Towards a Post-Critical Philosophy*. London: Routledge.

Qiu, J., Boukis, A. & Storey, C. (2022) Internal marketing: A systematic review, *Journal of Marketing Theory and Practice*, 30(1), pp. 53–67. DOI:10.1080/10696679.2021.1886588

Rafiq, M. & Ahmed, P.K. (1993) The scope of internal marketing: Defining the boundary between marketing and HRM. *Journal of Marketing Management*, 9, pp. 219–223.DOI:10.1080/0267257X.1993.9964234

Rafiq, M. & Ahmed, P.K. (2000) Advances in the internal marketing concept: Definition, synthesis and extension. *Journal of Services Marketing*, 6, 449–462.

Ramjaun, T.A. (2021) Corporate brand management in a charity context: The internal communications challenge. *Corporate Communications an International Journal*, 26(2), pp. 296–310. DOI:10.1108/CCIJ-05-2020-0083

Richardson, N. (2020) *Sustainable Marketing Planning*. Abingdon: Routledge.

Richardson, N. (2022) How new sustainability typologies will reshape traditional approaches to loyalty. *Italian Journal of Marketing. Special Issue:S.I. Sustainable Marketing and Performance Management*, February. DOI:10.1007/s43039-022-00047-y

Richardson, N. & Gosnay, R.M. (2022) Putting internal marketing into practice: To what extent can an Internal Marketing Orientation (IMO) be measured? *International Journal of Sales, Retailing & Marketing*, 11(1), pp. 17–31.

Richardson, N. & Gosnay, R.M. (2023) Is Internal marketing a declining field? If so, why? A literature exploration from a hermeneutic perspective. *Corporate Communications: An International Journal*. DOI:10.1108/CCIJ-10-2022-0123

Ruizalba Robledo, J.L., Bermudez-Gonzalez, G., Rodriguez-Molina M. & Blanca, M. (2014) Internal market orientation: An empirical research in hotel sector. *International Journal of Hospitality Management*, 38, pp. 11–19. DOI:10.1016/j.ijhm.2013.12.002

Ruizalba Robledo, J.L. & Vallespín-Arán, M. (2014) Empirical analysis of the constituent factors of internal marketing orientation at Spanish Hotels. *Tourism & Management Studies*, 10 (special issue), pp. 151–157.

Ruizalba Robledo, J.L., Vallespín-Arán, M. & Gonzalez, J.L. (2015) Analysis of corporate volunteering in internal market orientation and its effect on job satisfaction. *Tourism & Management Studies*, 11(1), pp. 173–181.

Sahi, G., Lonial, S., Gupta, M. & Seli, N. (2013) Revisiting internal market orientation: a note. *Journal of Services Marketing*, 27(5), pp. 385–403. DOI:10.1108/JSM-09-2011-0131

Tortosa, V., Miguel, M. & Sanchez, J. (2009) Internal market orientation and its influence on organisational performance. *European Journal of Marketing*, 43(11/12), pp. 1435–1456.

Tortosa-Edo, V., Llorens-Monzoniz, J., Moliner-Tena, M. & Sanchez-Garcia, J. (2015) The influence of internal market orientation on external outcomes: The mediating role of employees' attitudes. *Journal of Service Theory and Practice*, 25(4), pp. 486–523. DOI:10.1108/JSTP-11-2013-0259

Varey, R.J. (1995) Internal marketing: A review and some interdisciplinary research challenges. *International Journal of Service Industry Management*, 6(1), pp. 40–63.

Yu-Ting, H. & Rundle-Thiele, S. (2014) The moderating effect of cultural congruence on the internal marketing practice and employee satisfaction relationship: An empirical examination of Australian & Taiwanese born tourism employees. *Tourism Management*, 42, pp. 196–206.

Yu-Ting, H. & Rundle-Thiele, S. (2015) A holistic management tool for measuring internal marketing activities. *Journal of Services Marketing*, 29, pp. 571–584.

7 Relationship Marketing and Loyalty

Abstract

Chapter 7 addresses important themes around Relationship Marketing (RM). Increasingly organisations are gathering data so the issue of loyalty-related systems is addressed. The building blocks of BAU-based loyalty are identified. Loyalty is contrasted with satisfaction and readers are reminded that the two concepts are not synonymous. The widely used tools known as loyalty ladders are considered, leading to a discussion around the issues facing marketers wanting to utilise a TBL-based loyalty ladder. Issues relating to monitoring loyalty are discussed. The negative aspects of loyalty are acknowledged. Finally, the link between loyalty and IM is explored.

Learning Outcomes

At the end of this chapter students will be able to

- discuss the rationale for relationship marketing (RM)
- reflect on the role of Customer Relationship Marketing (CRM) within loyalty
- analyse the components of BAU loyalty
- appreciate how loyalty and satisfaction are related but different
- reflect on how a TBL-based loyalty approach can be adopted
- consider some of the issues related to online loyalty
- explain negative issues germane to loyalty.

Loyalty can be represented by the number of repurchases made by the consumer during a period of time (Mercadé-Melé *et al*, 2018). When the core activity of a company is highly integrated with its socially responsible activities, consumers take a favourable attitude toward the organisation (*ibid*). Similarly, poor sustainability practices can lead to corporate reputational damage (Gomez-Trujillo *et al*, 2020). Such reputational damage impacts on organisational attempts to engender customer and stakeholder loyalty. Companies that act responsibly improve company or brand reputation and customer loyalty (Kemper & Ballantyne, 2019). They must carry out responsible activities that fit their image because this will benefit their credibility, altruism attribution and how they are perceived (Mercadé-Melé *et al*, 2018). Crittenden *et al* (2011) suggest sustainability should be in the DNA of companies, embedded in their mission, goals, structure, operations and values (Rudowska, 2018). Clearly 'operations' covers loyalty programmes.

DOI: 10.4324/9781003434214-8

Example: Alpro has had sustainability in its DNA since the 1980s. Throughout its existence, Alpro's goal has been to continuously improve its products' ecological footprint and make them healthier (Alpro, 2023).

> "Following this long heritage and mission, it was just making sense to become a BCorp. BCorp strengthens our overall 'One Planet. One Health' vision which emphasizes our belief that the health of people and the planet are linked. We were at the time pioneering the global Danone ambition towards BCorp. In 2018, we finally certified with a BCorp score of 87 but this achievement was not the end. We focused even more on combining health & sustainability".
>
> (The sustainability team of Alpro, 2023)

In 2022, Alpro was recognised as 'Best for the World' in the Environment category. B Corps are leading the way towards a more sustainable and regenerative planet by putting their impact (on the air, climate, water, land and biodiversity) first in their business practices. B Corps excel in environmental performance by offering products or services designed to solve environmental issues or through their facilities, materials, emissions, energy use or the environmental impact of their supply chain. Their focus on the planet as a vital stakeholder has not gone unnoticed (*ibid*).

Marketers wanting to work sustainably are impeded by the dominance of traditional BAU models. They need to adapt existing models or adopt new versions a propos their marketing orientation, segmentation and loyalty.

7.1 Defining Relationship Marketing (RM)

Historically, marketers focused upon transactions and their survival and/or success depended upon repeat purchases. Repeat purchases suggest the development of confidence and trust leading to a relationship between buyers and sellers. Companies must balance (finite) resources when either acquiring new customers and/or retaining existing customers. Both are important but need different approaches: BAU acquisition requires companies to gain information about prospects, assess their value to the company and allocate resources to attract those with the greatest long-term value. BAU retention, by contrast, requires the maintenance of relationships with existing customers based on their long-term value.

Fuller (1999) insists credibility and trust are paramount in Sustainable Marketing (SM). Communicated messages based on facts and the credibility of the sender can influence the adoption of sustainable consumption. Consumers must trust the brand whether they receive communications via newspapers, online or by meeting representatives. Increasingly, they want to engage in mutually beneficial relationships. Mutual respect is the most effective way to develop a brand's reputation and build stakeholder relationships, whether they are customers, staff, investors, suppliers, community groups or even activist groups who oppose the activities of the business. Gaining this trust is important to building relationships.

Marketing, rightly, has its critics (see Chapter 2). Increasingly, marketers self-identify as being 'critical marketers' and their work has sought to 'keep marketing honest'. Since the 1970s marketers, especially the Scandinavians, have developed the notion of Relationship Marketing (RM) in a deliberate move away from transactional practices. That said, there is still much confusion regarding the nature of relationships.

Berry (1983) developed RM against the background of the rapid growth in services marketing in the 1980s. He argued for the need to move beyond the 'one-off sale' transactional sales-orientated model of marketing (see Table 6.1) to the development of longer-term relationships between supplier and customer. Questions that need to be asked at this point are:

- Can companies pursue the same level of relationship with every customer?
- Will all customers want the same level of relationship with their supplier?

There is no simple 'yes' or 'no' answer to either question. Customer engagement (whether B2C or B2B) varies from customer to customer and by type of product or service. RM in B2C marketing is desirable despite the lower level of engagement with most customers, contacts that are more routine and fewer opportunities for personalisation. Financial services companies, typically, use the value of a customer's business or size of their bank/savings account or their size of shareholding to determine the level of service that they will provide. The highest-value customers, often representing the smallest proportion of clients, receive a highly personalised service (Figure 7.1).

In Figure 7.1, customers lower down the pyramid receive lower levels of contact/support. A distinction must be made between frequency of transactions and their profitability. Furthermore, expectations still have to be managed. Marketers must monitor the monetary value of their customers' purchases/use of services to identify changing levels of activity which could trigger higher/lower levels of promotion or service and, thereafter, of RM management. In B2B marketing, the numbers of customers is smaller than in B2C. B2B features a greater emphasis on the importance of supplier relationships (or preferably

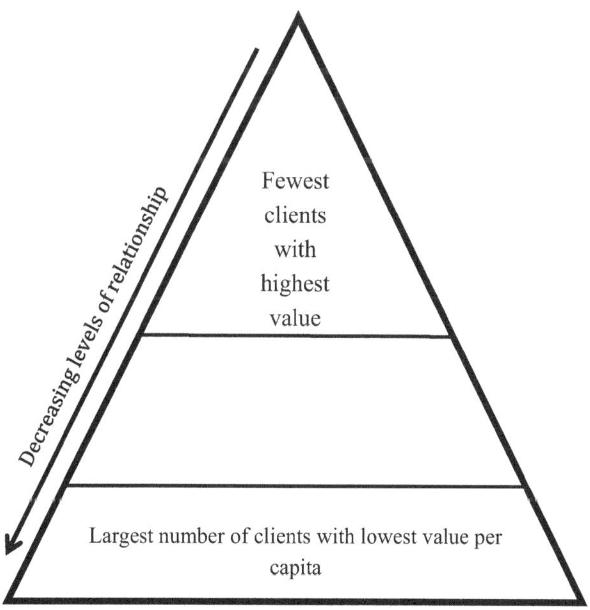

Figure 7.1 Customer value pyramid.

Source: Adapted from Richardson *et al* (2015, p 86).

partnerships) in terms of technology, quality and reliability. That said, the trend for companies rationalising (i.e. reducing) the size of their supplier base is set to continue, as is the adoption of 'one-stop shopping'. These developments have strengthened the importance and value of relationships. That said, not all organisations treat their suppliers fairly and equitably.

The Marketing Information System (MkIS) and Customer Relationship Management (CRM)

The importance of systems was introduced in Chapter 1. Since the advent of 'Big Data', it is increasingly necessary for other functions' systems to link to databases within the marketing function. Data relating to loyalty resides in the key system for marketers, namely the Marketing Information Systems (MkIS).

Figure 7.2 shows how a typical MkIS resides within the marketing function (designated by the dashed line) however it extends beyond the company into the stakeholders in the Micro-environment. As discussed, internally, the MkIS should overlap with systems in other functions (including HRM, procurement or Production). This is reflected in tools that evaluate the internal environment such as VCA (see Section 5.2). To be market-orientated (see Table 6.1) companies must develop their inter-functional communications and cooperation. Useful insights from non-marketers must be fed via the MkIS to the marketers making key decisions. Hollensen (2011) identifies how an MkIS can:

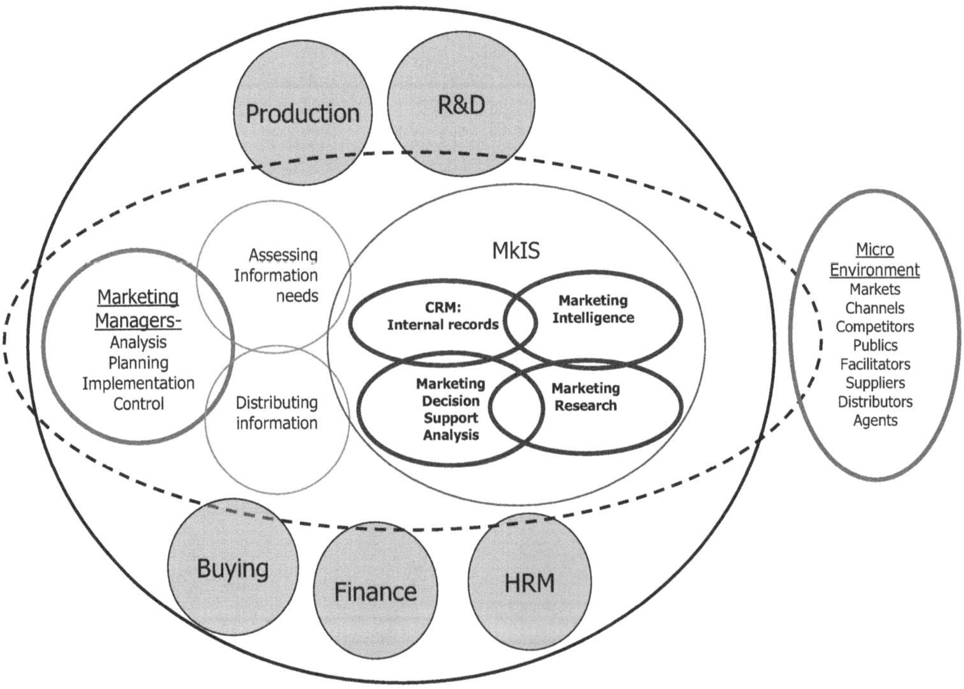

Figure 7.2 Marketing Information System (MkIS).

Source: Adapted from Richardson *et al* (2015).

- develop closer customer relationships
- avoid the increasing cost of making the wrong decisions
- take account of increasing market complexity (dynamism and turbulence)
- combat increased levels of competitor aggression.

Customer Relationship Management (CRM) was developed in the mid-1990s in the context of IT systems. The idea was for companies to use databases to maintain and develop customer knowledge and understanding. Improved understanding should lead to better relationships with customers, prospects and even suppliers.

CRM provides the necessary means to monitor levels of activity. It is regarded by some as the solution to many marketing problems, whereas others see it as the cause. Simply put, having an enormous database of contacts will not guarantee success if the customers cannot, or will not, take value from the brand. CRM should act as the platform to serve and nurture customers over their lifetime rather than in a single transaction. This makes good business sense, as existing customers are, on average, five to ten times more profitable.

Progressive marketers who promote customer centricity are not surprised that some companies misuse their data. Users of sites such as Facebook generate enormous amounts of data; marketers need to manage this data to produce information effectively and efficiently to make informed decisions. Hence, CRM programmes undoubtedly have something to offer but they are no substitute for genuine customer insight.

There is some debate whether CRM is the same as RM or merely reflects the technology used (to implement RM). A meta-analysis by Rababah *et al* (2011) concluded that some saw CRM as a philosophy (akin to RM) whilst others simply saw it as a technology. Most saw CRM from the perspective of IT-related strategies. With the advent of Big Data (data trawling, user-generated data etc.) the picture has become less clear. Having a substantial database of prospects and clients is pointless if they do not value what is offered. Value only resides with the customer, which is why many companies fail despite having substantial client databases. The term CRM is misleading as marketers should seek Customer Satisfaction Management (CSM) rather than simply hosting their customers' data in the internal records. Professor Michael Baker insisted the stress on CRM

> "suggests an imperfect understanding of the nature of relationships. Attempts to manage relationships are inevitably doomed to failure; far better to concentrate on CSM or customer satisfaction management".
>
> (Baker, 2009)

As customers change, their desires, needs, wants and information requirements also change. If companies do not respond to these changes, they will start to irritate customers and suffer attrition, i.e. lose them. Hence, databases must be 'massaged' to ensure the information extracted from the data is good enough to support decision making, knowledge management and, ideally, adoption of a market orientation (MO). Furthermore, data must be managed in accordance with the GDPR (see Section 5.2). Hence it is prudent to recognise that CRM alludes to the technology used to support RM but, on its own, this is no guarantee of customer loyalty or satisfaction.

7.2 The BAU Building Blocks of RM

Loyalty springs from the successful application of STP in the planning process (see Chapter 5). To move away from BAU loyalty practices, it is essential to consider segmentation's role through the prism of sustainability.

Identity

The issue of identity needs to be given serious consideration as brands increasingly use social media featuring groups, communities and tribes who share common interests, ideals and values. Organisations seeking to market themselves online, face fundamental challenges regarding the issue of 'identity'. Who are the 'users'? Are users and customers the same thing? Can Tik Tok users be treated in the same way as those on Facebook or LinkedIn? Segmentation will become increasingly harder as users (of Facebook, X, Instagram, Pinterest amongst others) 'disaggregate', i.e. present different versions of themselves. An individual's identity may vary across different social platforms on matters such as gender, age or nationality. Furthermore, online social behaviour is influenced by perceived anonymity. Undoubtedly the identities of social media users are multifaceted, fluid and often deceptive. Despite this it is still worth persevering as the customer's 'spending' is shaped by the thoughts, feelings and actions of those around them. Consumers adopt the attitudes, beliefs, opinions and values of their family, friends, communities, colleagues, reference groups, opinion leaders and so on. However, marketers using social media platforms are impeded by the ethically dubious practices of identity theft and fake profiles present on all social networks.

> **Example:** Statista (2020) reported that 16% of all Facebook accounts are fake or duplicates. Facebook estimates the proportion of duplicate accounts at 11% (circa 275 million profiles). The proportion of 'false', misclassified and/or 'undesirable' accounts is 5% (circa 137 million profiles). Furthermore, if someone wished to portray themself as more socially successful, they could simply 'buy' Twitter followers. A quick online search reveals companies who will sell followers accounts for as little as $10 per 1,000 or $279 for 30,000. In an era where online popularity is paramount, there will always be a supply for such demand.

Such practices are in the minority as most consumers are ethical and increasingly discerning about such behaviour. Social networks have to offer extensive privacy settings to help protect users' identities, even if at times these lack clarity and simplicity. The implementation of the GDPR (see Figure 5.6) was directly attributable to such questionable practices by digital marketers.

Segmentation and RM

As discussed in Section 5.3, segmentation is an important strategic part of the planning process. Many marketers use behavioural segmentation to consider attitudes, lifestyle choices or motivations. It is much harder to segment on the basis of such soft subjects compared to hard metrics, e.g. age, occupation or income. Many of the values attributed to sustainability change from generation to generation.

> **Example:** Generation Z includes those born since 1995. They are 'digital natives' and are constantly connected online. They use the mobile platform extensively and use smartphones as a hub for supporting social connectivity. To access this segment marketers must develop credible digital identities, through the branded website or social media. Generation Z are (unfairly) accused of having short attention spans and being easily distracted. Previous studies have suggested their attention spans to be less than six minutes. Hence more targeted sustainability strategies need to be developed, providing information, entertainment and other valuable content when and where it is needed. Gamification, bringing game-based mechanics such as leaderboards, competition and reward to interactions, is a useful approach. When dealing with minors, confirmation and support from parents is essential.

Generation Z often display high levels of environmental and/or societal concern. As discussed in Chapter 1, consumers who are concerned about sustainability issues can be mapped and thus segmented. The TBL provides a basis for value-based segmentation and mapping. Companies seeking to self-identify as sustainable may not necessarily prioritise the pursuit of growth; indeed, many sustainability start-ups prefer to keep standards undiluted and demanding. Being supported by idealistic stakeholders strongly committed to the sustainability mission, they may prefer to keep their niche at a size that does not attract undue interest from existing mainstream competitors (Hockerts & Wüstenhagen, 2010).

There is agreement that consumers experience involvement when objects or events 'connect' to important goals or centrally held sustainable values, e.g. being environmentally friendly often results in an intense emotional commitment (Richardson *et al*, 2015) which, in turn, increasingly influences their patronage decisions (Carpenter & Moore, 2006). Pro-environmental behaviour involves purchasing and non-purchasing behaviour (Jackson, 2005). Green consumers' contexts and values frame purchases apropos the motivation to pursue green criteria. It is influenced by the consumer's knowledge of the relevant issues as well as how previous purchase experience influenced the consumer (Young *et al*, 2010). Previous studies focused on segmenting 'elusive' green consumers (Peattie, 1992; Young *et al*, 2010; Worthington, 2013) with mixed results (Oates *et al*, 2008). Indeed, the term 'green' can be problematic as clearly different shades of 'green' consumers exist with some being 'light' green whilst others are heavily involved and self-identify as voluntary simplifiers (Oates *et al*, 2008; Young *et al*, 2010; Richardson *et al*, 2015).

> **Example:** In 2008 the UK government department DEFRA (Department of Food, Environment and Rural Affairs) developed a green segmentation based on self-reported public behaviours (DEFRA, 2008). The aim was to better understand and then drive 'green' or 'pro-environmental' behaviours. It received wide media coverage and was used by various organisations. In 2010 DEFRA commissioned CDSM (see www.cultdyn.co.uk) to apply Values Modes segmentation to the

DEFRA segments (Campaignstrategy, 2012). Based mainly on behaviour, standard demographics and social questions, the aim was to generate more effective strategy (for motivation, engagement and behaviour change). The analysis revealed that some segments were not 'real' at all, as they represent people with a variety of fundamentally different, even opposing unconscious motivations; any attempt to treat these people as a homogenous group based on common behaviours or standard demographics, would fail (*ibid*).

In their analysis of SM-related articles, Kemper and Ballantyne (2019) identified only five instances of green or ecological segmentation. They found none relating to TBL-based segmentation. Considerable attention has been given to companies being attacked online about aspects of their social and environmental performance (Belz & Peattie, 2009). The greater focus on 'green' segments is not surprising as consumers are increasingly exposed to information about sustainability issues such as climate change (*ibid*). Furthermore, a bias towards ecological and economic studies has always existed in the sustainability literature (Barkemeyer, 2009; Musgrave & Raj, 2009; White *et al*, 2019; Sinčić Ćorić *et al*, 2020). This may in part be because social SM activities have less significant impacts on brand image (Jung *et al*, 2020).

Sustainable segmentation is seen as an essential with SM (Wiscicka-Fernando, 2018) as it identifies how people perceive and respond to sustainability issues (*ibid*). As discussed in Chapter 3, the SST (see Figure 3.6) improves understanding of segmentation however Critical Scholars would argue that all such typologies have limitations. It does not forecast where the stakeholders may be in the future or that they may only have interest in aspects of an organisation's activities, say a project. The segments within the SST may need sub-sections to reflect other research and the reality. Young *et al* (2010) investigated voluntary simplifiers who strive to survive in a mode of sufficiency and demonstrated more complex decision-making processes than other consumers. Voluntary simplifiers were critical of certain sources and willing to search harder for information which, when provided by third parties, tends to be less biased (*ibid*). They would most likely be 'segmented' amongst 'Eco warriors' however depending on other values they could be Pro-Eco, Pro-Eco-Social or Sustainable Stakeholders. The SST is still relevant as it informs how IMC may need to be tailored (Porcu *et al*, 2020) to clarify, say, contradictory claims or terminological confusion.

As discussed, BAU frameworks focus on the traditional economic bottom line (see Chapter 5), however there is more to sustainable segmentation than is covered therein. Consumers may self-identify as sustainable. Hence segments' must be seen through a sustainable lens. The TBL-based APPROVES framework (see Table 5.17) embeds sustainability into the process that establishes a segment's viability. This aligns with the Critical School as it addresses the Developmental School's failure to offer a TBL-based alternative framework. It shares some limitations with its traditional predecessors. A segment's value will be wasted unless the whole organisation embraces it. Too often, critical insights are not realised because of a lack of senior management buy-in (McDonald, 2017). Furthermore, poor Internal Marketing (Rafiq & Ahmed, 2000) and IMC (Porcu *et al*, 2020) may result in other functions (not directly involved) feeling disconnected and lacking engagement. The APPROVES framework benefits from being more relevant to the increasing numbers of people who use ecological and ethical heuristics (Mitchell & Harris, 2005) to buy goods and services

7.3 Loyalty

The notion of loyalty has long occupied the minds and efforts of marketing academics and practitioners. Dick and Basu (1994) suggested loyalty is not just about attitudes towards products or services, but also behaviour, i.e. it includes the repeat(ed) purchase of said goods or services. This encouraged Marketers to consider the customers' Life-Time Value (LTV), i.e. the economic value gained during the time that the customer bought products or services. Subsequently, the definition has been expanded (see Oliver, 1997) however the basic concept remains unchanged. Worryingly, few companies have a working definition of what loyalty means (Aksoy, 2013) and, as such, many may not fully appreciate how it is engendered.

Loyalty starts with customer acquisition, i.e. converting suspects to prospects to customers. A number of tools can generate leads (a common first step in online customer acquisition) from real-time, say live chat, through to the forms used to capture user information, i.e. names and email addresses. Permission must be obtained to allow cookies and if retargeting, say, providing adverts on products previously browsed elsewhere. Retention of customers is a key loyalty concept. Customer acquisition is expensive and risky (until trust is developed) so marketers must prioritise customer retention (Table 7.1). This may involve migrating existing customers to an online platform (see Figure 4.4). This must only be done if satisfaction is maintained or enhanced. As long as customers are happy, marketers want them returning again and again. This may involve incentives, offers (sales promotions) or simply making them feel valued through dialogue and excellent customer service. Whatever the reason, marketers must focus on acquisition AND retention. Attrition is the final part of the loyalty triumvirate. All companies lose customers for a wide range of (often unpreventable) reasons.

A consumer using two sustainable brands at a similar time is not necessarily a sign of disloyalty. Rather sustainable consumers will have a 'repertoire of brands', e.g. buying Fairtrade goods in one category, MSC items in another and Soil Association goods in a third category. This will be welcome news to sustainable brands who do not necessarily want to ferociously compete with each other if their customers demonstrate multiple brand loyalties.

Example: Unilever have 1 million likes of Marmite on Facebook. They also have an 'I Love Marmite' page, user-generated content (UGC) via a 'Marmite Recipes' group and other measures. The Marmite brand community provided an alternative to the traditional 'push' form of marcomms. However, care must be taken when suggesting the community activities may have caused sales to increase.

A TBL-Appropriate Loyalty Ladder

Developmental Scholars (Christopher *et al*, 1991, 2002; Harridge-March & Quinton, 2009) have advocated loyalty ladders (Table 7.1) as a relatively easy way of understanding behavioural loyalty by helping companies to segment customers and prospects (Richardson *et al*, 2015). The BAU traditional 'ladders' still focus purely on

Table 7.1 Contrasting traditional and social media loyalty ladders with TBL-based sustainable segments

Traditional	*Social media*	*Sustainability*
Advocate – actively promotes brand to others	Evangelist – actively promotes social site to others	Sustainable stakeholder – advocate of brands that reinvest profits in People and Planet Influence others to adopt sustainability
Supporter – an influencer rather than a customer	'Celebrities' or 'Lead members' – very active. May influence others	Pro Eco/ Social – regularly buys brands that reinvest profits in People and Planet
Client – a customer who makes repeat purchases	Insiders – experts in specific topics and post regularly	Pro Eco – regularly buys brands that reinvest profits in Planet
Customer – an individual who purchases your product or service	Devotees – contribute regularly and developing social ties	Pro-social – regularly buys ethical brands that reinvest profits in People, say, Fairtrade
Prospect – finds the company's offer of interest	Mingler – mature tourist, perhaps, posts comments; no regularity or frequency	Social – committed to the notion of improving the human condition Critical of commerciality
Suspect – researches a brand but is not interested	Newby – an individual who has just started to post comments	Dark green – Eco warrior or voluntary simplifier. Wholly committed to a green lifestyle
	Tourist – posts comments; lacks engagement with the network	Libertarian – wants small gov't Sees tax as theft. Everything needed should be purchased
	Lurker – observes and may join the network	

Sources: Adapted from Christopher *et al* (1991, 2002); Harridge-March and Quinton (2009); Richardson *et al* (2015).

the customers' contribution to the 'bottom line' whilst ignoring customers' values (often ecological and ethical) and other stakeholders.

Table 7.1 illustrates how the segments in BAU loyalty ladders compare to those identified in the SST (Figure 3.6). In the BAU ladders the only value sought is economic. The segments therein are treated as homogenous (i.e. all 'prospects' are deemed the same). The fundamental idea, beyond segmenting the actual or potential customer base, is to remind marketers that they should try to move customers up the ladder. This is not straight forward with the SST segments as (once beyond 'Libertarians') some are fundamentally different (i.e. 'Dark Green' must be treated differently to say 'Pro-social'). The ladders present challenges as:

- it is not clear how to move customers up one or more rungs
- suppliers cannot have the same depth of relationship with each customer
- it is not possible to push every customer up the ladder
- it is difficult to identify suspects, prospects or lurkers before they have engaged
- differing marketing approaches will be needed for the different categories.

The TBL-based sustainability ladder (Figure 7.3) addresses the ecological and ethical omissions of its BAU predecessors. It should help companies seeking to align their sustainable values with their segments. That said, it presents other challenges. Many

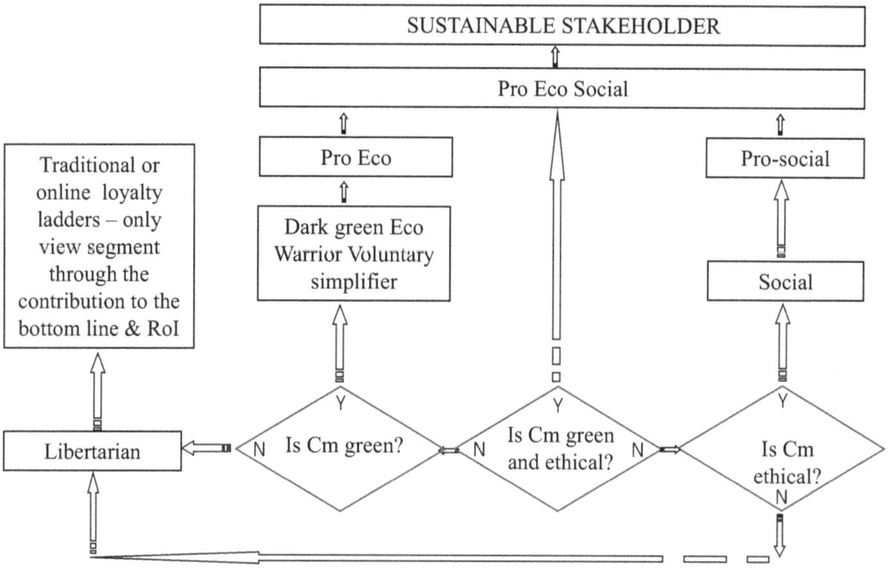

Figure 7.3 Sustainable Marketing (SM) loyalty ladder.

Source: Adapted from Richardson (2022).

of the values attributed to sustainable segments change from generation to generation, depend on involvement and vary across sectors. For example, younger generations may have higher levels of environmental concern, however some millennials may not (Bonera *et al*, 2020). The BAU ladders assume those at the bottom (say 'suspect' or lurker) are uncommitted, perhaps indifferent or ambivalent about the brand or site. As discussed, 'Libertarians' may have principled reasons for their attitudes and behaviours. Some consumers have negative moral values, associated with indulging in superfluous, unnecessary purchases, like those who buy luxury products (Guido *et al*, 2020). Someone who is 'Dark Green' may be an 'ecowarrior' or 'voluntary simplifier'. They may choose to value ecological considerations above all else (Young *et al*, 2010). Marketers may simply not be able to migrate these up the ladder to the ultimate 'Sustainable Stakeholder'. That said, as is often the case, the middle ground should be fruitful. Consumers deemed 'pro-social', could be encouraged to adopt environmentally friendly behaviour and migrated to 'Pro Eco/Social'. If they are satisfied and demonstrate loyalty to brands that are committed to ethical and environmental causes, in time they may evolve into sustainable stakeholders.

Loyalty Versus Satisfaction

Satisfaction is 'the emotional state that occurs as a result of customers' interactions with the firm over time' (Verhoef, 2003). Hence, genuine satisfaction may only come after repeated experiences (purchases); however there is still no clear link to the creation of loyalty. Academics generally agree that satisfaction is a matter of comparing expectations with experiences. Piercy (1991) warned against confusing loyalty with satisfaction. He

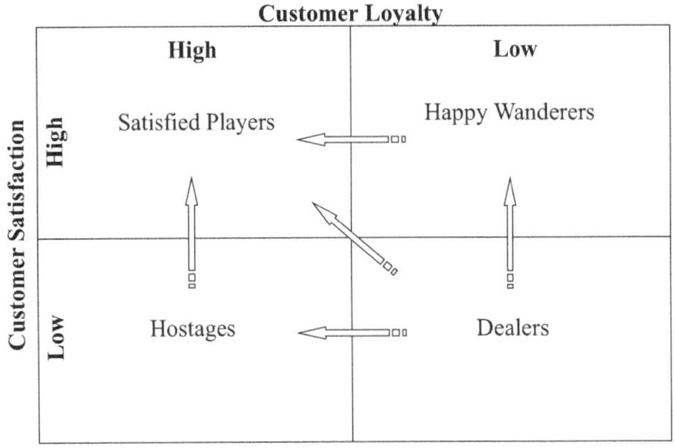

Figure 7.4 Customer satisfaction versus loyalty matrix.

Source: Adapted from Piercy (1991).

identified several states that could apply (Figure 7.4) and insisted that marketers should be precise in their use of language.

Figure 7.4 acts a positioning map germane to loyalty and satisfaction. It is useful as it reminds marketers that a key objective is to change customer behaviour, migrating them from Dealers (A) ideally to Satisfied Players (D). As is often the case with such exercises, this may need two steps, i.e. A-C-D or A-B-D. Clearly different objectives, strategies and tactics may be needed to improve loyalty compared to satisfaction. The challenge is persuading customers that there is value in a continuing relationship, which can only happen after dialogue. Marketers must sell the benefits and not simply list the features. Customers want to know how their problems can be solved. The oft-used metaphor is marketers are not selling drill-bits; rather they are helping customers to drill accurate holes easily, repeatedly and safely. Hence the value comes from specified value types (namely reduced risk, lower costs, greater accuracy and quicker completion). Loyalty will result from implementing this customer-centric approach if meaningfully supported by senior management. The right-first-time approach is customer centric and (by reducing the waste of energy and materials) sustainable.

Measuring and Monitoring Online Loyalty

Online services represent a challenge *and* opportunity for marketers to generate customer loyalty. Good communications and engagement are key to the implementation of RM. Aksoy (2013) identifies the following loyalty measures:

- indicators of customer perceptions and attitudes (satisfaction and commitment)
- indicators of customer loyalty behaviours (retention, share of wallet, frequency)
- customer financials (value of purchases, profitability, LTV)
- indicators of loyalty intentions (re-purchase intention; recommendation intention and Net Promoter Score).

This list shows areas of focus and measurement some of which (e.g. commitment, repurchase and recommendation intention) may be difficult to measure and/or predict accurately. Information can be gathered using tools, e.g. Google Analytics or Radian6 (a social media listening platform) to improve understanding of online behaviour through social media sentiment analysis. These insights into media consumption, customer needs, wants and desires (as well as considering competitor activity and future trends and emerging technology) allow marketers to support value-seeking customers and establish (or maintain) a competitive advantage.

Marcomms should be designed to encourage customer 'action' whether the first purchase, signing up for a newsletter, downloading content or taking part in competitions. Marketers must understand customer behaviour, i.e. which sites or platforms are used, browsing patterns and the most common search terms. Ultimately, marketers must monetise online provision in an ethical way. It is useful to consider the concept of conversion funnels. Google offers a funnels visualisation service via their analytics programme. Digital media channels have different advantages and disadvantages. The blend of channels being used must be economically viable and suitable for the customers. Furthermore, good content can increase the 'stickyness', i.e. dwell time on sites and promote repeat visits. Good content must be relevant, useful, unique (if possible) and current.

Negative Aspects of Loyalty

Marketers dedicate a great dealt of resource building relationships with customers by seeking increased satisfaction and loyalty. There may, however, be a negative aspect to loyalty. Critical Marketers identify 'unsustainable' aspects which (they argue) need to be discussed more frequently in academia. Many large service providers have customers who are not totally satisfied with their services. Some consumers' relationships with banks, insurance companies or energy providers are less than totally satisfying. Often the consumer feels "locked-in" (Sanne, 2002; Jackson, 2005; Murray & Haubl, 2007; Harrison *et al*, 2012) or a possibly unhealthy sense of compulsion (Guido *et al*, 2020). The effort needed to switch suppliers tends to make customers stay with the existing provider. This is 'unsustainable' and results from inertia, risk aversion, apathy and "working life conditions, which favour a work-and-spend lifestyle, the conditions of urban living or the effects of pervasive marketing" (Sanne, 2002, p 286). It would be instructive to know whether service providers factor in consumers' perceptions of feeling 'locked in' into their discussions with customers. In the EU and UK, legislation permits easy and quick switching between banking and energy providers. It remains to be seen to what extent these desirable developments impact upon customer behaviour and loyalty.

Loyalty and IM

The ideas for building relationships can also be applied to internal stakeholders who have power, ideas and insights. It is wise to engage with them to better understand their interests and needs. Internal marketing (IM) is essential and, despite being a well-established concept, it is often poorly practiced. Marketers must use IM approaches to sell the benefits of loyalty to their colleagues on an ongoing basis. Largely companies focus on managing their reputation externally, e.g. via their corporate websites and neglect sometimes conflicting messages being made public by employees and stakeholders in the Microenvironment. Sometimes there is a gap between managers' attitudes and behaviours. Those who claim to offer ethical and/or green brands will suffer more reputational damage should poor practices be exposed.

HR guides often identify expectations of behaviour and advise employees of the consequences of, say, misusing the internet in work time or posting negative messages about the brand. Negative comments should not be dismissed as the act of a curmudgeon. Some negative comments could result from whistle blowing where a company claims to operate in a certain way and the employee feels compelled to dispel any misrepresentation, especially if these concerns have been ignored through formal internal channels.

Example: In 2018 the CEO of Ted Baker was cited on Organise for inappropriate behaviour with staff. An online petition garnered 2,500 signatures; however it is not certain how many of these were Ted Baker staff. Whether guilty or not, investors sold Ted Baker shares resulting in a 15% drop, which wiped £123 million off the company's market value. It is safe to say that when a company's reputation is brought into disrepute by disgruntled employees, management will be faced with a challenging situation: how to deal with negative comments appearing publicly and how to deal with the employee.

Often user-generated content (UGC) appears above a company's website in search engine listings. Clearly organisations are no longer able to control the messages or brand-related discussions. They must engage with online debate or disgruntled employees to overcome any challenges. This may range from refining internal 'comms' to making fundamental changes to the company's modus operandi.

7.4 Benefits of RM

Loyalty derives from satisfying customers seeking benefits (Parasurman *et al*, 1991; Bitner, 1995; Mercadé-Melé *et al*, 2018) and values including co-creation of value (Richardson & Cassop Thompson, 2019; Coppola *et al*, 2020). Loyal (i.e. retained) customers increase income, buy additional products or services, generate Word of Mouth (or 'Word of Mouse' online), reduce costs and allow companies to amortise marketing (and sales) costs across the LTV. Clearly these benefits represent sources of competitive advantage which are difficult to copy. The implementation of RM should see increased trust and more equitable treatment of stakeholders. This clearly resonates with sustainability. Trust is central to the idea of loyalty and is built upon reliability, consistency, transparency, commitment and being treated fairly (with equity). Equity is particularly interesting in that research tends to underplay its importance.

Example: An illustration of trust is music festivalgoers' willingness to pay for the following year's festival during the current event, despite not knowing the 'line-up' and having no idea how the weather will behave in a year's time. This has two benefits, first the cash flow is improved; second, it leads to more commitment from festival goers who are given the opportunity to nail their colours to the mast and come back next year.

RM can lead to higher levels of repeat purchasing based upon increased customer satisfaction. Whether the most loyal customer is the most profitable customer is another matter. Loyal, satisfied customers who trust their suppliers:

- can increase a company's income
- are more likely to purchase additional products and services
- increase revenues through Word of Mouth (Word of Mouse online) recommendations
- help to reduce costs because they are less expensive to manage
- allow companies to set the cost of sales and marketing against the revenues generated during the whole period of that they deal with those companies (LTV)
- represent a source of competitive advantage which is difficult to copy.

In the B2C arena the sheer numbers of consumers make interactive marketing (see Figure 6.1) difficult apropos having identical 1:1 relationships with *every* customer. Social media has allowed companies to improve their customer engagement and has encouraged customers (users and influencers) to exchange views about brands. This has added both complexity and opportunities as customer relationships are not only influenced by the 'external marketing' but also the 'interactive marketing' and interactions with others (e.g. consumers, influencers and commentators).

The benefits may be clear, however engendering customer loyalty is anything but easy. Satisfying customers is seen as *sine qua non* for engendering loyalty. Verhoef (2003) defined satisfaction as the emotional state that occurs as a result of customers' interactions with the firm over time. This suggests that satisfaction involves comparing what customers expect will happen and what they actually experience. Genuine satisfaction often comes after repeated experience (purchases) (*ibid*). Furthermore, loyalty is predicated on trust which builds upon factors such as reliability and consistency, i.e. fulfilling the promises made (Bitner, 1995), to the same standard (Bertoli *et al*, 2020), 'being there' when required, going the extra mile, being treated equitably (Harris & Goode, 2004). The last of these is particularly interesting as the loyalty literature tends to underplay the importance of equity. Indeed, it is suggested that loyal customers may be less sensitive to price levels than first-time customers. Harris & Goode advocate the importance of equity, arguing that perceived value, satisfaction, service quality are key requirements of a relationship whereas trust is the key, central factor (*ibid*). Their finding that trust is key and loyalty may follow is supported by more recent studies (Bertoli *et al*, 2020).

Key Findings

1. RM relates to customer acquisition, retention and attrition.
2. Whilst RM is well-established, it is questionable whether effective implementation takes place.
3. RM can lead to higher levels of repeat purchasing based upon increased customer satisfaction.
4. Loyalty and satisfaction are not the same.
5. CRM alludes to the technology used to support RM but on its own is no guarantee of customer loyalty or satisfaction. Customer Satisfaction Management (CSM) is a different philosophical approach.
6. Measuring and monitoring online loyalty present challenges. Effective systems allow marketers to measure or monitor satisfaction and loyalty.

7 Differing BAU loyalty ladders exist and present differing challenges.
8 Good communications and engagement are key to the implementation of RM.
9 Some consumers' relationships with suppliers are less than totally satisfying. Often consumers feel "locked-in".

Activities

1 Identify 10 key sources that should be included in a MKiS for companies in B2C markets and B2B markets. How do the lists differ?
2 The "IT Toolbox" site (see https://it.toolbox.com/tags/crm) provides interesting insights into CRM and issues arising from poorly designed systems.
3 Regarding loyalty data in the digital environment, visit free off-site tools to look for conversations and posts about brands and organisations such as

- Social Mention (see http://socialmention.com)
- HowSociable http://howsociable.com.

References

Aksoy, L. (2013) How do you measure what you can't define? The current state of loyalty measurement and management. *Journal of Service Management,* 24(4), pp. 356–381.

Alpro. (2023) *Alpro: Promoting Healthier Eating and Sustainable Living.* https://bcorporation.eu/case_study/alpro-promoting-healthier-eating-and-sustainable-living/ (accessed 29-08-23).

Baker, M. (2009) *Aided Recall and Marketing Mnemonics* Guest Lecture presented by Professor Michael Baker to Leeds Business School, November 2009.

Barkemeyer, R. (2009) Beyond compliance – below expectations? CSR in the context of international development. *Business Ethics: A European Review,* 18(3) pp. 273–289.

Belz, F-M. & Peattie, K. (2009) *Sustainability Marketing – A Global Perspective.* Chichester: Wiley & Sons.

Berry, L. (1983) Relationship marketing in *Emerging Perspectives on Services Marketing*, Berry, Shostack, & Upah, (Eds), (2014), Chicago: American Marketing Association.

Bertoli, G., Busacca, B. & Imperato, M. (2020) Premium private label: How product value, trust and category involvement influence consumers' willingness to buy. *Italian Journal of Marketing*, pp. 143–161. DOI:10.1007/s43039-020-00012-7

Bitner M.J. (1995) Building service relationships: It's all about promises. *Journal of the Academy of Marketing Sciences*, 23(4), pp. 246–251.

Bonera, M., Codini, A.P. & Miniero, G. (2020) The great Millennials' trouble: Leading or confused green generation? An Italian insight. *Italian Journal of Marketing*, pp. 289–308. DOI:10.1007/s43039-020-00015-4

Campaignstrategy. (2012) *Analysis of DEFRA Green Segmentation by Values.* May 2012 http://threeworlds.campaignstrategy.org/?p=74 (accessed 12-09-23).

Carpenter, J.M. & Moore, M. (2006) Consumer demographics, store attributes, and retail format choice in the US grocery market. *International Journal of Retail & Distribution Management*, 34(6), pp. 434–452.

Christopher, M., Payne, A. & Ballantyne, D. (1991) *Relationship Marketing: Bringing Quality Customer Service and Marketing Together.* Oxford: Butterworth Heinemann.

Christopher, M., Payne, A. & Ballantyne, D. (2002) *Relationship Marketing: Creating Stakeholder Value.* Oxford: Butterworth-Heinemann.

Coppola, C., Vollero, A., Conte, F. & Siano, A. (2020) Self-production in an upcycling online community: Shared knowledge, collaborative ideas and creation of value. *Italian Journal of Marketing*, 2(3), pp. 231–248. DOI:10.1007/s43039-020-00010-9

Crittenden, V.L., Crittenden, W.F., Ferrell, L K., Ferrell, O.C. & Pinney, C.C. (2011) Market-oriented sustainability: A conceptual framework and propositions. *Journal of the Academy of Marketing Science*, 39, pp. 71–85. DOI:10.1007/s11747-010-0217-2

DEFRA. (2008) *A Framework for Proenvironmental Behaviours*. www.gov.uk/government/publications/a-framework-for-pro-environmental-behaviours (accessed 12-09-23).

Dick, A.S. & Basu, K. (1994) Consumer loyalty: Towards an integrated conceptual approach. *Journal of the Academy of Marketing Science*, 22(2), pp. 99–113.

Fuller, D.A. (1999) *Sustainable Marketing: Managerial-Ecological Issues*. London: Sage.

Gomez-Trujillo, A.M., Velez-Ocampo, J. & Gonzalez-Perez, M.A. (2020) A literature review on the causality between sustainability and corporate reputation. What goes first? *Management of Environmental Quality: An International Journal*, 31(2), pp. 406–430. DOI:10.1108/MEQ-09-2019-0207

Guido, G., Amatulli, C., Peluso, A.M., De Matteis, C., Piper, L. & Pino, G. (2020) Measuring internalized versus externalized luxury consumption motivations and consumers' segmentation. *Italian Journal of Marketing*, pp. 25–47. DOI:10.1007/s43039-020-00002-9

Harridge-March, S. & Quinton, S. (2009) Virtual snakes and ladders: Social networks and the relationship loyalty marketing ladder. *The Marketing Review*, 9(2), pp. 171–181.

Harris, L.C. & Goode, M.M.H. (2004) The four levels of loyalty and the pivotal role of trust: A study of online service dynamics. *Journal of Retailing*, 80, pp. 139–158.

Harrison, M.P., Beatty, S.E., Reynolds, K.E. & Noble, S.N. (2012) Why customers feel locked into relationships: Using qualitative research to uncover the lock-in factors. *Journal of Marketing Theory and Practice*, 20(4), Fall, pp. 391–406. DOI:10.2753/MTP1069-6679200403

Hockerts, K. & Wüstenhagen, R. (2010). Greening Goliaths versus emerging Davids – Theorizing about the role of incumbents and new entrants in sustainable entrepreneurship. *Journal of Business Venturing*, 25(5), pp. 481–492.

Hollensen, S. (2011) *Global Marketing: A Decision-Oriented Approach*, 5th Edition. FT/Prentice Hall.

Jackson, T. (2005) Motivating sustainable consumption- A review of evidence on consumer behaviour and behavioural change; *A Report to the Sustainable Development Research Network January 2005. Funded by the Economic and Social Research Council's Sustainable Technologies Programme (STP)*.

Jung, J., Kim, S.J. & Kim, K.H. (2020) Sustainable marketing activities of traditional fashion market and brand loyalty. *Journal of Business Research*, 120, pp. 294–301. DOI:10.1016/j.jbusres.2020.04.019

Kemper, J.A., & Ballantine, P.W. (2019). What do we mean by sustainability marketing? *Journal of Marketing Management*, February. DOI:10.1080/0267257X.2019.1573845

McDonald, M. (2017) *Malcolm McDonald on Marketing Planning – Understanding Marketing Plans and Strategy*, 2nd Edition. London: Kogan Page.

Mercadé-Melé. P., Molinillo, S., Fernández-Morales, A. & Porcu, L. (2018) CSR activities and consumer loyalty: The effect of the type of publicizing medium. *Journal of Business Economics and Management*, 19(3), pp. 431–455. DOI:10.3846/jbem.2018.5203

Murray, K.B., & Haubl, G. (2007) Explaining cognitive lock-in: The role of skill-based habits of use in consumer choice. *Journal of Consumer Research*, 34(1), pp. 77–88.

Musgrave, J. & Raj, R. (2009) Introduction to a conceptual framework for sustainable events. Chapter 1 in '*Event Management and Sustainability*'. Edited by Raj and Musgrave. Oxon: CABI.

Oates, C., McDonald, S., Alevizou P., Hwang, K., Young, W. & McMorland, L. (2008) Marketing sustainability: Use of information sources and degrees of voluntary simplicity *Journal of Marketing Communications*, 14(5), December, pp. 351–365.

Oliver, R.L. (1997) *Satisfaction: A Behavioural Perspective on the Consumer*, London: Irwin/McGraw Hill.

Parasuraman, A., Berry, L.L & Zeitmal, V.A. (1991) Perceived service quality as a customer-based performance measure: An empirical examination of organisational barriers using an extended service quality model. *Human Resource Management*, 30(3), pp. 335–364.

Peattie, K. (1992) *Green Marketing*. London: Pitman Publishing.

Piercy, N.F. (1991) *Market-Led Strategic Change – Making Marketing Happen in Your Organization*. Thorsons: University of California.

Porcu, L., del Barrio-García, S., Kitchen, P.J. & Tourky, M. (2020) The antecedent role of a collaborative vs. a controlling corporate culture on firm-wide integrated marketing communication and brand performance. *Journal of Business Research*, 119, pp. 435–443. DOI:10.1016/j.jbusres.2019.10.049

Rababah, K, Mohammed, H & Ibrahim, H (2011) A unified definition of CRM towards the successful adoption and implementation. *Academic Research International*, 1(1), pp. 220–228.

Rafiq, M. & Ahmed, P. (2000) Advances in internal marketing concept: Definition, synthesis and extension. *Journal of Services Marketing*, 14(6), pp. 449–462.

Richardson, N. (2022) How new sustainability typologies will reshape traditional approaches to loyalty. *Italian Journal of Marketing*. Special issue: S.I. Sustainable Marketing and Performance Management, February, DOI:10.1007/s43039-022-00047-y

Richardson, N. & Cassop Thompson, M. (2019) A new positioning framework for organizational value: Juxtaposing organizational value positions with customer centricity. *Strategic Change. Special Edition: Sustainable business models*, pp. 1–10. DOI:10.1002/jsc.2253

Richardson, N., James, J. & Kelley, N. (2015) *Customer-Centric Marketing: Supporting Sustainability in the Digital Age*. London: Kogan Page.

Rudowska, E. (2018) From sustainable market orientation to sustainability marketing (2018). Chapter 3 in *The Sustainable Marketing Concept in European SMEs-Insights from the Food & Drink Industry*. Edited by E. Rudowska. Bingley: Emerald. DOI:10.1108/978-1-78754-038-520180004

Sanne, C. (2002) Willing consumers – or locked in? Policies for a sustainable consumption. *Ecological Economics*, 42, pp. 273–287.

Sinčić Corić, D., Lučić, A., Brečić, R., Šević, A. & Šević, Z. (2020) An exploration of start-ups' Sustainable Marketing Orientation (SMO) *Industrial Marketing Management*, 91 November, pp. 176–186. DOI:10.1016/j.indmarman.2020.09.002

Statista. (2020) *16% of All Facebook Accounts Are Fake or Duplicates*. www.statista.com/chart/20685/duplicate-and-false-facebook-accounts/#:~:text=Social%20Media&text=The%20social%20network%20estimates%20the,about%20137%20million%20user%20profiles (accessed 08-08-23).

Verhoef, R. (2003) Understanding the effect of customer relationship management on customer share development. *Journal of Marketing*, 63, October, pp. 30–45.

White, K., Habib, R. & Hardisty, D.J. (2019) How to SHIFT consumer behaviors to be more sustainable: A literature review and guiding framework. *Journal of Marketing*, 83(3), pp. 22–49. DOI:10.1177/0022242919825649

Wiscicka-Fernando, M. (2018) Sustainability marketing tools in small and medium enterprises. Chapter 4 in *The Sustainable Marketing Concept in European SMEs-Insights from the Food & Drink Industry. (2018)* Edited by E. Rudowska. Bingley: Emerald.. DOI:10.1108/978-1-78754-038-520180005

Worthington, I. (2013) *Greening Business- Research, Theory & Practice*. Oxford: OUP.

Young, W., Hwang, K., McDonald, S. & Oates, C. (2010) Sustainable consumption: Green consumer behaviour when purchasing products. *Sustainable Development*, 18, pp. 20–31.

8 Themes

Abstract

This chapter contributes to the aims and objectives of the book by considering areas where the theories from previous chapters may inform academia and practice. Some see Sustainable Entrepreneurship (SE) as a major driver of sustainability adoption. Hence, the chapter first provides SE-related insights including value, norms and motivations (amongst others). Then branding is seen through the lens of sustainability with insights into brand positioning. Key factors in global marketing (i.e. Foreign Direct Investment, Vulnerable States and Sustainable Distribution) are evaluated. Aspects of the Mix and planning are revisited from the global perspective. The chapter concludes by explaining the role of small businesses and Not-For-Profit organisations.

Learning Outcomes

At the end of this chapter students will be able to

- discuss the rationale and benefits of sustainable entrepreneurship (SE)
- reflect on how branding tools can be used in relation to sustainability
- assess the nature of global Sustainable Marketing (SM)
- appreciate challenges faced by SMEs and micro-enterprises
- explain issues germane to non-profit organisations.

8.1 Sustainable Entrepreneurship (SE)

Many writers view Sustainable Entrepreneurship (SE) as the engine of sustainability, assuming its innovative power will bring about a more sustainable future. There is increasing interest in SE both as a phenomenon and a research topic (Shepherd & Patzelt, 2011). Traditionally, an inherent large-firm focus dominates corporate sustainability literature; however, entrepreneurs and small businesses have vital roles in managing global environmental and social resources (Moore & Manring, 2009). Sustainable entrepreneurs can bring skill sets to bear quickly, even more competitively than larger incumbents (*ibid*). SE research has traditionally focused on small firms, sometimes down to the level of individual entrepreneurs (Hockerts & Wüstenhagen, 2010) who face disadvantages when pursuing 'costly' sustainable actions, as such costs may not be borne by BAU competitors (Pacheco *et al*, 2010). They seek to balance social, environmental and economic dimensions requiring a specific orientation for guiding the venture design

DOI: 10.4324/9781003434214-9

process (Munoz & Dimov, 2015). SE embodies those who holistically integrate these dimensions into organisations that are sustainable in their goals and form of wealth generation (Young & Tilley, 2006).

Factors that drive SE are related to the individual entrepreneur and the context in which the behaviour occurs such as social norms, openness to sustainability practices and the nature of the value creation goals (Munoz & Dimov, 2015). A key SE objective is the realisation of successful businesses (*ibid*). Creating sustainable value may be subject to time constraints or may be impossible given resource allocations. Specifically, while some may implement sustainable practices immediately, others need to accrue the resources to initiate changes (Pacheco *et al*, 2010).

Not all activities to improve environmental or social performance can be characterised as SE. There is some debate as to what constitutes a sustainable entrepreneur as those who have no intention to broaden their impact on a wider market may be categorised as

> "incrementally innovative and hence not sustainable entrepreneurs ... (they) often come from the voluntary sector and sometimes tend to be opposed to consumerism and growth. They worry that mainstreaming requires them to abandon their ideals".
>
> (Hockerts & Wüstenhagen, 2010, p 484)

SE must be robust and resilient in face of anticipated and unanticipated economic, environmental and social challenges (Moore & Manring, 2009). Entrepreneurial activities performed in the pursuit of gains must not undermine the ecological and social environments and (when necessary) must restore or nurture such environments towards recovering the balance between nature, society and economic activity (Parrish, 2010).

Value, Norms, Motivations and SE

Entrepreneurs must quickly align their values with changing consumer perceptions and engagement. They must also engage with stakeholders in the micro-environment (see Figure 5.4). Entrepreneurial perceptions of value are not limited to financial profit or economic wealth creation but reflect personal and wider generalised value systems. Entrepreneurial processes are embedded in the social context. As social contexts, values and rules change, so do the entrepreneurial opportunities (Tilley & Young, 2009).

It is worth considering whether values influence behaviours; are special efforts needed by those who want to successfully commercialise sustainable innovation? As Hockerts and Wüstenhagen (2010) ask, how do they convince consumers that the product offering is not just good for society, but also good for them? Such desired value-creation pertains to the value that sustainable entrepreneurs aim to create both for their business and for society by offering combined social, economic and ecological value-types (Munoz & Dimov, 2015; Hockerts & Wüstenhagen, 2010).

Co-creation of value counters the idea of giving or proposing value by suggesting it is mutually created (Richardson & Cassop Thompson, 2023). The notion is not new; indeed Freeman (2008) suggests people have been creating value and trading with each other since long before there were corporations. He insists entrepreneurs are creating value, making our lives better, and changing the world (*ibid*). What sets sustainable companies apart is their pronounced value-based approach and their intention to effect social and environmental change in society. They seek to change market equilibria and (in the process) change the playing field for everybody by asking customers to pay a premium for socially and environmentally superior products (Hockerts & Wüstenhagen, 2010).

Value is not a permanent state, rather it can be created or destroyed. Cohen *et al* (2006) identified elements of sustainable value creation including economic performance, socio-efficiency, stewardship and eco-efficiency. These are consistent with Elkington's TBL, which sets the standard for business value that delivers economic, social and environmental benefits (Munoz & Dimov, 2015). The pursuit of such desired outcomes prompts the elaboration of business strategies and practices capable of tackling pressing challenges (*ibid*).

Individuals who attend to the social or ecological environments are more likely to recognise changes therein and the opportunities that arise. Therefore, compared to individuals more focused on the economic bottom line, those individuals are more likely to form beliefs about opportunities for sustainability even if they show no intention to personally pursue such opportunities (Shepherd & Patzelt, 2011).

Values and motives that give rise to SE may result in specific organising tensions that have the potential to challenge the viability of the enterprises (Munoz & Dimov, 2015). Ventures run by idealists are less likely to be caught in a specific technological mindset and are more prone to try out innovative approaches (Hockerts & Wüstenhagen, 2010). The pursuit of sustainability ideals through entrepreneurialism depends on the strength of the individual's intention to contribute to solving societal and environmental problems (Schaltegger & Wagner, 2011).

Entrepreneurs may be motivated for a number of reasons, e.g. their company being acquired can free founding entrepreneurs to develop new firms and pursue other synergistic alternatives (Moore & Manring, 2009). Motivations associated with BAU increased economic return may be deemed (by some) to be most important whereas those based on altruistic concerns for society or the environment may be less effective as institutional change is generally a costly endeavour (Pacheco *et al*, 2010). Entrepreneurs exist within a history or stream of ongoing action that gives meaning to and orientates their behaviour (*ibid*). As buyers, entrepreneurs can exert more pressure for sustainable supply chains (Moore & Manring, 2009).

SE transforms institutions by altering and/or creating norms. Examples of SE norms include codes of behaviour, partnerships and third-party certification programmes (Pacheco *et al*, 2010). Norms exist in a given social setting to the extent that individuals often they find themselves 'locked into' unsustainable patterns of consumption by social norms that lie beyond individual control (Jackson, 2005). In addition, norms (which are not exclusively related to monetary issues) can bring uniformity of behaviour, as their introduction encourages conformity. Many industries have witnessed the intervention of entrepreneurs in promoting self-enforced cooperative norms. Entrepreneurs may rely on sanctioned third-parties to devise and enforce industry norms (Pacheco *et al*, 2010). BCorp accreditation is an exemplar of enforced norms. Not all companies adopt normative notions of doing what is perceived to be right (Jackson, 2005). Hockerts and Wüstenhagen (2010, p 484) suggest SE firms

> "do not only see sustainability as central to core business activities, but at the same time aim for mass-market transformation beyond the eco-niche".

Entrepreneurs adopt ad-hoc approaches to engagement and exhibit diverse sustainability orientations. Within service economies entrepreneurial action can be found in various organisational settings, however Spedale and Watson (2014) argued that attention to context in mainstream entrepreneurial studies remained inadequate. Some sustainable actions are undertaken intuitively; however, intuition in itself may not be enough when promoting behavioural changes amongst stakeholders. This chimes with those critical of wealthy consumers enjoying being free riders while their immediate descendants and the world's poor pay (Kotler *et al*, 2009).

SE and Communities

Consumers often see and interact with 'sustainable' entrepreneurs who are essentially local, micro-enterprises, often featuring single persons including 'founding entrepreneurs' (Fisher *et al*, 2014). Sustainable entrepreneurs are often committed to supporting communities beyond the entrepreneurial activity itself, often highlighting the importance of welfare and quality of life in their locality (Tilley & Young, 2009). However, awareness of activities in the locale should not be assumed. Community engagement varies as, being heterogeneous, their needs vary. Some communities overlap and evolve which can provide opportunities for entrepreneurs who may seek to develop interdependence with differing sectors of the community (Vestrum & Rasmussen, 2013).

Traditionally viewed as a public (interested but no engagement) communities can evolve into 'engaged' stakeholders. They can foster good relations or a supportive atmosphere which may, in turn, improve consumer involvement. Social inclusion is an ethical objective for SE and should not be seen as purely altruistic as those included can make positive contributions. This chimes with the notion of enlightened self-interest (Haberberg *et al*, 2010) however there is a caveat to social inclusion as organisations may make social investments in the face of compelling economic reasoning not to do so (Margolis & Walsh, 2003).

Ownership and SE

Stakeholders often see ownership of sustainable practices as a value; where involved, consumers may share responsibility across aspects of their 'journey'. This 'ownership' can be linked to incentives (e.g. some music festivals incentivise litter collection – Boomtown offers an Eco Bond where, at the end of the festival, consumers receive a £20 refund on their ticket if they collect a specified amount of litter). Ownership is linked with the co-creation as value, i.e. 'safety' concerns are more likely to be addressed if, say, parents at an event think their peers will help care for their children onsite. Indeed, the emergence of consumers as co-creators has often been harnessed by firms in the creative industries (Richardson, 2020). It is always worth remembering that stakeholder theory is a very simple idea about how people create value for each other (Freeman, 2008). Hence entrepreneurs and consumers can develop different types of engagement with activities, objects, ideas or even social issues.

Growth

Growth is often a key concern for entrepreneurs; however, the differing modes of growth have risks, which ultimately may lead to increasing dissatisfaction amongst customers. The age of the enterprise will shape the attitude to risk and some entrepreneurs may not feel comfortable increasing this by taking onboard 'extra' costs of sustainability. This fits with Fussler (1996) who insisted most firms were not actively pursuing SE as a strategy to create market share. Ultimately, as consumers become increasingly sustainable, it will be easier for entrepreneurs to treat sustainability as an investment rather than a costly risk. Indeed, in time, the argument may evolve to become "How can entrepreneurs afford to not adopt sustainable practices"?

Growth can result from SE activities that represent disruptive, rather than incremental innovation (Hockerts & Wüstenhagen, 2010). This does, however, beg the question 'What is being disrupted?' Entrepreneurs may not be overtly 'sustainable' whereas some in their supply network may be. For the smallest, youngest organisations, the pursuit of growth is a key objective. It is difficult to survive when constrained by low turnover and cash flow. Such enterprises are subject to the capricious nature of the business environment. Many small companies failed during the crises of 2007 and 2020 whereas most multinationals were able to ride out the storm. Indeed, the FTSE 100 index rose as most incumbents were considered to be global and thus beyond the ramifications of local turbulence.

The growth may lead to specific SE tensions with the potential to impede the enterprises (Munoz & Dimov, 2015), e.g. whether to charge for car parking at an event, provide transport or include the socially excluded. For some sustainable entrepreneurs, motivations associated with increased economic return, whilst deemed important, are not of the highest priority as growth is not universally sought. A challenge is that growth is deemed by some to be the antithesis of sustainability. As sustainable enterprises grow, they may become more commercial and lose their attractiveness apropos sustainability. Hence, many sustainable entrepreneurs are happy to achieve a stasis where they are financially resilient but not dependent on growth. Resilience, of course, takes many forms.

Environmental Resilience

Sustainable Entrepreneurs seek to attract mainstream consumers, which may explain why so many just focus on niche, green consumers. The notion of resilience is key in SE. Often sustainability is seen to represent the regenerative use of resources. Indeed, many studies have found that individuals have a connectedness with the broader environment. Their environmental interaction features emotional commitment, which can affect their consumption decisions (see Figure 3.7). Regarding sustainability, stakeholders are often confused by the vastness of topics, e.g. recycling, energy saving, water saving or being environmentally friendly. The range of terms used may, in itself, be problematic when seeking to engage consumers. This might, to some extent, explain studies that (some time ago) identified increasing sustainability rhetoric but little progress is being made in addressing environmental and social problems facing society (Tilley & Young, 2009).

Jackson (2005) identified the need to change behaviour in relation to transport modes, eating habits and leisure practices, in order to reduce the damaging impact on the environment and on other people. These offerings fit with a 'biospheric' value orientation (*ibid*) and align with Young *et al* (2010) who found the environment was a key driver during purchasing decisions. Attitudes are linked with pro-environmental behaviour, which flows from pro-EcoSocial values (Figure 3.6). Hence stakeholders, like consumers, have a range of competing values that lead to dissonance when decision-making. Consumers are increasingly willing to pay a premium for socially and environmentally superior products (Ethical Consumer, 2022). Hence values based on altruistic concerns for society or the environment (whilst potentially costly) but are worthy of the investment. SE values may influence stakeholder engagement as they are not averse to the notion that green and societal endeavours are not just good for society, but also good for them (Hockerts & Wüstenhagen, 2010).

8.2 Sustainable Branding

Branding is a contentious area of marketing. Branding specialists insist it is the 'be-all-and-end-all' of marketing. However, they are often at a loss to explain why so many brands fail. de Chernatony *et al* (2011) describe brands as clusters of functional and emotional values which promise stakeholders a particular experience. It must be assumed that brands fail primarily because customers and stakeholders no longer see or take value. Brand loyalty measures a consumer's attachment to a specific brand. It is a function of several factors such as perceived quality, values, image, symbols, visual messages, non-verbal messages, emotional intelligence, the trust placed in the brand and the commitment the consumer feels towards it (*ibid*).

If, as Jackson (2005) suggests, consumption is socially constructed, then sustainable branding represents a social construct involving the brand, its ecological footprint and any ethical impact on society. This resonates with the marketing versus sustainability dichotomy –consumers may have a positive attitude towards sustainability, however this is no guarantee of changes in behaviour. Some consumers reluctantly pay more for sustainable brands whereas others see sustainability as an essential part of their social status.

Organisations not only sell brands but are also brands themselves. An organisation's brand is an amalgam of its reputation, product branding and image. Such branding helps to establish the positioning of products and companies. That said, positioning is perceived from the perspective of customers and stakeholders. Organisational branding can support Internal Marketing (IM) and the marketing of the brand itself. All employees, especially those who are internal customers (ICs), need to buy-in to the 'brand promise'. If the brand values, extolled externally, are not experienced internally, there is a risk of ICs feeling they are merely a 'channel to market'. Rather than the brand values being central to culture of the organisation, employees may perceive them as being superficial which, in turn, may lower motivation and morale.

Thomson *et al* (2010) identified the importance of communicating brand values to employees and suggest that they generally use a mixture of sources to draw information about the organisations' brand values. It is "necessary to develop brand knowledge among the company's employees" (Boukis *et al*, 2017, p 692). Brand performance is enhanced when employees are aware of their organisation's brand strategy and values. For this to happen both functionally, intellectually and emotionally, the brand values and message need to be communicated clearly and consistently (Thomson *et al*, 2010). Senior management are responsible for building a brand's identity and must create a culture of open communication throughout the organisation.

As brands become increasingly hard to control, managers should 'empower' employees to take responsibility for the brand. Employees who understand the brand can create relevant value for other stakeholders (Andersson, 2019). Seeking 540° feedback (see Section 5.3) will encourage more fluid horizontal and vertical communication to take place involving all stakeholders in a more involved manner. Marketers must work diligently and intelligently to build and maintain sustainable brands as part of sustainable consumers' social constructs. A sustainable brand management process will increasingly enhance an organisation's ability to acquire and retain custom. An added benefit is that it may also foster relationships with sustainable tribes, communities and networks.

As discussed in Chapter 4, services and product marketing are related but different. Service brands require greater emphasis on IM as they are reliant on boundary-spanning customer-facing employees who are subject to the differing characteristics of services. Branding can play a key role in building trust amongst service customers and stakeholders. Customers will trust a brand that they perceive can provide consistent quality over a period of time. That said, markets are often subject to hyper-competition, over-supply and fragmentation. In these circumstances brand differentiation is harder to achieve.

Brand Personalities

Gardner and Levy (1955) first suggested brands had personality characteristics in the 1950s. Aaker (1997) defined brand personality as the set of human characteristics associated with a brand. Consumer decision-making is informed by their perceptions of the product's functionally and based on brand personality perceptions. Indeed, consumers associate distinctive and relatively enduring characteristics with specific brands and these associations help (consumers) to form relationships with specific brands (*ibid*). Carlson and Donavan (2013, p 196) develop this, suggesting "brand personality is a dynamic amalgamation of unique attributes (i.e. brand adjectives) working together to create an overall personality for a brand". In tumultuous times all marketing activities must be dynamic rather than static. Introducing the link between human personality traits and brands was a significant contribution to brand management.

Aaker (1997) developed a brand personality framework (Table 8.1) that has been applied widely in branding research. Criticisms of the Aaker framework related to the lack of negative terms in the dimensions and attributes. Some attributes include degrees of overlap and clearly language and culture will shape perceptions. This raises questions regarding how the framework applies across international boundaries. A number of scholars have produced adapted frameworks to suit their scenario. One of which was Geuens *et al* (2009). Whilst their dimensions do not overtly refer to ethical or ecological matters, 'Responsibility', 'Simplicity' and 'Emotionality' could be argued to resonate with sustainability. These could be developed so the values within sustainable brands can be communicated (Table 8.1). Kapferer developed a brand-identity prism in which he considers a brand as a speech flowing from a sender to a receiver (Kapferer, 2008).

Figure 8.1 illustrates how the Identity Prism could be applied to an organisation wanting to open a vegan coffee shop. The brand identity dimensions (physique and personality (human personality traits)) imagine the sender. Reflection and self-image represent the receiver, whereas culture and relationship connect the sender and the receiver. The Identity Prism is largely judgement based; however, it can provide insights into how a segment could be supported.

Brand Equity

Aaker (1991) suggested brand equity occurs when brand associations are complemented with brand awareness, perceived quality and loyalty. Aaker suggests

> *Brand awareness* relates to consumer familiarity and recall. Marketers should not infer that this means the brand is 'superior'. Consumers may have high brand awareness and knowledge, however this does not necessarily shape their decision-making.
>
> *Perceived quality* reflects consumer perception of brand quality when compared to the competition. In high-quality markets a strong brand identity and personality are

Table 8.1 Contrasting BAU brand personality frameworks with a sustainable alternative

Aaker (1997)		*Geuens* et al *(2009)*		*Sustainable brands*	
Dimensions	*Core Attributes*	*Dimensions*	*Core Attributes*	*Dimensions*	*Core Attributes*
Sincerity	Down-to-earth Honesty Wholesomeness Cheerfulness	Responsibility	Down-to-earth, Stable Responsible	Responsibility	Down-to-earth, Durable Stable Responsible Collaborative
Excitement	Daring Spiritedness Imagination Contemporary	Activity	Active Dynamic Innovative	Activity	Dynamic Innovative Accountable Willing Collectivism
Competence	Reliability Intelligence Success	Aggressiveness	Aggressive Bold	Transparent	Communicative Listening Open Bold
Sophistication	Class Charm	Simplicity	Ordinary Simple	Contentment	Commitment Long-term Simple Voluntary
Ruggedness	Masculinity Toughness	Emotionally	Romantic Sentimental	Compassionate	Caring Considerate Honesty Sentimentality

Sources: Adapted from Aaker (1997); Geuens *et al* (2009).

essential. This applies to markets with low differentiation. The iPhone is the most profitable smartphone ever not because of its features, which are broadly similar to Huawei and Samsung, but because of its identity and personality.

Brand loyalty starts at an early age and can be both attitudinal and behavioural. Children are increasingly aware of charitable campaigns, specific charity brands and events. Targeting children is a contentious marketing activity. All research must comply with rigorous ethical standards.

Brand loyalty is an important outcome for many SM programmes seeking to change behaviours. Recycling programmes, for example, encourage people to separate their paper and food products, while healthy-eating programmes focus on increasing the number of people who sustain healthy eating habits.

Brand Positioning

Product positioning was discussed in Section 4.3. Brand positioning develops this by building on the brand's equity and characteristics. However, the need for customer centricity still applies. Brand positioning is only positive if the customer perceives it this way. A brand only achieves competitive advantage if customers think they are more likely to take value from the brand than a competitor. Kapferer (2008) offered a positioning framework based on four questions (Table 8.2).

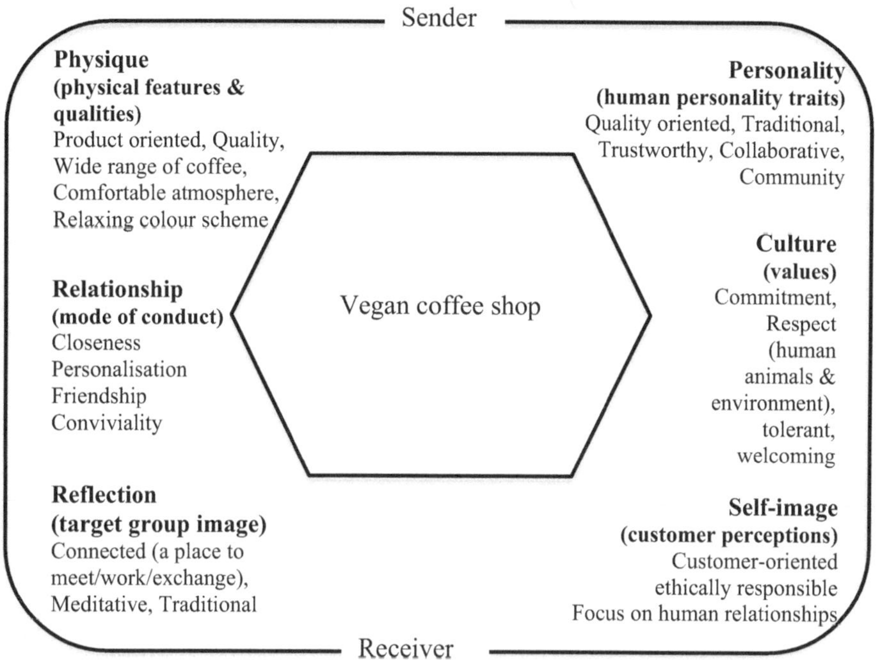

Figure 8.1 Kapferer's brand identity prism applied to a vegan coffee shop.

Source: Adapted from Kapferer (2008).

Table 8.2 juxtaposes three differing scenarios. The festival and agency are B2C and B2B service providers respectively. Whilst both are probably SMEs, their customer contact is wholly different. Festivals want repeat business – by definition, it is an annual event. The brand must reach value-seeking consumers who can choose between hundreds of festivals each season. The agency is looking to develop relationships with their clients (i.e. retailers) with whom they will have a high degree of contact and possibly online direct delivery to consumers. Finally, the stationery manufacturer has the added complication of dealing with raw materials and must meet waste and recycling standards. Sustainable brands need to counter the notion that they are perceived as being 'costly'.

Marketers must acknowledge the limitations of brand positioning. In competitive markets, brands must be able to position themselves against BAU competition who do not burden themselves with ethical or green practices. Sustainable brands often subscribe to building the 'sustainability pie' rather than engaging in a race to the bottom to seek a bigger slice of the BAU 'pie'. They often regard each other in a complementary fashion, which is appreciated by the brand communities. This reflects the concept of 'equifinality' where, regarding sustainability, there are many ways to reach the ultimate destination of sustainable consumption. All sustainable brands contribute to reaching the destination.

Table 8.2 Kapferer's positioning model applied to three sustainable scenarios

Positioning statements	*Scenarios*		
	Sustainable music festival	*Sustainable marketing agency*	*Environmentally friendly stationery manufacturer*
A brand for what?	A festival based on the rock music genre	Internal, B2B, Consumer & crisis communications	Personalised celebratory stationery
A brand for whom?	Both male and female professionals with interests in rock music and going to events	Sole traders, small budget charities & larger companies looking for regional and national brand exposure	Professionals with an inclination toward entertaining and/ or sentimental products
A brand for when?	Annual event for people to come together & enjoy rock music	Permanent projects or short-term consultancy work	Special occasions of friends or family
A brand against whom?	Hedonistic festivals with high eco and social impacts.	Agencies seeking to boost client profitability with no investment in social & green concerns. Unethical PR agencies offering spin.	Non-green suppliers of generic off the roll gift wrap. Those who promote single use wrapping.

Source: Adapted from Kapferer (2008).

Brand Communities

SM is inclusive and often seeks interactions with communities. Brand communities are groups of consumers with a shared enthusiasm for a brand. They have well-developed, collective identities (in-group, out-group) and engage in-group activities to achieve common objectives. Furthermore, they often share a common consciousness of a kind, moral responsibility for one another. They are akin to tribes in that they participate in shared rituals and/or events associated with the brand whilst co-creating value for each other.

Brand communities differ from standard brand relationships as the focus is on the inter-consumer relationships rather than between the consumer and the brand. Sustainable marketers will benefit from developing long-term relationships with brand communities. SM uses relationship-marketing techniques based on long-term dialogue and considering the customer's LTV, societal impact and eco-footprint. The synergies within the brand community will align with the brand, which should create stronger bonds. The advent of Web 2.0 and user-generated content (UGC) has enabled international brand communities to flourish, often overcoming linguistic and cultural barriers. Marketers must understand the structure within brand communities as some may be hierarchical. This should be coupled with an appreciation of sustainable segmentation (see Figure 3.6) as community members will have different degrees of commitment and motivation.

Reputation

A benefit of SM is that it may generate improved organisational and brand reputations. A reputation is generally what is said or believed about the character of a person, brand or organisation. With social media increasingly shaping marketing efforts, reputations can be the sum of the stories that people tell about a person (or an organisation). Urban myths can be associated with brands, which can be difficult to 'shake-off'. The old adage 'never let the truth get in the way of a good story' often applies. Brands can be 'trolled' online and often have little recourse. That said, libel and slander laws apply whether online or in print. Companies are increasingly concerned about reputational damage inflicted by their own employees. Bringing an employer into disrepute can lead to the rapid termination of a contract. Progressive employers understand the benefits of a sincere whistle-blowing programme. Reputations vary depending on whose perspective is being used, e.g. family, friends, employers, customers or suppliers. When does a strong manager become a bully? These can be fine lines. That said, bullying is never acceptable.

> **Example:** Reputations can have sub-reputations and constituent parts. The reputation of a city such as Leeds comprises the reputation of its people, its buildings, its location, its music, its history, its sporting teams and major events. Sometimes branding needs serendipity. Two of West Yorkshire's finest athletes (the Brownlee brothers) have been hugely successful in triathlon events at the highest level. They have brought triathlon events to Leeds. These events have seen the city of Leeds' reputation for sporting events enhanced on the world stage. Credit is also owed to the local authorities that supported these new ventures.

Trust in a brand is no longer just in terms of doing 'what it says on the tin'. Consumers increasingly want to be able to trust the people behind the product. They want to believe the brand represents the sort of people who 'do the right thing'. Sustainable brands can build win–win relationships, create a bigger sustainability cake and share the benefits of the best suppliers, partners, investors and customers. In treating people decently and ethically they will build a reputation for being good people with whom consumers can work. Some commentators are more cynical. Kotler suggested:

> "Ethical consumption is perhaps the biggest movement in branding today, (however) … consumers are confused. The public is not sure what an ethical brand actually is. There are so many angles to being ethical … The more optimistic British thought that supporting ethical brands could help make companies more accountable but were wary that ethical brands were for 'people with money'".
>
> (Kotler *et al*, 2009, pp 94–95)

This view is becoming increasingly outdated as brands align themselves to the social and ecological values of consumers. Consumers are indeed greener and more ethical (Ethical Consumer, 2022). Sustainable marketers must engage by communicating the brand's value and character. A key to many branding campaigns is (and always will be) 'word of mouth'. Ultimately power is largely a matter of perception. The mightiest of companies can be brought down by reputational damage caused by unethical practices (see Bell Pottinger for an egregious example). If marketers want consumers, prospects and influencers to see them as a powerful, sustainable brand, they need to act like credible leaders. Brands have evolved beyond their original role as a tool for sales oriented, transactional companies. Branding needs to become a management tool that creates clear, credible value for those who want to take it.

8.3 Global Sustainable Marketing

In the twenty-first century all marketers are global marketers who source goods, service customers and face competition globally. There are many push and pull factors relating to trading internationally (Table 8.3).

Table 8.3 is useful as it reminds marketers of some of the factors to take into account in global marketing endeavours. Clearly the global business environments must inform marketing objectives, strategies and tactics. The marketing mix may need to be tailored to suit international customers. Furthermore, different methods of entering overseas markets exist and companies must adopt suitable entry strategies. Hence, marketers must be able to analyse aspects of the business environment beyond the confines of their domestic market.

Table 8.3 Push and pull factors for global marketing

Push	*Pull*
Oversupply and hyper-competition in domestic market	Nascent and developing markets
Future economic recession or low GDP growth	Weaker competition
Unfavourable demographics- ageing population	Strong economic growth
Fragmentation of market	Increasing disposable income and living standards
High operating costs	Favourable demographics – younger age profile
Excessive shareholder power	Pro-business governments and bodies
Short-termism – government, City	Lower fixed and variable costs
Lack of differentiation in mature markets	Geographical spread of trading risks
	Positive attitude towards newness and innovation

Source: Author.

Example: Alpro, part of Danone, is headquartered in Ghent (Belgium) with three main production sites in Belgium, France and the UK. Alpro sells its products in Europe and beyond, contributing to the growth of plant-based nutrition. The global food production system has a huge impact on our planet, not only on the climate but also nature as a whole. Hence, Alpro pioneers adopting science-based targets for nature, expanding from targets for carbon only, to the Science Based Targets initiative (SBTi). SBTi drives ambitious climate action in the private sector by enabling organisations to set science-based emissions reduction targets (SBTi, 2023). Alpro use SBTi to measure impacts on biodiversity, water and land (Alpro, 2023). According to the B-Corp, there is a growing awareness amongst policymakers, international organisations, and scientists that plant-based products have a low environmental impact, and a shift towards a more plant-based diet is proposed as part of the solution for global environmental and social challenges humanity faces today and tomorrow (*ibid*).

Key Factors in Global Marketing

In the mid-twentieth century, the International Trade Organisation (ITO) and the World Bank were created. Under their auspices 22 countries signed up to the General Agreement on Trade & Tariffs (GATT) in 1947. GATT covered goods, the principle of Most Favoured Nation (MFN) and a commitment to rounds of negotiations to reduce tariffs. Founding members (largely rich countries) participated in many rounds and consequently have very low tariffs. The first 25 years of GATT coincided with the most prosperous in history. Rapid growth fostered liberalisation, which stimulated further expansion. GATT evolved into the World Trade Organisation (WTO) in 1995. A key WTO function is to prevent the exploitation of Intellectual Property Rights (IPRs) within set timescales. Sometimes long-term IPRs conflict with short-term public policy initiatives e.g. the South African government deliberately and justifiably violated pharmaceutical IPRs to better treat citizens with Aids. Substantive developments are associated with 'rounds' trade talks in specific locations, e.g.

- Paris – patents, trademarks and designs
- Rome – recording and broadcasting,
- Berne – copyright.
- Uruguay – anti-dumping measures, export and general domestic subsidies.

Uruguay saw the acceptance of Trade-Related Aspects of Intellectual Property Rights (TRIPs) which protect

- copyright, databases and computer programs (50 years)
- trademarks (7 years)
- industrial designs (10 years)
- patents (20 years) and
- trade secrets (indefinite).

Developing countries have 10 years' grace. TRIPs strengthen protection of IPRs almost worldwide with disputes subject to WTO dispute settlement procedures. Dispute procedures feature:

- panels of experts
- automatic adoption of reports
- time limits
- permitted retaliation.

The UN-based World Intellectual Property Organisation (WIPO) administers the 'rounds' and generally promotes IPRs. WIPO is (allegedly) a neutral forum (drawing on experts from government and industry) with arguably less political bargaining than the WTO ministerial conferences. The matters discussed are complex and ever changing; consider e-commerce, AI, genetically modified foods or biodiversity. The WTO seeks to harmonise measures, i.e. product standards, packaging provisions and labelling or assessment procedures. The agreements allow for some national flexibility; however, the aim is to reduce impediments to trade. The Uruguay round enshrined anti-dumping measures that still resonate today, e.g. President Trump's USA was open to charges of protectionism. Two broad types of subsidies are allowable, namely export and general domestic subsidies. Uruguay provided a RAG (traffic light) system for subsidies as follows:

- Red – those seeking to enhance exports or promote local content in preference to imports
- Amber (actionable) – actions that injure another country's exports
- Green (non-actionable) – e.g. areas of high unemployment.

Trans-National Corporations (TNCs)

A Trans-National Corporation (TNC) takes a long-term interest in or control of an entity in another country. It holds at least 10% of the shares. If it holds the majority of the shares it moves from being an affiliate to being a subsidiary of the parent company. In developed countries, incoming TNCs often pay higher wages whilst the outgoing TNCs shed jobs. TNCs play a key role global marketing and impact the host economy's trade performance directly (injecting capital, technology and/or management know-how) and indirectly with spillovers to local suppliers who have improved market access and can establish reputations on a larger platform. They can imitate the TNCs, recruit their staff whilst using infrastructure and institutions (created by the TNC). TNCs seek entry to markets using 'Greenfield' opportunities or mergers and acquisitions (M&A). Three modes of entry into global markets are

- Indirect – using domestic agents
- Direct – using overseas agents, licensing, distributors
- Direct investment – joint venture or wholly owned foreign enterprises (WOFEs or Woofies).

To do this they have to reflect on whether their Marketing Mix can simply be adopted or whether it needs to be tailored to the new market.

Foreign Direct Investment (FDI)

Foreign Direct Investment (FDI) occurs when an entity, located in one country, takes a long-term interest in and/or control of an entity resident in another country. The minimum proportion of equity that is needed is 10%. After a strong rebound in 2021, global FDI fell 12% in 2022 to $1.3 trillion, due mainly to overlapping global crises (the war in Ukraine, high food/energy prices and soaring public debt). The decline was felt mostly in developed economies, where FDI fell by 37% to $378 billion. But flows to developing countries grew by 4% – albeit unevenly, with a few large emerging countries attracting most of the investment while flows to the least developed countries declined (UNCTAD, 2023).

The 2023 World Investment Report reveals a widening annual investment deficit that developing countries face as they work to achieve the UN SDGs by 2030. The gap rose to $4 trillion per year in 2022 up from $2.5 trillion in 2015 when the SDGs were adopted. Developing countries need renewable energy investments of about $1.7 trillion each year (for power grids, transmission lines or storage) but attracted only $544 billion in clean energy FDI in 2022. Although investments in renewables have nearly tripled since 2015, most of the money has gone to developed countries (*ibid*).

The report highlights how international investment in renewable energy generation, including solar and wind, continued to grow in 2022, but at a slower 8% than the 50% growth recorded in 2021. Notably, projects announced in battery manufacturing tripled to more than $100 billion in 2022. More than 30 developing countries have not registered a large international investment project in renewables. Furthermore, FDI flows to Africa declined to $45 billion in 2022 from the record $80 billion in 2021 accounting for 3.5% of global FDI. FDI inflows to the least developed countries (LDCs) as a group declined by 16% to $22 billion. Flows remained concentrated, with the top five recipients (Ethiopia, Cambodia, Bangladesh, Senegal and Mozambique, in that order) accounting for about 70% of the total. FDI in the 33 African LDCs accounted for 58% of all LDC inflows (UNCTAD, 2023).

Vulnerable States

SM is predicated on ethical decision-making, particularly when supplying goods and services to vulnerable states and countries. Marketing decisions will be influenced by the characteristics of the host economy. Strategies and tactics may alter if the host is an LDC as against being 'developed'. Marketers targeting states with weak institutions will have to be wary of corrupt practices, particularly in the post-Sarbanes-Oxley Act world.

Countries with a greater dependence on natural resources, say oil, have long suffered poverty, civil war, dictatorship and corruption, compared to others. Sachs & Warner (1995) found 97 natural-resource-dependent nations had slower economic growth than the rest of world. The drivers for this were economic as oil revenues took resources from other export sectors, while corruption saw politicians receive money from outside sources resulting in conflict, deprivation, poor investment and high levels of debt. Marketers can potentially export to over 200 countries. For the 2022 fiscal year, countries were categorised using Gross National Income (GNI) per capita (a.k.a. income per head) as

1. High-income economies	$12,615 or more.
2. Upper middle-income	economies between $4,086 and $12,615;
3. Lower middle-income	economies between $1,035 and $4,086;
4. Low-income economies	$1,035 or less in 2022;

(World Bank, 2023)

Clearly the term 'high income' is relative. Marketers must recognise that US and European median salaries are substantially higher than $12,615 despite some of their citizens living in poverty. Seeking to change international consumer behaviour may be challenging as it involves paying a premium for 'costly' sustainable actions. Other characteristics that distinguish high-income economies from the rest of the world are growth trends, birth

Table 8.4 Dynamic versus static Foreign Direct Investment (FDI)

Dynamic	*Static*
• continually upgrade facilities and infrastructure • increase economic investment • raise economic value-add • create linkages with local communities and institutions • have positive spill-over into the host business sector	• not develop link ages with the host community • limit or stop future investment • not increase local economic value-added • be susceptible to sudden departure • lead to a race-to-the-bottom • cause job losses in local firms

Source: Author.

rate, average family size, infant mortality, disposable income, debt and the share of GDP coming from agriculture.

Most vulnerable states would welcome FDI; however the scale of benefits will be dictated by the incoming company's approach (Table 8.4). Whether adopting a dynamic or static approach there are micro-environmental matters to consider. These allude to stakeholders in the host country, e.g. labour markets, creditors, customers, competitors and forces therein including the cost of capital or export restrictions. Some organisations straddle the micro/macro divide, i.e. the UN, OPEC, EU etc.

Global Marketing and the 'Macro' Environment

The 'Macro' environment refers to the situation where the organisation has little control, i.e. strategic decisions have no effect on economic, financial, political, cultural and technological factors. Assessing a country initially involves 'hard' data, e.g. location, climate-zone, natural resources, population size and rate of growth. These complement the macro factors in PEST, which was adapted by Richard Stead to PLATFORM (Table 8.5).

Aspects of the PLATFORM macro-framework are useful as it focuses on natural resources eagerly sought by countries and companies worldwide. As is often the case, marketers can 'cherry pick' the best elements within models and frameworks to produce the optimum analysis. Economic factors, whilst not reflected in PLATFORM, are significant when dealing with international markets. Economic factors can include

- differing rates of growth
- changing balances of payments
- varying fiscal and monetary approaches
- inflationary/deflationary GDP trends
- price and/or wage controls
- the business cycle
- rate of domestic and foreign investment
- level of personal consumption
- variations in unit labour cost
- disposable income per household (or per capita).

Table 8.5 PLATFORM macroenvironmental analysis framework

Macro factor	*Questions posed by factor*
Politics	What is the political structure? Are gov't powers limited? Is a constitution in place? Is there meaningful opposition? Is there a tendency for rapid (or inadequate) gov't change?
Legal	How does the legal system operate? Are companies fully accountable or protected by the gov't? Do tariffs and/or quotas apply? Are there issues with product liability? Is there 'Home Country' legislation – think US Sarbanes-Oxley Act.
Accessibility	Is the sector public or private? Is it easy to access and assess gov't data? Do monopolies or other restrictive practices exist?
Technology	Does the gov't allow private-sector competition with the public-sector? Does the gov't control the infrastructure and/or media? Will foreign companies be forced to share IPR? Does the gov't fund pure or applied 'tech' research?
Finance	Is local capital available? Does the stock exchange have sustainability indices? Can NGOs support inward investment? If the target sector is private, will it be going Public? Is the gov't hostile to foreign capital? Is the tax regime benign?
Ores	Does the country have abundant, accessible natural resources? Are these resources unique or in high demand? Will infrastructure allow access to these resources? Is there a renewable alternative?
Regulations & Reform	How does gov't control private enterprise? What contributions does the gov't expect from the private sector?
Manners	Are foreign companies seen as threats to host sovereignty? Is nationalism rising? Do regions seek independence or recognition?

Source: Adapted from Stead (2003).

Marketers need to make research-informed decisions. International Bodies hold a lot of data, however care is needed. Within the EU, the Euro binds Member States' currencies together to reduce exchange rate fluctuations and supposedly create stability. Internal trade with/from the EU should be more attractive to marketers. The UK retains Sterling and marketers need to understand that the depreciating value of currencies can influence cash flow. However, foreign countries may have benign tax regimes and global marketers can benefit by declaring profits overseas. Larger companies can gain a competitive advantage over domestic-only competition by borrowing internationally where monetary policy is looser.

Care must be taken as reputational damage can result from negative WoM relating to tax management schemes. Apple has a vast amount of money banked offshore which does not generate tax for the US government. Amazon had to change their European arrangements as politicians and pressure groups noted that their original Luxemburg Headquarters meant little or no tax was paid where the profits were generated. The pressure on large, global marketing companies (e.g., Facebook, Apple, Amazon, Google etc.) will continue to increase.

Investment, SD and 'Environmental, Social and Governance' (ESG)

Policies and instruments designed to promote investment in sustainable businesses are an increasingly important feature of the global investment landscape. Market innovations related to SD attract interest from portfolio investors; the positive track record of sustainability-themed products is reinforcing asset managers' views that 'environmental, social and governance' (ESG) issues are material to long-term investment performance. As these sustainable investment trends expand, they will strongly influence operational policies and practices relative to SD (UNCTAD, 2018).

Under UN SDG 17 (see Table 1.4), Target 12.6 seeks to encourage companies, especially large and TNCs, to adopt sustainable practices and integrate sustainability information into their reporting cycle. The Sustainable Stock Exchange (SSE) initiative is a UN Partnership Programme organised by UNCTAD, the UN Global Compact, UNEP FI and the PRI. The SSE's mission is to provide a global platform, exploring how exchanges (in collaboration with investors, companies (issuers), regulators, policymakers and relevant international organisations) enhance performance on ESG issues, encouraging sustainable investment (i.e. financing the UN SDGs). They seek to achieve this through an integrated programme of evidence-based policy analysis, facilitating networks and fora for multi-stakeholder consensus-building, providing technical assistance and advisory services (SSE, 2023a). The SSE's goal is for all stock exchanges to provide listed companies with guidance on sustainability reporting.

When SSE launched its Model Guidance for exchanges in 2015, less than 10% of stock exchanges around the world were providing guidance on reporting ESG information. By 2023, 71 of the 122 stock exchanges (i.e. 59%) tracked by the SSE published ESG reporting guidance for their listed companies (*ibid*). These SSE exchanges collectively list over 45,000 companies with a market capitalisation of over $80 trillion (UNCTAD, 2018). The purpose of the Model Guidance compiled by the SSE is to help exchanges address this need by providing a model, or template, that exchanges can use to develop their own, custom guidance (SSE, 2023a). The gap in guidance on ESG reporting leads to incomplete corporate information, creating a challenge for investors seeking a comprehensive view of a company's material issues (SSE, 2023b).

Socio-Cultural Factors

Host countries and their consumers may resent the 'cultural imperialism' of foreign marketers, so cultural training and sensitivity are essential. Some simple steps are:

1. Be culturally sensitive and prepared.
2. Adopt the local language and customs.
3. Respect the host country's values.
4. Avoid ethnocentricity.
5. Recognise local complexities – avoid stereotyping.
6. Consider different approaches to time, i.e. westerners are mono-chronic whereas hosts may be poly-chronic.
7. Set realistic objectives.
8. Be willing to unlearn and be open to new experiences.

Example: Hollensen (2017) describes how Guanxi is deeply rooted in Chinese culture and is basically 'a tool to get business' and 'a way of getting things done'. It may take some considerable time (possibly years) to establish Guanxi. Exporters and importers must establish and maintain close relationships with their Chinese counterparts and relevant government agencies. Exporters must encourage strong Guanxi between their Chinese representatives and customers. A web of strong personal relationships can often help to ensure expedited governmental procedures and the smoother development of business in China.

Gender Balance

There is no room in marketing for sexism, nor for any of the 'isms' for that matter. In 2020, women accounted for approximately 28.3% of all managerial positions worldwide, compared with 23.6% in 1991. Apropos Marketing, the CIM has observed that, in the UK, women hold the majority of Marketing Manager positions, however at director level men still have the majority. This will no doubt change with the passing of time as there is a clear trend of increasing representation for women in managerial positions (Statista, 2023). By 2017, women held 22% of board seats in the top 100 global MNEs, and five corporations had female CEOs. The MNEs with the most diverse boards are from Europe, where some countries (i.e. Norway) have introduced quotas and targets, followed by North America, where the appointment of women is not regulated. South African corporations have a comparable share of women on their boards of directors. Companies in other economies, along with Japanese corporations, lag significantly behind their Western and South African counterparts.

Technology Factors

Marketers must evaluate whether returns can be generated using technology. Knowledge intensive companies tend to be highly profitable and are more willing to take risks and diversify. This can be done via M&As where companies can use in-house expertise in new markets. They can exploit the output of their earlier research, developed by in-house R&D. Alternatively, companies can develop overseas R&D facilities where the host country benefits from technology transfer and diffusion into the local institutions and markets. Sometimes local subsidiaries or partners can buy or licence the technology. That said, some countries adopt a more critical stance towards foreign takeovers, especially when they relate to national security or the sale of strategic domestic assets and technology firms (UNCTAD, 2018).

Global Marketing and the Marketing Mix

In global marketing, branding involves much more than product name selection. All 'comms' vehicles must be appropriate for the target market, including social media, websites, print media, packaging and documentation. Figure 4.1 shows the communication model and its realms of understanding. In Global Marketing one realm represents the context of the Country of Origin (CoO). The other represents the context of the foreign market. Linguistic and cultural mistakes are easy to make when seeking to move into new markets or simply refreshing the brand in an existing international market. Marketers must recognise that the brand name may mean something undesirable in another language and should undertake research to avoid faux pas in gestures, expressions and even dialect. Consumers of 'tech'-related products prefer to have domestic support including service centres and local representatives. Consumers prefer to have catalogues and user manuals in their mother tongue. Some global marketers (say IKEA) have worked tirelessly to produce wholly graphical assembly manuals with little or no written language.

Care must be taken when applying models across international boundaries. Take for example Maslow's 'Hierarchy of Needs' (see Figure 3.2) and the TBL DMP (see Figure 3.7). Developed societies have well-defined health and safety regulations so workers should feel physically safe in the work-environment. Largely law and order applies, so consumers should feel safe in society at large (with the emphasis on should). Wealthier consumers have greater disposable income to lavish on 'extended' purchases, fashion, events and activities. These may help their struggle towards self-actualisation. These conditions may not be replicated in LDCs. Marketers targeting LDCs may struggle with brands in the self-actualisation category. That said, even in LDCs there are segments who will have disposable income and care must be taken to avoid simplistic stereotypes.

Colours play a significant role in marketing materials, however they are not consistent across international boundaries and cultures. In some cultures, red is used to represent danger, whereas others use green or black. In some countries, white is the colour of funerals, whereas others use it for weddings. To avoid (accidentally) sending inappropriate messages, marketers must understand how colours are perceived in host countries.

The advent of new technologies is driving the latest wave of globalisation with increasing adoption of free-market styles of management. This presents marketers with key decisions, namely whether to adopt or adapt their Marketing Mix for the new foreign market. As discussed in Chapter 4, Customer Benefits (Product) and Comms could be adapted to influence sustainable product adoption. Table 4.14 can also be applied when accessing global markets. Marketers must choose which option will have the highest likelihood of success. As discussed, new FMCG products have a high failure rate. In Table 4.14 higher-risk options would involve adaptation when launching a new product into a new foreign market. Marketers may use this approach once they have established the influence of the Country of Origin (CoO) effect and the extent to which new products may be well received by the customers.

Sustainable Distribution

As discussed, the overlap between functions can determine the success of organisations. One such overlap is between Marketing, Sales and Logistics apropos international shipping. Goods can be shipped by land, sea or air and in each the 'terms' must be clearly communicated between stakeholders. Incoterms are the global standard for international trade and have been translated into more than 30 languages (Table 8.6).

Table 8.6, whilst not exhaustive, ensures marketers are aware of the rules for differing modes of transport. If involved in transporting goods internationally, seek advice from experts, say, in the Chamber of Commerce. They are often involved in producing documentation for exports. As a matter of interest, the Incoterms for using ships and/or boats apply to sea-based or inland waterway transport.

A major issue for the International Maritime Organisation was whether to set an emission reduction target for 2030 and if so, how high it should be. To aid the decision, CE Delft modelled (in 2023) the greatest technically achievable reduction potential for the sector. Assuming that ships take all possible technical abatement measures available,

Table 8.6 Incoterms for all modes of transport

Incoterm	*Seller's responsibilities*	*Buyer's responsibilities*
Ex Works (EXW)	Deliver goods to the buyer at the seller's premises or at another named place.	Load the goods onto collecting vehicle & clear for export (where needed).
Free Carrier (FCA)	Deliver goods to the carrier or person nominated by the buyer at the seller's premises or another named place.	Parties are advised to specify the point within the named place of delivery, as the risk passes to the buyer at that point.
Carriage Paid To (CPT)	Deliver goods to the carrier or another person nominated by the seller at an agreed place. Arrange and cover the costs of delivery	Collect the goods from a nominated person or at the named place of destination (after the seller unloads).
Carriage and insurance paid to (CIP)	Deliver goods to the carrier or another person nominated by the seller at an agreed place. Arrange and cover the costs to deliver the goods. Insure against the buyer's risk of loss of or damage to the goods during transport.	Under CIP the seller is required to obtain insurance only on minimum cover. Should the buyer wish to have more insurance protection, it will need to take appropriate actions.
Delivered at terminal (DAT)	Deliver and unload goods for the buyer at a place of destination (e.g. a quay, warehouse, road, rail or air cargo terminal). Bear all risks involved in bringing and unloading the goods.	Collect the goods at the terminal at the named port or place of destination (after the seller unloads).
Delivered at place (DAP)	Deliver goods ready for unloading to a named destination. Bear all risks involved in bringing the goods to the named place.	Collect the goods at the named place of destination (after the seller unloads).
Delivered Duty Paid (DDP)	Deliver goods when cleared for import and ready for unloading at the destination. Bearing the costs and risks involved in delivering the goods, providing export / import clearance, paying duties & covering customs formalities.	Collect the goods at the named place of destination (after the seller unloads and has cleared the goods for export/import, paid any duties and to carried out all customs formalities).
FAS Free Alongside Ship	Deliver the goods alongside the vessel (e.g., on a quay or a barge) nominated by the buyer at the named port of shipment. The risk of loss of or damage to the goods passes when the goods are alongside the ship.	Collects the goods at the named place of destination (after the seller unloads).
FOB Free on Board Ship	Deliver the goods onboard the vessel nominated by the buyer at the named port of shipment.	Bear all costs and responsibilities once the goods are onboard a vessel. The risk of loss or damage to the goods passes when the goods are onboard.
CFR Cost and Freight -Ship	Deliver the goods on board the vessel. Pay the costs and freight necessary to bring the goods to the named port of destination.	The risk of loss of or damage to the goods passes when the goods are on board the vessel in port.
CIF Cost, Insurance and Freight -Ship	Deliver the goods on board the vessel. Pay the costs and freight necessary to bring the goods to the named port and insure against the buyer's risk of loss or damage to the goods during the carriage.	Under CIF the seller is required to obtain insurance only on minimum cover. Should the buyer wish to have more insurance protection, it will need to take appropriate actions The buyer collects the goods on board the vessel in port.

Source: Adapted from ICC, 2010.

including the optimal deployment of wind-assisted technology, reduce their speed by 20–30% and use 5–10% zero-GHG fuels, the emissions of international shipping can be reduced by 28–47% (compared to 2008) by 2030. This substantial reduction over a seven-year period of implementation, would increase shipping costs by 6–14% on average, relative to BAU. Nearly half of the emission reductions result from lower speeds and other operational measures, a quarter from wind-assisted propulsion and other technical measures and another quarter from using zero and near-zero GHG fuels (CE Delft, 2023).

8.4 SMEs and Micro-Enterprises

The UK has over 2.5 million enterprises of which 99% are Small-to-Medium Size Enterprises (SMEs). The SME sector's annual turnover exceeds £1 trillion, representing over half of the UK's private sector economic activity. They are major employers who often provide the platform for new ideas (think technology spin-offs from universities). Clearly, they are vital for the economy and will play an increasingly important role in future. The EC definition (2003/361/EC) states that SMEs should be 'independent' and employ less than 250 people. Further to this companies who have nine employees (or fewer) are classed as micro-enterprises.

Many sustainability studies focus on larger manufacturers. Large and small firms play differing roles however it is largely agreed that SMEs (hereafter including micro-enterprises) are more flexible, can react quicker to changes in the marketplace and generally are more 'agile' enabling them to fill local, specialised or niche markets. SMEs have characteristics which dictate their approach to marketing namely:

- the inherent characteristics and behaviours of the owner/manager
- size limitations and the stage of development
- limited resources (such as finance, time, marketing knowledge)
- lack of specialist expertise (owners tend to be generalists)
- limited impact in the marketplace

(Gilmore *et al*, 2001)

Marketing planning is an essential activity for all organisations; however, many SME owners deem it unnecessary often regarding formal marketing as something more relevant to large organisations. This is often influenced by their own characteristics which do not necessarily remain constant. In many SMEs there is a third-generation problem. The originator may hand the business safely to their offspring, however by the third generation the ties are less binding. SME service providers need to train their staff to minimise variability. However, traditionally, they undertake less formal marketing training than their larger counterparts. If in doubt SMEs should seek external advice – their local Business School will often be able to provide cost-effective assistance.

Furthermore, the financial restrictions faced by many SMEs coupled with the time demands of the owner/managers undoubtedly contribute to the lack of coordinated marketing therein.

It is, however, impossible to apply a single rule to all SMEs as they are simply too diverse. Many exhibit entrepreneurial behavioural patterns whilst having little structure,

Table 8.7 Attributes in relation to company size

	Weaknesses	*Strengths*
SMEs	Poor Finances Weak Market Presence	Flexibility Speed of Response Independence
Large Enterprises	Inertia Politicised Slow Response	Strong Brand Financial Stability Economy of Scale Professional Management

whereas others are long standing and well-established, with structures comparable to larger companies (Table 8.7).

It can be inferred from Table 8.7 that an interesting paradox exists as larger SMEs could be in a 'win–win' scenario of having the benefits of SMEs and larger companies, or in a 'lose–lose' situation, having only weaknesses, or a combination of both. Whatever the scenario, it will impact their approach to marketing. All SMEs should engage in PR (see Section 2.1) and networking. PR has many benefits and few drawbacks for SMEs. Support is available from a wide range of third parties ranging from agencies, to consultants, to local business schools. One of these will be able to help within a limited budget.

Apropos networking, there are many events suitable for SME managers such as those run by local Chambers of Commerce. Furthermore, online networking sites are increasingly useful in helping SMEs to grow whilst adopting sustainable practices. Facebook and LinkedIn are generic networking sites widely used by SMEs. Increasingly SMEs are using Instagram to promote their brand. More specialist sites are gaining credence. Some SMEs look to share resources either through working collaboratively or using portals. SME booksellers use Abebooks as a portal (see www.abebooks.co.uk/) while others use eBay or Etsy (amongst others) to sell their goods to consumers and other businesses. Whilst eBay was originally a C2C platform it is now predominantly B2C and B2B sales, with B2B sales growing faster than C2C. People and business have always bought from governments (i.e. G2B and G2B). Now local government departments are saving money by buying items from sellers on eBay (i.e. B2G and C2G).

Whilst online buyers are typically younger, increasing social inclusion will provide services to all sectors of society. Interestingly, over half of eBay's buyers are over 45. Silver surfers (i.e. those over 55) are increasingly visible online. eBay also attracts a wide variety of sellers. Originally, sellers were consumers selling unwanted goods to other consumers in a classic C2C sense.

It is impossible to apply a single rule to all SMEs as they are simply too diverse. Many exhibit entrepreneurial behavioural patterns whilst having little structure whereas others are long standing well established, with structures comparable to larger companies. Whatever the scenario, it will impact on their approach to marketing (see Section 4.6).

SMEs and Sustainability

SMEs have a significant environmental impact. Walker and Preuss (2008) suggest they may be responsible for up to 70% of all UK industrial pollution. They have significant social impacts with behaviours and characteristics that are important in the evolution towards adopting sustainability. They may, however, tend to focus on their societal and environmental behaviours internally, rather than engaging with stakeholders in the supply chain (Moore & Manring, 2009). Kerr (2006) argues SMEs should develop strategies that incorporate sustainability and that the resulting skills would guide them to act in a sustainable way.

The benefits of sustainable strategic plans for SMEs are different from those offered to larger competitors (Moore & Manring, 2009). Barriers to SME adoption of sustainability do exist including:

- lacking awareness in terms of sources of assistance, e.g. grants
- perceiving the necessary skills problems as barriers
- feeling their company size is too small to have a meaningful affect
- thinking 'costly' sustainable actions are unaffordable or incompatible with existing in-house systems.

Tools and Frameworks

Historically, key marketing texts have concentrated on large organisations and it can be argued that they have failed to provide SME managers with meaningful marketing guidance. Certainly, many of the tools and frameworks are not easy to apply. Consider Porter's VCA (see Table 5.5). In a micro-enterprise it is highly unlikely that they will have both inbound and outbound logistics in their 'Primary' activities. Apropos the 'Support' activities, the 'Firm infrastructure' is less of an issue as they are flatter and more flexible. McLarty (1998) recognised the role of entrepreneurial drives in small firms. These are shaped by the characteristics and behaviours of the founding entrepreneur, the owner or the manager.

In small firms, managers must be leaders as well. They have to be creative and pragmatic. They have to deal with today and the future development of the company. The size and nature of their resource will shape their ability to grow. Often a key factor will involve the resource structure. Finally, SMEs and micro-enterprises are limited when it comes to technology development.

It is sensible to adapt VCA when applied to SMEs and micro-enterprises. In VCA the analysis of management is often subsumed within 'Operations' or 'Infrastructure' activities, which may be more appropriate for larger more structured enterprises than for SMEs. McLarty (1998) developed this concern suggesting that the model also failed to recognise that entrepreneurial drive plays a leading part in stimulating growth, specifically the owner/manager's role as the driving force within an SME. The traditional definition of support and primary activities were too limiting for his study. Imaginatively he redefined the support activities to be:

- Entrepreneurial Drives
- Management Capability and
- Resource Infrastructure.

McLarty's Small Firm Value Chain (Figure 8.2) may not be perfect, but it serves a key purpose. It reminds marketers that frameworks, models and tools are not precious things that are beyond reproach, but can and should be adapted to suit the company.

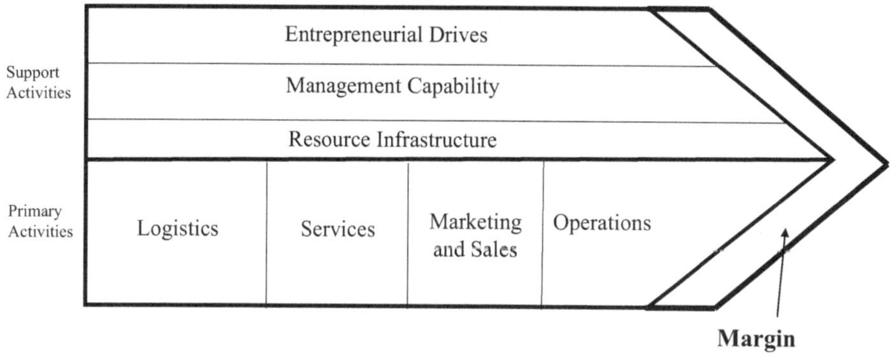

Figure 8.2 The small firm value chain analysis (VCA).

Source: Adapted from McLarty (1998, p 115).

Frameworks (see the SMBF in Figure 5.15) should be adapted to incorporate differing approaches. A large company may well have a CSR policy and platform. Research suggests many entrepreneurs have not even heard of CSR. In the SMBF a large company could be benchmarked using the traditional VCA, whereas an SME could use McLarty's adaptation ... or an updated version.

8.5 Charities, Not-for-Profit and Third Sector

Kotler recognised long ago that there is more to marketing than Adam Smith's idea of a simple transaction. Kotler's social marketing theory (see Chapter 2) extends to charities who are government funded (occasionally referred to as B2G, i.e. business-to-government). Even though charities do not sell in the traditional fashion they still provide services for which they receive funding. Today charity managers are under increasing pressure to meet stakeholder expectations so it is appropriate to consider them in more detail. Today, businesses are more like charities with CSR and sustainability platforms whereas charities are more like businesses with professionally run marketing campaigns. It is no longer a case of raising enough funds for a charity to achieve its objectives; stories exist of larger charities having extensive reserves and yet still heavily promoting themselves and driving fundraising campaigns. Their argument is that it is too risky to drop out of the public's view.

It is unlikely that the 'public purse' is going to increase to any great extent. Charities increasingly find themselves competing for resources and income. Smaller charities have been particularly affected with many closing in the aftermath of the 2007 global credit crunch and the COVID-19 pandemic. Increasingly charities are seeking to 'co-brand' with either larger, more established charities or private-sector companies. Clearly, any such exercises must be customer-centric and should only proceed if the customers' perceptions are positive. The compatibility between the charity and the corporate brand will influence consumer decision-making. 'Green' charities would have to avoid being tainted by any 'greenwashing' associated with the partner brand. The public is, however, often more forgiving of charities than private-sector brands.

Charities often struggle attracting appropriate partners. However, this is improving as more companies are on sustainable indices and undertake independent sustainability auditing. Benefits of co-branding include greater awareness through increased exposure, an enhanced image or reputation and greater financial security. The larger partner may be a source of volunteers. Indeed, some companies (e.g. First Direct) enshrine volunteering in their HR procedures. These volunteers may bring new skills (say website design) that will have a long-lasting impact on the smaller charity's brand.

> **Example:** The Marine Stewardship Council (see www.msc.org/uk/) is an international non-profit organisation that recognises and rewards efforts to protect oceans and safeguard seafood supplies. In short, they certify sustainable fisheries. They were founded in 1996 when Unilever collaborated with WWF to create this new brand. The MSC celebrated 20 years in 2016 and having certified an increasing number of key fisheries they have a widely recognised logo which consumers use to inform their decision-making.

Consumers' awareness and preference for ethical products are increasing. The Fairtrade Mark has become a well-known logo attached to over 6,000 Fairtrade products from coffee and tea to flowers and gold (Fairtrade, 2023). The growth of ethical consumerism has driven the growth of the Fairtrade market. Fairtrade is now on the agenda globally for leading retailers (and other stakeholders) and is being recognised by supranational organisations including the UN and the EC. The Fairtrade Mark was introduced in the UK in 1994 and within a decade the UK's Fairtrade market was worth more than £140 million; by 2012 it was £1.57 billion and by 2023 most UK adults could identify the Fairtrade mark (*ibid*).

Charities exist to create a better society. The vast majority of people consider charities to be trustworthy, which may not be the case with politicians (of various hues) or political organisations. Most people use charities in some way and the sector makes a substantial contribution to the UK economy, with over 200,000 registered charities generating a turnover of over £32 billion whilst employing almost 600,000 paid staff. Charities face increasing pressure from the constantly reducing life cycles of funding, processes and services. However, lack of resources and (often) heavy senior management workloads have stifled strategic marketing development. This confirms the need for charities to monitor the micro and macro-environments. Many charities became over-dependent upon external funding which often diminished their long-term marketing planning. In these days of challenging funding, financial security is often no longer guaranteed.

Marketing generally, and particularly research, are weaknesses for charities and many acknowledge the need for change. They need to market themselves in a co-ordinated way rather than rely on their usual ad-hoc approach. That said charities have always been willing to adopt a flexible approach to marketing and income generation, with staff often having the freedom to develop activities in effective and efficient ways. That said most charities are also SMEs with the challenges therein.

Key Findings

1 Sustainable entrepreneurship is a key driver of SD as the entrepreneurs seek to disrupt old market structures.

2 Sustainable communities can influence other consumers. They can be advocates or provide potent opposition.
3 Sustainable brands have traits akin to human characteristics.
4 All marketers are global marketers.
5 Sustainability should inform market entry methods.
6 SMEs and micro-enterprises represent 99% of all enterprises. They are a major contributor to the economy. They need support in adopting sustainable practices.
7 In a world of reduced public (government) spending, charities increasingly act like businesses whilst businesses act like charities. Third-sector organisations are growing in number and importance.

Activities

1 A wealth of information related to global trade is available free from the UNCTAD site. Visit their website (www.unctad.org/diae) or the organisation's investment policy hub (www. investmentpolicyhub.unctad.org).
2 See the works of Aaker, de Chernatony and Kapferer, all key branding authors.
3 Hollensen is a leading author on global marketing. Review his texts to gain insights.
4 A number of sources related to FDI exist, e.g.

- Transparency International – see Corruption-perceptions index
- World Bank – Data and Statistics – Statistics by country
- US Bureau of Labor Statistics has data on labour-costs
- IMF Publications 'World Economic outlook'
- OECD Main Economic Indicators
- US Trade Representative (USTR.gov National Trade Estimate Reports; pick a country).
- OECD 'Economic Surveys' on developed and larger developing countries
- CIA World Factbook (general background).

5 The Charities Commission provides extensive information on the sector. Visit their website at www.gov.uk/government/organisations/charity-commission

References

Aaker, D.A. (1991) *Managing Brand Equity*. New York: Free Press.

Aaker, J.L. (1997). Dimensions of brand personality. *Journal of Marketing Research*, 34(3), pp. 347–357. DOI:10.2307/3151897

Alpro. (2023) *Alpro: Promoting Healthier Eating and Sustainable Living* https://bcorporation.eu/case_study/alpro-promoting-healthier-eating-and-sustainable-living/ (accessed 29-08-23).

Andersson, R. (2019) Employees as ambassadors: Embracing new role expectations and coping with identity-tensions. *Corporate Communications-an International Journal*, 24(4), pp. 702–716. DOI:10.1108/CCIJ-04-2019-0038

Boukis, A., Gounaris, S. & Lings, I. (2017) Internal market orientation determinants of employee brand enactment. *Journal of Services Marketing*, 31(7), pp. 690–703. DOI:10.1108/JSM-07-2016-0272

Carlson, B.D. & Donavan, T. (2013) Human brands in sport: Athlete brand personality and identification. *Journal of Sport Management*, 27(3), pp. 193–206. DOI:10.1123/jsm.27.3.193

CE Delft. (2023) *Shipping GHG Emissions 2030. Analysis of the Maximum Technical Abatement Potential* https://cedelft.eu/publications/shipping-ghg-emissions-2030/ (accessed 20-09-2023).

Cohen, B., Smith, B., & Mitchell, R., (2006). Toward a sustainable conceptualization of dependent variables in entrepreneurship research. *Business Strategy and the Environment*, 17(2), pp. 107–119. DOI:10.1002/bse.505
de Chernatony, L., Mcdonald, M. & Wallace, E. (2011) *Creating Powerful Brands*, 4th Edition. London: Elsevier.
EC. (2005) *SME definition European Commission Recommendation 2005/361/EC* www.eusmecentre.org.cn/wp-content/uploads/2022/12/SME-Definition.pdf (accessed 25/08/23).
Ethical Consumer. (2022) *Ethical Markets Report* www.ethicalconsumer.org (accessed 09-08-23).
Fairtrade. (2023) *Fairtrade Foundation Website* www.fairtrade.org.uk (accessed 15-08-23).
Fisher, R., Maritz, A & Lobo, A. (2014) Evaluating entrepreneurs' perception of success-Development of a measurement scale. *International Journal of Entrepreneurial Behaviour & Research*, 20(5), pp. 478–492.
Fussler, C. (1996). *Driving Eco-innovation, A Breakthrough Discipline for Innovation and Sustainability*. London: Pitman.
Gardner, B.B. & Levy, S.J. (1955). The product and the brand. *Harvard Business Review*, 33(2), pp. 33–39. DOI:10.4135/9781452231372.n13
Geuens, M., Weijters, B. & De Wulf, K. (2009). A new measure of brand personality. *International Journal of Research in Marketing*, 26(2), pp. 97–107. DOI:10.1016/j.ijresmar.2008.12.002
Gilmore, A. Carson, D. & Grant, K (2001) SME marketing in practice. *Marketing Intelligence & Planning*, 19(1), pp. 6–11.
Haberberg, A., Gander, J., Rieple, A., Martin-Castilla, J-I & Helm, C. (2010) Institutionalizing idealism: The adoption of CSR practices. *Journal of Global Responsibility*, 1(2), pp. 366–381.
Hockerts, K. & Wüstenhagen, R. (2010). Greening Goliaths versus emerging Davids – Theorizing about the role of incumbents and new entrants in sustainable entrepreneurship. *Journal of Business Venturing*, 25(5), pp. 481–492.
Hollensen, S. (2017) *Global Marketing*, 7th Edition. Harlow: Pearson Education.
ICC. (2010) *The Incoterms* Rules *(2010)* https://iccwbo.org/publication/incoterms-rules-2010/ (Accessed 06-09-23).
Jackson, T. (2005) *Motivating Sustainable Consumption – A Review of Evidence on consumer Behaviour and Behavioural Change*; A report to the Sustainable Development Research Network January 2005. Funded by the ESRC's Sustainable Technologies Programme (STP)
Kapferer, J.N. (2008) *The New Strategic Brand Management*, 4th Edition. London: Kogan-Page.
Kerr, I.R. (2006) Leadership strategies for sustainable SME operation. *Business Strategy and the Environment*,15, pp. 30–39.
Kotler, P., Wong, V., Saunders, J. & Armstrong, G. (2009) *Principles of Marketing*, 5th European Edition. Harlow: Prentice Hall.
Margolis, J.D. & Walsh J.P. (2003) Misery loves companies: Rethinking social initiatives by business. *Administrative Science Quarterly*, 48, pp. 268–305.
McLarty, R. (1998) Case study: Evidence of a strategic marketing paradigm in a growing SME. *Journal of Marketing Practice. Applied Marketing Science*. 4(4), pp. 105–117.
Moore, S.B. & Manring, S.L. (2009) Strategy development in small and medium sized enterprises for sustainability and increased value creation. *Journal of Cleaner Production*, 17(2), pp. 276–282.
Munoz, P. & Dimov, D. (2015). The call of the whole in understanding the development of sustainable ventures. *Journal of Business Venturing*, 30(4), pp. 632–654.
Pacheco, D.F., Dean, T.J. & Payne, D.S., 2010. Escaping the green prison: Entrepreneurship and the creation of opportunities for sustainable development. *Journal of Business Venturing*, 25(5), pp. 464–480.
Parrish, B. (2010). Sustainability-driven entrepreneurship: Principles of organization design. *Journal of Business Venturing* 25(5), 510–523.
Richardson, N. (2020) *Sustainable Marketing Planning*. Abingdon: Routledge.

Richardson, N. & Cassop Thompson, M. (2023) How improved understanding of what constitutes 'value' may lead to better underpinning of Corporate Social Responsibility (CSR). *Journal of Global Responsibility*, pp. 2041–2568. DOI:10.1108/JGR-10-2022-0115

Sachs, J. & Warner, A. (1995) Natural resource abundance and economic growth. *National Bureau for Economic Research Working Paper 5398*, Cambridge, Massachusetts.

SBTi. (2023) *Science Based Targets Initiative Website.* https://sciencebasedtargets.org/about-us (accessed 29-08-23).

Schaltegger, S. & Wagner, M., (2011). Sustainable entrepreneurship and sustainability innovation: Categories and interactions. *Business Strategy and Environment*, 20 (4), pp. 222–237.

Shepherd, D.A. & Patzelt, H. (2011) The new field of sustainable entrepreneurship: Studying entrepreneurial action linking "What is to be sustained" with "What is to be developed". *Entrepreneurship: Theory and Practice*, 35(1), pp. 137–163.

Spedale, S. & Watson, T.J. (2014) The emergence of entrepreneurial action: At the crossroads between institutional logics and individual life-orientation. *International Small Business Journal*, 32(7), pp. 759–776.

SSE. (2023a) *About the SSE Initiative.* https://sseinitiative.org/about/ (accessed 30-08-23).

SSE. (2023b) *ESG Disclosure.* https://sseinitiative.org/esg-disclosure/ (accessed 30-08-23).

Statista. (2023) *Proportion of Women in Managerial Positions Worldwide 1991-2020.* Statista Research Department, Jun 7, 2023. www.statista.com/statistics/1259478/women-in-managerial-positions-worldwide/ (accessed 30-09-23).

Stead, R., Curwen, P. & Lawler, K. (2003) *Industrial Economics – Theory, Applications and Policy.* London: McGraw Hill.

Thomson, K., de Chernatony, L, Arganbright, L. & Khan, S. (2010) The Buy-in Benchmark: How staff understanding and commitment impact brand and business performance. *Journal of Marketing Management*, 15(8), pp. 819–835. DOI:10.1362/026725799784772684

Tilley, F & Young, W. (2009) Sustainability entrepreneurs — Could they be the true wealth generators of the future? *Greener Management International*, 55, pp. 70–92.

UNCTAD. (2018) *World Investment Report 2018- Investment and New Industrial Policies- Key Messages and Overview.* https://unctad.org/system/files/official-document/wir2018_overview_en.pdf (accessed 29-08-23).

UNCTAD. (2023) *World Investment Report 2023- Investing in Sustainable Energy for All.* https://unctad.org/publication/world-investment-report-2023 (accessed 29-08-23).

Vestrum, I & Rasmussen, E. (2013) How community ventures mobilise resources: Developing resource dependence and embeddedness. *International Journal of Entrepreneurial Behavior & Research*, 19(3), pp. 283–32.

Walker, H. & Preuss, L. (2008) Fostering sustainability through sourcing from small businesses: Public sector perspectives. *Journal of Cleaner Production*, 16(15), pp. 1600–1609. DOI:10.1016/j.jclepro.2008.04.014

World Bank. (2023) *World Bank Country and Lending Groups.* https://datahelpdesk.worldbank.org (accessed 30-08-23).

Young, W., Hwang, K., McDonald, S. & Oates, C. (2010) Sustainable consumption: Green consumer behaviour when purchasing products. *Sustainable Development*, 18, pp. 20–31.

Young, W. & Tilley, F., (2006). Can businesses move beyond efficiency? The shift toward effectiveness and equity in the corporate sustainability debate. *Business Strategy Environment*, 15(6), pp. 402–415. DOI:10.1002/sd.394

Index

ABEBooks portal 269
account manager (AM) 217
accountants 112–14, 153
advertising 48, 50, 56, 83–8, 94, 127, 133, 139, 176, 209, 210
advertisements (aka Ads) 80, 84–5, 127, 170
Agenda 21 19
Aldi 36, 113, 196
Alexa 89
Allbirds 124–5
Alphabet Inc 89
Alpro 23, 126, 134, 212–13, 226, 230, 258
Amazon 4, 89, 167, 170, 263
American Marketing Association (AMA) 37
Android 24, 188
Ansoff's matrix 189, 190, 202
APIC (Analyse, Plan, Implement, Control) 138, 140, 198
Apple iPad 49, 88, 109, 172, 210
Apple iPhone 38, 49, 94–5, 109, 158, 172, 181, 210, 254
Apple iPlayer 122
Apple iOS 49
apps 50, 85, 88, 117, 158, 160
aspiration 142, 174
Aston Martin 92, 182, 186
attitude 4, 14, 18, 36, 62, 69, 70, 72, 75, 123, 141–2, 146, 155, 165, 171, 174, 178, 182, 184, 191, 196, 217, 220, 222, 228–9, 234, 237, 239, 240, 242, 250–2, 258
augmented product 95
augmented reality (AR) 85, 88
austerity programmes (policies) 14, 165
Automated Teller Machine (ATM) 56, 119, 120

Baker, Michael (Prof.) 54, 60, 233
Balanced Scorecard 151–4, 172
banking sector 1, 3, 14–15, 49, 53, 117–19, 130, 158, 166, 210, 231, 241, 259
Barnum, P. T. 80
barriers to sustainable marketing planning 63–4, 69, 70, 128, 140, 158, 199, 202, 270
BBC 122
BCorp Beauty Coalition 155
BCorporation (BCorp) 3, 22–3, 27, 31–2, 74, 97, 124, 126–7, 129, 131, 134, 155, 226, 230, 244, 249, 273
Bell Pottinger 19, 258
benchmarking 17, 47, 148, 151–2, 154, 184–5, 188, 196–7, 217, 271
Beyond Greening (by Stuart L. Hart) 182
Big Data 30, 232–3
biospheric (i.e. pro-environmental behaviour) 69, 129, 251
bird 131
Blackberry 53, 210
Boston Control Group (BCG) matrix 108–11, 172, 182
boundary spanning employees (BSEs) 8, 123, 212, 215–19, 220–3, 225
Bowen's *Social Responsibilities of the Businessman* 4
B & Q store 126, 190
brand communities 63, 160–2, 230, 234, 237, 252, 255–6
brand equity 2, 127, 242–3, 253
brand personalities 253–5
brand positioning 114, 145, 181–2, 185, 220, 252, 254–6
Brexit 40, 156, 165, 174, 189, 191
'Brick' and/or 'Click' 91–2
British Petroleum (BP) 113
Brown, Stephen, (Prof.) 137
Brownlee, Alistair and Jonny 257
Brundtland Commission 14
business-as-usual (BAU) 3, 4, 10, 11, 13–17, 25, 29, 36–7, 45, 47, 56, 59, 61–6, 73–6, 100, 112, 138, 140, 149, 152, 175, 177–8, 182, 188, 229, 230, 234, 236–9, 244, 247, 249, 254–5, 268
business-to-business (B2B) 59, 61, 66–9, 85–6, 93, 96, 104, 114, 131, 152, 162, 175, 178, 180, 231, 255–6, 269

business-to-consumer (B2C) 59, 61–2, 66–7, 73, 85–6, 96, 104, 121, 133, 152, 162, 178, 180, 200, 231, 233, 244, 255, 269
budgets 14, 84, 89, 90, 140, 150, 156, 166, 195, 256, 269
buy one get one free (BOGOF) 83, 85
buy one get one later (BOGOL) 83

Cadburys 11, 100
cashback schemes 117
cash cows 108–9, 209
Carroll, Archie (Prof.) 5, 6, 17, 31
CASS Business School 147
CAST auditing mnemonic 147
charities 85, 124, 145, 164, 178, 190, 200, 210, 254–6, 271–3
Chartered Institute of Marketing (CIM) 37, 151, 160, 265
Chartered Institute of Public Relations (CIPR) 84, 134
Chartered Institute of Personnel Development (CIPD) 148
Chartered Institute of Purchasing and Supply (CIPS) 148
China 25, 29, 41, 105, 132, 151, 186–7, 265
Chloé 22–3
choice editing 126
circular economy 26–9, 73, 165, 167
Clarkson, Jeremy 82
climate conventions 123
closed systems 16, 29
co-creation 37, 52, 54–6, 61, 65, 72, 118–19, 120, 178, 242, 248, 250, 256
codes of conduct 61, 171, 192, 202
communications agencies 89, 90
communications channels 83, 86, 88, 224, 241
communications mix 71, 84–5, 87–8, 126–9
communications noise 65, 80–1, 85, 87, 127
communities 3, 6, 8, 10, 11, 14, 16, 18, 21, 42–3, 45, 52, 63, 65, 85, 103, 107, 117, 125, 132, 158–9, 160–2, 166, 179, 183, 196–8, 200–1, 230, 234, 237, 250, 252, 255–6, 262, 273
Companies Act (2006) 200
competitive pricing 112, 115, 152, 154
complaints 22, 63, 68, 84, 131, 154, 194
concentrated targeting 180
concentration strategy 186–7, 191
conspicuous consumption 4, 51, 94, 128
consumer generated media (CGM) 63, 212, 237, 256
consumer decision-making process (DMP) 59, 61–4, 67–8, 70, 72–6, 94, 266
consumerism 44
consumer purchasing scenarios 63–4, 93–5, 101
consumer-to-consumer (C2C) 61, 269
consumption (aspects of) 71–2
controls-hard and soft 149, 150, 152, 194–5
convenience (aka Place) 79, 90–1, 128, 177
convenience goods 93, 96
conversion 152, 157, 241
co-operative business model 8, 14–15, 201
co-operative retailer (The Co-op) 8, 14–15, 50, 71, 91, 119, 171
COP26 123
core competencies 19, 91, 141, 146, 151, 155, 157–8, 172, 174, 219, 223
core product 95, 118, 139
corporate failure 1, 147, 199
corporate governance 16–18, 141, 147
corporate objectives 7, 48, 107, 114, 140–3, 167, 175, 192, 195, 214, 223
corporate social irresponsibility (CSI) 17–19, 200
corporate social responsibility (CSR) 3–7, 17–18, 43, 70, 81, 91, 116, 131, 141, 182, 185, 196–7, 200, 271
corporate values 52, 56, 142, 147, 213
cost leadership 39, 152, 181, 189, 209
cost plus pricing 115
Country of Origin (CoO) 40, 191, 265
COVID-19 14, 53, 201, 271
credit crunch (2007–8) 14, 53, 104, 165, 271
crisis management 199
critical marketing (and marketers) 36, 49, 56, 73, 137, 183, 241
critical success factors (CSFs) 110
customer centric 13, 29, 37, 39, 52, 56, 58, 74, 79, 93, 109, 125, 141, 148, 154, 157, 172, 174–5, 183, 199, 202, 207, 209, 210, 233, 240, 271
customer life-time value (LTV/CLTV) 237, 240, 242–3, 256
customer linking 211
customer relationship management (CRM) 49, 154, 157, 180, 229, 232–3
customer satisfaction 1, 38, 91, 120, 126, 131, 133, 138, 145, 147, 158, 195, 201, 212–13, 219, 233, 240, 243, 250
customer satisfaction management (CSM) 233

DAMP segments 177
Data Protection Act (1998) 168
Data Protection Officer (DPO) 181
Davis's Iron Law 4
decision-making process (DMP) 59, 61–4, 67–8, 70, 72–7, 94, 133, 266
decision-making unit (DMU) 59, 66–7
Dell 49, 100, 210
deregulation 4, 53
differentiated targeting 180
direct distribution 90

Directional Policy Matrix DPM (aka GE Matrix) 110, 112, 172, 182
direct marketing 83, 85–7, 157, 195
directors, non-executive (NEDS) 147–8
discount pricing 104, 116, 139
Disney 119
display ads 85
disposable income 66, 71, 97, 103, 164, 172, 178, 180, 210, 258, 262, 266
distributed process control (DPC) system 29, 168
distribution channels 23, 50, 91, 138–9, 149, 150
distribution logistics 90, 130, 149
distribution networks 16, 48
Dominant Social Paradigm (DSP) 4, 43
Dow Jones Sustainable Index (DJSI) 22, 32
Drucker, Peter (Prof.) 138
dual factor theory of motivation (Herzberg) 65
DVD 39, 53, 102, 153
Dyson 67, 95, 105, 181

E7 40–1
easyJet 138
EAUC (Alliance for Sustainability in Education) 20
eBay 166, 269
economic systems 24
economics 5, 12, 54, 146, 164
economy of scale (EoS) 108, 130, 152, 191, 269
eco warrior 73, 128, 180, 236, 238–9
effectiveness *vs.* efficiency 138, 150, 202
EFQM service quality framework 134
electronic point of sale (EPoS) system 30
Elkington, John (Prof.) 14–16, 22, 249
enlightened marketing 43, 55
environmental scanning 147
environmental, social & governance (ESG) 2, 109, 113, 130, 196, 263–4
Environment Protection Agency (US) 171
EPISTLE framework 164
equity 2, 12, 127, 242–3, 253–4, 260
ethics 1, 4, 5, 6, 13, 17, 42, 43, 63, 69, 141, 146, 171
European Union (EU) 132, 168
exchange view 37
exclusive distribution 92–3
existing markets 39
expansion-based strategy 186
extended consumer problem solving 94, 97, 266
extended (expanded) 'Comms' Mix 84, 128
extended Marketing Mix for services 120–1, 125
extinction rebellion 12, 51
Facebook 4, 83, 89, 170, 233, 234, 237, 263, 269
facial recognition 88–9
Fairphone 24–5
Fairtrade Foundation 1, 61, 70–4, 171, 179, 182, 237–8, 272, 274
Fast Moving Consumer Goods (FMCG) 63, 93–4, 129, 266
festivals 30, 70, 122, 178–9, 242, 250, 255–6
Fill, Chris (Prof.) 81, 84
financial services 130, 134, 210, 231
fine jewellery 97
Finisterre 129
First Direct 119, 158, 222, 272
first-mover advantage 16, 50, 151, 172, 209
5G 49
5Ms 111, 151, 164, 172
Five Planets theory 24
focused targeting 180
focus groups 106, 112, 154
Ford, Henry 208
Ford, Model T 208
forecasting 38
Foreign Direct Investment (FDI) 260–2, 273
Forest Alliance 61
Forest Stewardship Council (FSC) 102, 126
Freedom of Information Act (2000) 168
Freeman, R. E. (Prof.) 7–9, 11, 31, 35, 248, 250
free riders 184, 250
Friedman, M. (Prof.) 3, 11–12, 15, 196
Friends of the Earth (FoE) 166
FTSE4Good index 22, 192, 201, 203
FUD (fear, uncertainty and/or doubt) 69
functional objectives 48, 142–3

gaming 83, 88, 119
Gantt Charts 175
gap analysis 145, 192
GE Matrix (aka Directional Policy Matrix (DMP)) 110, 112, 172, 182
gender 151, 265
General Agreement on Trade and Tariffs (GATT) 259
General Data Protection Regulations (GDPR) 53, 86, 89, 168–70, 180, 204, 233–4
Generation Z (Gen Z) 235
Glastonbury festival 122
goal setting 140–1, 145
Going rate pricing 115
goods classification 96, 121
Google Analytics 241
Google Assistant 89
Google Chrome 49
Gosnay, Ruth, M. 47, 207, 225
governments 14, 22, 42, 50, 53, 81, 104, 112, 121, 165, 180, 182, 185, 201, 210, 258, 269

green consumers 69, 73, 128, 170, 184–5, 239, 257
Green Gown Awards 20
greenhouse gases (GHGs) 28, 171, 179, 268
green marketing 41–5, 46, 56
Greenpeace 128, 160, 166
green segmentation 128, 179, 236, 238
green washing 2, 15, 70, 76, 113, 165, 182, 185, 200, 271
gross domestic product (GDP) 45, 79, 164–5, 191, 202, 258, 262
Groupon 120
Guanxi 264–5
Guardian newspaper 88

Hart, Stuart, L. (Prof.) 182–3
Harvard Business Review (HBR) 14, 45, 177
Heinz 91
Henderson, Bruce 108
Herzberg, Frederick (dual factor theory) 65–5, 125
heterogeneity (or variability of services) 120–1, 268
heuristics 62–3, 75, 184, 236
hierarchy of needs (Maslow) 64–5, 266
high learning (PLC profile) 101
HMV 53
Honda 40, 208
horizons 144, 150
Huawei 88, 94–5, 172, 181, 254
hybrid distribution 91
hybrid electric cars 179
hybrid systems 29
hyper-competition 1, 123, 253, 258

Idea Screening (NPD) 106
imitative products 105
incipient markets 38–9
Incoterms 266–7
India 24, 40, 153
individual influences 62, 64, 75
inertia 45, 47, 52, 157, 188, 202, 241, 269
influencer 8, 42, 67, 73, 75–6, 82–3, 103, 160, 178, 208, 218, 222, 238, 243, 258
information (macro factor) 164, 172
information search 23, 62–3, 70, 74–5
innovative products 104–5
input-transformation-output (ITO) model 146
inseparability (of services) 121
instant bust PLC profile 101
intangibility (of services) 120–1
integrated marketing communications (IMC) 63, 74, 76, 127–9, 236
intellectual property 53, 209, 259
intensive distribution 92–3
interactive marketing 208
interactive signage 88–9
inter-functional aspects 150, 153–4, 174, 209, 213, 217–19, 223–5, 232
intermediaries (use of) 90–1, 159, 201, 211
internal customers (ICs) 8, 125, 216–17
internal supplier–customer relationships (ISCRs) 216
internal marketing (IM) 207–25
Internal Marketing Orientation (IMO) 207, 213–16, 218, 220, 222, 224–6
International Monetary Fund (IMF) 12, 273
International Social Marketing Association (ISMA) 42, 56
International Trade Organisation (ITO) 259
internet of things (IoT) 53, 89
internet service providers (ISPs) 100
ISO 20121 202–3
ISO 14001 environmental management systems 202

Jackson, Tim (Prof.) 60, 71
Jaguar Land Rover (JLR) 40
JD Power car survey 63, 77
John Lewis 8, 161
just noticeable difference (JND) 54, 60, 95, 173
Just Stop Oil 12

Kaizen 187
Kanban 159
Keynes, J. M. (Prof.) 132
key performance indicators (KPIs) 140, 175, 193, 203
Kia 93
Kiosks 88
Kotler, Phillip (Prof.) 41–3, 55, 138, 182, 193, 198, 207, 271
Kuznets, Simon 164

latent markets 39
LEGO ideas 107
less-developed countries (LDCs) 261, 266
Lever Bros 11
Levy, S. J. (Prof.) 41, 253
Libel Act (1792) 19, 168, 257
libertarian 11, 15, 73, 238–9
Lidl 104
life-time value (LTV aka CLTV) 237, 240, 242–3, 256
limited problem-solving purchasing scenario 94, 96
linear economy 26
linear model of communication 80–1
Linux 49
LinkedIn 49, 234, 269
local government 42, 44, 133, 165–6, 269
locked-in (consumers) 47, 54, 61, 121, 241, 249

logistics 29, 37, 90, 130, 132, 133, 142, 149, 266, 270
'Long Tail', the 50
London Evening Standard 88
London North East Railway (LNER) 53
low learning product PLC profile 101
loyalty ladders 229, 237–9
loyalty versus satisfaction 239–40
Lucozade 100

mainstream (aka legacy) media (MSM) 88
Malthus, Thomas 4, 24, 51
management culture 38, 125
Marine Stewardship Certification (MSC) 126, 237
Marine Stewardship Council 272
market coverage 92–3
marketing agencies 48, 88, 158, 256
marketing audits 114, 140, 147, 175, 203, 221
marketing information system (MkIS) 152, 154–6, 232
marketing myths 36, 48
marketing myopia 45, 52
marketing orientation (MkO) 183, 207–9, 210–14, 230
market orientation (MO) 50, 140, 209, 211–12, 214
market revolutions (Elkington) 15–16
Marks and Spencer (M&S) 190
Marmite 237
Marx, Karl 4, 38, 51
Maslow, Abraham 5, 51, 64–5, 266
maturity (PLC stage) 99–102, 108, 127, 146
McDonald, Malcolm (Prof.) 47, 49, 123, 175
McKinsey 7S Framework 148–9, 151, 156
Mendelow grid 8, 162–3, 172
Metro newspaper 88
MG 40–1
micro-enterprises 5, 129, 150, 152, 201, 247, 250, 268, 270, 273
Microsoft 4, 49, 191
Mintzberg, Henry (Prof.) 29, 191, 196, 215
Mintzberg's deflected and realised strategies 188
mission statements 15, 46, 141, 200, 202
mobile advertising 50
Mondragon 8
Moneysavingexpert.com 85, 226
Monster 105
Moore, G. E. 52
Most Favoured Nation (MFN) 259
Motorola Dyna TAC 8000X 104
Mozilla 49
multi-taskers 50, 129
Mumsnet 161
mystery shopping 152, 154

National Audit Office (NAO) 13
Netflix 167
new product development (NPD) 104–7, 129, 133, 152, 154, 158, 209
niche (concentrated) targeting 173, 209
Nike 7
Nissan 41, 58, 103, 104, 186
Nokia 25, 49, 104
non-executive directors (NEDs) 147–8
norms 5, 12, 53–4, 59–61, 74, 166, 247–9
Northern Rock 145, 201–2
not-for-profit 164, 198, 247, 271–2

odd pricing 155
OECD 165, 273
online banking 119, 158
online communities 162, 197, 203, 234, 244
online loyalty 229, 238–45
open question argument 52
open systems 29, 3
operational gaps 145–6
opinion leaders and/or formers 62, 75, 81–3, 103, 127, 160
order processing 93
organisational culture 7, 185, 199, 215–16
'Organise' online HR petitions site 242
original equipment manufacturer (OEM) 131
Our World in Data 25
Out of Home (OoH) 88, 133

page pop-ups 162
Panasonic 167
Patagonia 28, 75, 113, 116
Pay Per Click (PPC) 85
Paysafecard 116
People-Planet-Profit14, 46, 61, 71, 73, 121, 131, 188, 192, 197–8; *see also* triple bottom line)
performance evaluation 68
perishability (of services) 121
personal selling 87, 195
PEST macro framework 61, 69, 164, 172, 188, 262
Piercy, Nigel (Prof.) 224, 229, 240
planning frameworks 138–41
PLATFORM macro framework 164, 262–3
podcasts 153
pop-ups 85, 162
Porter, Michael (Prof.) 55, 61, 111, 148–9, 151–2, 159, 189, 190, 270
Porter's 5 Forces framework 61, 111, 151–2
Porter's generic strategies 189, 190
post-purchase decision review 63
premium pricing 16, 48, 116, 149
Press Association 88
Privacy Law (1987) 168
problem recognition 62, 68, 75

Procter & Gamble (P&G) 97–8, 138
product anatomy 95
product adoption (aka diffusion) curve 82, 103, 133
production orientation 39, 208–11, 225
product life cycle (PLC) 99, 100–3, 107–8, 111, 116, 133–4, 144, 146, 172, 195, 201, 209
product portfolio management 79, 95, 97, 99, 108–10
product risk continuum 105
Public Relations Consulting Association (PRCA) 84, 132
Public Relations (PR) 7, 19, 84, 85, 87, 220
purpose statement 15, 46, 141–2, 202
push, pull and profile strategies 83

qualitative (aka Qual) data 63, 153, 162, 194
quantitative (aka Quant) data 153, 194

Radian6 241
Radio Frequency Identification Device (RFID) 30
RATIFI mnemonic for systems 30
raw materials 16, 26–8, 96, 114, 149, 150, 153, 164–5, 167, 187, 197, 255
REACH NEW planning framework 138, 140, 199
Red Bull 105
Relationship Marketing (RM) 87, 229–43
re-launch (including PLC) 101–2, 104–5
resource allocation 5, 15, 99, 140, 248
retail market 104, 131, 189
Return on Capital Employed (ROCE) 94, 142, 150, 152, 154, 195
Return on Investment (RoI) 47–8, 99, 114–15, 140, 142, 155, 178, 195, 239
Return on Marketing Investment (RoMI) 47, 114, 127, 144, 162, 178, 195
Return on Objectives (RoO) 47–8, 116, 127, 142, 155
Reuters news agency 88
revolutions of a sustainable future (Elkington) 15–16
Roads to Ruin (Cass Business School report) 147
Rosling, Hans 4, 24
Rover 40
Rowntree 11
Ruskin, John 4
Ryanair 138

Saatchi and Saatchi 89
Sainsburys 126
sales order processing systems (SOP) 93
sales orientation 199, 209, 210, 225
sales promotion 83, 85, 87, 96, 127, 237
Samsung 88, 167, 172, 254
Sarbanes-Oxley Act (USA) 261, 263
satisfaction (customer) 38, 91, 119, 126, 131, 133, 138, 145, 147, 158, 195, 201, 212–13, 228, 233, 239, 243, 250
satisfaction versus loyalty 239–40
scalloped pattern PLC profile 101
scenario planning 141, 144, 186, 191, 193
Schumpeter's creative destruction 2, 187
search engine optimisation (SEO) 84, 242
seat car manufacturer 131
segmentation targeting and positioning (STP) 137, 145, 175, 178, 180, 234
selective distribution 92–3
semi-open systems 29, 30
senior management 10, 30, 37, 107, 112, 158, 174, 180, 199, 208, 211–12, 215–19, 221, 236, 240, 252, 272
service characteristics 118, 121
Service Level Agreement (SLA) 180
Service Quality 63, 121–4, 133–5, 217
SERVQUAL 123–5
shareholders 4, 7, 8, 10–13, 18, 22, 45, 47, 53, 113, 142, 150, 199–201, 258
shopping goods 96
short-termism 199, 201, 258
single-step model of communication 82
situational analysis (aka macro analysis) 56, 61
situation review 61, 140–1, 202
Skandinavisk 13, 102, 155
small to medium sized enterprises (SMEs) 5, 268–71
Smartinsights.com 203
SMART objectives 115, 173–5, 195
smart phones 24, 38, 53, 88, 94, 100, 116–17, 122, 166–210, 235, 254
Smart TV 89
smart watches 88
Smile (Co-operative Bank) 119
Smith, Adam 3, 4, 51, 271
social marketing 41–3, 56, 271
social media 2, 6, 7, 50, 62, 83, 86, 95, 127, 133, 154, 157, 158, 160, 170, 174, 176, 192, 222, 227, 234–5, 238, 241, 243, 257, 265
social network 66, 83, 156, 162, 219, 269
Soil Association 61, 237
SolarAid 131
Sony Internet-enabled TVs 104, 167
Sony Walkman 38, 107
spam 85–6
speciality goods 96
stability-based strategy 186
staging 5, 102
stakeholder theory 3, 7, 9, 13, 31, 250
standard product cost (SPC) 107
STEEPLE and/or STEEL PIES framework 164

Strategic Business Units (SBUs) 109, 149–52, 158, 172, 223
Strategy Formulation 140–1, 145, 175, 186
supply networks 7, 16, 28, 129, 131–3, 149, 150, 152–4, 159, 196, 216, 234, 251
surveys 63, 77, 154, 156, 217, 273
sustainability (as megatrend) 13
sustainability continuum 11, 184, 193
sustainability ownership issues 200, 250
sustainability polar diagram 198
sustainable branding 28, 73, 182, 192, 237–8, 252–8
sustainable development goals (SDGs) 2, 3, 19–23, 26–7, 31, 74, 97, 125, 129, 131, 261, 264
sustainable development (SD) 2, 3, 13, 22–7
sustainable distribution 266
sustainable entrepreneurs 97, 187, 247–52
sustainable marketing benchmarking 47, 196–7, 271
sustainable marketing (SM) 36, 41, 45–6, 194, 196, 224, 230, 239, 256
SWOT summary 137, 172–5, 203
systems 25–35

tablets 38, 49, 50, 88, 172, 210
tactics 2, 9, 10, 46, 51, 79, 83, 85, 114, 123, 128, 137, 140, 142–3, 145, 153, 163, 173, 175, 189, 192, 203, 222, 258, 261
tangible product 95, 118, 133
targeted ads 85
targeting 104, 137, 182, 174–8, 180, 237, 254, 261, 266
technological factors 25, 39, 49, 50, 62, 75, 84, 103, 124, 151, 155, 164, 167, 172, 187, 262
Ted Baker 242
television (TV) 39, 50, 67–8, 81, 84–5, 89, 94, 104, 109, 121–2, 124, 153, 166–7, 237, 240, 242–3, 256
Tesco 91, 161, 190
Tesla 41, 186
third sector organisations 42, 145, 166, 271–3
360 and 540 degree reviews 152, 154, 194, 223
3D printing 167
3Rs reduce, reuse, recycle 24
Tik Tok 83, 168, 170, 234
Topcashback.co.uk 117
TOWS analysis 137, 142, 155, 174–7, 195
Toyota 104, 180
Toys R Us 38
Trade Related Aspects of Intellectual Property 259
Trade Related Aspects of Intellectual Property Rights (TRIPS) 259
Trans-national Corporation (TNC) 260, 264
tribes (including online) 161, 234
Tripadvisor 63
triple-bottom-line (TBL) 14, 22, 25, 43, 47, 59, 69, 71, 73–6, 121–2, 126, 138, 140, 175–6, 179, 185, 187–8, 191–3, 196, 229, 235–8, 249, 266
Trump, Donald 170–1, 260
Twitter (now X) 83, 234
two step model of communication 81–2

Unilever 115, 237, 272
unique selling point (USP) 54, 60, 95, 158, 173, 181
United Nations Global Compact 19, 20, 35, 264
United States of America (USA) 24, 43, 103, 105, 208, 260
United Repair Centre (URC) 28
University 20, 30
unsought goods or services 96, 118, 133
user generated c(UGC) 83, 237, 242, 256

value chain analysis (VCA) 148–51, 156, 232, 270–1
value co-creation 37, 52, 55, 61, 118, 120, 242, 248, 256
value for money (VFM) 49, 54, 104, 112, 117, 133, 154, 182, 189
value proposition (VP) 49, 56
value seeking (or sougt) 2, 5, 15, 37, 42, 46, 53–4, 71, 76, 91, 93, 103, 112, 118, 120, 122–3, 127, 161, 177, 180, 216, 241, 255
value systems 141, 159
variability (heterogeneity of services) 120–1, 268
Veja (BCorp) 74
Vestiaire Collective (BCorp) 27
Vine 83
viral marketing 87
Virtual Learning Environments (VLEs) 30
virtual reality (VR) 87
Volkswagen (VW) 7, 40, 182
voluntary simplifier 73, 127, 179, 180, 235–6, 238–9
Volvo 40
Vouchercloud 85
vouchers and cashback 85, 117, 120, 122

Walls Ice Cream (Share Happy) 89
warehousing 93, 133, 267
wearable tech 88
Web 2.0 64, 66, 83, 212, 256
website analytics 241
wicked problems 13
Wood, Donna (Prof.) 5, 12
Woolworths 52

Word of Mouth (WoM) of Mouse (eWoM) 6, 48, 63, 83, 87
World Bank 259, 261, 273
World Intellectual Property Organisation (WIPO) 259
World Trade Organisation (WTO) 12, 50, 259, 260
World Wide Fund for Nature (WWF) 272

X (formerly Twitter) 83

YouTube 122, 167

Zero Emission Vehicles (ZEVs) 41, 103–4, 161, 170
zero level channel 90–1
Zero Moment of Truth (ZMOT) model 77